Jc

Provoking
the Gospel
of Matthew

Provoking the Gospel of Matthew

A STORYTELLER'S COMMENTARY
YEAR A

Richard W. Swanson

THE
PILGRIM
PRESS
Cleveland

For Kathy J. R. Swanson:
a woman of meticulous insight,
courageous determination,
magnificent accomplishment,
and absolute integrity;
I am privileged to have her
as a teacher,
as an intellectual companion,
and as my sister.

The Pilgrim Press
700 Prospect Avenue
Cleveland, Ohio 44115-1100
thepilgrimpress.com

© 2007 by Richard W. Swanson

All rights reserved. Published 2007

✡ Printed in the United States of America on acid-free paper that contains
post-consumer fiber.

12 11 10 09 08 07 5 4 3 2 1

Library of Congress Cataloging-in-Publication Data
Swanson, Richard W., 1952-
    Provoking the gospel of Matthew : a storyteller's commentary : year A /
Richard W. Swanson.
        p. cm.
    Includes bibliographical references.
    ISBN 978-0-8298-1691-4
    1. Bible. N.T. Matthew – Criticism, Narrative. 2. Storytelling – Religious
aspects – Christianity. 3. Common lectionary (1992). Year A. I. Title.
BS2575.52.S93 2007
226.2′07 – dc22
                                                        2006035666

Contents

Preface

LIFE LEAVES MARKS:
TRUTH, INTEGRITY, AND PERFORMANCE

Jesus has a face.

Obviously.

But the thing about a face is, it looks the way it looks. Anger shows in the eyes and in the jaw. Joy shows in the eyes and in the softness of the mouth. Determination shows in the angle of the chin, or in the flat, focused gray of the eyes. Amusement shows in the twinkles and in the wrinkles. Poker players and police officers know what a liar does with the eyes, the head, the upper body. Parents know what fear looks like when it crosses the face of their child, even if it runs across so quickly that no one else sees it.

And Jesus has a face. If he played poker, someone at the table would have been able to read his cards out of his face. His mother would have seen hope and fear and joy and pain as they carved themselves deep into his face.

An actor has a face. Obviously. And shoulders. And a back. And elbows and knees. I have had the privilege of working for several years now with the actors who are my collaborators in the Provoking the Gospel Storytelling Project. I have learned to watch what happens to their bodies when lines from our scripts go into them. The words change their bodies. When they get the physics right, I scarcely need to hear them to understand what they just said: their

7

bodies tell me the truth, their bodies show me what they love and fear and feel and mean.

Their bodies also tell me when they are lying — as they sometimes do. Sometimes it is on purpose. I work with some very skillful actors who can make their character tell a lie. They do this many different ways, but always there is a moment of disjunction, sometimes between what is said and what is shown, sometimes between one part of the body and another. Words full of joy are delivered with a flat face, or the mouth will smile while the eyes will wait, crouched and ready to spring.

Sometimes the lying is unintentional, a result of not fully comprehending the bite of the lines that they are embodying. When that happens, the body knows, and the body always shows what it knows. Feet shift, torsos become rigid, faces freeze into caricatures of emotions that the actor imagines she should be feeling, and showing, to the audience.

And sometimes the lies come because Jesus has a face, a smiling face, a happy face that Christians have seen since they first started Sunday School. It is a face that has been shaped by centuries of seismic, tectonic theology that has shaped the geography of what things Jesus can be up to and still be Jesus and have Jesus' face. Put simply, on the continent of customary theology, Jesus is gracious and good and gentle, and even when he must be stern, it is always for the purpose of being gracious and good and gentle to the people to whom he is gracious and good and gentle. Which would be us. This face of Jesus smiles, and when it does not smile, we miss the smile and wait for it to return, knowing that it will, knowing that it will be warm and understanding.

Matthew's story causes all sorts of trouble for the face of Jesus that lives on the continent of customary theology. Some of the lines in the story work very well when an actor delivers them while smiling warmly and looking gentle. "You are worth more than many sparrows," says Jesus and laughs. "Pick up my yoke, and learn from me, for I am gentle and lowly in mind; you will find rest for your life." Jesus looks a lot like my grandmother when he says those words.

But there are other lines in the story as well. An actor embodying Jesus' lines in Matthew's story must also call a Gentile mother a dog, and cast Capernaum down to hell, and throw character after character into the outer darkness where people wail and gnash their teeth. I have been working for several years with a troupe of actors, performing biblical stories, embodying the characters and tensions that live within the stories. I have learned that embodied performance is a stern master. It is possible to imagine almost anything in the quiet of one's study. The standard-issue Jesus can have good reasons for anything he might say, and still maintain his composure. But when an actor attempts to perform the troublesome lines in Matthew's story with that sort of composure, audiences either conclude that he is lying or that he is quite insane. Neither is a comforting conclusion. My actors have taught me this.

The emerging field of performance criticism in biblical studies holds great promise because of the phenomenon I have encountered working with my actors. David Rhoads's fine sketch of this promising field is instructive.[1] Performance puts the words into bodies, and audiences can always tell when something is amiss on stage. An actor embodying the harsh lines that Jesus speaks in Matthew's story must find a way to play those lines for true[2] in front of an audience. At the very least, the harsh lines must distort the face of Jesus. If they do not, the actor creates the kind of disjunction that audiences and police interrogators read as lying. But what harsh hardness must carve itself into a face when it sends an entire city to hell? Find a way to perform this line before you answer.

Embodied performance confronts an interpreter with another reality in Matthew's story. The character Jesus emerges out of the chaos and blood of Herod's genocidal attempt to slaughter all of the children of Bethlehem. Ask an actor. Such a bit of backstory is going to shape the way the character can be played. Ask a counselor. Such a disastrous beginning will damage a human being. Life leaves marks, and actors have to explore those marks in order to embody the characters they are assigned to play. Even when the character is Jesus.

I know a few people who have come out of such disasters. Most of them navigate pretty well in ordinary society most of the time. Some don't navigate at all. But there are always moments when something else shows through. Maybe it is the flash of anger that seems disproportionate. Maybe there is a certain rigidity, a durable wariness, that shows through even in tender moments. Or maybe it is just the thousand-yard-stare that peeks out when they sit by themselves, alone but surrounded by people talking and telling stories at a party. Always there is something because life leaves marks, always.

In this commentary on Matthew's story, I incorporate what I have learned from my actors. My actors have taught me to look for the physical truth of the lines that must be performed. My actors have taught me to look for the marks left by the backstory that a character brings to a moment on stage. My actors have taught me the same lesson I have learned from every teacher worthy of the title: integrity will carry you farther than craft or cleverness, though the trip may be unsettling to comfortable ideologies. I have looked for the physical truth of this story, however unsettling that has been. In doing so, I have found dimensions to Matthew's story that surprise me. In particular, I have found a Jesus portrayed honestly, which means he is portrayed as damaged by the disaster that spun his life into motion. I have found a storyteller who shows clearly the effects of imperial violence on all aspects of Jewish faith and life, effects that marked all Jews who lived in that period and that place, all Jews specifically including Jesus. I have found a storyteller who puts forth a Jesus who has little in common with the standard-issue Jesus so familiar to Christian audiences, though one who should have been expected by anyone who took seriously the notion that he would be a "man of sorrows and acquainted with grief." I have found a fearless storyteller who does not flinch while portraying Jesus throughout his career as a damaged character, a storyteller who does not stop until he has brought that damaged character through an entire narrative arc and is transformed at his resurrection.

I have more people to thank than this slim volume would ever hold. Thanks especially to the members of the Provoking the Gospel Storytelling Project who worked with me to create "Rachel Weeping for Her Children," our performance of selections from Bach's St. Matthew Passion: Jason Dybsetter, Jennie Graves, Sandra Looney, Amanda Mitchell, Meghan Swanson, Mandy Younger, and Kris Zingler. Thanks also to James Johnson, director of the Augustana Choir, and to the members of the Augustana Choir, with whom we worked weeks and months to bring our shared vision of Matthew's story to life. Thanks also to my long-time collaborators, Michael T. Smith and Erika L. Iverson, whose judgment and insight are a gift from God. And thanks to my editor at The Pilgrim Press, Ulrike Guthrie, whose gracious good will has sustained me throughout our collaboration. Everyone should have the experience of working with such an editor.

Strap yourself in tight. This reading of Matthew's story is not going to be like any other you have encountered. Enjoy the ride.

Chapter One

AUTHORITY AND REVENGE

At least fifty mostly decomposed cadavers covered the floor, wadded in clothing, their belongings strewn about and smashed. Macheted skulls had rolled here and there.

The dead looked like pictures of the dead. They did not smell. They did not buzz with flies. They had been killed thirteen months earlier, and they hadn't been moved. Skin stuck here and there over the bones, many of which lay scattered away from the bodies, dismembered by the killers, or by scavengers — birds, dogs, bugs. The more complete figures looked a lot like people, which they were once. A woman in a cloth wrap printed with flowers lay near the door. Her fleshless hip bones were high and her legs slightly spread, and a child's skeleton extended between them. Her torso was hollowed out. Her ribs and spinal column poked through the rotting cloth. Her head was toppled back and her mouth was open: a strange image — half agony, half repose.

I had never been among the dead before. What to do? Look? Yes. I wanted to see them, I suppose.

— We Wish to Inform You That Tomorrow
We Will Be Killed with Our Families:
Stories from Rwanda[3]

Odette nodded at my notebook, where I was writing as she spoke. "So the people in America really want to read this? People tell me to write these things down, but it's written inside of me. I almost hope for the day when I can forget."

— *We Wish to Inform You*[4]

What do you do with a story like that?

Do you remember it? Do you wish you could forget it? Do you look at the corpses that do not smell? Do you imagine what the room smelled like three days after the slaughter, instead of thirteen months? Do you wonder if any of the corpses were still alive when the room smelled of death and the beginning of decay?

Do you wish you had never heard of such things?

Do you wish that you had not been required to imagine such things?

I do, too.

Such stories, however, claim our attention. They seize our imagination, and thus suggest something about the authority of story that needs careful consideration. What does it mean that there are some stories we cannot stop thinking about? What does it mean that some stories not only stop us and force us to listen, but, in fact, nail us to the ground, make us unable to run away?

These stories came to me first from a student of mine. My student lives in Kenya and works to resettle refugees. She frequently hears stories like the excruciating one I just told you and must sift through them to determine which ones are true and which ones are simply lurid. She works with people who are trying to reconstitute the universe after seeing babies ripped from their mothers' arms and smashed against the ground. She told me that every human being needed to read about such things, to imagine them vividly until we find the political will and the moral resolve to make them stop forever. She wrote to me recently: "I am on the coast letting the tides calm me. Sounds disgustingly poetic, but it's the truth. The refugees have worn me out. I am exhausted. Just came from Kigomatz and

14

the Burundis' stories are still chasing me. If they are this bad for me, I cannot imagine what life is for them."

These stories came to me also from my daughter. My daughter read Gourevitch's book as part of a course in her undergraduate education. She told me that if I was going to write on Matthew, I had to read about Rwanda.

She was right.

But before we can consider why she was right, I need to return to the question that has begun each of these storyteller's commentaries: What is the authority of biblical story?

This is the question that I have pursued in each of the two commentaries leading up to this one. The question is an old one, a traditional one with traditional answers. While the traditional answers have all manner of dogmatic value, as well as having the solidity of being rooted in the sediment of centuries of theological history, this is a storyteller's commentary, and storytellers encounter the issue of authority differently. What is it that allows a performer to continue telling a story? What is it that holds an audience, stops them as they drift past the story being told? In each of the two preceding commentaries in this series I have explored this question, this kind of authority. I have asked about the authority of biblical story by observing what actually happens when a story is told.

I wrote the commentary on the Gospel of Mark in the midst of trying to figure out the stories that were told to me by my father's friends from his unit in the 82nd Airborne. As I listened to the stories told by these old men who had gone to war as boys, I heard funny stories, terrifying stories, stories that were achingly sad. As I listened longer, I noticed that the essential characteristic of all of these stories, the thing that held both the storyteller and his audience, was a shared wrestling provoked by the story. These stories were not told as entertainment. They were not told as journalistic reports. The tellers and the audience told and heard the same stories that they had shared for over half a century, and they shared these stories because they needed to wrestle with what had happened, what they had suffered and done. This wrestling created the functional authority of the stories they told. They held an audience because they drew the audience into the wrestling that they could not finish.

These old stories told by these generous old men also held an audience because of the process of "true-ing" that I encountered as I listened and watched. The metaphor is owed to what I learned when I worked as a butcher. Knives are sharpened and then they are trued: a butcher strokes the knife back and forth on a sharpening steel and the edge is trued, worked back and forth until it stands up straight and cuts deep and clean all the way to the bone. The stories had the same effect as the sharpening steel. They worked the teller and audience back and forth, straightening them, sharpening them, creating a truth that cut to the bone. This was a lot to learn from a bunch of old men who told me their stories, whether I understood them or not.

The commentary on the Gospel of Luke grew out of the haunting silences that hung with me as I tried to understand the stories told me by my father's friends and comrades. Every story, even the funny ones, was wrapped in silences more eloquent than the words, more evocative than the presence of the storyteller. As I listened and remembered, I discovered that the authority of the stories lived in a powerful sense of absence that sat silent in each story. Sometimes the absence was the form of a friend who walked through the story on his way to a mission from which he would never return. Sometimes the absence was the face of an enemy soldier when he realized that the storyteller would kill him.

These silences still fill my ears. As I listened to them, I heard other silences also, silences from other moments of disaster and destruction. These silences marked, among other things, the boundaries between insiders and outsiders, between people who could not speak what they had seen and suffered and done and people who could never understand. I wondered in that second commentary about the authority of a story to compel silence. There are stories that demand memory at the same moment they compel silence. I heard such stories out of the disastrous decade of the Holocaust and wondered if the odd silences surrounding the story that Luke tells might be similar. What if the silences of Luke's story sit in the story as the absent form of the experimental community that attempted to mix Jews and Gentiles in a single community focused on Jesus as messiah; what if this community was absent and silent because it died in the ashes of the First Jewish Revolt against Rome? If Luke's written Gospel is silent because it is a relic of a crushed community, then the story has the authority to command memory and to compel silence. If Luke's written Gospel is such a story, then it leaves us to undertake a mandatory apprenticeship, to become apprentices to Luke's story and to the Jewish community that gave it its breath and hope. If we are also compelled to tell Luke's story, it will only be after we have completed our apprenticeship. That may take a while.

Matthew's story has a different flavor. Where Luke allows us to hear the silence that followed the devastation, Matthew points our eyes at the devastation itself. Where Luke leaves us to discover the sound of the wind whistling through empty ruins of Jerusalem, Matthew opens our ears to hear the wailing of Rachel weeping for her children. Where Luke shows us the warmth of family welcoming family in Bethlehem, Joseph's clan city, Matthew shows us the same city littered with the corpses of little children, and not just the corpses of the children, but the corpses also of family members who died trying to defend them against Herod, the stooge of Rome who was defending his throne against a baby. These differences matter for a storyteller.

I finished my study of Luke's story listening to the silences and trying to discern the patterns in that silence. I heard in that silence a call to reverent silence, and a call to an apprenticeship. The authority to tell Luke's story comes after an apprenticeship to the Jewish thought-forms and language and hope and offenses that shape Luke's story. Because this story comes to contemporary Christians after Auschwitz, we must wait and wonder, with George Steiner and Emil Fackenheim, whether our use of language, our complicity, might not compel a much longer silence. How long an apprenticeship must be served after Auschwitz? The answer to that question is not clear, even as we bowl merrily along, chattering all the way.

As I began to consider the authority of Matthew's story, I encountered a different problem, a different question, a different challenge. Where the stern gentleness of Luke's story compels silence, the harshness of Matthew's story compels something else. As I will argue, Matthew's story opens by establishing a deep violence in the narrative world, a violence that is there long before Herod's murderers show up with their swords. This constitutive violence shows up already in the genealogy, and this means that the rhythm of this narrative world is set by men with swords, or, more to the point, the power to use them. Even when no sword-play is involved, still the men in the stories use their power to divide and destroy. My daughter was right. I cannot read Matthew's opening slaughter without reading about Rwanda. My student was right. The stories of the Burundis chase me, too, just as the stories of the slaughter in Bethlehem will have chased Jesus throughout the story that Matthew tells.

This will complicate any attempt to talk about the authority of the story. If the driving reality of the narrative world is the authority of Herod to kill little children, the authority of Rome to kill any opponent it chooses (or creates), then what will it mean to talk of the authority of the story? The story cannot stop Herod, cannot even slow down the Roman power behind him. What is the authority of a story that tells of a refugee people swung and spun about and finally washed up on the sand of another culture, another community?

You will hear in the title of this chapter an echo of one type of authority held by such a story. Such stories can hold an audience when they call for revenge. Is that the authority of Matthew's story? This is a question to ask slowly and carefully. The answer will be awkward, at least, no matter what answer comes back.

Matthew's story does not simply paint a picture for us of the slaughter of the children. It does not simply narrate a news story about the numbers of the dead and the relative positions of their bodies. Matthew's story shivers with the shrieking of Rachel who will not be comforted. Her cries are often translated as weeping, or as wailing. These smooth, domesticated words slide through our ears without registering the horror that stabs in her cries. Shrieking is a better translation of the Greek word that Matthew uses. I have learned from working with my troupe of actors that the word is hard to say. Shrieking is even harder to hear: it chops its way through any stability and sense we normally muster in the face of disruption. Rachel does not wail, and she does not merely weep. Rachel shrieks.

And we hear.

What Do We Hear When We Hear the Cry of Rachel?

The question is: What do we hear? The question is: What does it mean? The question really is: What response must we make? To say that another way: What are we responsible to do? We hear Rachel shrieking. Such sounds change people. They change the people who discover them coming out of their mouths. They change the people who are startled when the sounds twist themselves into their ears. They change people who respond. They change people who do not respond. Surely Rachel is changed the most, altered beyond anything she could ever have anticipated, jerked into a shattered world where none of the laws of physics are what they used to be. Surely Rachel is changed the most, but after her, who? Maybe it is the people who respond, and thus hear and see things they can never forget. Maybe. But I think sometimes that it is the people who do not respond: they hear and then they learn not to hear. I think they are changed most because they must live in the diminished world that is left to them in the aftermath, must live with what they learn about themselves when they cut themselves off from a mother who needs a human response.

Philip Gourevitch makes this point in his reporting from Rwanda. He tells of a night that was suddenly torn by a cry of terror. The cry is answered by other cries, and he asks what is going on. A man from Rwanda explains:

[H]e said, "So there is responsibility. I cry, you cry. You cry, I cry. We all come running, and the one that stays quiet, the one that stays home must explain. Is he in league with the criminals? Is he a coward? And what would he expect when he cries? This is simple. This is normal. This is community."[5]

I explore this cry and its implications more fully in my discussion of the scene in which we hear Rachel's cries (page 76), but for now just notice the authority of this cry, this shriek that tears comfort and isolation into rags. "The one that stays home must explain." Indeed. The cry has the authority to divide human communities into separate groups: when you hear the cry, you either act as a neighbor or you tie yourself to the criminals and cowards.

This is true if you hear the cry in the night, camped alongside the road in Rwanda. It is also true if you hear the cry narrated in Gourevitch's story of the night in Rwanda. The story conveys the cry, and audiences are held to a related standard: Are you a neighbor or are you a coward? Are you, perhaps, a criminal? The story has the authority to ask the question and to expect an answer. Surely the edge is not as sharp, surely the experience of hearing the cry in the night is more terrifying, but the responsibility is the same because the authority of the story calls the audience to account.

But is that all there is to the call to the audience? Is the audience called to account, and to nothing else? This is not a simple question. When the act demanded by the authoritative story is to cry and run together, the ethical situation is clear-cut: either you cry and run or you do not. But what do you do with this authoritative story when the sun rises and you find yourself in the aftermath of the wrong that was done? What do you do when you must plan a response to the atrocity? What is the authority of the story in that situation? Then the story of the wrong that was done takes on a new authority, and a new complication.

Richard Fiske was a survivor of the attack on Pearl Harbor. I met him at the Pearl Harbor memorial. He was there, day after day, to meet with people who came to visit the memorial and to tell them the story of the day that his world turned upside down. Fiske was a young man, a marine bugler serving on the USS *West Virginia,* on the morning that Pearl Harbor was attacked. He saw the devastation. He escaped when so many did not. He tells of the aftermath, when he and the rescue crews could hear tapping from inside the capsized ship, tapping that went on until December 24, Christmas Eve. He tells of finding the bodies later in the last compartment to be opened in June of 1942. In drydock they opened the compartment and found the bodies, and with them a clock and a calendar. The men had lived for weeks after the attack. They could be heard, but they could not be rescued.

Fiske said:

> For me, that clock is one of the most precious artifacts found, because it reminds me of those guys. I often wonder what they were thinking about. Their lives were cut so short and they never had a chance to realize their dreams.[6]

When I met Richard Fiske, I was traveling with a group of students from Augustana College, where I teach. The students were participants in a course called "Peopling Paradise: Missionaries, Migrants, and Money," a course designed by my colleague Michael Mullin to explore the history of immigration and colonial contact in the Hawaiian Islands. As Fiske told his story, no one in the group was thinking of paradise anymore. He told us of the fury that drove him because of that experience, that experience woven into the thousands of stories that came out of that day. He told us of standing on the deck of the *West Virginia* and seeing an attacking plane flying so low that he could clearly see the face of the pilot. He told us how that memory gave him someone to hate, someone to kill, someone on whom he must take revenge.

"You can't believe the anger," he told us. "My brother was there, too. The anger killed him."

Our students clearly thought that they could believe the anger. My colleague and I could see the effect of the story on these bright and considerate students who had spent a month soaking up both the sunshine and the history of the islands. They were imagining the pain, the loss, the shock. They were imagining the face of the attacking pilot: "It seemed like as close as me to you, that's how I remember it," said Mr. Fiske. They were hearing the shriek in his story, and they were hearing a call for revenge. They could even see the face of the pilot who had become their enemy when they heard the story, the shriek, the call for revenge. "Nothing brings back the dead," said Fiske, and my students were sure they knew what he meant.

We have heard the shriek of Rachel, the wailing cry that has an authority to require human beings to jump and run, and to cry out as they run. We have heard the shriek from Richard Fiske. We have heard it from Philip Gourevitch. We have heard it from Rwandans who wish they could forget what they heard, and saw, and survived. My student in Kenya hears it day after day from people who fled the insanity. My daughter heard it and told me that I could not interpret Rachel's shriek until I had interpreted the wailing from Rwanda. She was right, but we have to figure out the consequences of what we have heard. We have to figure out how and why she was right.

The figuring requires that we understand what to do with the anger that arises when we hear such a call.

Memory and the Cry of Rachel

Perhaps we are called to remember. Richard Fiske surely remembers. He heard the tapping of the trapped men, the men who lived until Christmas but were not found until summer. My students surely remember: they heard Richard Fiske. My student in Kenya surely remembers: she hears stories that do not fit in any world most of us have ever lived in. Emil Fackenheim, in his *Jewish Bible after the Holocaust: A Re-reading*, argues that Rachel has become central for Jewish faith and must become central also for Christian faith. Her cries must spur remembrance of all the children, all the villages, all the worlds that were shattered in the decisive decade from 1935 to 1945. All over Europe, towns had echoed with the sounds of Jewish children at play, echoed for five hundred or a thousand years, and in ten short years these sounds of life were silenced. Fackenheim hears Rachel's cries stabbing through the empty synagogues, the empty streets of the Jewish sections of city after city in Eastern Europe.

But it must be asked if remembrance is enough.

I had the honor of being invited to participate in a Yom HaShoah service with the Jewish community in my city. The service was planned by two friends of mine, colleagues at my college who are members of the synagogue. The title of the event was powerful: "In Memory Lies Redemption." It was a stunning service. Singing was woven into reading, prayers were wrapped in memories. In the months since the service, however, I have been thinking about the title. It comes to us from the sayings of the Baal Shem Tov, which compels attention, but not necessarily agreement. Does redemption lie in memory? If it does, what is redeemed, and who? And how does the redeeming happen? As Fiske said at the Pearl Harbor Memorial, the grave of friends of his youth, "Nothing brings back the dead."

As I sat in the service, I listened to stories of a survivor who had lived in a stable Jewish world that was wonderfully knit into a whole and wholesome Europe, who discovered as the decisive decade stalked her that anything that can be knit together can be raveled and shredded. As I listened to her story, I wondered what it would mean to say that anything or anyone was redeemed. It pleased me as I sat there to note that the title was not "In Memory Lies Atonement." Aside from the problems that would be caused by the heavy Christian overlay that the word "atonement" wears, such a word would claim the wrong thing for the service and the remembering. Nothing was atoned for that evening. To suggest that there was atonement would imply that feeling regret amounts to acting to heal the damage done to God's creation and God's chosen people in that awful decade. Regret does not bring back the dead. Remembrance makes that clear, and perhaps it is remembrance of the irreversibility of murder that works the process of redeeming the human beings who are brought together to remember together.

But Is It Enough?

It is the simplest thing in the world to say, quickly, that of course nothing will be enough. But this question goes deeper than such a facile reply. Is it enough to remember? My student in Kenya calls for the moral courage and imagination that will lead to forceful intervention in an effort to prevent genocide so that we do not have to gather in services designed to remember the victims we could have saved. Voices out of the genocide in Rwanda call for justice, or at least for balancing.

> Now whenever the Hutus there see a car coming to my nephew's, they all hide. People will say I'm an extremist because I can't accept or tolerate the people who killed my family. So if they're afraid once in their lives — I was afraid since I was three years old — let them know how it feels.[7]

In the aftermath of the September 11 attacks on the World Trade Center and the Pentagon I saw a bumper sticker that I fear because I understand it. It said: "To Hell with Justice. I Want Revenge."

There is no suggestion in any of these calls that regret will atone for anything, no notion that memory will redeem anything that needs redeeming. *Of course* nothing will be enough, of course nothing brings back the dead, but the question about what will be enough is not a theoretical question. It is a question that aims to unleash proper action driven by carefully considered policy. Or it is a question that responds deeply and viscerally to the shrieks of Rachel and thus refuses to pretend that one can hear such wailing and remain unchanged. Rachel's cries alter the fabric of the universe. After one hears such cries, business-as-usual is revealed as a hobby for the pampered and protected. Walter Brueggemann comes closest in his reflections on the cries of Rachel when he posits an opposition between remembrance and the purposeful forgetting involved in doing triage.[8] Business-as-usual requires us to do triage, to systematically forget those bits of data (human beings! Rachel's children!) that are disruptive and awkward. But even after Brueggemann's point is taken, we must still ask if remembering is enough, if it actually yields the kind of moral courage and imagination, the kind of decisive action that counts as a human response to shrieks in the night.

Anger

Comfortable people seek to remain comfortable. This is not the worst goal in life; neither is it the best. While everything from sports magazines to self-help books to brochures for adventure tourism promotes "getting outside your comfort zone," it is worth noting that the privilege of choosing to "get outside your comfort zone" implies its own sort of comfort. The prevalence of such advice and sales pitches would indicate that we are pretty comfortable with the idea that we should get outside our comfort zones.

But that means that we are still able to remember selectively and safely, and to forget when we choose to forget, that we are still able to do the triage that preserves our safety and stability in a world that violates safety and stability daily. That implies that we can choose to hear, or not hear, the cries that shatter the night, or that we can listen to them for a while and then go back to planning our adventure vacation that will get us comfortably outside our comfort zone.

If that is the position from which we hear Matthew's story, we reveal that we do not and will not hear Rachel's authoritative cry. Hearing the cries in the night is indeed a decisive moment. Either you run together and cry out or you stay home and reveal either cowardice or complicity. Such is the authority of these shrieks and of the story that bears them. For those who hear the cries and run together, the world is changed forever, and it is not clear what it has become. The story has the authority to change worlds. For those who hear the cries and then choose to stay home, the world is also changed forever.

This is an odd sort of authority. The story changes the world, whether we choose to listen or not, and it changes it because it rings with cries that force the audience to divide. For those who are sorted into the company of cowards and criminals, the effect of this authority is clear enough.

My concern at the moment is more for those who hear the shrieks and respond. The call to remember seems never to be enough. The call for revenge seems always to be heard, and felt, and those who hear this call seem always to be ready to continue dividing the audience in response. In extreme cases, the purity of heart on the part of those who hear the cries and respond has led them not only to divide the audience, but to dismember them. Even where the response is more measured and well-mannered ("No blood on the rug, please"), still the anger affects everything, from the root to the fruit. I fear the anger that eats us as we swallow it. Purity of heart may indeed be to will one thing, as Kierkegaard said, but when that "one thing" is anger and revenge, that purity becomes a terrible thing.

Richard Fiske saw the face of a Japanese pilot who was attacking his ship in the Pearl Harbor raid. "Just as close as from me to you," he told us, "and I hated that face. All the years of the war and a long time after, I hated that face." This, my students could understand. But Fiske surprised us all when he continued. "Anger can kill you," he said. "Anger killed my brother."

This was clearly a story Fiske had told many times, a story he had practiced. It was still a story that tore him, even as he walked daily down its familiar paths. And then he surprised his audience. When he turned to talk about the death of his brother, he surprised us all. He did not tell us of a death in the Pearl Harbor attack: his brother went on to serve heroically throughout the South Pacific. He did not tell us of a death in combat: his brother survived the war. He told us about how anger killed his brother years later, how the desire for revenge ate him alive and finally killed him. "People said it was the alcohol," said Fiske, "and they were right, so far as that goes. But it was really the anger that killed him. Anger will kill you." And then he went silent, and his audience with him. "I woke up in the hospital one day and realized that the anger was going to kill me, too," he told us, "and so I decided to get rid of the anger. Revenge will kill you. Nothing brings back the dead."

And so he met and made friends with Zenji Abe, a pilot who participated in that raid. This friendship lasted for the rest of Fiske's life. From 1991 through 2004, when Fiske died at the age of eighty-two, Zenji Abe sent $500 each year to Richard Fiske, who bought two roses each month and laid them at the Pearl Harbor Memorial in honor of the people who died on the day of the attack, in honor also of all the people who died because of the attack.

> "People don't seem to understand that we did what we were told to do, both of us [us and the Japanese]. I'm sorry for all the deaths I may have caused," Fiske explained tearfully.[9]

My students were surprised. Having felt the call to respond, the call to seek revenge, they then heard Fiske tell of his friendship with the Japanese pilots who had attacked Pearl Harbor and of his work to establish links between Japanese and American veterans of that battle.

> "I want kids to understand that you don't have to hate forever," Dick says in a letter to Jennifer in *Pearl Harbor Warriors*. "I'm happy to tell you about my friendship with my former enemy. We can become friends with our adversaries."[10]

Perhaps the fifty years between the beginning of the war and Fiske's discovery is essential to the process. Perhaps Fiske was simply an oddity. "He just had a heart that was a forgiving one," said one of his friends, a fellow survivor of the attack on Pearl Harbor.[11]

The call out of Rwanda sounds different because the killing in Rwanda was different, completely different. Neighbor killed neighbor, husband killed wife, pastors surrendered parishioners to the death squads. "Do your work!" was the call that kept the murderers going through the long hard work of hacking people to death.[12] In the end, there were hundreds of thousands of people killed, and many thousands of people guilty of murder.

> "It's materially impossible to judge all those who participated in the massacres, and politically it's no good, even though it's

just," the RPF's [Rwandese Patriotic Front] Tito Ruteremara told me. "This was a true genocide, and the only correct response is true justice. But Rwanda has the death penalty, and — well, that would mean a lot more killing."

"In other words, a true genocide and true justice are incompatible."[13]

This remains the most disturbing aspect of this sense of the authority of a story, biblical or otherwise. Telling the story of the cries of Rachel changes the world. A call is heard, a call for justice, a call for revenge, a call for "a lot more killing." Not to respond is to join the cowards and the criminals. To respond is to feed the anger that already simmers under the surface of too much of religious practice. Richard Fiske is surely correct: nursing anger will kill you; forgiving your enemy will set you both free. But what do you do when you cannot understand your enemy as a soldier just like you who was, just like you, only following orders? The title given to the Yom HaShoah service is surely appropriate: "In Memory Lies Redemption." But does that offer any guidance before the killing has been stopped? What does memory mean for Rwanda? What does it mean for the next conflagration? Does it call us to quietism and resignation? Or does it demand that we strike first, that we attack on warning, knowing that some warnings will be mistakes, and some will be lies?

The authority of Matthew's story is the authority of a shriek in the night that calls us to cry and run together. We cannot hear the story honestly and with integrity and ignore Rachel's wailing. But once we have heard the wailing, we discover the painful truth that the world is full of such shrieks. Walter Brueggemann hears Rachel's cries in Jewish history and in Jonathan Kozol's revelations of the lives of children who live in America's inner cities. The same wailing is to be heard in Po Bronson's collection of vignettes, *What Should I Do with My Life?* Bronson tells the story of a young man who worked at a casino. One night he saw an old man shaking and crying as he put his last chips into a slot machine. The young man does not know how to respond. The old man fed the chips into the machine willingly. The young man needed the job at the casino. The old man needed the money that he lost, whether he lost it willingly or not, and his cries shook the young man's world. But he does not know how to respond.

His co-workers are not so conflicted. They know how to respond: they laugh at the old man. When the young man protests, they again know exactly how to respond: "Bleeding heart," they say. And they are probably correct. They are comfortable. They have done their triage. They have decided that only fools cry and run when an old man is weeping because of his own actions. But they recognize clearly that the young man in this story has also decided not to respond to the old man's cries. He feels badly about them. He deplores the callous response of his co-workers. But, after a suitable period of soul-searching, he goes back to work at the casino. The old man's cries have the authority to change the world, and the young man picks up his paycheck.

The question that matters for understanding the authority of Matthew's story is the question that comes to every audience: What is an appropriate response to the cries that change the world? Matthew's story will surprise every attentive audience, but in a way that mirrors and reverses the surprise my students heard from Richard Fiske's story. Neither action nor inaction solves the problem. Neither forgiveness nor revenge will bring back the dead, and neither will balance the damage that has been done. True genocide does indeed preclude true justice; it precludes even flawed and imperfect justice. And perhaps remembrance, as unsatisfying as that must be, is all we can get. If so, then the life (and death) of Primo Levi is called into this court. Philip Gourevitch calls Levi into his reflections on the genocide in Rwanda. Levi comes just as necessarily into our reflections on Matthew. After the war, after the aftermath, after the world had settled back to a broken normalcy, Levi said: "If there is one thing sure in this world, it is certainly this: that it will not happen to us a second time."[14] As desperate and damaged as this sounds, it carries a sort of exhausted hope: the disaster will not happen again. There is a relief to be heard even in the exhaustion.

Then, near the end of his life, Levi wrote: "It happened, therefore it can happen again: this is the core of what we have to say. It can happen, and it can happen everywhere."[15]

I cry, you cry. You cry, I cry. This is simple, this is normal. This is community.

In Memory Lies Redemption, but only if you cry and run together.

Chapter Two

MATTHEW'S NARRATIVE ARC: FROM RACHEL TO RESURRECTION

Never merely peripheral for Jews, the weeping Rachel has moved into the centre — and no shared Jewish-Christian reading is possible unless she moves into the Christian centre also: a Rachel weeping for children who have not returned, nor ever will return, from the land of the enemy.

—Emil Fackenheim
The Jewish Bible after the Holocaust: A Re-reading

Beginning and Ending

You have to begin somewhere.

For a storyteller, this is the simplest of all simple truths. And it is the most difficult.

There is always plenty of material that could go in the middle somewhere, too much material, really. As the writer of the Gospel of John said: if everything were told about Jesus that could be told, "the world itself could not contain the books." Storytelling is always as much about leaving things out as it is about including them. There is so much more that you could tell. There always is.

But none of this matters if you don't have a beginning, and beginnings are the hardest to create.

They are difficult because, if stories create worlds, there is a lot of work to be done in a very few words. They are difficult because the beginning of a story is the first clue that we are dealing with a work of art and not just raw, undigested reality. Real life does not have a beginning: things just flow from one to another in a dizzying swirl of complex interwoven causes and effects.

Think about a marriage. It is a simple thing, and it is real. Where does a marriage begin? With the ceremony? In a sense, yes, but few people in North America marry someone they have never been engaged to. And before engagement came dating, and before dating came interest, and before interest came noticing, and before noticing there maybe came hearing and wondering. And of course before all of that there were prior relationships, maybe prior marriages, and prior experiences with marriage, maybe in your own family, maybe with friends. At which of these moments did the marriage begin? The answer is yes, which is not particularly helpful.

If we were to decide that the marriage ceremony is the proper beginning point, I could tell you stories about my own wedding. June 21, 1975. That afternoon it was 98 degrees outside and 90 percent humidity. To understand this story, you have to know that in 1975 not everyone in our town had air conditioning in their homes, and not a single church had air conditioning at all. It was hot when the sun came up. By the time of the wedding, it was beyond hot. It was a whole new kind of temperature, ill-suited to the wearing of tuxedos and heavy dresses with trains. I remember the feeling of sweat rolling down the small of my back and collecting at my belt as we stood in front of the church trying to remember to keep our knees flexed so we wouldn't pass out.

Another thing you have to know about 1975 to understand this story is that no one in those days used the service that was printed in the service book. We all created our own wedding services. (This was the '70s, after all.) Our pastor had taken careful notes on everything that we had planned for the service and had written it all down on a note card. Especially the vows. He used a fountain pen. With washable blue ink.

The service proceeded normally enough. Someone sang some-thing, and someone read something else. I remember being surprised by each part of the service even though we had created the whole thing ourselves. It was like I had never heard it before. All through the ceremony, I mostly remember being overwhelmed. I remember sweating. A lot. Our pastor was sweating, too. The sweat would build up on his forehead in drops. From there it would roll down his face, particularly his nose, and from his nose it would fall in big drops. I remember wondering if I could predict when the next drop would fall.

As the time for the vows approached our pastor began to look distressed. He looked at his notecard and shook his head. He showed us the card. It was an even blue wash with some fascinating splash marks spread around on the card. Hardly a word was legible. He looked up at the two of us and whispered, "We're on our own now. Just follow me." So we did. From that point on, he made it all up as he went along. He made up new vows, that were, I think, a little like the ones we had written. He made up new parts of the service, drawing on whatever resources he could remember in that steamy heat. And so we finished the service. And so began our marriage.

If I tell the story of our marriage with that beginning, you expect that the story will have a certain shape. Maybe there will be a lot of improvising. Maybe there will be a lot of puzzlement. Maybe there will be a lot of sweating. All of those things have been part of our marriage, and such a beginning would ensure that those bits would become prominent in the story that would be told.

But I could begin the story differently. During the wedding cere-mony a thunderstorm erupted. It was a huge storm, with shots of lightning followed immediately by cracks of thunder. The tempera-ture dropped 30 degrees just during the course of the service. It even hailed a little. There are parts of the service that cannot be heard on the tape we had made because of the wind, the thunder, and the hail. If I began the story with the storm, you might expect that there would be more storms to come. Of course there have been, as there will be in every marriage, but beginning with the storm would guarantee that the storms would be heavily featured in the story.

I could also choose to begin the story with something about the first time we met. That seems a good place to begin, but it is difficult in our case since my wife is my sister's best friend since forever. I have no idea when I first met her. I do remember the first time I recall speaking to her. I was sitting in the cafeteria at school. My sister (two years younger) came up with a group of her classmates and asked if they could sit with me. (I used to think it was because I was the cool and charming older brother and my sister wanted to show me off, but my sister and my wife both tell me that had absolutely nothing to do with it.) They sat down. My someday wife sat directly across from me. She looked vaguely familiar. I must have seen her someplace, I thought. Then I thought: I should say something. Something cool and charming. "You should eat your cheese." I said. "It will make you constipated."

It would be rather a different story if I began there. Each of the options would yield a true story, but they would be very different true stories. The differences all have their roots in the ways the stories begin. Storytellers always have to pick what to leave out and what to include, storytellers always have to make choices, but it is the beginning of the story that creates the pattern that will govern the picking and choosing and weaving that make the story.

The only part of the story more important than the beginning is the end. When stories begin they explode, sending energy and plot developments whizzing off in every direction. The only thing that keeps a story from simply dissipating into empty space is the end. The end is where the story stops; it is the goal of the story. But even more significantly, it is the force that creates all the turning points that make for dramatic tension and resolution. The end of a story is like a magnet. It reaches out across the middle of the story and grabs each bit of energy and plot and character and yanks them so that they fall into place when the story is finished.[16]

A good place to see this operating is on American television. Think of an hour-long drama. If you have watched such shows regularly, you already know a lot about how the end of the story pulls everything toward it. Imagine a crime drama. Sometime during the first ten minutes someone is killed. This may not be the last person killed in the story, but with only sixty minutes to work with, this first crime will be crucial. After you come back from the commercial break, you will be led through another ten minutes of complications. New data will fly around in every direction and the characters who are charged with solving the case will become increasingly confused. During the next ten minutes the detectives will begin to get the data in order. They will begin to stabilize the chaos.

Suddenly everything will become clear. The murderer is identified and all the forces of good are mobilized to corner the criminal before he can strike again. You look at your watch and there are twenty minutes left in the show. A question: are the detectives right? Have they cornered the right criminal? In my experience as a watcher of American television, if it is twenty minutes to the end of the hour, you can be sure that they are wrong. You can be sure that this last rush is not a rush to end the story, but rather a rush to increase the tension and complication. The real killer is still undetected. In fact, at twenty minutes to the hour, the real killer is not only undetected, he is probably a trusted person who has been left to protect the vulnerable next victim while everyone else rushes off across the city.

At ten minutes to the hour the last reversal comes. The end reaches out one last time and yanks the story to its conclusion. The killer is revealed and the forces of good race to remedy their mistake. At this point, American television dramas differ. The mistake is sometimes corrected, sometimes not, but always the tension is released, and the story comes to its resting place, its goal. It is finally pulled in by the magnet that has tugged on it from the beginning.[17]

The end creates the tension and provides the resolution. The beginning provides the energy and all the material for the end to pull on. Between these two powerful poles the arc of the story is shaped. Episodes are selected and rejected. Tensions and themes and hopes and frustrations all dance in the middle of the story, but all of these are brought into being by the interaction between the beginning and the end. A storyteller will, therefore, pay exquisite attention to both the beginning and the end when analyzing the story because they are the forces that create the arc that the story follows.

In what follows I will sketch one possible narrative arc for the story of the Gospel of Matthew. This is not the only sketch possible, to be sure, but this one pays careful attention to what the audience is handed at the beginning and to where and how the end reaches back and yanks the story to its conclusion. Readers are heartily encouraged to argue with the sketch I present and to carry out their own close investigating of the ways Matthew's beginning and end might shape the arc of the story. Remember, however, that proper storytelling will pay attention to the actual shape of the story being told and not to ideological forces outside the story that already know what things a Gospel story is allowed to be and mean. A basic rule for storytellers and other interpreters: Always make sure that you are reading the story that you are studying and not what everyone else thinks the story has to mean. Even if everyone else is right, still you should read the story and not their predigested ideological interpretations. Biblical stories are stronger, and more interesting, than our ideologies.

Matthew's Beginning

Matthew begins his story with a genealogy, with a list of birthings. This beginning is significant, as are all beginnings. Commentators often link this beginning to the genealogies that inhabit other Jewish writings, and with good cause. Matthew is a story continuous with the other stories that have breathed life into Jewish faith in all centuries. Matthew's list is like other lists: it contains (mostly) men and establishes links between a rather anonymous present and a historic past. Joseph may be an unknown (except for this story), but David and Abraham are not. The genealogy arrays itself in ordered ranks from Abraham to David, from David to Exile, from Exile to

Jesus. The present moment, however fragile and provisional it may seem, is the culmination of centuries of orderly preparation. There is a rhythm underlying the cacophony of history, and it is not just any old rhythm. Matthew begins his story by establishing a rhythm based on multiples of seven. He tells us that it is fourteen generations from the father of all fathers (Abraham) to the king of all kings (David), fourteen generations from the king of all kings to the disaster of all disasters (the Exile), and fourteen generations from the disasters of all disasters to the one anointed by God to set all things right (the Messiah). These multiples of seven are significant. There are seven days in every week, and there have always been seven days. Torah specifies observing a week of seven days, six to work and one to observe as Shabbat (a word that itself means "seventh"). Even God followed this rhythm in creating the world.[18] For the generations to order themselves in multiples of rhythmic sevens testifies to the readiness of the creation for the coming of Messiah who will put things right.

Of course, if you count the generations as listed they don't quite add up, which is odd. The first two blocks of generations add up nicely enough, at least if you decide to count Tamar's son as levirate progeny to her first husband Er, who died without impregnating his wife (more on that in a moment). But no matter how you count, Jesus arrives one generation too early, at least by a count of the generations as listed in the current text. It is always possible that, somewhere in the textual history of this list of birthings, one went missing. It is not too surprising that this might happen in the last block, since the people contained in that block are largely unknowns, at least to contemporary interpreters. It is also not particularly surprising that the last two blocks depart almost completely from Luke's genealogy, or that the first block does not. The further things recede into the mythic past, the easier it is to regularize them.

But it is a surprise that the genealogy is out of rhythm. People use genealogies to establish a firm and regular foundation under the blowing and shifting present moment.[19] Genealogies are supposed to provide stability and order, but this one frustrates that expectation before the story even gets started. Perhaps that should indicate that we should expect other frustrations as Matthew tells his story. Perhaps Matthew puts Jesus a couple of generations off the beat on purpose. In any case, such a surprise at the beginning of this story should incline us to expect more surprises. In this, Matthew does not disappoint.

Surprising Women

We meet the next surprise even before we leave the genealogy, and this surprise is even bigger than the disturbed rhythm. Matthew's real surprise comes in the form of women who pop out of the list of birthings. This ought not be a surprise, since this is a list of birthings, after all. But ancient genealogies do not typically include mention of the women involved, as odd as this may sound to contemporary ears. Matthew mentions several women, and it is rather surprising. Commentators who have cared to notice their presence (and not all commentators do) have offered various explanations for their inclusion. Perhaps they are representatives of outsiders who have been included in Israel, thus making Jesus' list of birthings to foreshadow the composition of the church that developed from his movement.[20] Perhaps they are sinners who have been included to show that the Messiah comes from common human stock, including sinners like those he will forgive.[21] Both of these explanations have their own merit. It has been interesting to the rabbis that David had a Moabite among his mothers. And establishing a link to humanity as it actually is would be a worthy task for any messiah.

There is a problem with the second explanation, of course, since it would be odd to single out women as sinners and pass over the men who also had earned such a classification. This is particularly true in the case of "the wife of Uriah." In her case, the sinner is David the king who takes her and rapes her, and then arranges to murder her husband (her protection in a patriarchal society). Any interpretation that chooses to call her a sinner is simply inattentive, or too willing to invent ways to blame women for trouble.[22]

Especially Tamar

If the case of Bathsheba weakens the argument that these women are sinners, that of Tamar destroys it (Genesis 38). This last statement might appear unsupportable, at least at first. Tamar did, after all, dress herself as a prostitute and walk the streets. In her case, as in so many others, it is the rest of the story that is determinative. Before she could dress herself as a prostitute, she had to take off her widow's garments. She was dressed as a widow because her husband had died. The storyteller in Genesis 38 carefully informs us that her husband was wicked and that God killed him. What this wickedness might have been, we would have to imagine. Tamar would not have had to use her imagination, which makes her like many women who know wickedness in the person of a husband.

Tamar, further, changed her clothing in her father's household, not in the household of her husband's clan, where one would expect to find a widow in those days. She was back with her father because her father-in-law, Judah, had sent her away after the death of both Tamar's husband (Er) and of her brother-in-law, whose clan responsibility it was to impregnate her so she would bear children for her husband's name and for the clan. Onan, the brother-in-law, refused to impregnate Tamar, and God killed him as well.

Older commentators sometimes imagined that God was angry with Onan because he "spilled his seed on the ground." This interpretive line lies behind the name given in the past to male masturbation: onanism. While this reading may catch something of the ancient reverence for the mystery of life and procreation, it explains little else in the text. Such an interpretive line seems unpromising because it proceeds without noticing the obvious. Onan "spills his seed," the storyteller informs us, *whenever*[23] he went into his brother's wife. Responsible telling of this story will have to make sense of the word "whenever." How many acts of penetration are required to establish a pattern that deserves the word "whenever"? Again, the storyteller leaves that to our imagination. Again, Tamar will not have needed to use her imagination. She will simply have had to wait for Onan to use her yet again, "whenever" he wanted his pleasure and release.

Shall we notice, just for the moment, that Onan has created Tamar as his private prostitute? As long as she does not become pregnant, he is bound by brotherly duty (and probably patriotism, that other refuge of scoundrels) to try ever so hard to impregnate poor infertile Tamar. So he tried ever so hard, and ever so often. How often? I imagine he cast himself as the ultimate brother. I imagine he did his duty to the clan repeatedly. All for the good of the family. And Tamar has to be available. Repeatedly. All for the good of the family.

God kills Onan, though not until the "whenever" has had sufficient time to become a "whenever." Judah, now having lost two sons (both of them wicked, by the way) now decides to turn Tamar out, which leaves her as an unproductive mouth in her father's house, permanently unavailable to marry and bear children, and so also unavailable to secure her own future by having children who will honor her and feed her when she is old.[24] Judah promises to send for Tamar when his next son comes of age. He is lying, and Tamar knows it, but she can do nothing about it. Or so it seems.

Tamar takes off the clothes that mark her mourning for a wicked husband. She covers her face. This act marks her, Gerhard von Rad tells us, as a "devoted one,"[25] a woman who may be presumed (if cultural practices extended across ethnic borders as may be assumed) to be available for sex with strangers.

That she covers her face to indicate such responsibility is significant, at least in terms handed us by Emmanuel Levinas. Levinas, in *Totality and Infinity,* argued that ethics are born in the face of "the other." A single human being, acting and moving in splendid isolation, can plan and do anything. But then this single human being encounters another face, another set of eyes, another "mirror of the soul" (to echo an old, perceptive understanding), only this mirror does not reflect back; it reveals the depth of another's being, a depth into which she can barely see, a person she cannot control. Levinas argued that with this startling face-to-face encounter comes the first absolute ethical prohibition: this is the Other whom you must not kill.[26]

For all of the complicated problems that go with this insight, Levinas has caught something here. There is something riveting about a face-to-face encounter, whether the other face is that of a stranger or that of a lifelong family member. There is something about that encounter that reveals the limitations of all the plans and projects you cook up in splendid and abstract isolation, and ethics, Levinas argued, grow out of limitation. Years ago, just before my wife and I were to be married, I asked an old man, a pastor with whom I worked, what I needed to know about being married. He and his wife had just celebrated their sixty-fifth wedding anniversary, so I figured he might have something important to tell me. He thought for a while, and then he said, "Here's the only thing I know about being married: I wake up in the morning, roll over in bed and look my wife in the face and I realize in that moment that I have not the slightest idea what she is going to do next." At the time I thought this rather thin, which only demonstrates my own limitations. Now that my wife and I have been married more than thirty years, I realize the ethical wisdom of what Pastor Mueller said so many years ago. Levinas would have agreed. With the face of the Other comes an encounter with another world of infinite possibility, none of which can be predicted or controlled, and with this encounter comes obligation, connection, and life.

All this helps crack open the story of Tamar. Interpreters frequently note that Judah acts improperly in this scene because he treats Tamar as if she were a nobody, not his daughter-in-law. They are correct about the impropriety of his actions, but wrong about the reason. It is not that she is no-body. Rather, she is "no-face." If she has no face to be seen, she has no face to be encountered, no face to exert an ethical demand on those she meets. Men can exhaust themselves in her body and not be bound by any obligation beyond the payment of the agreed-upon price. As the story develops, however, the issue is not "men" in the plural, but a single man, Judah. Judah hires her for a promise. This puts Tamar in exactly the position over against this representative of the patriarchal clan system that she has always been in: her future depends on a promise. If Levinas is right, however, this promise is an uncertain thing. If Tamar, and all "devoted ones," are "no-faced" in this interchange, then they have no ethical claim on the man who penetrates them. This also puts Tamar in a position with which she is quite familiar. It would appear that Judah and his clan have never (to this point, anyway) seen her face and acknowledged her claim. This time, however, Tamar takes trophies. Judah promises (there is that word again) to pay her, and to do it soon. Tamar asks how she has any way of believing this man who is standing there ready for sex but not for responsibility. Judah gives her his staff, his cord, and his signet, signs of his promise. Interpreters may be right in noting, with Leon Kass,[27] that the staff, cord, and signet were public signs of a man's promise, power, and integrity. But if that is the case, Judah is no more a man of character than were his sons. When he sends a servant around to deliver the promised kid-goat, only to find no one there to collect the payment, the storyteller does not even hint that Judah is distressed to have his promise, power, and integrity loose and beyond his control. Imagine not caring that your PIN number for your bank account was lost and in someone else's hands, someone whose face you had never seen. Either the staff, cord, and signet are of less significance than is sometimes argued, or Judah does not care about the possible unauthorized use of his name and authority. Either way, Judah looks more and more like his sons.

It is also worth noting, in passing, that Judah does indeed attempt to keep his promise to the prostitute he found himself needing to use alongside the road. Why he would feel himself bound by a promise made to a "no-faced" woman, but not bound by a promise made to his daughter-in-law, is puzzling, to say the least. Perhaps it is that his concern for his wicked sons has blinded him to all the faces surrounding them. Perhaps it is that the faces of women in his own clan are to him not faces but property, breeding stock. Perhaps it is that a transaction made along the public roadside might be observed, and thus enforced, while promises touching on private family matters always offer the opportunity to create convenient excuses for not keeping inconvenient promises.

Or perhaps it is all of these possibilities. This seems the most likely judgment, given the behavior of Judah and his clan when Tamar is discovered to be pregnant. The storyteller establishes a careful silence around the dismissal of Tamar after the death of her second wicked husband. To send her home without cause is a clan offense. Promises had been made. Deals had been struck. It may be that Judah has manipulated the system by pleading that his younger son is too young, but the hollow silence in which Tamar is consigned to a bleak and barren future hints that, though all is not well, all is quite normal. Such abuses of power are part of the real game of clan politics, especially where women are concerned. When Tamar turns up pregnant, this hollow pretense is punctured. Judah (speaking for his clan) rushes in with righteous wailing about the terrible offense committed by this monstrous woman. Now it is clear, he can argue at last, that Tamar's wickedness killed his wicked sons. And though wickedness is, often as not, a public category (which is to say the neighbors knew all about the sons and their character), the public appears to have decided to go along with "poor long-suffering Judah." Tamar, the no-faced woman, is to be executed, put down like so much damaged livestock.

But they had not reckoned on Tamar's understanding of the game. They had not imagined that she understood that the power of a public promise given to a "devoted one" along a road exceeded that of a public promise given in marriage to a daughter-in-law (read: brood mare). They had not thought about the staff and signet ring that the storyteller showed us as they passed between a sexually excited Judah and a no-faced woman alongside the road. They had not reckoned on Tamar at all. For Judah, she seems to have been no-faced all along. When he saw her alongside the road he did not recognize her, not her stance, not her way of walking, not the way she moved her hands, not even her voice during their negotiations. This last failure may be understandable. As the comedian Robin Williams noted, men have two heads, but only enough blood to operate one of them at a time. It is not that Tamar has no face. It is simply that Judah is blind to it. But, as the storyteller makes clear, blindness is no excuse.

"The man who impregnated me is the man who gave me this staff and this signet," Tamar says, careful to make her declaration in public. "You're smarter than I am, lady," says Judah (though not exactly in those words). And he is right. Tamar is indeed smarter, and she is more determined not to be pushed out of what is rightfully hers. And so she is included in the list of birthings.

Especially Mary

The last woman in the list is often not much mentioned, even by those who pay some attention to the other women included in the genealogy. This is odd, since the last woman is Mary, the mother of Jesus. In Luke's story Mary is a speaking character who moves independently about at the beginning of the story, a character who has mobility and also relatives. Matthew's Mary is silent and without connections. In Matthew's story, all she is is pregnant.

And she is in danger. To be inconveniently pregnant in her generation puts her at risk of being stoned. Tamar was to be stoned when she was inconveniently pregnant. Bathsheba's husband was killed when David made her pregnant. And now Mary faces the same danger. Her betrothed husband, Joseph, is most commonly treated gently by interpreters:[28] he is imagined to be compassionate in choosing to put Mary away quietly (either *because* he is strictly observant, or *despite* it, but that is another argument). What such interpreters do not mention (perhaps because they are not interested in it?) is that this covert action by Joseph will serve to keep his name clear. He will emerge from the whole unfortunate affair with his reputation for being strictly observant intact. What is too often passed over is that, at the end of the unfortunate affair, Mary is still pregnant, and thus still at risk of being killed.[29] Even with the very best outcome, she will be another unproductive mouth, another woman with no secure future, another woman who has been put away by the practices of a patriarchal clan. Joseph looks more and more like Judah, who also wanted to be rid of an inconvenient woman as quickly as possible.

Joseph looks far too much like other males in the list of birthings who push women out of what is rightfully theirs. And Mary looks far too much like the other women in the list of birthings. Each of them was pushed out. Though we know little about Rahab, we know that she was a prostitute, which means she existed in the midst of patriarchal clans as an unprotected woman available to all men as long as she was desirable. We know a little more about Bathsheba, enough to see that the system did not offer her anything like adequate protection. We know even more about Ruth and Tamar because the stories we have inherited allow us to hear their voices. In each case we see and hear them as they refuse to be pushed out of what is rightfully theirs.

In the case of Mary, we do not hear her voice or see her actions. This time it is God who speaks, through an angel, and informs Joseph that he is not to put Mary away. He is not to be afraid (of a pregnant woman!). He is to accept Mary and her inconvenient child. He does. It is perhaps important for a storyteller to notice that, in Mary's case, God does what has been done by a woman before. Naomi coached Ruth. Tamar took care of herself. Now when it is Mary who is made vulnerable, God does for her what has been a woman's job to this point. If figuring God as a warrior (for instance) must incline interpreters to speak of God as a male,[30] then perhaps this way of figuring God ought to incline us to speak of God as a woman who has learned how things really work. In any case, Mary fits into the list of birthings nicely. She also is pushed out of what is rightfully hers by a male who does it because he can, and like the other women in the genealogy, she is brought back to what is hers.

Especially Rachel

There is another woman's voice coming in this story. There is another call back through history and memory. There is another criminal abuse of power, another shameful exercise of brutality, and this abuse calls Rachel into the story. Rachel, the wife of Jacob. Rachel, the mother of Joseph and Benjamin. Rachel, the mother chosen by Jeremiah to weep for all the Jews being dragged into Exile in Babylon after the destruction of the first Temple in 587 BCE. Rachel, ever since Jeremiah called on her, was designated the chief mourner for all Jewish children killed by dangerous enemies in every generation.[31] Now Matthew calls this same Rachel, this archetypal mourner, into his story as well. No sooner is Jesus born than Mary and Joseph are forced to flee. Herod will not have a rival. He will kill infants in order to preempt any future attack on his position. He will kill all the children, or maybe all the boys, living in and around Bethlehem, Jesus' hometown, all who are under two years old.

The description of the age of the children killed is important to Matthew's story. No storyteller should attempt to tell any part of Matthew's story before she has sat and played with a two-year-old child, before she has had her hair pulled, her fingers chewed, and her neck hugged by an energetic toddler. No one should attempt to tell any part of Matthew's story until she has watched a toddler learn to walk, talk, and eat with a spoon. Matthew tells us that the intended victims were two years old and younger. The detail matters.

Matthew does not tell us if there were other victims. Why? There would surely have been other victims, and many of them. When Herod's surrogates arrived to kill all the toddlers, mothers would have fought them, fathers would have fought them, as would sisters, brothers, grandparents, and neighbors. And the murderers would have killed them, too.[32] Why does Matthew choose not to tell us the story of their deaths? Perhaps he simply lacks imagination. Perhaps he is in a hurry to get on with the rest of his story. Perhaps. But it seems far more productive to assume that Matthew is silent about the "collateral damage" because he, like the storytellers of the whole biblical tradition, chooses to leave gaps that require interpretation. All these storytellers trust their audience to imagine what must have happened.

What Matthew does show us is crucial. While Rachel weeps for yet another generation of Jewish babies killed by men with power, Matthew shows us Mary, Joseph, and Jesus as they barely escape to Egypt. How narrow was the escape? Once again, Matthew does not tell us. The angel warns Joseph, and the family flees. As they flee, Herod sends his murderers to kill all the toddlers in Bethlehem. There is more to be explored in this episode (see the fuller discussion on page 76), but notice for now that Jesus enters this story on the run with the cries of Rachel drifting on the breeze behind him. Notice that Matthew's story emerges out of a hard and violent past into a present moment that is just as dangerous. The story is barely two chapters old and already the stage is littered with the corpses of little children. Already those with the power of Empire are hunting Jesus.

What Kind of Story Is This?
A Hunting Story?

This beginning is important because into the beginning is compressed all the energy, all the tension, all the conflict that will explode and become the whole story that Matthew is telling. In the beginning is everything. If this is true, then notice that Matthew is telling a story driven by violence. Notice that Matthew is telling a story of hunting. Though Herod dies before he could know that he had missed his target, Joseph is not particularly comforted by his death. Joseph assumes that Herod's successor is as dangerous as was Herod, perhaps since both serve in the shadow of Rome, of Empire, of domination. Herod hunts for Jesus. Archelaus hunts for Jesus. Behind them, however, we see the real hunter. Herod, the king of the Jews, is just a dog sent into the field by his Roman master. It is important that a storyteller remember who whistles in this story, and who has to obey.

If Matthew is telling a hunting story, then the ending of the story is the moment when the prey is finally run to ground. Jesus is caught by another group of his countrymen (the chief priests and the members of the Sanhedrin) that live in the overpowering shadow of Empire. Whatever their own views on Jesus might have been, they knew that Pilate (and Rome) would not tolerate anything that could be construed as rebellion. The stakes were high. Pilate had no problem provoking the Jewish community and then killing anyone who got in his way. Empire was always hunting for rebels to kill. In Matthew's story, Empire has been hunting for Jesus from the beginning. It is fitting (in an Aristotelian sort of way)[33] for Jesus to finally be caught and killed here at the end of the story. The beginning is the moment of the explosion of all the energy of the story. The end is the magnet that draws everything to itself. The end provides the goal that the beginning had begged for. At the end of Matthew's story, the last baby of Bethlehem is finally hunted down and killed.

If the story ended there (and it could), Matthew would be telling a story about the inexorable power of Empire to get its way. Momentary escape is possible, and it is even possible to live a whole life in this moment of escape, but in the end Empire will always catch its prey and kill it. "Resistance is futile," as members of the Borg used to say on the *Star Trek* television series. Herod was succeeded by Archelaus and neither caught Jesus. But in the background waited Empire, working and watching at all times. After a whole life devoted to resisting everything Rome stood for, Jesus was finally caught and delivered to Pilate. He was caught by Roman surrogates, but these surrogates were themselves caught in the web of Empire. They could do nothing else. Pilate and Empire had complete control. And Pilate killed Jesus, adding a jab at Jewish life and faith to his act when he nailed both Jesus and his taunt ("King of the Jews") to the cross outside Jerusalem.

Surprises between the Beginning and the End

The story could have ended there, but it did not. Matthew goes on to tell the story of Jesus' resurrection. Before considering this fascinating ending, we ought to revisit the middle of Matthew's story. The middle hangs between the decisive beginning and the powerful end. The middle is the field on which the discoveries and reversals of the story are played out, the space in which the tensions of the story spark and crackle.

The middle of Matthew's story is fascinating. As has been long noted, the middles of the Synoptic Gospels (Matthew, Mark, and Luke) hold in common most of their material, each arranging and deploying it as the storyteller sees fit. As has also been long noted, Matthew has what source and redaction critics called "special material." This material is of various sorts. Some of it seems to indicate that Matthew knew of episodes that the other storytellers did not. Other times Matthew's special material takes the form of characteristic phrases or flavors that are stirred through the telling of otherwise shared material. As redaction critics pointed out, Matthew's special spin on the story contributes a hard-edged rigor to Jesus' teaching and healing. In Matthew's telling of the story, Jesus makes harsh demands. He tells sharply worded parables of sorting, and those who are sorted out and rejected are thrown into the outer darkness where people wail and gnash their teeth. This last phrase is nearly unique to Matthew's Jesus, and he not only uses the phrase, he delights in it. Every time Jesus encounters a crowd whose commitment, understanding, or faithfulness is mixed or ambiguous, he divides them into sheep and goats, wheat and weeds, good fish and waste, and every time the waste is burned. Jesus in Matthew is hard-edged and harsh. Jesus in Matthew, however, is also gentle and warm. If Matthew's middle opens our eyes to a harsh and demanding Jesus, we see also the gentlest Jesus in any of the Gospels. "Come to me all those who are exhausted (by work) and loaded heavy. I, even I, will rest you. Pick up my yoke on you. Learn from me because I am gentle and lowly in mind. You will find rest for your life.

My yoke is serviceable; my lead is light." So says Matthew's Jesus in the middle of his story (chapter 11).

What is a storyteller to make of this sharp disjunction? For the middle of a story to work, there have to be physical causes for the reactions that drive the episodes of the story. The effects must have adequate causes. It is, of course, always possible to do every scene in "gentle Jesus, meek and mild" mode, but real storytellers will have trouble with this mode, if only because the harsh lines spoken by Jesus sound much worse when they are spoken with a smile and a slight laugh.[34] I wondered about this for a long time. Perhaps, I thought, this would be a good time to retreat to the old, comfortable notions of early redaction critics. Perhaps Matthew was simply a scissors-and-paste man, and not a particularly skilled one at that. I imagined that I might be able to dress up this dodge in a theoretical flourish (perhaps something about the insistent incompleteness of all textuality). But it did not seem like enough. I give the old storytellers more credit than did Martin Dibelius, and I know enough about the deconstructive fraying of texts to recognize that this is not an instance of that. Jesus is sharply inconsistent in the middle of Matthew's story. The question is, why?

In the midst of wondering about this difficult storytelling problem, I found myself in conversation with a colleague in the Education Department in the college where I teach. She was talking about the effects that violence and family disruption have on children. Such children typically act out the effects of this disruption. They are typically excessively demanding, both of themselves and of others. They typically divide the people around them into groups of heroes and enemies. The heroes are saints to be loved and the enemies are devils to be hated above all else. And, most typical of all, they tend to snap back and forth between love and hate, and all it takes for a hero to become a devil is a single disappointment. Such traits, my colleague told me, persist into adulthood.

Suddenly Jesus made sense. In the middle of Matthew's story he looks exactly as one would expect someone with his beginning to look. The sharply different texts, the extremes of gentleness and harshness, the call to perfection (see the Sermon on the Mount), all fit together if Matthew is telling a starkly honest story about the damage done by Rome and its subordinates, by imperial brutality. Suddenly I have something that works for a storyteller. Jesus becomes a whole and rounded character, not a collage of pious images held together by an audience that agrees never to ask questions. The Jesus we see in the middle of the story, jagged and inconsistent, makes most sense if we read him as both hunted and haunted by the violence with which his story began. What child would not have asked why it was that he had no cousins near his own age? What child would not have seen the pain and residual fear that his mother's face could not hide when he asked? What child would have been unaffected when his father stormed out of the room whenever he brought up the matter of Herod and the innocent children? Such a violent assault leaves marks, and attentive storytellers can see those marks in the middle of Matthew's story. Though commentators are correct when they note that Matthew does not explicitly refer back to Jesus' birth stories once you have finished with them,[35] the story of the slaughter of Jesus' innocent cousins (and aunts and uncles, too, to be sure) has left its palpable marks on Jesus character.

What Kind of Story Is This?
A Martyr's Story?

This damaged Jesus, this hunted Jesus is, in the end, caught. He is killed. His death could make of him a martyr. This also is material a storyteller can use. There are many martyr stories that we all know. Even without thinking about it, most audiences will recognize the parts of such a story. Martyr stories require an atrocity. Martyr stories require a capture. Martyr stories require an execution. And martyr stories require an executioner who is reduced to muttering wonder at the calm and control exhibited by the hero, the martyr. Jews of Jesus' era knew many martyr stories, and collected them in texts like 4 Maccabees. The story of Eleazar is a good example. Throughout the agonizing torture it is the torturer who feels the agony. Eleazar speaks with a remarkable calm, and finally dies, as he has lived, for the sanctification of the Name (haShem). His calm is what marks him as a martyr. His quiet courage is what makes his story into an example story, fit to tell children.

So a storyteller must ask: If Matthew is not simply a hunting story, is it more properly a martyr story? The answer will be found in the death scene. Does Jesus die a martyr's calm death? At this point a contemporary storyteller must shake free from all the accumulated assumptions about what the Gospels are and simply look at Matthew's story and see it for what it is. However much we may be inclined to view Jesus' death as a martyr's death, however much Matthew has set us up to expect exactly such a death, it is my judgment that Matthew frustrates that inclination. The problem comes with the death itself: if Jesus is to be a proper martyr, he dies incorrectly. To be sure, many of the elements required for a martyrdom are there. He has obvious executioners. One of his executioners has a line that could be played as torturer's agony.

But then comes his death. In the very event that would have made him indisputably a martyr, it must be noticed that Jesus simply dies wrong. At the moment of death he does not look into heaven and see hosts of welcoming angels. He does not regret that he has but one life to lose for his faith. He does not hold his integrity quietly intact. He shatters and with his last breath accuses God of deserting him.

The impact of this last collapse is hard for practiced Christian readers to assess. Millennia of explanatory theology have padded the scene, making it into a demonstration of Jesus' humanity, or of the depths of the pain of burden of sin, or of the reality of the pain of death.[36] Each of these explanations has its value and its place in the history of Christian theology. But each of these explanations clouds the story that Matthew is telling. They are all later theological growth that grew up in the aftermath of Matthew's story. Contemporary storytellers are, of course, quite free to use this later growth as the substance of a story they are telling. But a storyteller ought also to pause and reflect on what the story might have been before it was made into a theological object lesson.

Matthew sets up what *ought* to be a martyr story, and then just when the curtain is ready to go down to the applause of those who will honor, remember, and emulate the heroic martyr killed by Empire, Matthew gives Jesus lines that must choke a storyteller. "My God," says Jesus, calling on the guarantor of narrative sense and predictability.[37] "My God," cries Jesus, "why have you abandoned me?" Eleazar says no such thing. The mother of the seven sons says no such thing. In fact, not even her youngest, least prepared son says anything like Jesus says. If he had, he would have revealed that he, alone of all his brothers, was not equipped to be a proper martyr. Such an outcome would have had tragic effect. The executioner would have been scorned as the killer of ill-prepared children. But he would not have been a proper martyr. In 4 Maccabees the little boy dies as a fully approved and proper martyr.

Jesus does not. When he collapses at the end, his integrity collapses with him, and the storyteller is left with a tense disaster that will resist any simplified telling of the story.

Once again Matthew has told a story with more tension than simple Christian ideology expects. Once again Matthew has told a story with more complex texture than most portrayals of Jesus ever attempt. Once again Matthew tells a story that demands a storyteller with powerful skills and insight.

Surprises in the Raggedy Ending

The death scene ends with a messy aftermath. There are earthquakes. Old, dead holy ones appear in the holy city. There is a barely managed effort to guard Jesus' tomb. None of these ragged events flows smoothly. The pieces of the story are picked up, one after another, like debris scattered on a smoking battlefield. Then Shabbat intervenes and passes in silence. Nothing is resolved. As the sun begins to rise on the day after Shabbat, women wander onto the battlefield. The ragged events continue: another earthquake, a messenger of the LORD, a message that overwhelms the women who hear it, a plot and a lie. In the midst of this chaos Jesus appears. And then, apparently, disappears.

The raggedness of this aftermath impresses itself on anyone who would attempt to honor this story by telling it. The flurry of chaotic fragments defeats any attempt to tell a smooth story, though smoothness is what tellers and audiences alike take as a sign of truth.[38]

Then Jesus appears again. His followers see him. Some worship, doing what well-trained Christians know is appropriate. But others doubt. The raveled edges of Matthew's story have prepared the audience to appreciate the rationality of the doubters. No matter how ready an audience might be to settle down and acclaim Jesus as lord and messiah, the raggedness of his death and its aftermath (properly honored) will have unsettled them. They will understand how even Jesus' followers could doubt at such a moment.

If the audience has been following Matthew's story closely, they know what has to come next. Jesus has encountered doubters before. He has acted with marvelous regularity in the face of such unbelief. He has looked on crowds of listeners and has, like Gideon before battle, chosen a worthy few and sent the many home in shame. That puts it too lightly. Jesus, faced with people of flawed integrity, has consistently sent them to the fires of condemnation (see Matthew 8:12, 13:42, 22:13, 24:51, 25:30). An attentive audience will know to expect this.

And now comes the real challenge for anyone who would tell Matthew's story faithfully. Now comes the challenge that demands real skill, real insight, real craft. Now comes Matthew's biggest surprise. Jesus does not send anyone to Gehenna. No one burns. No one is left to wail in the outer darkness. Jesus commissions the whole mixed lot, without making any distinction. He sends the whole lot out as his emissaries to make disciples. He does what he has never done before: he sheaths the sword of division and embraces all those gathered on the mountain, welcoming them all, flawed as they are, into his mission.

Embodied storytelling requires storytellers to pay exquisite attention to the physics of the text. Nothing can happen without adequate cause. Such a dramatic change in such a central character must have an adequate cause. But what could that cause be?

I have argued elsewhere that the cause of all this change is the resurrection of Jesus. Jesus the perfectionist knew the consequences of his collapsed integrity.[39] Such imperfection marks him for the outer darkness. In terms he himself had laid down, such a failure to achieve mythic martyrdom disqualifies him for the kingdom. It does not matter that such a collapse is exactly what one ought to expect out of the horror of crucifixion. Mythic martyrs and brittle perfectionists make no such allowances. In Matthew's story, Jesus dies aware of his failure and expecting nothing. And then he finds himself raised from the dead.

Such impossible events are dangerous to think about. What would the experience of resurrection be like? Martin Luther imagined that God, before all creation, was whittling switches to use on people who asked such meaningless questions. We may be able, however, to know something about what resurrection would have meant to a Jew of Jesus' generation and faith. From texts written both before and after Jesus' career, it comes clear that resurrection was understood as the last and final victory of faithfulness, faithfulness to the sanctity of the Name of God despite a world that made that Name an emptiness, an ineffective protection against the power of the sword and the cross. Rome could well scoff at Jewish faith (remember Pilate's taunt was aimed at all Jews and all Jewish faith, not just Jesus) because they could kill anyone they chose. Resurrection provided a field on which God's promises, long blocked, could finally have full effect. Resurrection was the final effective consequence of faithfulness.

And so Jesus, the broken perfectionist, found himself raised. He found himself sharing in God's gracious care for a crushed creation even though he had not managed a martyr's death, even though he had violated his own standards for faithfulness, even though in his own terms he was more goat than sheep. And he seems to have drawn conclusions from his experience. Resurrection changed him. The effective promises of God have a way of doing that.

Provisional Conclusions

There are other ways to sketch the narrative arc that Matthew's story follows. This is one way. This sketch implies that anyone telling, interpreting, or hearing Matthew's story of Jesus should pay careful attention to the violence of the story. The story begins and ends in violence, from the deep remembered past, to the contemporary slaughter of little children, to the hunting down and killing of the last of the babies of Bethlehem, Matthew's story is haunted by violence and its consequences. Any attempt to embody this story will need to explore the physics of the violent scenes, and the physics of violence in general, in order to tell this story truthfully. This story cannot be told calmly. There are powerfully gentle moments, but around these moments swirls violence, both linguistic and physical. Any truthful telling of this story will have to solve the problem of how to embody the tension between the gentleness and the rage. Even in scenes that seem unrelated to either of these opposed poles, a storyteller will have to find ways to physically re-member the violence out of which the whole story springs. Jesus *must* remember the death of his cousins under Herod, and the ensemble playing this story must continually re-member what those deaths would have meant to every character and every scene.

The story begins and ends in violence, but then Jesus is raised from the dead, raised from collapse, and brought into the life that is God's (too-)long awaited promise for a creation hunted by death. The story ends, and then the story ends again, but very differently. If the end of the story is truly the magnet that pulls everything into motion, then this end of the story that comes after the end of the story changes everything. Now we shall turn to key scenes from Matthew's story to see how they play as part of this provisional sketch of the narrative arc.

Chapter Three

THE TEXTS IN THEIR CON-TEXTS

Section 1:
ADVENT, CHRISTMAS, AND EPIPHANY

First Sunday in Advent
Matthew 24:36–44
(see translation, p. 399)

Ritual Text: The Life of the Worshiping Community

The school year begins with new shoes, new schools, new joys and fears. The calendar year begins with parades and football on television. The fiscal year begins with a resetting of budget lines after the annual flurry of spending or cutting that finished the last fiscal year.

The year of the Christian community's cycle of celebration begins with a raising of the eyes. Customary preoccupations are set aside, or at least that's the idea. Short-term plans are noted, and transcended. At least that's the plan. At the beginning of Advent, Christians lift their eyes to the horizon beyond the horizon.

At least that's the ritual direction we are given.

This scene is filled with language about arriving, and seizing, and coming, and preparing. The usual assumption is that we are preparing for the "End of the World," whatever that might be. This is not a bad assumption, though Jewish and Christian hopes are better characterized as expecting the Beginning of the World, not the end, the freeing and fruition of creation, not its destruction. It is a good exercise to raise your eyes to the horizon of this event, which must (by definition) always be somewhere over the horizon. This pregnant expectation of the Beginning of the World reminds Jews and Christians that the customary injustices that we so easily accommodate are offenses against the creation that our central stories tell us this world is meant to be.

But most of what passes for expectation of this coming, this arriving, is better left untouched. Most of it would offend the Jesus who speaks out of Matthew's story. "No one knows the hour," says that Jesus, responding to yet another calculating schemer who will take advantage of popular expectation of some sort of Second Coming. "If ever anyone should say to you: 'Look, here is the Messiah,' " says that Jesus, "ignore them." He is responding perhaps even to his own overheated followers who are sure that they know who Jesus is and exactly what he has come to accomplish.

Lift up your eyes. Look to the horizon. But do not miss those people whose world is ending (or beginning) somewhere between you and that eschatological horizon. Lifting your eyes is a good exercise for Advent. Just don't overlook the people who cannot lift their eyes.

Intra-Text: The World of Matthew's Story

The clash in Matthew's story begins in Jerusalem. After the genealogy has rung out the rhythm of life in a world that routinely abuses power, after Joseph has been brought up short by a messenger from God, after Jesus has been born in his hometown, his father's hometown, his family's hometown, then Herod is shaken and all Jerusalem with him. Because Herod is shaken, he launches a campaign to protect his throne by killing toddlers. Such tactics are not new in the history of clashes over dominance. Herod wants to destroy the possibility that there would rise a king of the Jews other than him, so he aims to slaughter the children and the hopes of the people who live in Bethlehem, the city where David was born. From this beginning, Matthew's story moves carefully toward Jerusalem. Along the way, we are reminded that the death of Herod does not imply that his campaign has died. His successor in Galilee hunts John the Purifier, and the story Matthew tells is structured so that after John's story is told in three installments, the audience can hear the three predictions of Jesus' final clash with the forces that have been hunting him since his birth. Three sections for John; three for Jesus: all ending in execution at the hands of enemy forces. These forces are finally Roman forces, since Rome works all its Jewish puppets skillfully and carefully to maintain its technology of control in good working order.

One particular consequence of this technology of control is the subversion of the Temple in Jerusalem. Rome, like any effective colonial power, selected an organ of liaison when it set up the governing structure in a conquered land. This organ of liaison needed to be one that ordinary people would listen to. That would guarantee that when Rome spoke through its new mouthpiece, the conquered people would be likely to have heard the message. The organ of liaison needed also to be simple and centralized. This would guarantee that Rome could control things efficiently.

But the most important characteristic of this organ of liaison was that it needed to be somewhere near the center of the hopes and dreams of the conquered people. This would guarantee not only that Roman messages emanating from this center would be heard, but also that this cultural and religious center would undermine itself every time Rome used it to convey messages about its domination over the conquered people's nation. By undermining the cultural center of the conquered people, Rome effectively weakened the beating heart of the conquered people. And by weakening the people's beating heart, Rome made it less likely that the conquered people would revolt. This administrative task was further helped every time Rome rewarded its compelled servants. By paying handsomely for the service of subverting Jewish culture and community, faith and hope, Rome guaranteed that popular resentment would turn on its organ of liaison.

In the case of the Jewish people, the organ of liaison was the Temple organization in Jerusalem. Rome suborned the priests, the Sadducees, and most important the Temple itself. The center of the universe, the holy place where God touched the earth to hold it still in the midst of chaos was destroyed and remade, by Roman action, into the center of Roman control. The Temple was made into the focus of resentment that ought to have been directed against Rome. It was an ingenious scheme.

This matters for this week's scene in Matthew's story because Jesus has just emerged from teaching in the Temple. Early in the story, he taught his followers on a mountain in Galilee (Matthew 5–7, the Sermon on the Mount). Now, after a long narrative approach to Jerusalem, the Temple, and the center of Roman domination, Jesus has delivered the Sermon on the Temple Mount (Matthew 21–23). At the beginning of chapter 24, Jesus steps back out of the Temple and surveys this situation. His disciples point out Herod's improvements. In a deliciously ironic touch, the storyteller does not indicate whether the disciples are impressed or offended. An observant Jewish audience would have felt both reactions. The Temple was, after all, a beautiful reminder of God's provision of stability and safety in a dangerous world. At the same time, the Temple's beauty was an accomplishment of the Roman stooge who had been hunting Jesus (even from his grave) since the beginning of the story. "There will not be left here stone on stone," says Jesus, again ironically celebrating and mourning at the same time. The Roman organ of liaison will be destroyed; the edifice built by the slaughterer of Jewish children (all of them Jesus' cousins) will be razed. The narrative structure of tension and release requires this balancing of accounts. But when the account is settled, the Temple will be gone, and with it, God's stabilizing presence that holds the Jewish world still and links it to a history that grows out of David and Solomon.

Inter-Text: The World We Think We Live In

His disciples ask when this will happen. The storyteller is creating a tense moment for the audience. The audience knows the answer to the disciples' question. They have already lived through that catastrophe, whether as witnesses to the event or as participants in the stories told about the event. In Matthew's story, the audience is carried back to a moment before the catastrophe, a time when no one knew how bad things would be when the Temple would be destroyed. At such an innocent moment, it was still possible to ask about the moment of destruction and imagine that it would be also the moment of deliverance, of the completion of the aeon.

"When will these things be?" they ask.

The simple answer that Jesus gives is that no one knows. Not anyone, not under any circumstances. No one.

The complex answer reveals an awareness of how bad things got in the run-up to the First Jewish Revolt. Leaders emerged, each claiming anointed authority. The result was chaos and destruction. Nation fought against nation, people against people. The wise choice was to flee Jerusalem, to run without regard for common sense or community responsibilities. Even ordinary daily life was disrupted when Romans seized ordinary people engaged in ordinary activities of daily life, working the fields, grinding grain into flour. One is seized, one is left. This is not a picture of the "rapture" with pilots vanishing off the flight decks of airliners. This is a picture of the disastrous depredations that attended Rome's attempts to crush rebellion.

"Stay awake," says Jesus. Indeed.

Provoking the Story

One month ago, my sister was diagnosed with ALS, Lou Gehrig's disease. In the month we have had to get used to that idea, I have heard from many people who have gone through the same slow, falling dance with a family member who was caught by the disease. There seems to be someone in almost every group who knows and loves someone who has danced down to death with this jackal of a disease, which is invariably debilitating, invariably fatal, variable only in its pace and progress in ways that are maddening even as they are terrifying.

One month ago.

The other day I was thinking about conversations with my sister from two months ago. Then we were talking about the things that aging baby boomers talk about when they complain recreationally: the onset of arthritis and menopause, the advent of creaky knees, the ears that show the signs of too much Jimi Hendrix in our youth. Some of those conversations were serious, even disturbing. I would love to have those problems again. Just now it would be delightful to be looking ahead to languid decades of grumbling and getting a good laugh out of it. Her diagnosis changed everything. Oh well.

Listen to this scene in Matthew's story. Listen for the same wistful memory of a time when Jesus' disciples could ask, "When will this be?" and not know the answer, not know the painful details of the destruction that had damaged the world forever.

Play the scene so that your audience catches a glimpse of the wistful grief that looks back to a time when the Temple still stood.

Second Sunday in Advent
Matthew 3:1–12
(see translation, p. 285)

Ritual Text: The Life of the Worshiping Community

When John enters the story, the stage shakes. He brings with him a weight of history and hope, of the words of old prophets long dead whose words have been worked and worked and worked over by Jews who knew that God could not accept the depredations that had become Israel's regular life. Old words that had once heralded a return from Exile in Babylon now were heard by Jews to promise the rise of the dominion of God. It was not clear exactly what this would mean, and could not be clear, since God had never sat on any earthly throne, nor had God yet overthrown the last earthly tyrant ever to oppress creation. It was not clear what this would mean, but it was clear the approach of this overturning of tyrants, this approach of

God's dominion, required washing, an act of preparation suitable for religious devotees or warriors.

When John arrives, Jerusalem and all Judea comes out to him. We will hear later that Jesus also arrives to be washed. The word about John and the reaction to the approach of God's dominion reached even to Galilee. Jews everywhere heard. Jews everywhere came. Jews everywhere confessed their sins, set aside the burdens that would otherwise encumber them in the upheaval that would come with the approach of God's dominion.

Jews came together to John to be washed. But that does not imply that distinctions between Jews vanished in the water with John. Many of the Pharisees and Sadducees came to be washed. Pharisees and Sadducees come to Christian sermons all the time, and when they do they come disguised as rich hypocrites, as rigid legalists, and as misunderstanders of their own faith tradition. This portrayal is funded by John's words in this scene, so Christian interpreters feel justified in taking shots at any Pharisee or Sadducee they encounter, charging them with hypocritical devotion to rigid purity.

There surely were hypocritical Sadducees and legalistic Pharisees. You can't have a crowd of one hundred serious religious people without including at least ten hypocrites and a handful of legalists. It is statistically and sociologically impossible, and that has funded the usual sermonic take on these Jews who also come out to hear John and be washed.

But in the rush to preserve a convenient sermonic reflex, interpreters miss the most interesting facet of this scene. Pharisees and Sadducees come out to be washed, along with all the other Jews who have been waiting for the world to be turned right-side-up. Of course, it could be the case that they show up for this event for the same reasons that politicians show up for the latest flavor-of-the-month social cause and give speeches filled with stirring platitudes, full of sound and fury, signifying that they are and have always been strong supporters of the downtrodden common people on this issue as on all other issues. This is possible. But what if John's harsh words to them simply reproduce the proclamation that has led all the others to confess their own sins? Now Pharisees and Sadducees approach, and they are met, in their turn, with a ringing revelation of the depth of washing required to be part of the movement of God's dominion.

Or what if their approach surprises even John, who had drawn his own conclusions about who would and could be part of the arrival of the dominion of God? What if his reaction reveals a split within the Jewish people rather like the split that will lead (in part) to their defeat during the First Jewish Revolt in 70 CE?

There are several possibilities in this scene. Do not cut off exploration too soon.

Intra-Text: The World of Matthew's Story

John emerges out of the wreckage of murder and flight that is the beginning of Matthew's story. He emerges also out of the boiling mix of hopes and grievances that was Jewish life in the first century of the Common Era. Christians who imagine, unconsciously, that John arrives in the wilderness to prepare the way for Sunday School Christmas programs and classical oratorios will miss what this scene in Matthew's story actually reveals. John arrives and suddenly the audience glimpses the wild hope that seethes just below the surface of Jewish faith in first-century Judea. The glassy crust on the lava flow is broken through, and suddenly you see the red-orange surge that is racing toward an explosive encounter with the ocean. You can feel the heat, and you realize, disconcertingly, that it was not the sun that made the rock beneath your feet warm. John opens a skylight on the dangerous flow of hope just beneath the surface of the story. It is not surprising that Rome would kill him in an effort to keep the rock beneath their feet from melting.

As Matthew tells the story, John accomplishes his run in three stages. This is the first. He will return in Matthew 11 with a report from prison. In Matthew 14, he will be murdered by Herod.

This three-step progression sets up the three-step rhythm of Jesus' own dance with crucifixion. That is not the only link between John and Jesus in Matthew's story. John establishes the practice of deploring the worthless generation to which he speaks; he calls them snakes. Jesus picks up this practice and carries it forward. He picks it up after John is in prison, but before he is murdered. This splices his career into John's. Both emerge as resisters, as opponents of Rome and all its stooges. Both call anyone who disagrees with them a snake. Both are hunted by Herod (remember that Rome pulls the strings on all the Herodian puppets). Both are murdered in the end.

In the Gospel of Luke, Jesus and John are some sort of cousins. There is no hint of any such relationship in Matthew's story, and this difference must be noted. But also note that Jesus and John are linked tightly together in this story: both of them call for faithfulness in a way that leads Rome (or its stooges) to kill them. This is a deep and durable comradeship.

Inter-Text: The World We Think We Live In

If Jesus and John are linked by their shared program of resistance to Empire, consider how this linkage sounds in the story. In each case, their resistance draws the attention of Empire. In each case, their resistance leads to arrest. In each case, the resister is executed: Jesus as a Roman object lesson on a cross, John (oddly enough) given the sort of execution accorded to Roman citizens who could not be crucified: beheading.

Matthew tells a story that interweaves John's story of resistance and provocation together with that of Jesus. This makes the two characters into comrades. Consider what comradeship means. For help, consider Henry's speech on the eve of the battle of Agincourt, as staged in Shakespeare's *Henry V*. Jesus and John may not be related in Matthew's story, but their shared resistance and their shared execution make them brothers.

> This day is call'd the feast of Crispian.
> He that outlives this day, and comes safe home,
> Will stand a tip-toe when this day is nam'd,
> And rouse him at the name of Crispian.

He that shall live this day, and see old age,
Will yearly on the vigil feast his neighbours,
And say 'To-morrow is Saint Crispian.'
Then will he strip his sleeve and show his scars,
And say 'These wounds I had on Crispian's day.'
Old men forget; yet all shall be forgot,
But he'll remember, with advantages,
What feats he did that day. Then shall our names,
Familiar in his mouth as household words —
Harry the King, Bedford and Exeter,
Warwick and Talbot, Salisbury and Gloucester —
Be in their flowing cups freshly rememb'red.
This story shall the good man teach his son;
And Crispin Crispian shall ne'er go by,
From this day to the ending of the world,
But we in it shall be remembered —
We few, we happy few, we band of brothers;
For he to-day that sheds his blood with me
Shall be my brother; be he ne'er so vile,
This day shall gentle his condition;
And gentlemen in England now-a-bed
Shall think themselves accurs'd they were not here,
And hold their manhoods cheap whiles any speaks
That fought with us upon Saint Crispin's day.

— William Shakespeare, *Henry V,* Act 4, Scene 3

Provoking the Story

Every Christian audience knows to cheer for John. The more he rants, the more we cheer. We assume with John, as we always assume with Jesus, that if he is ranting, we should be agreeing. Play this scene differently. Do not make John into some sort of stereotypical apocalyptic preacher. Above all, do not give him a cheap Southern accent. That is far too easy, and unproductive. But play this scene differently.

Before you play John in this scene, listen carefully to his last words in this scene, his words about incineration, his words about fire. These words sound different in a world that has smelled the fires of Auschwitz, or surveyed the wreckage left by the incineration of Hiroshima and Nagasaki, or wondered at the bits of burned paper that floated out over New York City after the World Trade Center was attacked, bits of paper that had been scattered on desktops or tucked in files up to the last ordinary moment before the disaster.

Understand this carefully: these dreadful events are not similar to each other. These moments in history do not resemble, or balance, or counteract, or interpret each other.

But all of them involve fire.

Because all of them involve fire, all of them contribute to what we are able to hear and play out of this scene from Matthew's story. Imagine the ashes spinning in the breeze before you play this scene about chaff that will be incinerated in unquenchable fire.

Third Sunday in Advent
Matthew 11:2–11

(see translation, p. 322)

Ritual Text: The Life of the Worshiping Community

John is in prison, shortly to be executed. He has been caught by Rome and its stooge, Herod. Herod has the palace. He has the prison. He does not control the hopes of the people. John has been arrested in an effort to let the ground cool and harden into territory that can be dominated by Rome. It has not worked. Even from prison, John sends a delegation to study this newest eruption of Jewish hope. "You are the coming one?" he asks, though we do not know in what tone of voice.

What we do know is that even in prison John is a volcanic vent through which flows erupting Jewish hope. "Is this the eruption, or is something else coming?" he asks. It is the correct question.

In our century, this erupting hope has hardened into a religion of personal salvation and pet projects (like the banning of gay marriage or the once-a-year staffing of soup kitchens, especially around Christmas). It is a question that must be asked again. John erupts in the wilderness, the messenger preparing the road for God's act to turn the world right-side-up, and we celebrate this eruption by hoping for the best shopping season of the decade. Somehow one would have thought there would be more to it than this.

Intra-Text: The World of Matthew's Story

This is the second scene in the three-step dance that John does in Matthew's story. In Matthew 3 we met John and found him to be a fascinating and dangerous character, and judged him to be a staunch opponent of Empire. In this scene, he enquires whether Jesus is an ally or a distraction in the movement against Empire, the movement that gave John life, and for which he will shortly give his life. John expects something, and expects it with all his might, and expects it in the midst of the present moment. He expects it even from his prison cell, or maybe particularly from his prison cell. If Empire is interested in someone who calls the Jewish people to faithfulness, sufficiently interested to lock him up, then something large is moving in the world. Perhaps Jesus is that large thing, the movement to turn the world right-side-up.

Jesus reports back to John, which is significant all by itself. He sees in John the same movement that he finds himself called to. His answer, however, requires some examination. Christians have long ago made peace with the career of Jesus. Of course he was a healer. Of course he cleansed lepers. Of course he raised the dead. What else would a messiah do?

The problem is that there is a great deal else that a proper messiah ought to do. Chiefly, a messiah ought to turn the world right-side-up, and that would require ridding God's people of the overbearing presence of the Romans. "Are you the one who is to come, or will we have to continue waiting, perhaps without end yet again, for God to set God's people free?" It is a large question.

When Jesus' answer is understood to reject politics in favor of a campaign of taking care of immediate medical needs,[40] his answer is misunderstood. Jesus is not dulling the political edge of John's question; he is sharpening it.

Jesus' answer echoes all the way back to the songs sung by the people who returned from the Exile in Babylon in the years following 538 BCE (see Isaiah 40, 35, and 25 for examples). Jesus' answer sounds echoes that may be heard in 2 Esdras and 2 Baruch, Jewish writings that were composed at roughly the same time as Matthew's story.[41] Jesus' answer echoes also in Revelation, another Jewish work from this same tense moment in history. Jesus' answer claims that this moment in a tense and disastrous history may be larger and more significant than even John has guessed. Jesus, by his answer, implies that kicking the Romans out is the least that he will accomplish. The hopes he calls up are expected as benefits that will follow the establishment of peace in God's creation. "Not only will the Romans be eliminated," Jesus implies, "but so will everything that binds and restricts the flourishing of life in God's creation." The last enemy to be defeated, Paul tells us in 1 Corinthians, is death. Jesus says that's just next on the list.

Christians who are accustomed to blowing Jesus up into the heavens will have no great trouble with this intense answer. They ought to ask why it is that Jesus needs to finish his answer by warning people not to be scandalized by him. What possible cause could there be for offense?

Perhaps it was because he could not raise the dead children of Bethlehem.

Inter-Text: The World We Think We Live In

Jesus speaks strongly and warmly of John to the crowds around him. His words are easier to hear if they are translated into submission. "What did you go out to see?" asks one translation, "A blade of grass bending in the wind?" The image is good enough, if a little unclear. "Was he someone dressed in fine clothing?" asks another.

The problem is that the word that describes John's clothing in this question is μαλακος. When this word is translated as "fancy" or "fine" the basic sense works out, but Jesus' question then seems to emerge out of some sort of economic resentment. "John (and I) aren't your fancy-dressers, no not us," Jesus chuckles, "you won't see neither of us living in no palace."

It's always possible that this is exactly what Matthew means to imply.

But the word μαλακος means more than that. Some translators read the word as "soft," which is a perfectly workable translation. The word does indeed mean soft, and the reference could be to clothes that are not made of crudely woven cloth that is rough to the hand.

"We wear workin' clothes, John and me," growls Jesus, and then he spits.

But the word carries other implications, as well. The word is often used to mean "weak," and so the question could mean to distinguish John as a "manly man" from the pencil-necked geeks that manly men love to ridicule.

It gets worse. The word μαλακος is used as a code word for "woman-like." If this is what Jesus means to imply in this scene, he is doing what resentful men often do when they look across the line between Us and Them. He slams his male opponents by calling them women. When such things happen, men are supposed to laugh crudely at the de-sexed males on the other side of the line, and women are required to be glad that the men on our side of the line are "real men," not the pale, wilting imitation on the other side of the line. If you play the text this way, you may expect that young men who enjoy testosterone jousting will respond favorably. You may also expect that many of the rest of us will simply be tired of such antics. You might want to ask women who will tell you the truth what such jousting sounds like to them. Be sure to ask what it means that being "woman-like" is an insult. Listen carefully. There are many answers to these questions.

Provoking the Story

In the end, Jesus healed only a few, cleansed only a few, raised only a very few. The hopes that gave John life, that animated the Jewish families who called Jesus "messiah" did not expect such a limited delivery on the old, strong promises that belong to the title "Anointed One of God."

Consider the problems examined in Nils Dahl's essay "The Crucified Messiah."[42] Of all the titles that might have been given to Jesus, messiah is surely the poorest fit and causes the most focused conflict. You could easily call Jesus a teacher. You could call him a wonderworker. You might get away with calling him a revolutionary leader (though that will be a harder sell). People who disliked what his movement contributed called him a sorcerer, and the title stuck. But calling him a messiah guarantees that any speaking about Jesus as messiah will be, as the apostle Paul says, either scandalous or moronic. He did not use those words lightly. Paul testifies to the problem that lurks behind this scene from Matthew's story. "You are the one?" asks John. Jesus gives an answer that promises a righting of the world.

Look out the window. Does the world look right-side-up to you?

Fourth Sunday in Advent
Matthew 1:18–25

(see translation, p. 281)

Ritual text: The Life of the Worshiping Community

"His mother was promised. . . . "

"She was found having a baby in her belly. . . . "

Notice that all the verbs are passive. Jesus' mother will not even be given a name for a few verses. Before she has a name, she will be the respondent in a planned divorce proceeding.

Every customary Christian knows that everything turns out all right, and that it only takes a few verses. What not everybody thinks about is the precarious balance Mary hangs in until Joseph changes his mind in response to being visited by a messenger of God. Joseph, who will later become a saint and (as such) have a town in Missouri and an orange-flavored aspirin product named after him, is at this point in the story a strict man who does not want to go through the trouble of a public divorce proceeding. His honor is affronted and he intends to leave Mary to her own devices. If she can get herself pregnant, she can also fend for herself from now on. Interpreters, who are anxious to get Joseph ready to become the namesake of a town, leap over what Mary will have seen in Joseph in this pre-sainthood moment: he is a strict man who is perfectly glad to leave her to the gentle mercies of a society that seems to have practiced honor killings.[43] After the private divorce, Joseph will be free and clear. But Mary will still be pregnant and out of place, abandoned by the one man who could have protected her, though it would have cost him honor points. He intends to decline either to protect her or to publicly confront her. This saves him from having to throw one of the stones that will kill her, but it does not spare her from her fate. He just gets to avoid getting blood spattered on his robes. He gets to miss hearing her cries as she dies. What a guy. What a saint.

Intra-Text: The World of Matthew's Story

In the genealogy with which Matthew's story begins, only sons are listed. Of course baby girls are born. Of course they are the ones who grow up and give birth to this long line of baby boys who later father baby boys (and girls, though they won't be mentioned). But the genealogy is a males-only party, as is customary in patriarchal societies. At least it is nearly males-only. Four women from the deep history of the Jewish people are brought in to specify out of whom some of the baby boys in the genealogy came. Three of these women predate David the king. One is a victim of David the predator.

There is a fuller discussion of these women in chapter 2 (page 38), which explores the narrative arc of Matthew's story. There is a long history of wondering what these women are doing in the genealogy. Interpreters imagine that they are forgiven sinners, or welcomed outsiders. Such roles are potentially useful, but finally inattentive to the stories told about the women. Their status as outsiders may be important but adds nothing to this genealogy. Perhaps it matters because that status makes them vulnerable to the crimes committed against them. To call them sinners contributes nothing significant, except the slanderous insult that would blame women for the crimes of the men who attacked them.

To view them as women who are pushed out of what is rightfully theirs sets up an important consideration of the scene for this Sunday. Tamar is abused and pushed out. Rahab has no stake in the people once she is not attractive to men who want selfish intercourse that entails no clan responsibilities. Ruth is left to starve until she uncovers Boaz's "feet." And the "wife of Uriah" suffers an attack and the murder of her husband, both carried out by David the predator king.

And now Mary is set to be abandoned by Joseph. I imagine that there have been clan negotiations that led to the promise of marriage. I understand that Joseph is put in a difficult position by Mary's unexpected pregnancy. I am struck that we hear nothing from Mary, nothing from Gabriel (who enters Luke's story, but not Matthew's), nothing that establishes the pregnancy until just seconds before we hear of the choice to divorce her. The pregnancy comes out of a "holy breath." That links it to God's creative act in Genesis 2, which breathed life into the intricately made, but still inanimate, mudguy who lay lifeless on the ground from which he had been formed. After Joseph makes his plan, a messenger speaks to him in a dream. The unborn child is given a name, a mission, a prophetic backing, and a title. The title, Emmanuel, is echoed at the end of Matthew's story, when Jesus promises to be with his followers until the end of the aeon. This echo, however, is twisted in important ways. At the end of the story, it is Jesus who will be with his followers, though it is not altogether clear how this will be accomplished, or what exactly it means. Here at the beginning of the story, it is God who will be with the people. The title lends to the story of Jesus the status of an enacted prophecy. The rejected children of Hosea acted out the cutting off of God's people when they were named Lo-Ruhamah

(Not Loved) and Lo-Ammi (Not My People).[44] Jesus, by contrast, is given a title that embodies God's commitment to the Jewish people. What remains to be seen is what this presence of God will mean for God's people in Matthew's story. Notice that Herod's slaughter of the innocent children and families of Bethlehem (Jesus, Mary, and Joseph's kin) leaves "God-Is-With-Us" a refugee while still a toddler and gives to him the hunted face of a shocked survivor who must puzzle out why he is alive when all his contemporary cousins are dead.

Inter-Text: The World We Think We Live In

In the world we think we live in, we imagine that Joseph in this story is St. Joseph and that he is preparing to become the model for fatherly care, for statues and hospitals. In our world, Joseph is not a husband; he is an icon. These aspects of the "culture of reception," the world in which Matthew's story is read and heard, make it difficult to hear this scene in its full integrity. Honest playing and hearing of this scene require us to pay attention also to the culture of origin. Remember that Matthew's story comes to us out of a regional culture that, then and now, values male honor very highly. That is why the genealogy contains only male heirs, except for the jarring intrusions of the strong women "out of" whom the male heirs came. That is also why Joseph's actions in this scene pass without comment in the text. This scene simply assumes that it is appropriate for an affronted male to put away a "damaged" woman. If Joseph carries out his plan, he will not be censured for his action. If anything, he will be remembered as a protector of his, and his family's, honor.

To understand the tensions in this scene, read about the practice of honor killing, which is still practiced in traditional cultures in the Near East. Because these cultures believe that you must maintain your honor, because "if you do not live with honor, you have nothing," a woman who is judged to be "damaged" is liable to be killed for the sake of honor. Thus it was that a young woman in Iraq was kidnapped in order to force her brother to resign from the police force. The threat was that she would be raped if her brother did not resign. Rape would render her unmarriageable and useless. Her brother resigned; the young woman was released. But because it could not be determined that she had not been "damaged," she was killed by her own family. Her father could not bring himself to do it, nor could her brother. Thank goodness she had a cousin who saved the family's honor by killing her.

"She was so dear to us," he said. "I had taught her to read and write. She was our finest girl."

The casual use of the possessive is not an accident. Fatima, the young woman who was killed, was possessed by the men of her family.

"She knew the custom but I don't think she expected we would kill her. She was crying. I saw it in her eyes that she thought we would take her in our arms and say, "Thank God you are safe," but she got bullets instead."

Of course, no contemporary audience will be glad to be required to imagine that Joseph would do any such thing. He was Jewish, after all, and we are Christian, after all. Neither Jews nor Christians practice such things. Both Judaism and Christianity call such acts murder. But it is worth noting that legal texts from the culture of origin do make reference to execution by stoning as a possible sentence for a woman found to be inappropriately pregnant. And it is worth remembering that Islam also condemns this practice, but patriarchal culture has its own logic, its own demands. As Fatima's cousin, her executioner, says, "The traditions of the tribe are even stronger than religion. Islam forbids this but our culture runs deep. Anger is like a strong wind that sets the mind on fire."[45]

Against this background, this scene reveals a Joseph who cannot bring himself to kill Mary. He resolves to put her away quietly. This does not end the matter for his family, and nothing in the scene implies that it does. Remember that Joseph probably has a cousin, and if he doesn't, Mary does. Remember that Mary knows this cousin. Perhaps he even taught her to read and write.

Provoking the Story

Do not lose Mary when you play this scene. Remember the tears of Fatima, remember her expectation that her family would gather her into their arms, and her shock when it became clear that they would not. Because angels are genderless, according to Jewish understandings, the scene ought to be played with a female angel. That allows this scene to echo the scenes in the genealogy that lead up to it. Since angels, as messengers of God, were understood in the culture of origin to be the virtual embodiment of God,[46] such a playing of the scene would ring the right echoes: God is now doing what has been done in Jewish story by women who had been pushed out of what was rightfully theirs, pushed out by men (patriarchs!) who had the power to push and protect their honor any way they saw fit.

First Sunday after Christmas Day
Matthew 2:13–23
(see translation, p. 283)

Ritual Text: The Life of the Worshiping Community

When Christmas is celebrated in Christian congregations, it is the Christmas created by the Gospel of Luke. (Well, actually a combination of Luke and an overheated American holiday economy.) Matthew contributes only the Magi, who generally show up at the manger along with Luke's shepherds. These characters eye each other uneasily and then go back into storage, along with their costumes, until the next Christmas pageant.

The scene for this Sunday is often ignored, and nearly never played as part of the Sunday School Christmas pageant.

You can see why.

Sentimental celebration of Christmas has little place for shrieking mothers[47] and the corpses of toddlers. But if Christmas is the season during which Christians explore what it means for God to enter human existence, Matthew's scene is crucial to the exploration. In

Matthew's story, Jesus (explicitly identified as "God is with us": Emmanuel) is born into a village that suffers slaughter. Herod launches a preemptive strike to block any future challenge to his authority. Jesus emerges safe out of the dust and smoke and flowing blood of this slaughter. He emerges safe, but not untouched. All of his cousins are killed, and with them we must assume he has lost also aunts and uncles, neighbors and perhaps even grandparents. When Herod's murderers enter the village to kill the children, the village will have resisted. At the end of this scene, the stage is littered with corpses, and only some of them are toddlers.

Jesus will have inherited from this scene the hunted look of people who have lost family members in other slaughters, other preemptive strikes, other attacks carried out to crush a people and their hopes. In Matthew's story this is precisely where God enters our story. Emmanuel appears among the victims of genocide.

Intra-Text: The World of Matthew's Story

Matthew's story begins with the long rhythmic rocking of the genealogy. Generation follows generation; ancestor follows ancestor. If the purpose of genealogies is to build a solid foundation under the present family, to establish the deep continuity of the clan, then Matthew's rendition of this story of birthings deserves close attention. We have noticed the women, and the decisive (and surprising) role that they play (see the second chapter of this book, pages 38–47). The disruption of the rhythm that they represent is by itself important, but it becomes more important when we notice that each interrupting woman pushes her way into the genealogy because she was pushed out of what was rightly hers. Always the pushing was done by men who had the power to do what they did.

A closer look at the genealogy, however, reveals more violence. The whole rolling record begins with Abraham, the father of all fathers, and runs to David, the king of all kings. But with David comes the memory of his attack on Bathsheba. The storyteller makes it clear that there was an attack involved: Bathsheba is identified as the wife of Uriah. In a patriarchal culture, this identification matters.

Of course the crime is understood as having been committed against Uriah, but the preceding women shape the way even this is heard. In this list of birthings, women are presented as refusing to be pushed out even when the man in question has both the power and the patriarchal right to do exactly what he did. Women are not simple ciphers in this list of birthings. They are people who establish the character of the foundation of this family. This is a family that has had to learn what it means that power can be abused. Women have suffered from that abuse, and have fought their way back, even when the opponent was David, the king of all kings.

The next measured chunk of the list of birthings runs to the time of the Exile into Babylon. This confirms what we have felt about this genealogy up to this point: it is a story of power and abuse, of pain and survival. It has run from the father of all fathers to the king of all kings, and now stops at the disaster of all disasters. The Babylonian Exile left deep scars on Jewish faith, and life, and scripture. The memory of the Temple in ruins, the wall of Jerusalem breached, the land of promise lost to foreign domination, these memories mark every mention of the land of promise in Jewish scripture. Even Rachel is summoned from her tomb to wail for the exiles as they are led past on the way to the foreign land, the land of the devastator, Babylon. Look again at Psalm 137 to see what this exile meant to those who survived it. "O Daughter Babylon," sang the survivors, "Happy shall they be who dash your little ones against a stone."

Against this backdrop, Herod's murders look like what God's people ought to expect in a world ripped by violent abuse of power. Herod is not the first to kill simply because he could. He will not be the last. Remember that when Matthew's story was first told, the Romans (the real power behind Herod) had again destroyed the Temple and Jerusalem, and had killed thousands of Jews. Some sources claim that a million were killed. Rachel's shrieks ring now as they have rung through the centuries, birthing after birthing, children born and slaughtered.

Inter-Text: The World We Think We Live In

A few weeks earlier, in Bukavu, Zaire, in the giant market of a refugee camp that was home to many Rwandan Hutu militiamen, I had watched a man butchering a cow with a machete. He was quite expert at his work, taking big precise strokes that made a sharp hacking noise. The rallying cry to the killers during the genocide was "Do your work!" And I saw that it was work, this butchery; hard work. It took many hacks — two, three, four, five hard hacks — to chop through the cow's leg. How many hacks to dismember a person? . . . What sustained them, beyond the frenzy of the first attack, through the plain physical exhaustion and mess of it?[48]

These painful descriptions come from Rwanda. They could have come from many other places. They will come from other places in the future. We have not finished with genocide, no, not nearly, not yet.

Imagine the same questions being asked in the aftermath of Herod's attack on Bethlehem. How many hacks would it take to dismember a mother who was trying to protect her baby? How could human beings hack and hack and hack, killing steadily until they were sure (enough) that they had killed all the babies in and around Bethlehem two years old and under? Did they need to rest to recover their strength? I can imagine situations in which a person might find herself hacking and hacking, killing in desperation, but how could anyone come back to this operation after taking a needed rest?

Provoking the Story

"Every survivor wonders why he is alive," Abbé Modeste, a priest at the cathedral in Butare, Rwanda's second-largest city, told me. Abbé Modeste had hidden for weeks in his sacristy, eating communion wafers, before moving under the desk in his study, and finally into the rafters at the home of some neighboring nuns. . . . "I had eighteen people killed at my house," said Etienne Niyonzima, a former businessman who had become a deputy in the National Assembly. "Everything was totally destroyed — a place of fifty-five meters by fifty meters. In my neighborhood they killed six hundred and forty-seven people. They tortured them, too. You had to see how they killed them. They had the number of everyone's house, and they went through with red paint and marked the homes of all the Tutsis and of the Hutu moderates. My wife was at a friend's, shot with two bullets. She is still alive, only" — he fell quiet for a moment — "she has no arms. The others with her were killed. The militia left her for dead. Her whole family of sixty-five in Gitarama were killed." Niyonzima was in hiding at the time. Only after he had been separated from his wife for three months did he learn that she and four of their children had survived. "Well," he said, "one son was cut in the head with a machete. I don't know where he went." His voice weakened, and caught. "He disappeared." Niyonzima clicked his tongue, and said, "But the others are still alive. Quite honestly, I don't understand at all how I was saved."[49]

Play the scene interwoven with these memories of others who survived an attempt at extermination.

Epiphany of the Lord
Matthew 2:1–12
(see translation, p. 282)

Ritual Text: The Life of the Worshiping Community

Religion is a funny thing. Every faith I know anything about prays for peace on earth and good will to all, and at the same time draws a sharp line between Us and Them, between people whom God favors (Us) and people God rejects. The peace we pray for, each in our separate gatherings, is for Us, and the good will of God will come, we each imagine, when every one of Them agrees with Us.

Thirty years ago, the churches in my hometown joined in an ecumenical project. We met together, studied together, worked together for months. Afterward we were asked what had surprised us most. One person said he was surprised that there were some Christians in denominations beside his own. It was an awkward moment.

January 6 is Epiphany, the twelfth day of Christmas. Lords are leaping, ladies are dancing, and the partridge is still stuck in the same old pear tree. More important, Epiphany is the day Christians tell the story of the Magi who honor the baby Jesus. It is not clear who these strangers are; it's only clear that they are strange. They are from the East; they watch the stars. Perhaps they come from Babylon. Certainly they are pagans.

Epiphany is the season of surprises, so stop and think. In a religious world that is very careful to distinguish Us from Them, this group of Them arrives as pagans, and they leave as pagans. What is more, these pagans appear to be astrologers. They know about the birth of Jesus because they study the stars. If you want to find out what the Bible thinks about pagans and astrologers, check Leviticus. Leviticus doesn't much like either one. There is a lot that Leviticus doesn't like, and people concerned about the line between Us and Them tend to read Leviticus a lot, maybe because it tells them whom to ignore, whom to reject and dislike. Why would anyone pay attention to Them? They're just wrong.

And then here come the Magi, no matter what Leviticus says. And they're not ignored.

Here's an exercise for Epiphany: find someone with whom you disagree and listen to that person. With all the lines drawn between Us and Them, red states and blue states, pro-this and anti-that, it shouldn't be too hard to find someone you are supposed to reject. Find someone and really listen. You might be surprised.

Intra-Text: The World of Matthew's Story

For the First Sunday after Christmas, the community listened to the story of the Slaughter of the Innocents, the name given to Herod's attempt to kill Jesus before he could rise against entrenched power. Now on Epiphany the community hears the beginning of that story.

While this disordering of the scene makes liturgical sense, do not lose the cries of the families of the slaughtered in an attempt to capture the joy of the revelation of Jesus to the Magi. Epiphany is the season for surprises, and it is certainly a surprise to discover travelers from the East, Gentiles who are looking for the king of the Jews. East of Judea is the Tigris and the Euphrates. East of Judea is the Garden of Eden. East of Judea is Ur of the Chaldees. East of Judea is Babylon, where Jews lived in Exile after the destruction of the first Temple. East of Judea is the Jewish community who stayed behind when Jews returned to rebuild the Temple and Jerusalem, the Jewish community that would later produce the Babylonian Talmud. But this surprise brings with it a village full of slaughtered children and their families. And these deaths would not have taken place had the Magi not alerted Herod to Jesus' birth. Do not forget this in the midst of celebrating the wonder of pagan discovery of Jesus.

Inter-Text: The World We Think We Live In

No matter who these pagans are, they come from the same direction as did the conquerors who destroyed the ancient kingdoms of Israel and Judah. Assyria came from the East in 722 BCE and obliterated the Northern Kingdom, Israel, removing it forever from history, but not from memory. All of the Jews of the Northern Kingdom were forced into exile, dispersed throughout Assyria's vast imperial territory. They were lost forever, to be found only on the Discovery Channel, year after year, when yet another researcher discovers traces of the Lost Tribes of Israel. One outcome of this dispersal, in Jewish memory and expectation, is that people learned to expect that there might be a leavening effect even in the most dangerous of Gentile enemies as a result of having the memory of the God of Israel kneaded in after the dispersal of the northern tribes. Humane actions might be expected even from enemies and were taken as a sign of the hidden influence of the God of Israel. On this model, the

Magi arrive because something hidden in their cultural DNA drew them to honor the king of the Jews.

After Assyria came Babylon, also from the East. Babylon also conquered God's people, by then reduced to a much smaller Southern Kingdom, Judah. In 587 BCE this remnant was conquered, the Temple was destroyed, and the wall of Jerusalem was reduced to rubble. Once again the people were driven into exile, though this time it was only the leaders of Jewish society who were deported. And this time the exiles were not dispersed and lost. They were allowed to maintain their own communities in Exile, and they took the occasion to maintain also their language, their stories, and their faithfulness to the God of Abraham, of Isaac, and of Jacob. This community lived in Exile, lived as Jews, until Cyrus King of the Persians (also from the East), conquered Babylon and offered the exiles freedom to return to their home, the land of promise.

In 538 BCE some of the exiles did return, and they rebuilt the Temple (more or less, mostly less). They rebuilt also the city of Jerusalem, including its wall. They rebuilt their version of Jewish tradition on the land they believed God had promised to their ancestors. Not all of the exiles returned. There remained in Babylonian territory a sizeable Jewish community, one that persisted even into very recent times. In the early centuries of the Common Era, this community produced the Babylonian Talmud and the scholarly and observant community out of which it grew. One outcome, in Jewish understanding, of this persistent Jewish community was that those who had been violent conquerors, dangerous Gentiles, were civilized (to an extent) by the humanizing effect of living with an observant Jewish community. On this model, the Magi come from the East because they had been trained to raise their eyes to the horizon of God's activity in the world, trained by their association with the Babylonian Jewish community.

These pagans arrive and bring gifts to honor Messiah. Jewish hopes expect exactly that. But these pagans bring more than the gifts one would expect from a world that waits impatiently for God to turn it right-side-up. These pagans from the East, from the land of exile and conquest, bring with them also the attention of Herod, the king, the killer.

Remember this second sort of gift. The storyteller, by the time Matthew's story is told in this form, knows of other Gentiles who have been drawn to the community that honors Jesus as messiah. The storyteller knows, by this time, that the gifts brought by these Gentiles are not unmixed. Roman attention brings the destruction of the Temple. It may be that Gentiles, even wise ones, cannot help but bring exile and conquest along with whatever other gifts they bring.

Provoking the Story

If the Magi had returned to Herod, perhaps he would have killed only Jesus and his family instead of needing to kill all of the toddlers in and around Bethlehem. Play this scene so that the audience sees and feels the cost of considering such a terrible calculation. Would it have been better if Jesus had been turned over? Can a faithful community save itself by betraying itself? Is there any way to defend against Herod without becoming as bad as Herod? Tell the story so that the community's risks and losses come clear. This is not just a story about one baby, but about all the babies.

Baptism of the Lord — First Sunday after the Epiphany Matthew 3:13–17

(see translation, p. 287)

Ritual Text: The Life of the Worshiping Community

Still this is Epiphany, still this is the season of surprises and revelations. After Jesus came up out of the water, we encounter a surprise: God opens the heavens and breathes into the world again. To read this breath as a spirit, or as the Holy Spirit (as is customary), misses the way this scene calls back to Genesis 2, when God blew into the nose of Mudguy (one translation of "Adam" who was made from *adamah*/soil and the water that welled up) and created him as a living being. The Hebrew makes it clear: when God blew into Mudguy's nose, he was created a *nephesh chayah*. This is usually (and properly) translated as "a living being," but the word *nephesh* actually means "throat." Of course, it makes no sense in English to describe anyone as a "living throat" so it is not translated that way. But the throat is the organ of aspiration as well as respiration, and the term means that Mudguy not only breathes, but also desires.

Now in this scene, God breathes into the world again. One ought to expect that the result will be the creation of lively aspiration. The voice out of heaven calls a name to Jesus: "my son, the beloved." This also calls back to Genesis 2. In that story, Mudguy got his name, and so did Chavvah (Eve, Mother-of-All-the-Living), along with all other living creatures. This time Jesus is named and is thus given an identity, a nature, a purpose, and a place in God's work in creation. He is "Beloved Son." This may give some shape to the aspiration that God breathes into life. The words may link Jesus with Isaac, the son whom Abraham loved, and for whom Sarah waited into her very old age. The promise of a future, land, and a blessing waited for the birth of a beloved son, but this beloved son, given by God, was taken to the mountain in the land of Moriah where Abraham bound him in order to slaughter him and offer him as a burnt offering. We are not told if Isaac wrestled with his father on the mountain. We are not told because Isaac nearly vanishes from the story after he is bound and placed upon the altar by his father. After that scene, Abraham (the father of a multitude) and Isaac (the beloved son named for laughter) never again share a scene. Before he disappears completely, Isaac becomes father also to Esau. Isaac becomes father also to Jacob, who wrestles his way to a new name: Israel. Esau, in his turn, becomes father to the multitude of rampaging Gentiles. Any child marked for slaughter will have mixed offspring. This surely applies to Isaac. It may also apply to Jesus, who barely escaped Herod's knife.

To call Jesus "beloved son" also marks him as the anointed one, the king of Israel, the messiah. When God speaks to the anointed and newly crowned king in Psalm 2, God calls to the king as son. By breathing this call into the world, this scene hopes for the creation to be turned right-side-up.

This hope can only be ill-defined. When the topic at hand is the correcting of all of creation, the sheer number of variables defeats any simple list of performance objectives and objective measures that we might propose for this task. When the area of operation is the whole of the creation, how would you ever measure enough factors to determine that the task had been completed?

But though the hope is ill-defined, it is not diffuse. The hope that God would anoint a human being to turn the creation right-side-up amounts to a global demand for justice that leaps to life in the face of all the offenses that make the demand necessary.

This is not the end of the aspirations that are breathed into life in this scene. What matters is that the creation stirs to life and hopes for things that were impossible when it lay inert on the ground, fully formed but not yet a *nephesh chayah*. With the eruption of life, everything changes.

Intra-Text: The World of Matthew's Story

Once Jesus is established as a refugee who is named "God-Is-With-Us" (Emmanu-el), we leave his childhood and meet Jesus as an adult. In Matthew's story of Jesus as an adult, the first three sections (chapters 3, 11, and 14) are kicked into motion by John, who erupts, explodes, and accuses each time he enters. And then he is killed. The pattern established in the John scenes sets up the rest of Matthew's adult story, because the next three sections of the story are kicked into motion by announcements of the death that stalks Jesus, the death that has stalked him since he was created as a refugee.

The scene for this week follows immediately upon the first eruption of John and foreshadows the tight link that will exist between Jesus and John throughout Matthew's story. Apart from the patterned flow of the story, the baptism scene could be played (in isolation) as a calm story of self-discovery. It could be played with a humble John deferring to a superior Jesus. It could all finish with a swell of organ music and a deep baritone God announcing that henceforth God will be a Trinitarian theologian.

It could be played that way, but it shouldn't be.

Moments before Jesus arrives, John is erupting about snakes and judgment and fire and strength and fire and winnowing and fire, and fire, and fire, unquenchable fire. Then Jesus arrives. John's words are still arcing through the air, you can see the lava stream still glowing, you can still smell the sulfur in the clouds of gas that explode when the lava hits the seawater. Even the rock that has hardened under your feet has not yet altogether cooled; its surface is jagged with shards of volcanic glass, sharp as scalpels. Then, and only then, the adult Jesus arrives (with his winnowing fork in his hand, John tells us). This will be a Jesus who will make sharp divisions. This will be a Jesus who erupts just as John erupts. The face of the earth will change.

In the next scene, Jesus is driven up into the wordless wilderness, back to a place and time before God spoke to chaos and brought forth order and life. He is driven there by the same breath that just breathed into the world when he was washed, the same breath that breathed life and hope and aspiration into Mudguy. Jesus is tested to determine whether he can control his impulses, his *yetzrim*. The rabbis read the story in Genesis 3 as a story demonstrating the difficulty of controlling human appetites and impulses. Genesis 3, as the rabbis read it, illustrates the necessity for balance between the impulse toward altruism (*yetzer ha-tov*) and the impulse toward acquisition (*yetzer ha-ra*). The work ahead of one who is called "Beloved-Son" will require that he be able to manage his appetites and his drive to accomplishment. It all starts with the washing.

Inter-Text: The World We Think We Live In

Interpretations of this scene that begin by reading and playing it as a direct link to our practice of baptism (no matter what form of Christian baptism your community of faith practices) will always misread the scene. Jesus is no infant in a baptismal gown with sponsors standing by. He is no adult believer who has decided to follow

Jesus ("no turning back, no turning back"). He is no catechumen who has been trained and taught and brought to confess the creed that will separate him from his former pagan life and link him to a whole new life and a whole new community.

Jesus in this scene is a faithful Jew who is drawn to John's eruption along with crowds of other faithful Jews. Who came out to John? Jerusalem came out, and all Judea, and all the region surrounding the Jordan. That is a lot of faithful Jews. They did not come out to participate in an outdoor religious service; John's spot in the Jordan is an induction center, and the people came out to volunteer for service, to be washed, purified to participate in the long-awaited new thing that God was doing in the world. If the military tone of that image makes you nervous, that may be a sign that you have finally caught the disturbing force of John's eruption. The face of the earth was changing. Jews came out to enlist.

Pharisees came out. Sadducees came out. It is not too surprising that Pharisees would come out to be purified, set apart for special service to God and creation. Their name, after all, refers to this same setting apart. As stable middle-class folk,[50] they will not often have come out to share the risks of such an eruption. It is more surprising, at least initially, that Sadducees should have come out. Because they were the group tied most tightly to the Temple and its service, they were also the group chosen (and rewarded) by the Romans to be the organ of liaison between imperial power and the Jewish community. Matthew finds observant, faithful Jews everywhere, even among those people most compromised by Roman power, and Matthew brings all of them out to John for purification.

John calls them snakes. John tells the Pharisees and the Sadducees that they cannot come this close to the fire and expect to go home with only a stirring experience, an amusing anecdote, a memory of time spent with God. Service in this movement in God's creation requires purification. There is water available for that purpose, but there is also fire, and both appear to be necessary for the purification that John requires.

Jesus comes out with this crowd, and he comes for both the water and the fire. If images of Jesus with a fanatic's fire burning in his eyes trouble you, you may finally have caught the bite of Matthew's story. Jesus lost all his cousins in Herod's murderous attempt to defend Empire by burning hope out of the Jewish people. Now he steps into the story, steps into a movement that fights fire with fire.

Matthew's audience will know what this fire feels like and looks like. Matthew's audience will have seen this fire in the eyes of people who rejected Roman domination.

Matthew's audience will also have seen the smoke from this fire rising over Jerusalem when the Temple was destroyed along with the First Jewish Revolt against Rome in 70 CE. Fire is a complicated image in this story, and for the generation that first heard it in the form we now have it.

Provoking the Story

Amos Oz has written about fanatics. See, for instance, his *How to Cure a Fanatic*.[51] Play this scene with recognizable fanatics in the water and on the banks. Do not make them into fire-breathing caricatures of fanatics. Play them as quiet, determined, terrifying fanatics who have had enough and who are sure that they are right.

Third Sunday after the Epiphany
Matthew 4:12–23
(see translation, p. 289)

Ritual Text: The Life of the Worshiping Community

In Epiphany you should always look for the surprise. This season that began with the arrival of Gentiles from the East, from the ancient land of Exile, now continues with the eruption of light and hope in Galilee of the Gentiles. Those leaping to life are Jews, as their names make clear, but they are Jews who live surrounded by dominant Gentiles. Traditional communities always ask questions about assimilation and cultural accommodation when faced with people living in the Diaspora. European Christians who emigrated to the United States worried lest they become too "Americanized." Colonial administrators take pains to avoid "going native" no matter where they are stationed or in what century. Jews who lived in Galilee of the Gentiles were suspected (by some) of being more "Gentilish" than Jewish.[52]

And that is where the career of Jesus, continuing the work and proclamation of John, erupts. That means that the area, however dominated by Gentiles, maintains a strong and expectant Jewish population. John spurred a reaction in the wilderness near the Jordan and near Jerusalem. Jesus finds the same sort of response among Jews living far from that place.

Intra-Text: The World of Matthew's Story

The essential transformation in this scene involves abandonment. Simon and Andrew abandon their nets. James and John abandon their father. Both acts of separation are surprising and set up the audience to hear Matthew's story as a story of sharp division. Both acts are surprising, but the first is more surprising than the second. James and John abandon their father. This is surprising. One ought assume that they were together practicing the inherited family trade, and that their abandonment of their father leaves him and the family business without an assured future. This abandonment is an earthquake. It leaves the nets unmended; it leaves the future untended. But children do leave home. In any century, children leave home, and family, and even the family business. As shocking as this separation would have been for Zebedee, when the dust settled he would have been able to look up and down the shore of the Sea of Galilee and see a handful of other fathers whose children had left them behind.

More surprising is the action of Simon and Andrew. We do not hear that they have a father. We do not hear that they have partners. We only hear that they have nets and that they are throwing them into the sea. They abandon their nets, Matthew tells us.

These nets were the tools that they used every day to practice their trade. They knew their nets as well as they did their children, maybe better.[53] If they did not make their own nets, they surely picked them out, bought them from the best netmaker they could afford. Tools matter. My grandfather was a carpenter. I have his hammer, the last one he used on the job. I remember when he first let me use it. Before I could use it, he made sure I understood that there are dangers involved in using tools. Before I could use it, he made sure I understood that he valued this hammer and wanted it back in good shape. Before I could even hold it, he explained why the handle was made of hickory, and why the head was shaped the way it was. He held it in his hands and felt the balance. My grandfather was fully ambidextrous. He could hammer and saw equally well with either hand. But I could see as he held his hammer, and as I watched him use it, that each hand knew this hammer differently and used it differently. Before he handed it to me, he looked carefully to make sure that I had understood even a little of this. And then he handed me the hammer.

Tools matter. And Simon and Andrew abandon their tools and follow Jesus. When James and John leave their father, at least they know that he will bring the nets home at the end of the day. They know that he will tend the nets and preserve them, that he will respect the tools of their trade and care for them. I am trying to imagine a circumstance under which my grandfather would leave his tools out in the rain. I cannot think of one.

Simon and Andrew abandon their nets.

Matthew's whole story is a story of division and departure, of separation and abandonment. This scene builds that theme.

Inter-Text: The World We Think We Live In

I still see the nets lying where they were dropped. I still see my grandfather holding his hammer until he was sure that I had caught something of what tools mean to a craftsman. I can still hear the man who taught me to cut meat explaining to me, more with his actions than with his words, that a butcher learns to know his knives so that they work with him, not against him. As I watched him true the edge on a boning knife, it did not even occur to me to chuckle at the way he gave life to an inanimate object. Tools are alive, at least for the person who has learned to use them. And Simon and Andrew's nets are lying on the ground. Perhaps another person picked them up, arranged and ordered them, and put them in storage. No one who fishes for a living could simply ignore abandoned tools. But Simon and Andrew abandoned their nets.

I have been wondering about abandoned things. I read stories out of Rwanda and I hear of houses found with meals prepared and tables set, the people all gone, vanished, probably killed. I wonder about the houses in Bethlehem at the time of Herod's slaughter. How many cooking pots were left where they sat in the last ordinary moment before the murderers arrived? As I write this, the partial transcripts of 911 calls from the World Trade Center have just been released, revealing voices from the instants before and after people learned that the ordinary world through which they had ridden the subway to work had vanished, for them forever. My friends who live in New York City tell me of the scraps of paper, the ordinary debris of ordinary life, that drifted on the breeze in the days after the collapse of the Twin Towers and lay abandoned on the ground until they were swept, collected, gathered up to be saved or destroyed, depending on the day. I remember the empty echoes of Lamentations 1:

> the ways of Zion mourn,
>   because no one comes to the festivals.
> How lonely sits the city that once was full of people.

After Babylon carried the people "into captivity because of affliction," what echoes of ordinary life still wandered the empty streets looking for a living sound to respond to? I read in Tim O'Brien's book on Vietnam of Alpha Company, which found itself under fire in the middle of the mire of a rice paddy.[54] As the men fled for cover back across the paddy, canteens were abandoned, along with radios and weapons, and the armored personnel carriers, in backing away from the rocket-propelled grenade fire, ran over soldiers and killed them. I wonder how many of Matthew's audience knew of the silence that greeted the Romans when they entered Masada at the end of the Jewish Revolt. The last defenders of Masada, having seen the Revolt crushed in defeat after defeat, killed themselves rather than allow Rome the honor of victory. When Roman soldiers entered the fortress, they found the bodies of the last defenders lying on the ground, surrounded by their weapons and tools, abandoned.

Provoking the Story

Play this scene as a swirl of abandonment. When Simon and Andrew abandon their nets, the nets should fall on a pile of other things left abandoned, perhaps from Masada, perhaps from the Warsaw Ghetto, perhaps from any place that people lived ordinary lives until they did not. Perhaps play this scene in front of pictures of abandoned farmhouses and barns. You might even weave Josephus's description of the "terrible solitude" that the Romans encountered when they entered Masada armed for battle only to find all the defenders dead by their own hand. As Simon and Andrew, James and John abandon ordinary life to follow Jesus, perhaps a character could tell other stories of abandonment.

Fourth Sunday after the Epiphany
Matthew 5:1–12

(see translation, p. 291)

Ritual Text: The Life of the Worshiping Community

The strange old words of this scene have been read as the outline for a program of otherworldly spirituality. They have been taken as a guide for living a happy and fulfilled life. At their worst, these statements of blessing have been called the "Be-Happy-Attitudes." Epiphany continues to be the season for surprises, and the surprise this time is that all these spiritual interpreters, these engineers of attitudes, seem never to have read what Matthew has Jesus say.

The first thing I notice when my troupe of storytellers plays this scene is that different lines in this scene taste different. Some lines

Matthew 5:1–12

taste sweet and mild: Godlike in their happiness, the gentle ones, the merciful ones, those making peace. Some lines taste a little sharp: Godlike in happiness, the hungry ones, hungry and thirsty for strictness, those who have been hunted on account of strictness. Some lines taste a little strange: Godlike in their happiness, the mourners. And some taste even bitter: Godlike in happiness you are whenever they reproach you and hunt you and speak all evil against you. Once the bitterness has been tasted, other lines start to pop out as well. The mention of inheriting the earth catches the ear because the known world was in the hands of the Roman overlords when the words were spoken and when the scene was first played. Against that backdrop, the words about the dominion of God draw attention because "dominion" is a word that, even when thoroughly spiritualized, carries a physical, geographic, territorial metaphor with it. The blessing of the mourners carries a sharp bite in the aftermath of the crushing of the First Jewish Revolt against Rome, and the possibility that παρακληθησονται (usually translated as "comforted") ought rather to be read in its courtroom context as "be called as witnesses" sharpens this bite. There were indeed many mourners among the Jews who survived those days. And the fact that the whole scene begins with blessing the poor in breath, those whose life has been sucked out of them and sweeps to an end that invokes images of being hunted and killed makes even the word "happiness" taste bitter and ironic. This is no simple sketch of how to live a happy Christian life.

My storytellers notice when they play this scene that the tastes of the lines jump back and forth, with the bitter attacking the sweet, the gentle resisting the angry, until the whole scene is swept into a history of being hunted and hurt. There are plenty of surprises to be had in this scene, and perhaps a few epiphanies.[55]

Intra-Text: The World of Matthew's Story

When John entered Matthew's story, he harangued the crowds that came out to be purified for the fight that lay ahead. When Jesus entered the story, he came out to John. When John was arrested,

Jesus traveled and taught and healed in Galilee, and crowds like those that had come out to John came out also to him.

In the scene for this Sunday, Jesus appears to withdraw from the crowds to teach his disciples, who come to him after he goes up into "the mountain." By the end of this protracted period of teaching (see the end of Matthew 7), however, it seems that the crowds have rejoined the audience. The scene at the end of Matthew 7 shows us crowds driven out of their minds by his teaching and his authority. So is the Sermon on the Mount delivered to crowds or away from crowds? The text offers both possibilities. This inconsistency is important. Does this imply that the group of disciples is a very large group? Does it imply that a smaller group of disciples spread the word of what he was teaching and the crowds that heard it were driven out of their minds? Or is the statement at the end of Matthew 7 a summary statement that is meant to echo the summary statements that attended the work of John? In that case, consistency is less important than the coherence of Jesus' program in the story with John's. Both are presented as being greeted by eager people who have been waiting for God to intervene in the ordinary world.

But if that is the case, notice how Jesus' teaching pushes these eager people back and forth. The list of blessings begins with a blessing for those who have had the life sucked out of them. In Matthew's story there are plenty of these people; they stretch all the way back to Tamar and Ruth and the wife of Uriah in the genealogy. They are not blandly blessed in this story. Matthew recognizes them and speaks his blessing with a kind of bitter irony that knows the reality of their desperation and honors their refusal to be defeated. Jesus then blesses the mourners. There are plenty of them in this story as well, including characters throughout the genealogy and including especially the families of Bethlehem, Joseph's (and Jesus') hometown. This mourning is extended all the way back to Rachel, who shrieks for her children. In traditional readings of this scene, all these mourners are comforted. One can see why: there has never been, and will never be, human community without mourners, and (consequently) the work of comforting mourners is always going on, as it must always be going on. There are always more mourners, and more comfort will always be needed. But the term translated as "comfort" refers more properly to exhortation than to any activity involving "tea and sympathy." On that model, the passage could be translated, "Godlike in happiness, the mourners, because they will be told to cheer up." Such exhortation might be appropriate, but it does rather change the tone of this scene if the audience is to imagine someone trying to silence Rachel's shrieks by telling her to cheer up. If that is the playing of this scene that is to be chosen, then this scene tells an audience that is tired of hearing the wailing of a distraught mother that it won't be long before they won't have to listen to it anymore. Somehow that seems a little cold, wouldn't you say?

The word that is translated as "they will be comforted," however, offers a richer set of meanings than the customary translation picks up. The word, παρακληθησονται, also appears in legal contexts, where it is translated as "they will be called as witnesses." While this translation (the one that I have indeed chosen) pushes this word about as far as it can possibly go, it does fit rather nicely into the story that Matthew is telling. The mourners we have met in this story are not the everyday mourners who inhabit every human community in every human century. They are not simply mourners created by the ordinary depredations of mortal human life. In Matthew's story, mourners enter the story in response to imperial abuse of power. This is true in Bethlehem as it is true in the genealogy (consider Bathsheba's mourning for Uriah, and the possibility that Matthew is echoing Samuel's warning that kings are dangerous (1 Samuel 8), which may imply that David, as king, acts like Herod the king). But it is also true in the case of John, who will be mourned by his followers, and by all those who heard in John a call to bring something better than submission to the Empire. There will be mourners at the end of Matthew's story, as well, and these mourners will take up the wailing that has echoed in Jewish story since before the time of Rachel. In Matthew's story, all this wailing is caused by Roman abuse of power. In such a context, mourners will indeed be comforted if they can be called as witnesses against the abuses that make Empire work. There would indeed be a bitter sort of happiness in such a call.

The next blessing responds to the threat of violence that comes when mourners are called as witnesses. "Godlike in happiness, the gentle ones," blurts Matthew's Jesus. But in the next line he retorts that happiness properly belongs to those who are hungry for strictness. The word could surely refer to religious righteousness, but the element of strictness must play through this word when it is spoken, and that element knows no particular boundaries. When the matter of revenge is placed on the table (as it is here and throughout Matthew's story), then any hunger for "strictness" will relate also to a demand for justice and legal, retributive balancing.

The next blessing honors mercy, again a reply to the threat of the previous blessing, only to be pushed back when an echo of John's ranting purification in the wilderness is called back into the story. "Make peace," calls the next blessing, only to be scolded by two consecutive blessings that specifically recall Herod's murderous hunting for Jesus, or any toddler he could find.

In this first extended section of teaching, Matthew sets the tone for the clash that will erupt repeatedly in the story he is telling. Watch for how mercy and justice smash into each other in this story. Watch for release and for revenge in the scenes that follow.

Inter-Text: The World We Think We Live In

In Rwanda, with eight hundred thousand people slaughtered in such a short time, calls for justice are necessary. Calls for balance and retribution, however, run into the reality of what so many trials would mean. Voice after voice notes that no legal system on earth could accommodate the thousands of trials that would be necessary. Philip Gourevitch talks with Tito Ruteremara of the RPF:

> "It's materially impossible to judge all those who participated in the massacres, and politically it's no good, even though it's just," the RPF's Tito Ruteremara told me. "This was a true

genocide, and the only correct response is true justice. But Rwanda has the death penalty, and — well, that would mean a lot more killing."[56]

"In other words," concludes Gourevitch, "a true genocide and true justice are incompatible."

Do not assume that this conclusion is a simple, settled judgment. Gourevitch is not suggesting that justice can be set aside because it is impractical. He does not imagine that what is called for is some kind of cynical blessing of the crunching and grinding of "real life." Gourevitch knows that justice is a basic human demand and that it calls most forcefully out of the bitter aftermath of genocide. But Gourevitch also knows that the very situation that demands absolute justice makes it absolutely impossible. The clash implied in Gourevitch's conclusion is the same clash that may be heard in Matthew's bitter blessings.

Provoking the Story

Tim O'Brien tells terrifying stories of Vietnam. He tells stories of night patrols. He tells stories of land mines. He tells stories of hand grenades that skip and bump across his helmet and land next to him. And he tells stories of the day villagers silently allowed Alpha Company to walk into an ambush in a rice paddy. No one said a thing; no one hinted. No one looked up from the ground. And then, as O'Brien says, "the bushes erupted." At night, the mortar shells walked in from two sides, bracketing Alpha Company, forcing them to crawl back and forth in the deep darkness as they tried to break out of the box that was closing in on them, step by step. And the next day, a booby-trapped artillery round blew up two popular soldiers in the unit. And the next day a friend stepped on a land mine. And again at night came the mortar fire, and Alpha Company could not fire back for fear of betraying their position more exactly. And still the villagers were sullen, silent, and impossible to distinguish from the enemy. O'Brien writes:

In the next days it took little provocation for us to flick the flint of our Zippo lighters. Thatched roofs take the flame quickly, and on bad days the hamlets of Pinkville burned, taking our revenge in fire. It was good to walk from Pinkville and to see fire behind Alpha Company. It was good, just as pure hate is good.[57]

Before you are shocked by this passage, reflect on the deep need for revenge in response to day after day of deadly chaos. Before you make peace with the need for revenge, be shocked by the practice of pure hate in this passage.

Now look back at the battle between revenge and mercy in the scene from Matthew. Remember to be shocked and to reflect, and to be shocked again.

Play the scene so that the offense of O'Brien's language is felt by the audience.

Transfiguration Sunday — Last Sunday after the Epiphany
Matthew 17:1–9

(see translation, p. 355)

Ritual Text: The Life of the Worshiping Community

A small group of people. A high mountain. They are all alone. One of the small group is changed in form, right in front of them: his face shines like the sun, his clothes become white as light. These last two images have become clichés. To recover their metaphorical power, stare at the sun on a bright, clear day. Do not stare too long; it will damage your eyes. Notice that the shining of the sun makes you blind if you walk into ordinary shadows. Notice the persistent image of the sun that follows your field of vision when you look away from the sky, a floating blue dot that shows that your eyes cannot easily forget things that shine like the sun. Now reflect on what it would mean for something to be as "white as light." These images are stronger than one would imagine when you first encounter the cliché.

Moses and Elijah enter the scene. They enter though they are long dead. They are eligible to enter the scene, and continue in human history, because they (like Enoch) do not have locatable graves. Enoch walked with God and then was with God. Elijah was swept up to the heavens in the "sweet chariot" when it swung low. Moses was taken by an angel and buried, but his grave was hidden and this sufficed to link him with Elijah and Enoch as a character who could still interact with living human beings. People who have graves live on in the memory of the people of Israel. People who do not have graves live on in a more active sense. And so two of them appear in this scene.

Worship is a proper time to consider that status of these appearances, these epiphanies. Ritual functions (among other things) to mediate between ordinary life and the insights into the depths that are difficult to talk about in ordinary language. These depths are part of ordinary life, ordinary experience, but we need ritual, hymns, and drama because they are the medium that allows us to express what is otherwise inexpressible. This scene comes to us as an event in ordinary life. Fortunately it comes to us as a scene to be performed. That allows us to peer into its depths without needing (at least at the outset) to settle the matter of how dead people can show up in ordinary life. Such matters are important, but they are for another time.

Intra-Text: The World of Matthew's Story

The first thing to notice about this scene is the presence of Elijah. Elijah also appears in Matthew 11, 16, and 27. The first two appearances are explicitly tied to John the Purifier. The discussion of Elijah in the scene that follows this one in Matthew 17 also ties him to John. The appearance of Elijah in the Transfiguration scene warrants consideration. No matter what is going on here, Matthew has knit this scene into the pattern he is using to link Jesus and John.

The story of John's career, arrest, and execution (chapters 3, 11, and 14) sets the rhythm for the story of Jesus' approach to Jerusalem and death at the hands of the Romans (chapters 16, 17, and 20). The string of Elijah/John references ties the middle episode of John's story to the middle prediction of the passion in Jesus' career, and the final linking of Elijah with the death of Jesus confirms both the link between Jesus and John and the link between John and Elijah. And all three are wound tight around execution at the hands of the foreign oppressor.

This is a good time to remember that Elijah killed his opponents. When he entered the contest with the prophets of Ba'al to see whose deity would respond and kindle the burnt offering (1 Kings 18:17–40), he risked his life. When God consumed his offering with fire, Elijah emerged victorious. But the next thing he did was to kill the four hundred[58] prophets of Ba'al who had entered the contest against him. This is not an incidental element of this scene, nor is it incidental to the scene for Transfiguration Sunday. Jesus is linked to Elijah, and Elijah kills his opponents. The killing is figured as a purifying of the people. It comes in the middle of Ahab's hunting of the "troubler of Israel," Elijah. But before justifying Elijah's act, imagine the look of such a character; imagine the fury; imagine the blood. John is linked explicitly to Elijah, and Christians seem comfortable enough playing John as wild-eyed and fire-breathing. But Jesus is also explicitly linked to Elijah (and to John). When Jesus asks who people say that he is, his disciples report that people say that he is John, or Elijah, or Jeremiah, or one of the prophets. If he looks like a prophet, he looks like a troubler of the people. If he looks like Jeremiah, he looks like a mourner for Israel. But if he looks like Elijah, he looks like someone who could order, and carry out, the execution of four hundred of his opponents.

Jesus has plenty of opponents in Matthew's story. All of them stem from the murders committed by Herod (king of the Judeans, stooge of the Romans).

Inter-Text: The World We Think We Live In

This is a good time also to remember the threats made against Elijah's life. Elijah, like John, fought against a ruler who was accused of contaminating God's people. Elijah, like John, was uncompromising in his attacks. Elijah, however, unlike John (and Jesus), was not killed. His opponents, powerful and numerous though they were, were slaughtered and Elijah survived and was taken up in a fiery chariot. That each of these linked characters faced credible threats against their lives matters for how their stories dance together. Note, though, that the old stories of Elijah end with escape and victory. Perhaps this is simply the effect of weaving old stories of legendary stature together with events closer to hand: the old stories will generally be cleaner, smoother, more clearly heroic, the stories closer to hand will still be gritty and not so neatly resolved. If that is the case here, then the death of John and the death of Jesus are bits of historical data that have not yet been polished into conformity with the Elijah legends. Or perhaps Jesus' resurrection is understood to provide escape and victory to him, thus making him a good parallel to Elijah. If this is a productive reading of these interwoven characters, then John comes off looking like the small guy in the group.

Provoking the Story

Play this scene with Elijah still wild-eyed and disheveled after killing the four hundred prophets of Ba'al, perhaps still with blood on his hands and robes. Play Moses so that the audience can hear the screams of the mothers of the firstborn sons of Egypt that ring in his ears. Such sounds change people. Play Jesus so that Rachel's shrieks ring in his ears.

Notice how this changes the words from the cloud about a beloved son?

Section 2:
LENT AND EASTER

Ash Wednesday
Matthew 6:1–6, 16–21
(see translation, p. 297)

Ritual Text: The Life of the Worshiping Community

Ash Wednesday enters the traditional spiral of the Christian community's exploration of its texts and truths as the beginning of a long exercise in honesty and integrity. This long exercise prepares the way for Maundy Thursday, Good Friday, Holy Saturday, and Easter. It begins with honest and patient reflection on the real failures that haunt human lives. There are things we have done that we ought not to have done. There are things we have avoided that we ought not to have avoided. There is damage that we need to repair. This repair work requires honesty and integrity, and it begins with Ash Wednesday. In communities that celebrate this day in its traditional form, the Ash Wednesday ritual involves an extensive confession of sin. This confession is unique because of its length and detail. It is also unique because it is the only act of confession in the traditional spiral that is not immediately answered with an act of absolution, an enactment of forgiveness.

This ritual structure needs to be carefully understood. Absolution is not omitted because of some sadistic desire to crush and control worshipers. Such a theological offense has no part in the ritual spiral. In fact, absolution is not withheld at all. As in all traditional rituals, forgiveness is enacted immediately following the completion of the act of repentance, but this service of confession is not completed until Maundy Thursday. Lent, this season of honesty and integrity, is a ritual of careful and patient confession, from beginning to end. Ash Wednesday begins the work of repairing damage, but this work does not end until the community is on the very edge of Easter, moments before the crucifixion, only days from the celebration of the resurrection. Before a traditional community can productively explore Jesus' death and resurrection, we need to be carefully honest.

The scene from Matthew helps in this practice of honesty.

Intra-Text: The World of Matthew's Story

The Sermon on the Mount (Matthew 5–7) is echoed in the Sermon on the Temple Mount (Matthew 21–23). This echoing is part of the way Matthew's story holds together. Scenes are doubled, sometimes almost exactly. Themes are reproduced and reconsidered. Parts of the story are linked together so that perspectives can be clarified and complicated. And around the whole story is the link between the promise given on the mountain at the end — that Jesus will be "with them" (whatever that means, exactly) — and the name given to Jesus at the beginning of the story: Emmanuel. The surprise of the resurrection is tied back to the shock of naming the fugitive from Herod's murderous campaign "God-Is-With-Us." This embracing of the story by "God-Is-With-Us" is tied back to the scene for Ash Wednesday because of the mountain on which it takes place.

The pattern of link and crosslink is tangled and may not simplify to anything that settles down to one scheme, but the links do tie things together. For instance, just before this scene in chapter 6 Jesus gives instructions regarding swearing on the Temple. ("Don't do it," he says.) In chapter 23 he also deals with the matter of swearing as it touches the Temple. In that case he does not forbid swearing with the Temple as witness, but blasts those who would assign greater weight to the gold in the Temple or to the gifts on the altar than to the Temple and the altar themselves. The scenes are not identical, and their bite is different, but both "Mountain Sermons" pick up the theme of swearing as it touches the Temple.

Further, immediately after the scene for Ash Wednesday Jesus addresses the matter of an eye that is "worthless." It is not altogether clear what he might mean in this cryptic saying (verses 22f.), but it appears that he is using physical blindness as a metaphor for other kinds of inability to perceive. This would link this scene, at least by thematic similarity, to the doubled healing of two blind people (chapters 9 and 20) and to the reported healings of other blind people (chapters 11, 15, and 21). This all would be linked, as well, to the doubled blasting of those Jesus calls "blind guides" (chapters 15 and 23). In all of this talk about blindness, however, there is only one other scene that mentions an eye that is "worthless," and that occurs in chapter 20. Here it is not physical blindness at all that is being referred to. Here, a "worthless eye" leads workers to resent a landowner who pays his workers unevenly. Those who work long hours in the sun are paid the same as those who work only a single hour at the end of the day. How does seeing things for what they are make an eye worthless? It is a good question. These patterns of linkage are also complicated and tangled, but they tie this theme in the Sermon on the Mount to the whole flow of the developing story up to the Sermon on the Temple Mount.

Perhaps the surest link in all of this is the one established in the scene assigned to Ash Wednesday, because it picks up seeing and being seen and links it to role-playing. This also is a theme that is echoed in Matthew's story. It comes back in chapter 7, and in 15, and in 23, where it is explored relentlessly. Once again the Sermon on the Mount is linked to the Sermon on the Temple Mount. Once again seeing and being seen is linked to the charge that the guides are blind. There is something here to follow carefully.

Inter-Text: The World We Think We Live In

When Jesus points to hypocrites (role players) who make a show of their devotion, he is pointing to characters that exist in every community. It is impossible to gather one hundred people from any community of faith and not have a big handful of hypocrites in the crowd. Sermons on this scene typically pick up on this and blandly urge people not to be hypocrites. Who could object to such urging?

The problem with this scene comes when you notice the Jewish practice during Yom Kippur of not showering, not brushing hair, all for the sake of observing this solemn day carefully. Some interpreters jump on such practices and see in them the hypocrisy that Jesus is said to point to. The sermons that grow out of such a beginning become anti-Semitic rants, even in the hands of well-intentioned preachers. Go carefully here. It is possible that Jesus is doing something simpler here, that he is only targeting religious play-acting. If so, there will always be plenty of targets to shoot at. There is no current shortage of hypocrites, and none looks likely in the future. But it is also possible that Jesus is shooting precisely at ordinary Jewish practices. This would be much more troublesome. No matter how many times interpreters quibble that such an attack would (or could, or should properly) be the result of a class-borne antagonism between hick Galileans and hoity-toity Judeans, it never quite holds as long as it takes a preacher to get into the pulpit. The distinction vanishes, in any case, before the audience gets back home. The result is that the whole attempt is transformed into a rant devoted to proving that Christian Gentiles who can't keep kosher on a bet are somehow superior in the eyes of God to Jews who are instructed by God to keep the commandments.

Go carefully here.

Provoking the Story

There are many ways to play this scene. Jesus can speak gently and calmly to his earnest listeners. Try it that way. Jesus can speak sharply to the imagined hypocrites. Try it that way, too. Jesus could make sarcastic fun of the role players. If you play it this way, make sure that the sarcasm is sharp and bitter. And Jesus could speak these words as a wild-eyed rant. This way of embodying this scene is quite frightening.

Make sure that, no matter what other ways you play the scene, you play also the frightening rant.

First Sunday in Lent
Matthew 4:1–11

(see translation, p. 288)

Ritual Text: The Life of the Worshiping Community

This scene is hopelessly overlaid with assumptions that are foreign to it. Christian interpreters assume that Jesus is being tempted, so this

scene is understood to be somehow parallel to instances of temptation that Christians experience in ordinary life. The "tempting"
is understood to be conducted by The Devil, who is understood to
be SATAN, who is understood to be an evil power engaged in cosmic and eternal conflict with God. The universe is understood, on
this model, to be a cosmic no-man's-land blasted between these two
equally matched powers. Of course, such construals of the universe
have been rightly rejected as heresies.

These assumptions might have roots (of some sort) in the first
century of the Common Era, though this is not so certain as is sometimes assumed. What is clear is that the kind of full-blown dualism
is more properly rooted in medieval Christendom than in any ancient Jewish monotheism. What is further clear is that the figure of
SATAN as it appears in customary readings of this scene is altogether
distant from the character who tries Jesus.

This is not a temptation scene. This is a scene in which an appointed agent tests Jesus' solidity. The tester is a prosecutor, not a
demon. He is an inspector with official responsibilities before God;
he is not a cosmic force arrayed against God. He is not Satan; he is
the satan, the inspector and tester.

Look back at the book of Job, and at the figure of the satan that
is found there. Though Job is much older than Matthew, the satan
plays a similar role in the two stories. And since Job is much closer to
Matthew, both in time and cultural development, than is our world,
it is worth considering whether the similarities might be greater than
interpreters assume.

The first thing to notice is that Jesus is brought to the place of
testing by "the breath," presumably the breath of God. That means
that no matter how the cosmological furniture is finally arranged
in our construal of this scene, Jesus is not ambushed; he is examined. The next thing to notice is that this examination begins with
a ritual weakening of the candidate. Jesus fasts for forty days and
forty nights. We are told that at the end of this rigorous fast he was
hungry. No kidding. But this simple and obvious statement deserves

another look. Hunger is not simply a biological state; it is a theological and anthropological index of what it means to be a human being. When God blew into Mudguy's nose in Genesis 2 (see the discussion of Matthew 3 for the First Sunday after the Epiphany, page 00), Mudguy became a *nephesh chayah,* a desiring being. That means that Jesus, as a result of his ritual fast, has become fully alive, a human being at the most basic level, capable of the greatness and the depravity that aspiration (hunger) brings to life.

It is in this state of basic human life that the tester approaches him. He addresses him as a "son of God." This name could mean many things. In any story about someone anointed, someone who is messiah, it is wise to remember that both "messiah" and "son of God" are terms used for the royal figure who rules Israel, the king of the Jews. But "son of God" triggers other echoes as well. At the end of Matthew's story there is reference to washing in the name of the father and of the son and of the holy breath. This becomes a root out of which trinitarian theology will grow, though such fully developed dogmatic notions are surely not yet present when Matthew's story is first told. But though this notion will need another few centuries of growth before a stable doctrine of the Trinity will be produced, still this use of father, son, and breath language seems to indicate that the name "son of God" creates Jesus as a personage of impressive stature. If indeed this is evidence of an early, and very high, Christology, one that links Jesus to the Creator of the universe, then he could indeed be expected to speak to stones and create them as something else entirely. If God can speak to formless chaos and bring out an ordered world, a (or *the*) son of God can speak to solid stone and bring forth something that a woman could knead, form, and bake.

There is another echo that might shape this scene. In Genesis 6 there is reference to "sons of God" who also are characterized by desire. In this case the objects of desire are young marriageable women, and the "sons of God," ill-defined beings read by Enoch as angels, mate with these women and giants are produced.

Which of these echoes matters? As usual, the answer is "yes."

Intra-Text: The World of Matthew's Story

The character opposite Jesus in this scene is "the tester," the prosecutor, the satan. He is doing his job, testing the integrity of Jesus here at the outset of the story. We have met Jesus in the context of his family history, both his immediate family (that suffered slaughter) and his centuries-long extended family, the Jewish family extending back to Abraham and Sarah. We have seen Jesus emerge from this history when he is drawn to John in the wilderness, when he comes to fill up all strictness. All the factors that led up to the birth of Jesus have prepared him and his family for this moment in history, the moment when God's people struggle under the weight of Empire. Jesus' whole history has prepared for his birth at such a time, and now he has been born and now has grown to adulthood. And now he is tested.

The question that matters with any testing is, What is he being tested for? Every test measures one sort of thing and not another. Consider the LSAT, the GRE, the MCAT, the SAT, the licensing examination for electricians, and the training and testing that precede the awarding of jump wings for paratroopers. Every test reveals one sort of weakness and not another, and each reveals its own sort of strength. But what is the tester looking for?

In Matthew's story the tester pokes at Jesus when he is hungry. Because he is a "son of adam," because he is (in terms drawn from Genesis 2) a *nephesh chayah,* a living, desiring being, and because he has been fasting for forty days and forty nights, it is a safe bet that he is hungry. But the real test is whether he will desire to leap above being a *nephesh chayah,* a living being, a "son of adam," and claim status as a son of God. Christians, of course, hear the Trinity in these words and pay little further attention. But every Jew is a child of God, and the tester is not merely asking for a demonstration of Christological pyrotechnics; he is testing to see whether Jesus will expect special privileges, expect the laws of nature to change so that he will have bread to eat without relying on someone to bake it, someone to grind the meal, someone to harvest the grain, someone to plant the grain. Will Jesus ask something of the world that it does not give? This is an important test.

Then the tester sharpens the test. Will Jesus step off the highest place on the Temple and dare gravity to do its work? Later in the story, Peter will step out of a boat onto the water, and sinks like a rock. Will Jesus do something similar here at the beginning of the story? Here the tester examines Jesus to see if he is inclined to do stupid things on the basis of a trust in God.

Then the test gets sharper still. The tester shows Jesus the kingdoms of the beautiful world.[59] He offers Jesus dominion, and all he demands is that Jesus worship him. Both the offer and the requirement need reflection. The tester offers Jesus dominion and glory, and he offers "all" of each, all there is in the world. My ear hears echoes of the customary closing that was added to the Lord's Prayer after it left Matthew's storyteller: "for thine is the kingdom, and the power, and the glory, forever and ever. Amen." Read this way, the tester is offering to Jesus the power of God and, with it, the place of God. Read this way, Jesus' answer reveals that he rejects the place and power of God, that he is no Trinitarian.

It is also possible to read the scene as if the real testing is camouflaged. The offer of kingdoms and glory is nothing; the test comes with the bowing down to anyone other than God. On this model, Jesus sees through the camouflage and refuses to honor any but God.

There is at least one more possible reading of this scene and of the test contained in it. It is possible that what the tester is offering Jesus is dominion, dominion on a scale unknown before Alexander the Great and his Roman successors. It is possible that the tester is offering Jesus domination, domination of the land on the model of Roman domination of the known world. On this model, he is offering Jesus a chance to replace Empire with his own rule, presumably more benign. Under this new rule, no more innocent children would be slaughtered. Under this rule, Israel would never again go into Exile. Under this rule, all of the remembered wrongs, recorded in the genealogy, would be corrected and balanced. All Jesus need do is honor the one who gave him power.

On this model, Jesus' answer becomes fascinating. Is he rejecting the whole offer on the grounds that closing the deal will require idolatry? Or is he rejecting the whole deal as idolatrous from the heart out? It makes a difference.

Inter-Text: The World We Think We Live In

In the play *The Maids,* by Jean Genet, Claire and Solange serve Madame. Madame is beautiful, powerful, dominating woman who is overwhelmed by how much her maids love her. When Madame is out of the house, Claire and Solange, the sisters who serve Madame, spend their time plotting to kill Madame. It is not clear why they must kill her. She is Madame. She is capricious, self-absorbed, and given to bullying. But we see nothing that rises to the level of a capital crime on Madame's part. She is Madame. And her maids plot to kill her.

But that is not all there is to it. Genet's plays are never that simple.

The instant Madame leaves the house, Claire and Solange begin an elaborate game of role playing. One plays Madame, brutal, demanding, sadistic, and the other acts out the plot to kill her. The violence escalates, the sadism explodes, and they are always interrupted before they can reach the climax of the game. They never quite get to the killing. This inability to finish the game is mirrored in real life. Each maid has an opportunity to kill Madame. Neither can do it. They play their games in order to practice the murder they dream of committing. They play their game to practice taking revenge.

And then Madame returns again and they become subservient.

One day they finish the game. One day Claire loses control and kills Solange. Madame is still alive, and will return home in due course. When she does, she will find the sisters lying on the floor, cuddled together as they were when they slept together as little girls, with Solange's dead arm draped around Claire.

Their dreams of revenge will have touched Madame not at all. Their game will have killed Solange and made a murderer, liable to be hanged, of Claire. And Madame will hire new maids and believe they love her even as she abuses them.

Provoking the Story

Play the scene from Matthew's story as a game of revenge. For hints as to how this might be done, read Genet's play *The Maids*. Play it as a ritual in which the satan offers to Jesus the chance to avenge all the wrongs done in the world since the time of Abraham and Sarah. The offer of dominion over the nations of the world is an offer of a chance at payback. To get a clearer sense of what is at stake in the scene, play it with Jesus taking the bait offered by the satan. What would be the consequences of such an outcome? Do not stop with any of the first five answers that come up as you play.

Second Sunday in Lent
Matthew 17:1–9
(see translation, p. 355)

Ritual Text: The Life of the Worshiping Community

See the discussion of this scene for Transfiguration Sunday, beginning on page 99. In addition, consider how playing this scene is different when the focus is the Lenten exercise of honesty and integrity instead of the Epiphany season of surprises. I notice that my ear is drawn this time to the words spoken by the voice out of the cloud. In Epiphany it is my eye that draws me: I see the face and clothing of Jesus; I see that they are changed in form. In Lent I hear a call to hear, a call to obey. Explore what it means to lead an audience by the eye, and how this is different from leading them by the ear. Notice also that the voice out of the cloud echoes the naming of Jesus as son, presumably of God.

Intra-Text: The World of Matthew's Story

See the discussion of this scene for Transfiguration Sunday, beginning on page 99.

Inter-Text: The World We Think We Live In

See the discussion of this scene for Transfiguration Sunday, beginning on page 99.

Provoking the Story

See the discussion of this scene for Transfiguration Sunday, beginning on page 99. Play this scene so that your audience feels the contrast between the way you play it this week and the way you played it a few weeks ago.

Liturgy of the Palms — Sixth Sunday in Lent
Matthew 21:1–11

(see translation, p. 375)

Ritual Text: The Life of the Worshiping Community

Matthew's story is written in Greek. This is not surprising, given that Greek was the language that had bound the Mediterranean basin together since the time of Alexander the Great. But not all of the words in Matthew's story are in Greek, and those few exceptions pop out of the text and demand attention. This scene contains one of those surprising words, spoken in Aramaic in the face of Roman power that would not have understood what was being said. The word is left untranslated in English translations, which means that the word stands a fair chance of being misunderstood also for contemporary audiences. The word is "hosanna." It does not mean "hip-hip-hooray," though such readings are common in Sunday School lessons. It means "Lord, save." It is an appeal for release from Roman domination, spoken at the gates of Jerusalem, the site of so much carnage during the First Jewish Revolt against Rome. This revolt is still in the future for Jesus, but it is in the past for the audience of Matthew's story. That makes the cry sharply poignant.

Why is this cry in Aramaic? Sometimes people use foreign words to conjure with. Foreign words can be magic words. They not only

113

add that little bit of frisson that makes a story sizzle; they carry the power of strangeness to move things and change them. If that is what is going on here, it is worth noting that the magic words are Jewish words.

Another possible reason to use Aramaic is that Rome did not understand the language, at least not well. The people see the approach of Jesus and cry out to the God of promise for rescue. Rome, if it deigns to listen, hears only "Jewish jabbering," not a call for revolution, for overturning, for turning things right-side-up. Some things are not meant for the ears of Empire.

Intra-Text: The World of Matthew's Story

The last time someone was described as "gentle" (πραυς) in Matthew's story, it was in chapter 5 at the beginning of the Sermon on the Mount. Now the word enters the story again just prior to the Sermon on the Temple Mount. The last time this word was used, it referred to the ones that will inherit the earth now dominated by Rome. This time it is spoken at the gates of Jerusalem, the city David established as his capital, the city in which Solomon built the Temple, the city claimed by the Romans as their organ of liaison. By the time Matthew's story is told and heard, the city has fallen to the Romans, its wall has been breached, and the Temple has been destroyed.

The first thing to notice about this scene is that in a very few moments Jesus will be anything but gentle. In Matthew's story, Jesus rides into Jerusalem in the company of crowds who acclaim him as a prophet and as the son of David. These identifications do not fit together, but they do work together. Together they make it clear that Jesus stirs hopes that have lived deep in the Jewish people, hopes that have helped them resist domination through all the centuries since the Babylonian Exile. These hopes live, for the most part, out of the sight of the Roman authorities, if only because they do not breathe the language in which the hopes are expressed. When the crowds cry "Hosanna" the Romans will have understood the emotion, but will not have caught all the echoes. Even when the dominant Romans catch a glimpse of the hopes that Jews breathe, they miss more than they see. Matthew identifies Jesus as the king who is coming. This simple identification, drawn from the remembered words of the prophets, rings with depths the Romans will not have heard at all. Once they understand that Jesus is being acclaimed as a king, they will kill him. Their approach is simple: there is one king, and it is not Jesus.

When Jesus enters the city in Matthew's story, immediately he attacks the Temple. Customary interpretation is always ready to justify Jesus' actions. Determining whether he is justified (or not) can wait for another time. For now notice the violence of his actions in the Temple; notice that this is an attack on the sacrificial dance that God's people do with God, the dance that they had done for millennia, in some form or other. Interpreters seem always ready to give Jesus credit for inventing post-sacrificial religion. Other interpreters, more helpfully I think, point to the way this action prepares the way for observant Jewish faith to survive the destruction of the Temple, the destruction of the possibility of continuing the sacrificial dance.

Even this, though, blunts the storyteller's contrast between the portrayal of Jesus as a gentle king on a donkey and the portrayal of his violence inside the confines of the Temple, making himself a whip since he would not have been allowed to carry other weapons into the Temple, the place where God maintained the peace and stability of the world.

Even if we grant in its entirety the customary suggestion that overthrowing the sacrificial system and its attending corruptions was a good and proper goal, even if we grant all of that dubious notion, still his attack is violent, and erupts out of nowhere. We could suppose, safely, that this is a tatter of old "oral tradition" that has been dropped into this context out of the sky, but such a bland reading refuses to recognize the oral reality of Matthew's story. If this story was performed for an audience, the audience would see Jesus enter the city, gentle and humble, and then suddenly erupt, make a weapon, and attack the dance that God had done with God's people since the days of Abraham and Sarah, even Cain and Abel, only now Jesus looks more like Cain than Abel. This is a frightening thought.

Inter-Text: The World We Think We Live In

Of course there is another possible way to read the "gentle" approach of Jesus the humble king. James C. Scott has tracked the ways that dominated populations learn to protect themselves under the watchful eye of their dominators. Anything that can be read as rebellion will be punished, so anything that is said or done has to be readable as flattery to the dominator, as safe and non-threatening. That does not, however, preclude the performance of what Scott calls a "hidden transcript." Every public utterance must simultaneous reassure and undercut the party in power. Thus it is that people who were held as slaves developed ways of seeming to comply while undercutting their "masters' " success at every turn. Thus it is that an old Ethiopian proverb developed: "When the great lord passes, the wise peasant bows deeply and silently farts."[60] Perhaps Jesus is described as gentle because the audience knows that this dodge would appease the Romans. On this reading, an insider audience is expected to know well ahead of time that this characterization of Jesus as "gentle" is simply a set-up. The deceptive dance of submission sets the Romans up to miss the powerful provocation that Jesus represents.

Oddly enough, even a supremely skilled reader like Paula Fredriksen may have taken this bait in her reading of the story of the entry into Jerusalem. Fredriksen, in her *Jesus of Nazareth, King of the Jews,* reads the entry into Jerusalem as the moment when Jesus loses control of his audience. On her model, he is a teacher, a faithful Jew, a Galilean. When he approaches Jerusalem for Passover, Judeans hear him and see him as the trigger for their revolutionary hopes. Jewish officials, forced to be Rome's organ of liaison, hear the crowds and see Jesus as a threat to the order of the city, a threat that might lead to Roman retaliation, and so they turn Jesus over to the Romans. Pilate, on this reading, knows that Jesus represents no threat, and thus crucifies Jesus to make a political point. But because he knows that Jesus is, in fact, no threat, he crucifies only Jesus. Why waste good crosses on insignificant rabble who will scatter when Jesus dies?

To my ear, Fredriksen's reading is most promising. It offers a way to understand why Jesus was crucified, and why his followers were not, and this is a huge gain in historical understanding.

Fredriksen's reading is strong and promising, but it may also offer us a glimpse of how Pilate has misunderstood the public transcript of the Jewish people. He looks at Jesus and sees a gentle Galilean on a donkey, and he kills him (though he is sure he is no real threat) to make a point to the uppity Judeans who are getting out of their place. He does all this because he thought that "gentle" meant gentle. He missed the hidden transcript. He had no idea what the followers of the guy on the donkey said when they were out of earshot. "Gentle" indeed.

There is, of course, another possible reading of this whole "gentle" business, a reading also suggested by Scott's analysis. This reading draws on the clash that I see in the beginning of the Sermon on the Mount, a clash between anger and restraint, between brittleness and flexibility, between revenge and realism. On this model, Matthew is providing a script for Jesus (the gentle king) that Jesus does not follow. He may enter the city on a donkey, he may hear the warning echoes that Matthew sounds, he may even be restrained by them, at least temporarily, but as soon as he enters the Temple, all warnings are forgotten and all restraint is leapt over. He makes a whip out of cords and drives people and animals out of the sacred precincts, thus attacking the Temple, the ancient faith of his family, and the organ of liaison of the Roman Empire. Such acts draw Roman ire. How could they not? Such acts are better gentled into hiddenness, but Jesus erupts, and Matthew's story will subsequently show the effects of such lack of restraint. Rome crucifies such uppity Jews. Such conflict is better avoided.[61]

Which is the correct reading? Yes.

I know that such an answer does not satisfy, but it does help. This is a complicated scene, and seeing the complications is better than ignoring them.

Provoking the Story

This scene is too simple if it is played simply as if everyone who is a "good guy" is cheering for Jesus and everyone who is not cheering for Jesus is a "bad guy." This simplification of narrative structures (an effect of cowboy movies on Russian formalism, I am convinced),[62] falsifies this scene.

Play the scene with faithful followers who are uneasy with the cheering crowds. Explore the different possible backstories that could contribute to this faithful uneasiness. Play the scene also so that the audience sees some members of the cheering crowd who are simply egging Jesus on so that he will overstep the limits. Let the audience see these *agents provocateurs* for what they are: Roman stooges who want to encourage Jesus to do in public what he teaches in private, to act out the hidden transcript. If he acts out the hidden transcript, he will be killed. Both the faithfully uneasy and the treacherously enthusiastic know that this is what happens when dominated people get uppity.

Liturgy of the Passion — Sixth Sunday in Lent
Matthew 26:14–27:66 or Matthew 27:11–54

(see translation, p. 409)

Ritual Text: The Life of the Worshiping Community

You have a choice. If this is the scene you have chosen to explore for this Sunday, it may well be because members of your community cannot attend Good Friday services with any solid regularity. That is a good reason to make such a choice. The resurrection scene makes no sense by itself; it even makes anti-sense. The pain of the death by torture tempers the joy of the resurrection. I do not say that it diminishes the joy, I say that it tempers it: hardens it, toughens it, makes it more suited to life and work in a hard world.

Both the longer and the shorter text focus attention on the stark death of Jesus. For Christians in our century, this is the first encounter with crucifixion since last Holy Week, unless you count all the casual references to "getting crucified" and "excruciating" pain. In the world out of which Matthew's story comes, the situation would be exactly reversed. Audiences would know more than they wanted about crucifixions, perhaps from having witnessed several. More important, there were no casual references to crucifixion ever to be heard. Crucifixion, for people who knew what it meant, was not a metaphor, it was a crime and an obscenity.

Celebration of this day in the ritual cycle of the church requires regaining a sense of how impossible this day would have been in the ancient world where people knew what crucifixion meant. This day brings a vile obscenity into the heart of the community's sanctuary. This is never done casually. People are properly hesitant about profanity in church. Crucifixion is far beyond profanity. It was an active obscenity. And it is explored on this day. Explore carefully.

Intra-Text: The World of Matthew's Story

At the beginning of Matthew's story, Herod began the hunt for the babies of Bethlehem. He killed almost all of them on his first foray. Matthew tells us that Herod then died, but that the hunt did not die with him. Joseph, when he saw that Herod's son was in power after his father, concluded that the danger persisted and that Bethlehem was no longer safe. God, being warned by Joseph, finally agreed and sent an angel to second Joseph's notion. The family fled to Nazareth, and Jesus grew up in hiding.

Now at the end of the story Jesus again returns to Judea, the region where he was born. He returns not to Bethlehem, the city of David's birth, but to Jerusalem, the city of David's kingship. Herod is no longer a factor in Matthew's story. His hunt ended when the next Herod killed John the Purifier in chapter 14. But when Jesus comes to Jerusalem it comes clear that the real hunter is still very much in the field. It was not just Herod that hunted the babies of Bethlehem; it was Empire. Behind Herod stood Rome. Now that

Herod is out of the way, the audience sees Pilate waiting to kill the one baby who escaped so long ago. Time does not matter to Empire. Empire may grind slowly, but it grinds exceedingly fine.[63] In this long scene, Empire finally catches Jesus, finally catches the "king of the Jews" that it has been chasing since his birth was revealed by the star and the traveling pagans. Notice that the Romans (who are the "they" in this scene, the ones who do the crucifying) mock Jesus and Jewish hopes simultaneously when they identify the cause for Jesus' crucifixion: This man is Jesus, the King of the Jews (27:37).

Empire is not seeking simply to crucify one man, whether gentle or troublesome. Rome is seeking to demonstrate that, though it may take a lifetime, it will catch and kill anyone who stirs Jewish hope. In Matthew's story, Rome finishes Herod's hunt and nails Jewish hope for a reversal of fortunes to the cross where it can watch it die. The ridicule from the Romans was glad and voluntary. But this scene also includes involuntary ridicule. The chief priests and the scribes and the elders also ridicule Jesus in this extended scene. Remember that they are pinned in place by Rome's choice of them as the organ of liaison. (See the fuller discussion of this fact of colonial life that begins on page 59.) To play their ridicule as freely chosen is to misunderstand what it means to live under domination. Empire in every century requires such public displays. It is part of the mechanism of domination.

Most painful in this scene, beyond even the physical pain, is Jesus' recognition of Empire's ability to dominate even God. From his first entry into the story he has been assured of God's partisanship, assured that he and God speak with one voice. This comes as no surprise to contemporary Christians or to customary interpretation, since both are convinced of the applicability of the doctrine of the Incarnation to all things touching Jesus. He speaks with God's authority because he is God in the flesh. Christians will, and ought to, read this way.

But Matthew wrote before this dogmatic scheme was fully worked out. Though I am convinced that the Christian movement operated with a very early, very highly exalted view of Jesus and his career and origin, still the Gospels predate the full articulating of this understanding. And still Matthew tells a story that does not simply exemplify later dogma. In fact, Matthew tells a story that significantly complicates later stable dogma.

In this scene, Jesus (who had always identified his voice with God's voice) accuses God of abandoning him. Go slowly here. Again there is a deposit of dogma on Jesus' accusing words, a deposit that blurs the outlines of the words, and softens their force. To make sense of (and with) these words you must vigorously honor the story that Matthew is telling. Jesus escapes death in Bethlehem, though his cousins, aunts, and uncles do not. Jesus grows up as a refugee, hunted by Empire. Jesus sees John likewise hunted, and finally killed: John the Purifier, John the prophet, John the re-presentation of Elijah, John who identified Jesus as stronger, as the one who would complete the burning that John began. Jesus conducts his career in a way that carries out John's expectations. He demands rigorous moral and religious perfection of his followers, and of all people, and condemns to the outer darkness and fires of Gehenna those who do not measure up. His rigid demands are what one would expect of a person who learned so early and so devastatingly the dangers of life under Empire. (See my fuller discussion of this matter in chapter 2, page 50.) Throughout his career he has met crowds of people and each time he has sorted them into groups of sheep and goats, wheat and weeds, good fish and bad, and each time he has conducted his sorting, he has consigned those sorted to his left to the fire. The criteria of sorting are finally simple, Jesus states them off-handedly in the Sermon on the Mount and applies them rigidly in the Sermon on the Temple Mount: You must be perfect as your father, your heavenly father, is perfect (Matthew 5:48). Christian interpreters have developed theological ways to dodge the force of this demand, mostly involving notions of the economy of the Atonement. Jewish interpreters, not being saddled with the responsibility to "make nice" with Jesus, are shocked by the saying. Jesus arrogates to himself a perfection that is proper only to God and demands that his followers do the same. It is a central affirmation of Judaism that "God is God, and you are not." Jesus' words contravene this central, wise understanding. Humans are humans, and not perfect. Thus it is that they have sins to confess, and forgiveness to ask, of each other and of God. This is a normal state of affairs, and one that God has provided for in every era of dealing with creation. Now Jesus is demanding that his followers reach for, and assert, a kind of perfection proper only to God. The hubris is stunning.

This scene demands that you have recognized the hubris. The scene of Jesus' death has its full dramatic bite only if the audience catches the deep disaster represented by Jesus' dying accusation. Jesus who has demanded perfection of everyone he has encountered accuses God of not measuring up to that standard. Jesus, who has calmly weathered every storm that he encountered after the loss of all his cousins, aunts, and uncles, now collapses at the moment he should, at least, embody the dignity of a martyr. To see how a martyr ought to die, read the story of Eleazar in 4 Maccabees, or read the story of Nathan Hale.[64] Proper martyrs hold their integrity to the end. Jesus collapses and goes so far as to blame God for the collapse. It does not improve things that he is quoting Psalm 22, which ends with a confession of confident faith in deliverance. As Matthew tells the story, Jesus quotes only the complaint and gives no voice to confident faith, either because he chooses not to do so, or because he dies incomplete and unable to finish the prescribed course from complaint to confidence. In either case, his death scene is a scene of collapse and not martyrdom. Martyr stories clothe the hero in perfect, calm integrity. Matthew's story holds the audience's head and forces it to look at an imperfect death that shreds Jesus' earlier rigid integrity.

Inter-Text: The World We Think We Live In

What conclusions would Jesus have drawn from his manner of death? It is a painful and awkward question, but it is a question that cracks open this scene. Given Jesus' rigid and demanding character in Matthew's story, a character that is consistent with his early experience of disaster in the assault on his extended family, he will have drawn fearful conclusions as a result of his collapse in the face of death. My colleagues tell me that children who survive such disasters, and live with the resulting chaos and uncertainty, demand great certainty and absolute integrity from those around them. They typically look at companions as either heroes or as the most despicable villains, and this opinion will snap from hero to villain in response to the first and slightest failing. My colleagues tell me that such people are significant risks for suicide, because they judge themselves even more harshly than they judge their companions. The first failing, long feared and barely kept at bay, delivers damning evidence. Anything that falls short of calm demonstration of wholeness and integrity induces deep despair, and can lead to a self-imposed death sentence.

If Christians are to take the doctrine of the Incarnation seriously, then the truths that apply to human life apply also to Jesus' life. He is affected by social and psychological laws as certainly as he is affected by the law of gravity. In the case of his death scene, this means that Jesus must see his manner of death as a disgrace to the principles that drove him throughout his career. This means that Jesus, the great sorter of sheep and goats, wheat and weeds, dies having drawn the conclusion that he is not perfect as his father in heaven is perfect, and that he is more goat than sheep.

Provoking the Story

This year, take the disaster of Jesus' death seriously. Do not play it as a price to be paid. Such a reading plays it as the death of a martyr, expensive but well within budgeted expectations. Do not play it as a substitutionary surprise. Such a reading plays it as a meritorious death that steps in front of a speeding auto to push a baby stroller out of the way. Both of these readings, and all the rest of the customary readings, are powerful and important, and they are well represented in the history of Christian interpretation.

But neither of these readings captures the depth of the disaster that Matthew captures through the way he tells his story of Jesus.

Matthew sets up the death scene to be the conclusion of the hunt for the babies of Bethlehem and prepares the audience for a story of an exemplary death. Having thus set the audience up, Matthew trips them. Matthew baffles them, stuns them. Matthew sorts Jesus to the left with the goats and consigns him to the outer darkness where people wail and gnash their teeth.

Play the scene so the audience catches the stunning force of Matthew's story.

For a sharp provocation, consider the story told by Tim O'Brien of the Vietnam war. After a long lapse during his time in combat, O'Brien begins corresponding again with a friend from training, a friend who has also been in Vietnam, but not in a combat zone. The friend is nearly done with his tour of duty. He writes about what he has seen, what he has watched:

> This morning, coming out of the hooch, I watched as a junior officer literally kicked a Vietnamese woman out of the company area adjacent to ours. I watched. The observer, the peeping tom of this army. Doing nothing. I was suddenly sickened by the thought of the near two thousand years that separate my life and that of a Roman centurion who stood by a narrow alley leading to Golgotha and who also watched, doing nothing.
>
> What difference then? What earthly change have centuries of suffering and joy wrought? Is it only that Christ is become a yellow-skinned harlot, a Sunday-morning short-time girl?
>
> Needless to say, I am uncomfortable in my thoughts today. Perhaps it's that I know I will leave this place alive and I need to suffer for that.
>
> But, more likely, what I see is evil.[65]

Holy Saturday
Matthew 27:57–66

(see translation, p. 425)

Ritual Text: The Life of the Worshiping Community

There were rituals associated with crucifixion. The one that matters most for this scene is the ritual of the abandonment of the corpse. The pain and offense of crucifixion did not end with death. The torture continued. The point of crucifixion was that Rome had the power to make *anyone* into a nobody who could be crucified, a nobody that no one would claim. To make this point, the corpse was dumped in a ditch and left for dogs to eat, and birds. To enforce the point, Rome made it clear that it could crucify anyone it chose, and that group might include anyone who associated themselves too closely with the nobody nailed to the cross.

That makes the act of Joseph of Arimathea more significant. He is not just burying Jesus. He is risking his own life to claim connection with someone Rome had decided to crucify. When he has placed Jesus in the tomb, he departs, leaving Mary Magdalene and the other Mary watching at the tomb. This waiting and watching at the tomb is also is an act of strong courage. Rome could crucify anyone it chose, and it would make good crushing sense to choose to punish anyone who would sit and wait by the grave of one who had been tortured to death. Still the women sit there and wait.

After Shabbat, they return to wait some more. This is not, as it is in Mark's story, an approach to the tomb to perform the proper burial customs. It appears in Matthew's story that such things have been properly attended to. Instead, they are simply sitting and watching the grave. They arrive early, the day is just dawning. How long would they have continued to come to watch the grave? Matthew does not give us any hint, but they appear to be made of stern stuff, so one may safely assume that the ritual of watching would go on for a long time. If they are watching until the breath is understood to have departed irrevocably from the body, they must wait into the third day before they have cultural proof that he is really and finally dead. If that is the purpose of their waiting, the resurrection catches them just after they have finished this officially recognized period of waiting for confirmation of death.

Intra-Text: The World of Matthew's Story

It is not surprising that this scene revealing the courage of Joseph of Arimathea should be wrapped in scenes that point out the steady courage of women in this story. Neither should it be ignored.

From the genealogy forward, Matthew has told a story of the durability of God's people that depends always on the durability and courage of women. Tamar refused her expulsion. Ruth refused to starve to death. These refusals set the tone for the story that followed. Even when the story was exclusively about Jesus and the hunt for the babies of Bethlehem, still in the background the audience must remember the women who refused and endured. Now at the end of the story, we see them again. They watch with Jesus as he dies. They do not leave him. Even when he accuses God of having abandoned him, still they do not leave. And they watch over his grave. They watch even past the limit of resuscitation, past the border of life into the time of certain death. Their waiting for the period of time when it was judged that he might spontaneously revive is remarkable and courageous. Rome had just crucified him and still they were waiting to claim him if Rome's murder should prove incomplete. But their waiting extends beyond this culturally defined period, a testimony to the deep durability that Matthew's story has shown in women back in the beginning of the story. Women have not figured prominently in Matthew's story since then, but the storyteller wraps the whole story in a web of courage and persistence with this return to a picture of women who do not give up.

Throughout his story, Matthew has enclosed stretches of the story inside arcs of repetition. The center of the story is wrapped five times in doubled references to blindness. Blind men are healed in chapters 9 and 20. Blindness and muteness are overcome in chapters 9 and 12. Repeated reference is made to the blind who now see (chapters 11, 15, and 21). While all this is going on, Jesus calls those who question him "blind guides" (chapters 15 and 23) and ties it all together with references to eyes that are "worthless" (chapters 6 and 20). There is other doubling, as well (the tree and its fruit is called to witness in chapters 7 and 12, crowds of people are fed in chapters 14 and 15, and the matter of swearing by the Temple arcs across the story from chapter 5 to chapter 23).

This arced reference to courageous women is subtler than the examples just cited, but more important. The women who watch the story as it begins (Tamar, Rahab, Ruth, the "wife of Uriah," Mary, and Rachel) see the beginning of the Empire's attempt to kill all the babies of Bethlehem. The women at the tomb (there are many, among them are Mary Magdalene and the other Mary) see the end. Jesus is dead and guarded in his tomb. The women are watching, just as they have watched throughout the story. Anyone who expects them to do otherwise has not been paying attention.

Inter-Text: The World We Think We Live In

This is a day devoted to waiting at the grave of one person who was tortured to death two millennia ago. This act of waiting is at the heart of the Christian faith. It is also dangerous.

On Holy Saturday, Christians wait by Jesus' tomb, in their imaginations, wait for Easter and the resurrection. This is dangerous because Easter comes tomorrow, and everybody knows this. The women waiting by the tomb did not have a calendar that told them they would be waiting for another three hours (no, wait: another two hours and fifteen minutes) before Easter dawned and the waiting was over, the resurrection had arrived. When Christians read this scene, and celebrate this day, they do so knowing that the resolution to the tension is only time away.

In the world we think we live in, this is never the way it is. The waiting is indefinite. The resolution is, too often, delayed, and then delayed again.

To play this scene responsibly (that is to say: to play this scene in a way that is answerable to the world we think we live in), weave in the instances of waiting that do not lead to "Easter tomorrow."

For instance, consider all those who are waiting at tombs in Rwanda, waiting still, but waiting for what?

> In one hundred days, between April 6 and July 19, 1994, they murdered roughly eight hundred thousand individuals. For the statistically inclined, that works out to 333 ⅓ deaths per hour, 5 ½ deaths per minute. The rate of murder was even greater during the first four weeks, when most of the deaths occurred. The Rwanda genocide, therefore, has the macabre distinction of exceeding the rate of killing attained during the Holocaust. And unlike the Nazis, who used modern industrial technology to accomplish the most primitive of ends, the perpetrators of the Rwandan genocide employed primarily low-tech and physically demanding instruments of death that required an intimacy with their victims. The genocide was executed with a brutality and sadism that defy imagination. Eyewitnesses were in denial. They believed that the high-pitched screams they were hearing were wind gusts, that the packs of dogs at the roadside were feeding on animal remains and not dismembered corpses, that the smells enveloping them emanated from spoiled food and not decomposing bodies. One is reminded of Primo Levi's observation about the Holocaust: "Things whose existence is not morally comprehensible cannot exist."[66]

Jesus' death is a real death, but it is one death among very many others.

Provoking the Story

To play this scene, gather instances of waiting at tombs that will remain closed. Gather instances of waiting in hospitals that will not resolve into joyful homecomings. Gather instances of waiting with disease that do not finish as stories of healing, miraculous or otherwise. Catch the way such waiters sit, the way they hold their faces, the way they see each other and ignore the irrelevant bustle around them. The women at the tomb look like these waiters. Play the scene with them waiting together. Do not play the scene as if the women have good news to share with the others who are waiting for other things. They do not. All they have to share is the waiting, and the waiting wears you out, if only because it is clear that the people who are bustling around you, the people so obviously and importantly busy, are busy denying that your waiting has any real claim on their attention. Bodies decompose all around us, and we, too, attribute the smell to spoiled food. Play the scene so that this is clear.

Easter Day
Matthew 28:1–10

(see translation, p. 426)

Ritual Text: The Life of the Worshiping Community

This scene embodies a resurrection of a dead body. Pay attention to the strange way this happens. The tomb is closed, and watched, both by opponents and by women who would not abandon Jesus, not even in death. A messenger appears, the stone is rolled away, the tomb is empty. Jesus has already come out of the tomb; in any case, he is not there. Jesus has already come out of the tomb, but, oddly enough, not by going out of the tomb. It was sealed and watched, but when it was opened, it was already empty. This is a scene that embodies a bodily resurrection: at the end of the scene Jesus has feet that the women can hold on to. But how can this body that can be held (and is therefore physical and corporeal in an ordinary sense) be absent from a tomb without exiting that tomb. This is a strange scene.

It is strange also because it involves an interchange, a changing of places. When the messenger enters the scene, the opponents who are watching the grave become like corpses, just at the moment that it is revealed that Jesus is no longer among the corpses. Death-like-ness is traded for life, and life for death.

And in all of it, the women do not flinch in the presence of a messenger from God. The watchers are shaken, but not the women.

The messenger tells them to stop being afraid, so it is possible that they too became like corpses, only to be revived by the word of the messenger. But it is also possible that the women bear all of this with the same strong, unflappable courage that brought them to the tomb in the first place.

Intra-Text: The World of Matthew's Story

When Jesus dies in Matthew's story, he dies with words of accusation on his lips. God has abandoned him, and Jesus screams out his agony. His death in the story is not the calm death of a martyr who is sure of God's control of all things. His death is not the exemplary death of a hero who has practiced dying every day of his life so that when it comes he steps through the door as easily as he steps out of the front door of his house on the way to his appointed work. When Jesus dies in Matthew's story, he is neither a hero nor a martyr. And everyone who watches him die knows that.

It is not just that Matthew tells the story of the death with a fearsome honesty. This is, indeed, just what death by torture looks like: messy, protracted, absurd, ugly, desperate. There is something else here that must be caught. Jesus, in Matthew's story, has set standards for the conduct of the faithful: be perfect, as your Father in the heavens is perfect. Anyone who is perfect (and Jesus means every bit of what is implied by the word "perfect") is gathered into the good graces of the master. Anyone who is not perfect (and Jesus never misses even the smallest imperfection) is thrown into the outer darkness where people wail and gnash their teeth.

Jesus' performance at this death is not perfect. This is not surprising, given the realities of death by torture, but it is a costly breakdown. Jesus has failed to live up to his own standards.

Inter-Text: The World We Think We Live In

YOU WILL BE SCARED.

Lt. Col. Dave Grosman, in his book *On Killing*, notes that soldiers being trained to fight in World War II were given a booklet that introduced them to army life. One important introduction that was included was the introduction to fear. Many of the men being trained would very shortly be in combat, and the army told them, directly and honestly, YOU WILL BE SCARED.[67]

This will not have come as a surprise to anyone who was handed the booklet.

As Grosman notes, soldiers of course fear death and dismemberment. What might be a surprise is what researchers have found as a result of studying soldiers. The fear of death and dismemberment is highest among those soldiers who serve in rear areas, soldiers who have not been in combat. Research done with Israeli soldiers who have just come out of combat indicates, however, that they do not report having been much afraid of death or dismemberment. They report that they were indeed afraid, but that they primarily feared letting their unit down. This fear, apparently, outweighs all others.

With this in mind, listen again to Jesus' dying cry in Matthew's story. He has spent his adult life demanding perfection of his listeners, requiring of them that they never let down at any point. He has been unflinching in this demand. And now he dies, crushed, exhausted, despairing, destroyed. Some years ago I was teaching a course, and we were reading the Gospels. A young woman came up after class one day and needed to talk to me. We had just been reading Jesus' death scenes in the four Gospels. The young woman was a serious Christian, and she had a serious concern.

"I don't think you should have students read that part about Jesus accusing God of abandoning him," she said. "It sets a bad example for weak Christians."

She was quite serious. She felt let down by a Jesus who died in despair.

One can only imagine how Matthew's Jesus, moral rigorist that he is, felt when those words came out of his mouth. He dies and disappoints moral rigorists everywhere and forever. He dies and succumbs to the deepest fear of people in desperate danger: he lets his unit down.

And now he is raised from the dead.

It will not do for this resurrection to be simply a resuscitation. If Jesus is dead and then finds himself again alive, he is simply returned to the shame and despair in which he died. The resurrection in Matthew's story cannot be a mere resuscitation; it must be a transformation. The change must go deeper than a simple return of death, or the tension of the story, so carefully built up, goes nowhere.

See the discussion of the scene assigned for Trinity Sunday to follow this matter further.

Provoking the Story

What would it take to transform the Jesus who died in the last chapter? What would it take to truly raise him to life? Too many imaginings of Easter make resurrection as natural as springtime, and forget that resurrection must be a surprise or it is not a resurrection. Too many imaginings make the resurrection of Jesus into a revelation of his godhood, forgetting that God (being immortal) would not need resurrection. Resurrection, to be resurrection, is a supremely human event. Only mortal beings need to be raised to life after dying, and to them such a transformation must always come as a surprise.

Play this scene with Jesus shocked to find himself alive. Play this scene with Jesus remembering what his words meant when he accused God of abandoning him. Play this scene with Jesus shocked that such blasphemy would be the prelude to a resurrection. Jesus knew very well what his last words meant. So did the women who heard them as they watched him die. What if Jesus feels driven to apologize for what he said? How would the women react to that? What transformation would then take place?

Section 3:
SUNDAYS AFTER PENTECOST

Trinity Sunday
Matthew 28:16–20
(see translation, p. 428)

Ritual Text: The Life of the Worshiping Community

This scene is chosen for this Sunday in the ritual cycle, of course, because it contains a reference to the Father, the Son, and the Holy Spirit, the Trinity that makes it hard for Jews to take us seriously when we insist that we are, like them, strict monotheists. It apparently also makes it hard for Christians, since a few weeks ago I worshiped with a Christian congregation that included in its worship a locally written benediction that blessed the congregation "in the name of the Three." This unfortunate theological construction does, in fact, ricochet off the rock of monotheism, with its glancing reference to one Name for Three "somethings," but you can see why Jews might be puzzled.

I will not settle two millennia of puzzlement (Jewish or Christian) in the next few paragraphs. I will, however, make a few suggestions that might help make sense of this scene as it dances with Matthew's story.

First, while this scene is, indeed, one of the seeds out of which Trinitarian theology will grow, we will misread it (and thus misinterpret and misplay it) if we read into it a full-blown, fully articulated notion of God's essential "triunity," in which "threeness" and "oneness" coexist inseparably but do not co-mingle.

Second, any playing of this scene that will be historically and theologically responsible will proceed from a firm grasp of the absolute commitment to the absolute Oneness of God. In Jewish thought, and therefore in Jesus' thought and in that of Matthew, God (to borrow language from astronomy) is a singularity. Anything that is God cannot be separate from God. Anything that is not God cannot be confused with God, and must not be. To push the metaphor a little further, there is an attractive power to the God of Abraham, Isaac, and Jacob, the God who alone is God, the God who cannot be limited by any idol or image. This God who radically resists all iconic representation attracts linguistic metaphors irresistibly. The God who cannot be painted or sculpted pulls word-pictures out of the storytellers of Israel, and these storytellers paint and carve with every metaphor (appropriate and otherwise) that they can find, borrow, or create. God becomes a bridegroom and a mother hen. God is painted with deep darkness and blinding light. God is pictured as a warrior and as a betrayed husband who abuses his wife and gives to his children insulting names. God is a nursing mother and loves Israel the way a pregnant woman loves the baby in her belly. God is dry rot. And, of course, God is painted as a father. Once a metaphor is pulled past the event horizon, it becomes an inseparable part of the singularity, the black hole that pulls image after image out of the people that must wrestle with the God who is One. This is part of the creative power of the God of Israel, the God with whom people are called to wrestle. This God pulls artistic creation out of human beings, and explodes into a vast theological universe of productive thought.

Third, in this scene a new image has been pulled into God: the son. God had been painted as parent for centuries, with results that are both comforting and frightening, depending on the painter and the times. Now this father had a son. This is not, itself, an innovation, since it pulls language from Psalm 2, from the coronation of a king who was anointed to serve, and named by God as "son." What is new with Christian storytellers is that Jesus is painted into the picture as that son, that king, that anointed one (meshiakh, messiah, or Christ, depending on the language of the painter). If storytellers must not lose their grip on the absolute Oneness of God, they also must not picture the exaltation of Jesus as a later scribbling on the original picture of Jesus as a mere human.[68] Already when Paul wrote to the Philippians he could quote a hymn that painted Jesus as refusing to seize equality with God. This is a complicated passage because it can be read either as Paul's affirmation of the divinity of Jesus or as Paul's refusal of such violations of the absolute Oneness of God. The problem with Philippians comes when an interpreter has to figure out what it might mean that Jesus did not count equality with God as a "thing to be seized." Does Paul mean that Jesus held such equality, but did not insist on holding on to it? Or does he mean that some people have seized such status for Jesus inappropriately and Jesus' own self-emptying is being used as an argument against such compromises of monotheism? The answer is probably "yes." When you get to heaven, ask around. What matters for our playing of this scene from Matthew's story is that either reading of Philippians reveals the existence of a very early, very highly exalted view of Jesus that makes it appropriate to paint him into a word-picture of God.

And finally, remember that when Jews talk about the "spirit" of God, they are talking about the *ruach*, the *pneuma*, the wind that ruffled the waters of creation (Genesis 1), the breath that God blew into Mudguy's nose (Genesis 2), the life that God blew into speakers and ecstatics to make them speak and act as prophets. The Jewish storytellers who shaped the Christian movement heard the creative rustling of God's wind, felt the life-giving force of God's breathing, shared the expectation that God would perturb Israel with prophets, and painted the resurrection of Jesus as another moment when God blew something new into the creation. Where the Empire had created death (dishonoring Jewish hope in the process), there God blew life and raised Jesus from the dead. To mention the father, the son, and the life-giving breath of God as the identifying mark and meaning of baptism is to continue the washing for battle that John began back in the beginning of Matthew's story, only this time the washing inaugurates not only resistance but resurrection. God has indeed blown something new into the world. Rome will not like it much.

Intra-Text: The World of Matthew's Story

In this scene Jesus appears to his eleven closest followers and they worship him. At least some of them do. Some of them also doubt.

It is easy to make sense of this doubting. Jesus had been tortured to death by Rome, a power that had considerable experience with such matters and was unlikely to make mistakes about death. Jesus was dead. And now he comes to them alive. Some doubted. If they had not, I would have questioned either their sanity or their judgment, or perhaps both.

In Matthew's story, however, this doubt ought to have consequences. Jesus has seen such hesitation before. He has encountered uncertainty. He has looked at people who were divided between worship and doubt. And he has sent them into the outer darkness where they wail and gnash their teeth. Throughout Matthew's story, Jesus has encountered imperfection, and he has burned it in fire.

This time he does not. Why?

In fact, this time he sends the whole mixed lot of worshipers and doubters out, sends them out without making any distinctions among them, to instruct the Gentiles by washing them and teaching them. Why?

Interpreters sometimes make space for this surprise by supposing that Jesus is delaying the judgment on the doubters until the culmination of the aeon. According to this reading, there will indeed be fire, but not just yet.

Inter-Text: The World We Think We Live In

When Rome started its campaign against God's people in Matthew's story, it imagined that all it had to do was wipe out a few Jewish babies (and whatever assortment of mothers and grandmothers, brothers, fathers, and grandfathers threw themselves into the bargain). Though that campaign was not successful, technically, it was probably counted as close enough. The body count was high, with few (if any) casualties suffered by the forces of Empire. The mission was accomplished (nearly) and the lesson had been taught: this is what happens to pretenders to the throne of Empire.

When it came clear to Empire that the initial campaign against God's people was not quite successful enough, Rome responded brutally and efficiently. Jesus, the sole survivor of the raid on Bethlehem, is singled out and crucified. The mode of execution aims to complete the lesson begun in Bethlehem: this is what happens to those who place their hope in anything other than submission to the will of Empire. Jesus was tortured to death, the breath twisted out of him. The aim was to twist the breath out of any Jewish hope that looked to God to provide deliverance, rescue, an anointed king who would remove Roman repression.

And now Jesus has been raised from death. As I have argued, it was likely a surprise to him.[69] If it was a surprise to him, for Empire it was worse. The resurrection blunts Rome's sharpest tool. If it can twist the breath out of a Jew who embodies Jewish hope in a God who promises deliverance for all creation only to have God blow life back into that Jew and that hope, then crucifixion no longer is enough. If Jesus had died heroically, as a martyr, that would have been bad enough. Empire (in any century) misunderstands the power of martyrs to galvanize resistance. But Jesus failed as a martyr, only to be resurrected as a messiah. For Empire, this is worse, because resurrection is stronger than resistance. Torture no longer delivers the goods. This will be a problem.

But this scene makes it clear that Rome's problems are even worse than we have seen. Jesus, the resurrected anointed king, is gathered together with eleven followers who are witnesses to the resurrection. The contagion of resurrection has spread. And that's not the end of it. At the beginning of the story a group of pagans wandered into the story looking for the king of the Jews. This was a storyteller's foreshadowing of the eruption that happens in Matthew's story. Jewish hope, fed by resurrection, will spread beyond the borders of Israel. In the scene for this Sunday, the storyteller shows the audience just how far this eruption will spread: all Gentiles will be baptized in the name of God's program of resistance and resurrection. Even the children of Esau will abandon Rome and become allies of Israel. Now it will be impossible to kill Jewish hope.

Now even Gentiles will remember the cries of Rachel weeping for her children, at Bethlehem, in Jerusalem, and throughout Jewish history.

Now Jews and Gentiles will together hear the cries of every Rachel and respond together.

At least, that's the hope at the end of the story.

Provoking the Story

Play this scene so that it pulls themes from the whole arc of Matthew's story. Bring the Magi back onstage, those old pagans who were somehow ready, as pagans, to look for the king of the Jews. Bring back Rachel, who will not forget the children of Bethlehem and the disaster created by Herod's abuse of power. Bring back the women from the genealogy, who likewise know what happens when people imagine that force can solve any problem. When my actors and I staged the story of Matthew's Passion, we listened to the odd moment in Jesus' death scene, the moment where the graves are opened and holy ones who had fallen asleep emerged and walked about in the city. Since Matthew does not specify which holy ones these might have been, we played them as the women from the genealogy who had come back to witness, with Rachel, another abuse of power, another disaster. This worked nicely, and made this scene into something more than a kind of weird Christian zombie movie.

While you are at it, bring into the story also those people who hear the cries of other embodiments of Rachel and respond to them. Bring in those people who heard the cries of the victims of genocide in Rwanda. Bring in those who heard the cries out of Sudan and Somalia and Cambodia.

To poke this scene hard, bring in the voice of Francis Fukuyama, a leading neoconservative theorist, who looked at the war in Iraq and said that you cannot kill enough people to win that sort of war.[70] While you are at it, bring in the voice of one of my actors, Erika Iverson, one of the founding members of the Provoking the Gospel Storytelling Project, who has gone on to work in Africa to help to resettle refugees. She has heard the cries of Rachel in several centuries and in many languages. She writes: "The stories of the Burundis are chasing me."

This is not easy.

The commission at the end of Matthew's story is not simply a charter for seminaries, Sunday Schools, and outreach ministries. The messiah who promises to be with us always was the messiah who was a refugee, the messiah who was tortured to death, the messiah who buckled under the strain, and who was raised, a changed man. But he is still the messiah who is given the task of turning the world right-side-up in response to the cries of Rachel.

This will not be easy. The refugees are indeed chasing us.

Proper 4 (9)
Matthew 7:21–29

(see translation, p. 304)

Ritual Text: The Life of the Worshiping Community

This scene is a dangerous scene for Americans, dangerous maybe for anyone with philosophic roots in Western Europe. For all of us, "authority" is a loaded word, a fighting word, a word that marks the field on which we come of age, both as individuals and as cultures. People of my cultural background tell journey myths when we tell stories about what it takes to become an adult. We expect that you have to leave the cocoon, break free from your childhood, cut the apron strings, strike out on your own, if ever you are to take on the responsibilities and authority that go with being an adult. Sometimes we even tell stories in which young men kill their fathers.

Thus is it that we "go away to college." Thus it is that we expect, and ritualize, and make movies about, adolescent rebellion. Thus it is that we value mavericks and elect leaders who convince us that they are courageous pioneers.

This understanding of what it takes to come of age has served us well. It has taught us to invent and to honor innovation. It has taught us to value honor and courage and intelligence.

It also makes it hard to read this scene and understand it.

Westerners, and perhaps especially Americans, see in this scene a divide between Jesus and the scribes. Jesus has set out on his own and the scribes have not. Jesus has broken free from tradition and the scribes have not. Jesus has come of age and the scribes have not. Jesus is a courageous, innovative, forward-thinking leader, and the scribes . . . You get the picture.

Because we begin with the cultural expectation that having authority comes from breaking away from tradition, we read this scene and imagine that Jesus' words break free from tradition, survey new territory, and lead his followers into a new integrity that was not possible for the backward-thinking scribbling scribes.

Intra-Text: The World of Matthew's Story

Matthew has kept Jesus up on the mountain teaching for almost three chapters when this scene begins. The discourse in these three chapters has rocked back and forth. Warmth has given way to sharp rebuke, tenderness to harsh demand. The tone throughout has been serious, and strictness is honored, but sometimes the voice in the scene is serious about the trustworthiness of God, and sometimes the voice demands that the audience be perfect as God is perfect. It would be possible to homogenize the voices in these three chapters, to put them in a blender and pour out an even gray-brown goo of a voice that can say everything contained in these chapters. It's possible, but I am not a big fan of gray-brown goo. Better results are to be had if you explore the separation between the voices heard in these scenes.

This is especially true when you come to play the scene assigned for this Sunday. The voices have thrown the conversation back and forth through the Sermon on the Mount, but as chapter 7 begins, the voice demanding hard-edged perfection gets louder and more demanding (as I hear it). We no longer hear long speeches full of warm reassurance about God's care for lilies. Instead we get quick exchanges back and forth. "Don't make divisions," one voice says. "You have a log in your eye and your neighbor does not," says the other. "Ask and seek and knock," one voice says. "Next to God you are worthless," says the other. "Do to others what you'd want them to do to you," says one voice. "Go in through the narrow gate because the road divides and down the other fork lies destruction," says the other voice. "Beware of false prophets who are wolves," warns one voice, "because a worthy tree bears worthy fruit." "And a worthless tree is burned," cries the other voice. "And besides, not everyone who seeks entry into the dominion of the heavens will be admitted, but only those who do the will of my father. Many will claim that they did the will of my father, but I will reject them. There is a rock to build on, and that rock is perfection, and building on sand leads to disaster." The audience hears this last voice and comments on its authority. And then Jesus goes down the mountain.

If you have honored the back-and-forth exchange of the previous chapters, the sharp volleys of this scene will pop into relief. One of the tasks of an interpreter of this scene, and an essential task for anyone who will perform this scene, is to figure out how one person can speak both sides of this debate, at least without sounding like a lunatic.

Inter-Text: The World We Think We Live In

The problem is that most of what Jesus has been saying is pretty traditional. The problem is that the parts of what Jesus has been saying in the last two chapters that are not traditional are troublesome. The first lines in this scene are quite traditional: what you do matters more than what you say. A Jewish colleague of mine tells me that it is simple: if you want to find out what persons believe, you watch their feet, not their lips. People can say anything, confess anything, claim to believe anything, but what they actually do tells you what they actually believe. This is functionally the same as what Jesus says in this scene. So far, so traditional. But Jesus adds two words that change everything. The words are "to me." Jacob Neusner notes this problem. Much of what Jesus says simply upholds the tradition. So far, so good. But some of what Jesus says and does displaces God and puts Jesus in God's place.[71] The words "to me" do this. This idolatrous displacement is sharpened by the way I have translated κυριος in the scene. The word is usually translated as "lord," and this is a good translation. But Christian audiences miss that κυριος is the Greek word used in the Septuagint to translate the Divine Name.

Provoking the Story

Play this scene with two voices. Divide up the lines different ways until you get the argument so that it feels right. Some of the dividing will be easy. Some could go either way. Don't worry about getting it exactly right; just go for a rough division that arrays the tougher sayings over against the softer sayings. Exaggerate the energy on both sides. It may be that there is, indeed, an argument preserved in this scene, or it may just be that these two sides temper each other. Exaggerate things to get a clearer view.

To sharpen the clash even further, weave in texts from outside Matthew's story that are, themselves, tough or soft. Pick pieces out of political debates, pieces out of Rwanda, pieces out of any serious scrap. Listen for voices that call for revenge and those that call for restraint. Weave them into the flow of the scene. Even if this never becomes part of the eventual performance of the scene, you will discover some things that might help you reflect on the scene.

Proper 5 (10)
Matthew 9:9–13, 18–26
(see translation, p. 312)

Ritual Text: The Life of the Worshiping Community

Jesus is in his own city. This city is not Bethlehem: his family was driven out of there by Herod's murderous attack on the children of that town. The city is not Nazareth, where his family finally fled and lived as refugees in Matthew's story. The city is Capernaum, to which he moved in chapter 4. It was in Capernaum that he encountered a centurion in the last chapter and healed his boy. It is in Capernaum that Jesus encounters Matthew, a tax traitor, and invites him to follow.

It is not surprising that he should invite such a person to eat with him. It is not surprising; it is astonishing.

This scene makes no real ritual sense unless you play it so that the audience is dismayed at Jesus' behavior. Remember, Jesus' family suffered the loss of all of Jesus' contemporary cousins when Empire (in the person of the puppet, Herod) launched a campaign to make it clear that only those sanctioned by Empire can aspire to the title of king. Every symbol of Empire will have been a reminder of the loss he will have discovered throughout his childhood when he saw his mother flinch when he asked why they did not live where his family had roots, why they had no aunts and uncles and grandmothers living near them, and why he had no cousins his own age. And now he eats with a tax traitor. Those who gathered taxes did so for the Roman overlords: they made their living by collaborating with the conqueror, the pagan power that made the demand for the dominion of God more insistent. It is not revealed why Matthew got up and followed. It could be curiosity. It could be a long suppressed Jewish faithfulness. We are not told. We are told that other tax traitors, many of them, and other people who are sinful eat with Jesus in his house.[72] This is even more surprising. Meals are swaddled in rituals. Observant Jews, then and now, understand that meals center the world; they bring stability and joy back into an inhospitable world. But that means that one must be careful, especially under the domination of Rome, with whom one eats. There were economic advantages to be had from playing along with Empire, from fitting smoothly into the roles created by the dominator. But such advantages come at a high price, and the Pharisees in this scene know this. They are correct.

This is an odd scene in Matthew's story. Jesus is frequently prickly and brittle; he customarily demands perfect observance and absolute integrity from his listeners. In this scene he eats with traitors who play along with Rome and made a tidy profit in the bargain. In playing this scene, you will want to capture not only the Pharisees' astonishment, but also that of Jesus' disciples, who will have been attracted to him (in significant part) because of the sharp edge of his message and demands. You will also want to capture this astonishment and deliver it to the audience. Otherwise they will mis-understand this scene and imagine that Jesus is just being a really nice guy.

Maybe you can capture this by including Jesus' mother in the crowd. Let her react to Jesus as he shares a meal with representatives of the Empire that chased her from her home on the eve of her wedding. Let her face and body show what it meant to her to remember the wedding ceremony that never was, all the empty places filled with the absent corpses of her friends and relatives.

Maybe you could bring in Joseph. Maybe this scene provides an explanation for why he does not appear among the followers of Jesus. A man who could not protect his relatives would have powerful reactions to the sight of his son eating with the allies of the murderers. This time the kid just went too far.

Intra-Text: The World of Matthew's Story

The person with leprosy, the centurion with a boy, the mother-in-law with a fever, the storm in a boat, the demoniacs in Gadarenes, the paralyzed man in Capernaum, the two blind men somewhere on the road who call him "son of David," the man outside his house who was unable to call him anything. And into the middle of this string of healing stories that runs from chapter 8 to chapter 10, the storyteller drops the story of Matthew and the other tax traitors.[73]

The scene that is cut out and selected for this Sunday preserves something of this oddity. It pairs the scene with the tax traitors with the scene in which the little girl is raised from death after the hemorrhaging woman is rescued. Perhaps they are all of them healing stories and thus gathered under Isaiah's promise that weaknesses and illnesses would be lifted up and taken away (quoted in Matthew 8:17). This makes collaboration with Rome into a kind of cancer on the body of Israel, a disease that must be cured because it threatens the life of the people of God. Most times when Jesus encounters such a disease in Matthew's story, he prescribes radical surgery ("if your hand scandalizes you, cut it off"). Perhaps he is here attempting an alternate therapy? Later in the story when Jesus meets others who have been remade as Roman collaborators (the chief priests and Temple authorities), he does not continue with his attempt at "meal therapy." One ought to wonder why.

Inter-Text: The World We Think We Live In

I have spent this whole section so far focusing on Matthew the tax traitor. He is indeed fascinating.

I have not yet said a word about the two women in this composite scene.

One ought to notice my omission.

It is the genius of the Gospel of Mark to get the audience rolling gladly down its self-chosen alley of interpretation and then jerk it to a halt with an obvious question that it cannot answer because it has chosen to be blind to that answer.[74] This storytelling strategy does its work by engineering surprises that create quandaries with which the audience must wrestle in order to make sense of (and with) the story that Mark is telling.

We are not reading Mark just now. Just now we are reading and poking at the Gospel of Matthew. But discoveries from reading Mark might be useful just here. Matthew's story also has surprises, and the history of reading and interpreting his story is littered with evidence that readers roll down their own self-chosen alleys and make themselves blind to parts of Matthew's story that ought to be obvious and easy to read.

This is one such moment. Matthew very simply and straightforwardly weaves women into the family history of this story, and tells stories in which women play decisive roles, stories that do not simply rely on women as set dressing or wallpaper behind the scene. And yet interpreters of this story miss (or mess with) the women in the genealogy. Interpreters miss the women throughout the story, even when the storyteller hasn't hidden them so that the audience will have "Mark-like" surprises when Matthew's story is performed.

It matters that I have been distracted by Matthew, the male tax traitor.

There are two women in this scene. The first woman is a little girl, and she is dead. The second woman is not identified as a little girl, and she has been bleeding for twelve years. We do not know why. What we do know is that both women are figured as daughters. This probably matters.

In the case of the first woman, it matters because her status as daughter provides her with a father who can go to Jesus for help. Of course she cannot go by herself for help: she is dead, which radically limits what a character on stage can do. But because she is characterized as a daughter the audience knows that she may well have limited freedom of movement. Some readings of the patriarchal culture out of which this scene comes will note that calling her a daughter confines her to the interior spaces of the house just as surely as does her death bed. Such readings note that, because she is a daughter, she must wait for a patriarch to take up her cause and intercede for her, whether she is alive or dead. In this scene, she has a father, and he intercedes for her, though it is to be noted that he does not do so until after she is dead. Perhaps she died suddenly, leaving no time for early intervention. Or perhaps she did not die suddenly. Perhaps she died slowly. In that case, perhaps her father was busy with more important things earlier and simply did not notice her worsening condition.

The second woman in the scene is different. She is not a little girl; she is identified as a γυνη, which makes her older, at least of marriageable age, and perhaps a good bit older than that. We do not know anything beyond that about her. In particular, though we know that she is bleeding, we do not know that her bleeding is menstrual.[75] It may well be, but people can bleed in all sorts of ways, and being a woman does not confine her to menstrual bleeding only. In fact, the scene would work just as well if there were no indication at all of her age. If the word γυνη were not used, we could play the scene just as well with a hemorrhaging little girl as we could with a grandmother. As it is, only the possibility that she is a little girl is ruled out.

But there is another difference between the women in this scene. The first woman does not act for herself, which is not surprising because she is a daughter and because she is dead. The second woman in this scene, however, is pictured as she forms her own plan of action and carries it out successfully. She acts independently in her own interest. Notice this. This independent strength makes her look a lot like the women who act in the genealogy. Most of the scenes in Matthew's story may feature male characters, but the women who move through the story are not painted as passive or submissive. They act and make things happen that would otherwise not have happened.

Notice also that, once she has acted independently in her own interest, Jesus turns to her and calls her "daughter." Why? The line will seem natural enough if she is quite young, though she cannot possibly be young enough if her bleeding is menstrual. If she has been menstruating (somehow) for twelve years, she is at least somewhere in her twenties. Jesus is generally figured (on the basis of Luke's story and because he is sandwiched in Matthew's story between Herod and Pilate) as being about thirty years old. Play the scene with a thirty-year-old Jesus calling a twenty-five-year-old woman "daughter." The oddity is striking. Of course, she could be older than that. Play the scene with a thirty-year-old Jesus calling a grandmother "daughter." This is odder still.

Provoking the Story

Why does Jesus address her as "daughter," this woman who acts independently and touches him?

Here is where this scene gets tricky. In Matthew's story, the woman touches Jesus, but she has no indication that she is healed, or that anything has changed until Jesus, turning and noticing her and addressing her as "daughter," acts and heals her. The scene, unlike Mark's scene, is not constructed so that the woman's act draws power out of Jesus. In Matthew's story, the woman's act may draw no more than attention out of Jesus. On this reading, once he sees her he heals her. On this reading, his choice to call her "daughter" takes on a sharp, and rather disagreeable edge. The woman may have a plan, and she may carry it out all on her own, but in the end all her plan and action add up to is an appeal to a patriarch who deigns to act graciously when he is so moved.

However you finally choose to play this scene, remember that the woman has to react to the way Jesus has figured the scene. If he calls her "daughter" in order to put her in her place, she will react to it. If he calls her "daughter" to establish a relationship that allows touch without sexual implication, she will react to it. If he calls her "daughter" because he is surprised by her bold independence and needs, somehow, to regain patriarchal control of the situation, she will react. She will react most strongly, especially in this last case, if you play her as an older woman, perhaps even as a woman in her seventies or eighties. Such a woman, I imagine, would be glad enough to be healed, but she would also be amused that a young man needed to pretend to be her father in order to salvage the situation.

You might even try playing the scene so that Matthew (the tax traitor, not the storyteller), the focus of all the early attention, becomes increasingly jealous as the scene progresses and he (along with his tax traitor buddies) become more and more irrelevant.

Proper 6 (11)
Matthew 9:35–10:8, (9–23)
(see translation, p. 316)

Ritual Text: The Life of the Worshiping Community

In this scene workers are sent out. We are told that the harvest is large. This image sets the tone for this whole section of Matthew's story. This is harvest time. The field was prepared long ago. The crops have been planted. They have grown, and the process of growth has been both a cause for wonder and a cause for despair. Farming is a gamble that the implanted gift of fruitfulness will escape the depredations and diseases that hunt every crop. Always there are insects and other pests that consume some of the crop. Always there is enough rain, then too much, then too little, or it comes at the wrong time. Rain comes when it comes. And even when the growing season has gone very well and a bumper crop stands ready, soon to be harvested, all it takes is one hailstorm and everything is gone, at least for this year.

This gamble adds to the pressure of harvest time. Farmers work long, unreasonable hours, sleeping as little as is manageable until the crop is off the field. If you drive around farming country during harvest, you will see lights going up and down the field deep into the night. Farmers are out getting the beans off, getting the corn in, some of them working their day jobs and then harvesting most of the night, and then working their day jobs, and then harvesting some more, around and around until the crop is off. All it takes is a hailstorm, or a big snowstorm, and the yield and all that work over many months has little or nothing to show for it.

When my father was a child, harvest was a time when workers showed up at the farm to work the harvest and then move on. In those days, corn was picked by hand, and the job took more hands than it had taken to plant it. Wheat was shocked and the bundles were loaded, again by hand, onto wagons to be hauled to the threshing machine.

During harvest time, my father's mother, and her mother-in-law, and her sister-in-law, and all the daughters they could round up cooked all day long to feed the harvest crew. The work was hard. Good food was part of the pay. It was also part of the hospitality. Some of the workers didn't eat so well other times of the year. The family wanted them to eat well during the time they were responsible for feeding them. My father tells me that this was a duty to the workers and to God.

This whole enterprise was wrapped in rituals of working and welcoming. The scene for this Sunday sounds those same echoes. Jesus sends the twelve out because there is work to do. The harvest stands ready, the workers are few, so the twelve go out to add themselves to the crew. They go out expecting to work hard. They go out expecting hospitality and support. This is harvest time, after all, and hospitality is part of the ritual. Any house that knows that this is the time of harvest is a house that has been prepared, perhaps by John, perhaps by other workers. The hard work of cooking and feeding has been begun in such a house in order to support the hard work of the harvest. Any house or any city that does not offer the ritual of hospitality sees no harvest, no workers, no need for any change from the imperial norm. There is a ritual also for such places. The twelve are told to refuse to accept even dust from such a place. If they are not offered the gift of hospitality, they will accept no gifts at all.

Intra-Text: The World of Matthew's Story

The first thing to be noticed in this scene is that the usual translations miss the force of what Jesus sees when he looks at the crowds he encounters in synagogue after synagogue. The original Greek says that the crowds were εσκυλμενοι and ερριμμενοι. Most translations understand the original text as a metaphor, and translate it accordingly, making an effort to connect with their imagined contemporary audience. Thus the NIV and the NRSV find the crowds to be "harassed and helpless." The NASB decides that the crowds are "distressed and dispirited." The NKJV sees the crowds looking "weary and scattered," but the Good News Bible sees them "worried and helpless." The New Living Bible says, picking up on the tendencies in the other translations, that Jesus felt great pity for the crowds "because their problems were so great and they didn't know where to go for help." Each of these efforts is an honorable attempt to render the metaphoric force of the Greek words in a form that responds to perceived needs in our century. Each imagines that the crowds are scattered and wandering around sheepishly, without a shepherd.

The original words have a stronger force than that. To be without a shepherd does not simply imply that you might be nervous and worried; it implies that you might be at risk of being actually worried in the etymological sense: grabbed in the jaws of a predator and ripped, twisted, and torn to bits. This is the metaphor (usually lost) behind the common word "worried."

The original Greek is (if that is possible) even stronger and more violent than that. Jesus reacts in his gut because the observant Jews in synagogue after synagogue appear to him to have been skinned alive and thrown down, caught in the jaws of predatory Empire, unable to defend themselves. When the metaphor is softened in translation, Jesus feels bad for people who just don't feel that they have a real purpose in life. "That's okay," he responds. "I have a program and a purpose, I'll give them a mission in life and they'll feel more productive. They'll like that." Phooey.

When the metaphor is left vigorous and violent Jesus' words have a different bite. Everywhere he looks he sees the aftermath of the slaughter in Bethlehem, the slaughter he and his parents barely and inexplicably escaped. Everywhere he looks he sees crowds of people skinned alive by the violence that reminds them always that Empire will do whatever it chooses to do in order to shock and awe people into docile subjection. When the metaphor is preserved and not softened the mission that Jesus set for his disciples makes more sense. They are to heal all illness, to be sure. But they are also to heal all μαλακιαν. The word is generally translated as "sickness," so that the mission is to heal "disease and sickness," a doubled reference that would make sense only if it were understood as some sort of intensification through poetic repetition. Perhaps that is what Matthew's storyteller means to do. But the word does not simply mean "sickness." It means "softness" or "penetrability." It is the word used to identify and blame gentleness when severity is called for, to reject civilized manners when harsh hardness is desired, to ridicule people who bathe regularly and groom themselves. Real men don't smell good. Real men are not soft. Real men are invulnerable, impervious. Real men are impenetrable; real men are hard men.

Yes, the force of the word is exactly that disturbing. Ancient people, just like contemporary people, sometimes linked sexual potency with brutality. The question is: How do you play this scene so that you respect the violence of the original words? The question is: What do you do with a Jesus who calls for revenge?

Inter-Text: The World We Think We Live In

The phrase "sheep without a shepherd" has come into standard English as a cliché. The phrase has a history and an extended pattern of use. When the storyteller used it in this scene, it already had a history.

The history goes back to the time of King Ahab and the prophet Micaiah.[76] Judah and Israel were preparing to go into battle against the Arameans. They sought the advice of prophets before they set out on their campaign, and all the prophets encouraged them to attack and be victorious. All the prophets except one. Micaiah, son of Imlah, announced defeat and death for Ahab. In particular, Micaiah saw all of Israel scattered on the mountains, like sheep without a shepherd, like an army without a leader, like a kingdom without a king. Micaiah saw truly and spoke honestly. Ahab was killed by chance in the battle, and the army was scattered and fled like sheep. When the storyteller looks at the crowds around Jesus, something recalls the time of Ahab's death. Perhaps more to the point, when the storyteller looks at the audience assembled to hear Matthew's story in the years after the crushing of the First Jewish Revolt against Rome, something recalls the time when the people scattered and fled from the field of battle because they had no king. Remember that some sources suggest that up to one million Jews were killed in that failed revolt, which is easily enough to leave the people lost and leaderless.

Hear again these voices from Rwanda, from a time of similar loss, similar destruction, when people were similarly torn apart and helpless, like sheep without a shepherd.

"I had eighteen people killed at my house," said Etienne Niyonzima, a former businessman who had become a deputy in the National Assembly. "Everything was totally destroyed — a place of fifty-five meters by fifty meters. In my neighborhood they killed six hundred and forty-seven people. They tortured them, too. You had to see how they killed them. They had the number of everyone's house, and they went through with red paint and marked the homes of all the Tutsis and of the Hutu moderates. My wife was at a friend's, shot with two bullets. She is still alive, only" — he fell quiet for a moment — "she has no arms. The others with her were killed. The militia left her for dead. Her whole family of sixty-five in Gitarama were killed." Niyonzima was in hiding at the time. Only after he had been separated from his wife for three months did he learn that she and four of their children had survived. "Well," he said, "one son was cut in the head with a machete. I don't know where he went." His voice weakened, and caught. "He disappeared." Niyonzima clicked his tongue, and said, "But the others are still alive. Quite honestly, I don't understand at all how I was saved."[77]

Then the pastors sat down together and wrote letters to the mayor and to their boss, Pastor Elizaphan Ntakirutimana, Dr. Gerard's father, asking them in the name of the Lord to intercede on their behalf.

"And the response came," Samuel said. "It was Dr. Gerard who announced it: 'Saturday, the sixteenth, at exactly nine o'clock in the morning, you will be attacked.'" But it was Pastor Ntakirutimana's response that crushed Samuel's spirit, and he repeated the church president's words twice over slowly: "Your problem has already found a solution. You must die." One of Samuel's colleagues, Manase Bimenyimana, remembered Ntakirutimana's response slightly differently. He told me that the pastor's words were "You must be eliminated. God no longer wants you."[78]

Provoking the Story

Hear these voices out of Rwanda:

The fact of willful indifference continues to amaze. The Rwandan genocide is not only about the evil that is possible. It is also about the complacency exhibited by those who have the responsibility to confront that evil.[79]

Nobody ever talked seriously about conducting tens of thousands of murder trials in Rwanda. Western legal experts liked to say that even the lawyer-crowded United States could not have handled Rwanda's caseload fairly and expeditiously. "It's materially impossible to judge all those who participated in the massacres, and politically it's no good, even though it's just," the RPF's Tito Ruteremara told me. "This was a true genocide, and the only correct response is true justice. But Rwanda has the death penalty, and — well, that would mean a lot more killing."

In other words, a true genocide and true justice are incompatible.[80]

But if the guilty could never be fully punished and survivors could never be properly compensated, the RPF regarded forgiveness as equally impossible — unless, at the very least, the perpetrators of the genocide acknowledged that they had done wrong. With time, the quest for justice became, in large measure, a quest for repentance.[81]

Imagine them as voices out of Matthew's story world.

Proper 7 (12)
Matthew 10:24–39
(see translation, p. 319)

Ritual Text: The Life of the Worshiping Community

Beelzebul, the lord of the flies. There is a ritual universe revealed in this odd old title. This character is not The Devil, not the ultimate cosmic opponent of God. Jewish faith is insistent in its monotheism. God is God, and God alone is ultimate. Beelzebul is the name of a much more limited creature, a master of the maladies that plague life in the world. This creature is a lesser being, a master of nuisances, if we are looking at this on a cosmic scale. He is the lord of the flies, not lord of the universe. But he is the lord of all that plagues human beings, and his flies buzz around the corpses of his victims and crawl on the faces of hungry children who starve in his famines. He is a formidable foe for humans, but not for God. I am guessing that the starving children do not care much for this distinction. I am guessing that the corpses do not care much for anything.

This scene notes that Jesus has been linked to the lord of the flies, the director of demons. Presumably this was because people charged that his deeds of deliverance were put-up jobs arranged with the demons themselves. Perhaps this charge is to be understood in the terms suggested by Jesus in chapter 12, in the immediate aftermath of being charged with being in league with Beelzebul. Jesus says that when an unclean breath goes out of a person, it travels through waterless places and finds no home. It then returns to the person from whom it had been cast out, bringing seven breaths worse than itself, and the temporary respite of the person who had been exorcised is ended. If that was the usual result of casting out demons, you can see why people would be suspicious of those who plied that trade. Christian readers begin with the assumption that, of course, Jesus' exorcisms were permanent. But Jesus' own words make no such provision. He simply speaks about what happens when a breath is cast out of a person. Does he mean to say that his practice as an exorcist provides only temporary relief? Surely this was the nature of his feeding miracles. There is no implication that the people fed in the wilderness were never again hungry. Is there also no implication that the people who had demons expelled had no further need of an exorcist? This would be an odd conclusion indeed. But even if his words apply only to the work of other exorcists, you can see why people would ask hard questions of him.

The other set of rituals to keep in view in this scene is the set that governs the ways that parents and children dance with each other. The obligations are absolute, and this is made clear when you look at situations involving abuse. Such actions are crimes, not mere legal offenses. Abuse between parents and children is a crime that goes deep down to what must be honored for the world to hold together.

Jewish faith is very clear on this point, and so is the Christian faith. Torah observance means many things, but one thing it surely means is that there is a dance done by parents and children that acts out the stable and orderly love of God so that people grow up knowing in their DNA that God is good and loving. This holds the world together.

Which makes it surprising when Jesus intrudes himself into every parent-child relationship and claims a prior obligation. This is not so surprising, perhaps, for Christians who understand Jesus to be the second person of the Trinity. Perhaps God can demand whatever God wants to demand. In my experience, however, people who begin by asserting God's absolute right to intrude between a parent and a child finish by having enormous trouble with the story of Abraham and Isaac in Genesis 22. Can God even demand that a father kill his son, his only son, Isaac, whom he loves? If a father does that in any country I would live in, he goes to prison, and people (Christians included) cheer mightily. So what is Jesus doing here? Jacob Neusner, in his engagement of Matthew's story, *A Rabbi Talks with Jesus*,[82] is hooked by the way Jesus insists on interposing himself between parents and children, between person and the people. While he imagines that most of Jesus' teaching and practice would engage his attention and fit nicely into a Jewish life, the insistent elevating of himself as the criterion for everything will always cause trouble. I wonder if most parents wouldn't say the same thing.

Intra-Text: The World of Matthew's Story

This scene continues the angry rant that Jesus began last Sunday. To play this scene with integrity, you must capture what happens to any crowd that hears such words from a speaker. "Whoever denies me, I will deny." "I came to divide a person against his father, a daughter against her mother." "The one who loves father or mother over me is not worthy of me. The one who loves son or daughter over me is not worthy of me." Play these words to an audience of real fathers and mothers, daughters and sons, and see what happens. The danger is that we will play and interpret these words, giving them the "Jesus-Pass," that all-inclusive exemption that allows Jesus to say and do anything and then be greeted by smarmy adoration. Taking the Bible seriously requires much more than that. Taking the Bible seriously requires imagining this scene with real people listening to the words and reacting to them. Taking the Bible seriously requires applying what my actors call the SGNB (pronounced "sig-nib") principle: in a scene, you must react to the words as if Some Guy Named Bob (SGNB) said them. We can work out our reactions to the Savior of the Universe later. For now, we are just trying to feel the impact of the words.

It would be devastating.

Notice that Jesus introduces his talk about dividing families by saying that he came to swing a sword in the midst of human affairs. Most interpreters work mightily to hear a metaphor here, and for good cause. But remember that Matthew's story started with the swinging of real swords when the babies of Bethlehem were killed. After such a beginning, a metaphor is not just a metaphor. More pointedly, after such a beginning, a sword is a sword, and only later can it become a domesticated metaphor. For now the violence is still too fresh to be tamed. Matthew's Jesus swings a sword and families are cut in pieces.

Inter-Text: The World We Think We Live In

You may recall my saying earlier that this year my sister was diagnosed with ALS, amyotrophic lateral sclerosis, Lou Gehrig's disease. You may know the disease. It seems every time I mention her diagnosis, someone in the audience comes up to me later on and tells me about her mother, or friend, or cousin who also has ALS. ALS is a degenerative disease that affects the nerves controlling the voluntary muscles. Progressively the nerves die, and the muscles that they controlled become useless. Progressively simple voluntary tasks (walking, picking up silverware, talking, swallowing) become impossible. When the muscles that control breathing become useless, other complications kick in. Eventually the person with ALS dies. So do we all, but mostly not so young or under such ugly circumstances. Already my sister has discovered that when she uses a wheelchair (which she sometimes must), clerks in stores talk over her head as if her brain and determination were atrophied, not her legs. Someday in the future my sister will have to cope with clerks who refuse to listen to the computer-generated voice that will replace her own voice when voice and breathing are attacked by this jackal of a disease.

Along the way, people with ALS and their families and friends and support-network learn to cope with such things and adapt to situations that no one imagined until the moment of diagnosis.

I mention all this because of an email that I received from a good friend just today. "I will continue to hold you and your family in my thoughts and prayers," my friend wrote. "I cannot imagine what it is like, although my brief encounter with cancer certainly made me aware of how quickly life can be re-oriented, and focused on the essentials. I'm glad you can face this as a family, and, I hope, derive courage from each other. If distant friends can provide any kind of additional support, let me know."

"I'm glad you can face this as a family," she wrote.

Customary interpretations of this scene from Matthew's story spend time thinking about the heroic aloneness of the first Christians, and often imagine that keeping the faith is always a task for solitary, rugged individuals. This may sometimes be true and helpful, and examples from Søren Kierkegaard to Dietrich Bonhoeffer leap immediately to mind. But I am struck by my friend's kind and gracious email. She wishes for us the courage that grows out of family solidarity, precisely the kind of courage that Jesus says will be made impossible because he came to separate parents from children and children from parents. In this scene in Matthew's story, Jesus demands that his audience adhere to him before, and instead of, their families, the God-given source of support, endurance, and courage.

The customary readings of this scene surely have their place. But we ought to be clear: If anyone comes to me and demands that I choose between them and my sister just now, the choice is simple. I choose my sister. And I choose my brother-in-law. And I choose my wife, my sister's best friend since they were girls in school together. I choose my family and expect that we will find, together, the support, and endurance, and courage that will allow us to cope and adapt, to live together as creative human beings, created by God.

The odds are good that there were people in the crowd listening to Jesus who also had a sister with ALS, or an elderly mother, or a child with a fever. You can't throw a rock but you hit three people who are silently praying for someone they love and will not abandon, no matter who tells them to do otherwise. You ought not to play this scene until you discover this truth and honor it.

What would you do if it were your sister?

Provoking the Story

If the raw demands of this scene are reduced to bland encouragements to love God a lot, then we might as well stop trying to read, interpret, and honor the Bible and the old strange stories that peek out of it. We ought to admit publicly that we really intend only to interpret the messages written in uplifting greeting cards.

Of course, you might be stuck with a commitment to the Bible that is stronger than your commitment to greeting cards.

How inconvenient.

Just for the moment, imagine that the Bible is more substantial and interesting than a greeting card. Imagine that biblical stories are more challenging than uplifting, that they give life by provoking their audiences out of their dogmatic slumbers.

Now play this scene with characters around Jesus who react honestly to his demand to stand between parent and child, mother and daughter, between any and all family members. Honor the challenge of this disruptive scene by honoring the integrity of people who listen to Jesus' demands and reject them. This scene only works if the audience sees and feels how extreme the demands actually are.

It will take some experimentation to do this. The customary reading has dug deep trenches and is hard to displace. The customary reading pops up out of tunnels in places you'd never expect it: before you, behind you, in the middle of your most interesting experimental readings all of a sudden there is the old standard greeting-card reading of the scene. "Love God a lot," it says.

It will take experimentation and exploration, trial and error. Try it, even when it involves making mistakes.[83] Your initial goal is to develop a playing of this scene so that an audience feels the sharp edge of the sword when Jesus says that he comes to bring division. Perhaps you need a character with integrity to listen to Jesus' words and choose to hold on to her child instead. Perhaps you need the opposite: perhaps you need a character whom the audience will not easily trust who gladly abandons a parent who needs her in order to "follow Jesus." Don't settle for simplicity here. In your explorations, include ways of playing that bring many different characters into view so that they can react to what Jesus says. The customary reading only works with heroes who abandon their families and cowards who do not. Let them trade places. Find some smarmy religious types (George Orwell called them "creeping Jesuses," a particularly apt name), and let them both follow and refuse. Find some solid characters who find good reasons to be on both sides of the division.

Dietrich Bonhoeffer had been teaching at Union Theological Seminary in New York City. It was clear that the situation in Germany under Hitler was troubled and dangerous. Bonhoeffer had decided to return to Germany to participate in the destructive pain of the church under Hitler in order to be able to contribute to the rebuilding that would be needed after the disaster of Nazism. Customary readings of his heroism give him clear eyes and a determined smile as he makes his choice. His easy courage came to him because he loved God a lot. Maybe so. But the woman who cleaned the room he had been staying in at Union Seminary reported that the floor was littered with hundreds of cigarette butts. Bonhoeffer spent his last night before returning to Nazi Germany terrified and chain-smoking cigarettes. This should be no surprise, not in the face of real life and real death. Perhaps you might let the audience see the cigarette butts and the sleepless, smoke-reddened eyes that go with the division Jesus calls for so easily. A German pastor that I met said (at his retirement party) that his friend Bonhoeffer might have been a "hero" but that he had failed his family because he was not there after the war to take care of them.

Catch the complications when you explore and play this scene.

Proper 8 (13)
Matthew 10:40–42
(see translation, p. 321)

Ritual Text: The Life of the Worshiping Community

The ritual of welcome has deep roots in Jewish faith. Back behind it all is the ethic of a nomadic people. When all are wanderers, extending hospitality becomes the chief necessary act. This necessary virtue weaves itself through the stories of Jewish scripture, with Sarah and Abraham and their family welcoming wanderers and feeding them. The benefits of the virtue are paid in the form of incognito angelic visitors, and the expectation that any visitor might be angelic is offered as a prize that might foster further hospitality. One hears an echo of the same practice when rabbis commend the honoring of women who are expecting babies: they might, after all, give birth to the messiah. In the end, the prize is not what motivates hospitality and honor, at least not to my eye. The stories about angels and messiahs are told to convey a sense of the deep delight that arrives when human beings treat each other as human beings, with honor and respect, and perhaps a little food.

The added note in this scene is that welcome is taken as a sign of a co-worker in the dominion of God. This old sign of Torah faithfulness is taken as a sign, house by house, of who expects God to keep the old promises. Those who have given up on God's promises and have cast their lot with Rome (which was, by the way, very effective at keeping its promises) will reveal themselves by refusing welcome. They would not welcome a prophet. They would not welcome one who is carefully observant of Torah. They would not give water to a child. They would not welcome the Messiah, or the one who anointed and sent the Messiah. The thing that matters in this scene is the ritual of recognizing who welcomes God's promises and who does not. The matter of rewards is entirely secondary.

Intra-Text: The World of Matthew's Story

This little scene comes at the end of a chapter-long rant. By itself, it is a warm little set of instructions about being good to prophets and children. In the flow on this part of Matthew's story, the flavor of this scene is a bit different.

Interpreters often see in such scenes the traces of the development of fictive kinship relationships in the earliest church.[84] Such relationships are understood to have been a source of the support and solidarity that made the emerging movement durable in its difficult early years.

All of this may well be true.

But do not miss the disaster that is implied if actual kinship relationships are to be supplanted with fictive kinship relationships. Matthew's story begins with a genealogy that pointedly includes women who have been pushed out of supportive family relationships. Tamar is abandoned by Judah's family after she suffers the attentions of two of his sons who are identified by the storyteller as evil. Rahab meets us at the edges of a patriarchal society, which is where prostitutes have to live to be sexually available to all men but protected by none. Toni Morrison maps this border territory in *Sula*. Whores in the old days, she says, are likely to have been widows with eight children and no man to provide for them. Such women lived back in the woods where they could get up from dinner with their children to go into the woods with a client and come back to the table, just as natural as seeing to the birthing of a colt.[85] Morrison expects the reader to be able to count the cost. So does Matthew. Ruth gleans grain from the edges of a field and forces Boaz to act as kinsman. And Bathsheba stands up silent in the story, brought in as the raped wife of the man David murdered.[86] At the end of this chain of violated families hangs Mary, the woman inconveniently pregnant who stands alone. Her man (a phrase usually and properly translated as "her husband" but requiring a longer sociological pause than is afforded by that translation) is strict and plans to leave her alone and pregnant to deal with whatever reprisals patriarchal culture, in all its eminent gentleness, will visit upon her. From ancient statute and modern traditional practice, these gentle visitations could have included stoning her to death.

Matthew's story makes it clear that family is thin protection against the ravages of life. Any sentimental nostalgia for "traditional family values" is shredded long before Herod sends men with swords to kill toddlers (and whoever tries to defend them) in his effort to preserve the right of Empire to name and control anyone with the title "King of the Jews." Jesus enters Matthew's story as a member of a family that has been shredded repeatedly by hostile forces, some outside his family and some inside. Before he is done being a toddler, he loses all his same-age cousins, probably most of his relatives all together. We meet Jesus in the story as a character who could well need fictive kinship relationships, since he may well have no living kin left to him beyond his mother and immediate family. See Matthew 12:46ff. to see how he acts as a member of his own family when his mother comes to him and wants to see him.

Inter-Text: The World We Think We Live In

Interpreters who focus on the creation of fictive kinship relationships in the early Christian movement tend to concentrate on the ways that these relationships would have supported people who had been pushed out of their birth-families because they had "decided to follow Jesus." Such readings, valuable as they are, forget the impact of the crushing of the First Jewish Revolt against Rome in 70 CE. Some estimates of the death toll of this disaster run as high as one million Jews killed when Rome retaliated against those audacious enough to challenge Empire in the name of the dominion of God. Every family would have suffered irreplaceable losses. Every family would have huge holes chopped in it, and every family gathering would be a reminder of all those who had been lost. This adds a sharper edge still to Jesus' words about hospitality and welcome. Those who welcome God's prophets and messiah welcome also God's promises. Those who act as family at such a critical time honor also the memory of all those who were lost because they welcomed God's promise of deliverance from foreign oppressors.

Provoking the Story

This scene concludes with the giving of a cup of water to a little child. Customary interpretation brings to mind the shy smile of a little kid who was thirsty until the kindly lady next door acted as fictive grandmother and gave her a glass of water. I lived next door to such an all-purpose grandmother-to-the-world when I was a child, so I am particularly susceptible to the customary reading at this point. I can't read this scene without seeing "Grandma Carpenter" bringing out glasses of what she called "nectar" for all the kids of the neighborhood (all of whom called her "Grandma Carpenter" even though none of us were related to her, not even distantly).

These days this scene sounds different to me.

A student at Augustana College, where I teach, is one of the Lost Boys from Sudan. That makes him a member of a group of survivors of the slaughter of the Second Sudanese Civil War. Two million people were killed. Families were cut in pieces. Children who were away tending the herds came home to find themselves to be orphans. These children wandered and hid, sometimes alone, finally in groups with other children who became family to them, brothers and sisters, parents and protectors, each to the others, fictive kinship groups, if you will.

This student, now in his middle twenties, is a delightful young man and a capable and determined student. He lives with some of the "brothers" he acquired in those terrible days. He welcomes other students at Augustana College as new friends and gladly joins into the life of the campus.

And always there is a distance in his gaze. Always you see that he is looking deeper and more warily, always he watches carefully, always he sees through things that other people aren't even looking at. These days when I read this scene about giving a cup of water to a child, I see a group of Lost Boys, each with the same distant, penetrating gaze, each with the same calm wariness. Welcoming such a child is a fascinating and complicated matter.

Proper 9 (14)
Matthew 11:16–19, 25–30

(see translation, p. 323)

Ritual Text: The Life of the Worshiping Community

Why would children sitting in the market play the flute? Why would they mourn? Why would they expect someone else to join them? The surface of this complaint makes enough sense. Children expect that the things they find fascinating ought to fascinate everyone. For that matter, so do adults. But why mention flutes and mourners? And why specify that all this takes place in the marketplace?

Perhaps the place to start is with the mourning. This is not simply play-acting. It is not just that children play at having a funeral and expect others to join them, just as they joined them when they played wedding, or school, or going-shopping. Mourning is a specific part of playing funeral, a part that appears to have been elaborately acted out in the ancient Jewish world. Funerals required a death. They required an extended family. And they also required professional mourners, people who practiced the art of keening, the achingly high shrieking that allowed the grief of the family to be shared by all in hearing range. This is important in traditional cultures with no daily newspaper in which to publish the obituary. Keeners let the community know that they had cause to mourn. This art takes a life of practice, and that practice starts in childhood. Even for those who would not become professionals, such play teaches people to grow into their own culture, to play the role that will make them a member of their community when they grow up.

You remember I told you earlier about the practice seen in villages in Rwanda: when someone was under attack, she would begin a wailing call that would carry to the next house, the next farm, the next valley, the next human being who, upon hearing the call, was obliged to join the wailing and run to help. This is what responsible members of a traditional community do.

Jesus' little story is, therefore, not so innocuous as it would seem at first. The children are playing a game, and they are pouting when others (notably John, who would not dance, and Jesus, who would not mourn) do not join. This is clear enough. But the refusal to join in the practice of mourning is more serious than refusing to play football. The one who refuses is opting out of her culture. This will always be a problem.

Notice that when Matthew's story was told there was plenty to mourn. When the First Jewish Revolt against Rome was crushed, perhaps a million people were killed. Every family will have lost people; every family will have mourned. Notice that the Temple in Jerusalem was also a casualty in that Revolt. Every Jew would have had cause to mourn, whether she had ever been to Jerusalem or not. And remember that Matthew's story begins with the stage littered with the bodies of toddlers and the members of their families who tried to defend them against Herod's murderous campaign. Bach's St. Matthew Passion begins with the choir calling: "Come O daughters, share my wailing." The voice of the choir is, to my ear, the voice of Rachel who is wailing for her children, refusing to be comforted, Rachel, whose children are no more.

To refuse to join the mourning at such a time is a serious problem.

Intra-Text: The World of Matthew's Story

Pericopes are funny things. A community of faith comes together on Sunday for what will be (for many) their main episode of Bible reading during the week, sometimes their only episode of Bible reading. Because the community is coming together and will expect to hear something from the Bible, the preacher fishes for a scene to read. Fortunately (?) the lectionary-creating committee has helped with the fishing and has caught a pericope for the preacher and the people to listen to. The preacher casts about, catches the assigned pericope, pulls it out for everyone to see, and there you have it: the Bible has been read and studied and proclaimed for the community of faith.

And through it all, the pericope flops about on shore, a fish out of water.

Every scene from Matthew's story swims in the stream of his whole story, and swims there with all the other scenes that swirl and shift and flow with and against the current. When you pull them out they gasp and struggle and flop about, but they miss being in the water.

That is the case with today's scene. Taken by itself it is a scene that begins with jab at childish opponents who reject anyone who isn't as formless as they are. John is too strict, Jesus is too lax. They have no principle except extreme moderation: don't be "too" anything and you'll be fine. Jesus wraps it all up in today's scene by calmly and gently offering a light burden and an easy yoke.

What a guy.

But this scene follows one scene and precedes another. This scene is part of a narrative arc that carves a course from one part of Matthew's story to another, a course that traces the line of tension among forces that push and pull the whole story. Those forces and that tension matter.

Beyond that, there is a hole in the middle of this scene. The scene itself is cut out of part of the sweep of Matthew's story, and left to flop on the shore, but there is a gaping hole chopped right out of the middle of the scene. As cut, the scene presents a calm Jesus who chides opponents who are inert and tend to stay that way.

But in the first omitted verse Jesus begins to revile his opponents. He had been chiding people for inertia. There is a difference between chiding and reviling. And he is not merely reviling identified opponents; he is reviling whole cities where he had done deeds of power. He reviles them because they had not responded vigorously enough to his acts. Chorazin is reviled, and Bethsaida. Tyre and Sidon, pagan strongholds that had provided key support for Antiochus IV at the time of the Maccabean Revolt, are held up as models of more faithful response than Jewish cities in which Jesus had worked. Of course it matters that Jesus says "if" when he talks about Tyre and Sidon: if the deeds of power had been done in Tyre and Sidon, they would have repented, but those deeds were not done in Tyre and Sidon, and they did not repent, so these pagan strongholds will still be judged harshly, but it will be worse for Chorazin and Bethsaida. And then he turns and throws his adopted hometown, Capernaum, down to hell. Capernaum is the place Jesus shifted to after growing up as a refugee in Nazareth. Now he places this city below Sodom, that mythic example of the consequences of violating hospitality.

This reviling rather changes the flavor of the words that conclude this scene. Now when Jesus portrays himself as gentle the audience has to reconcile those words with the memory of the appearance of his face when he was throwing the town that welcomed him after Nazareth into the depths of hell. Now his words about a light burden bump against the echoes of his angry words. But maybe he spoke in a calm voice, quiet and controlled, when he ranted against the cities that had disappointed him. Maybe he didn't yell. Try it. Play the scene with those words spoken quietly. In my experience, the echoes ring louder, and the scene is more frightening. Jesus begins to sound like a father whose anger races like lava just below a surface that could shatter at any moment. His claim to be gentle and lowly sounds even more threatening.

Now look at the flow of Matthew's story as it races past this pericope. Jesus has jabbed at the people who rejected John, jabbed even at the people who had been fascinated by John. John was no softie, says Jesus, and he didn't dress like one, and you shouldn't have been surprised by what he said and did, nor by his harshness. If you want to see civilized people who bathe and cut their hair and eat quiche, go to the house of kings. That is where the softies live.

There is a nasty jab concealed in the word "softie."[87] It doesn't just refer to people who don't have good honest dirt under their fingernails and don't have calloused hands. It is a word that was used by men who bathed only when they happened to be outside during a rainstorm and expected women to adjust to the way a "real man" smelled. Such odorous men used the word to sneer at the "softies" who always seemed to get the girls. In this context, the word meant something like, "Well, sure, I could sleep with all the women I wanted if I wasted my time shaving and bathing and using deodorant. Some women are just afraid of the way a real man smells. Who needs 'em?"

Of course, the sneering did not stop there. It never does, not then or now. Men who bathe were called softies not just because real smelly men assumed that bathing made your hands soft. The word also implies "penetrable," which doesn't just mean that they had got in touch with their vulnerable side. Smelly men slandered those men who bathed by charging that they not only bathed so as to sleep with a lot of women, but that they also allowed themselves to be sexually penetrated by other men. There is in the word itself a reminder of the use of rape (of women and of men) in order to punish and humiliate opponents and conquered enemies.

Think back to the movie *Deliverance*. Citified outsiders come to the backwoods to ride down a wild river. They laugh at the rubes who live there and make jokes about in-breeding. The locals punish them by raping them. That is what it means to call someone a softie, in the ancient world and now.

In Matthew's story, Jesus plays this offensive language game. Maybe he means nothing other than, "John was rugged and real, the dandified Romans and their sycophants are not." Such a meaning would have a natural home in Matthew's story. He could mean a great deal more, and his meaning could be a great deal more offensive. No matter how broad and deep his intended offense, you cannot play him as a calm, gentle, quiet man who was good with children and would offend no one. Such men were called softies. Matthew's narrative arc has Jesus ranting before he ever starts talking about the children in the marketplace or the lightness of his burden. When Jesus reviles the cities in which he has done deeds of power, his reviling continues a tone that he has already established and will continue for many verses to come.

When the Pharisees react to the actions of his disciples in the next scene (12:1–8), they are reacting to a durable pattern of behavior, one that would trouble most people. When they ask him a reasonable question, Jesus responds with yet another rant. Of course his words can be played with calm and eminent restraint, but only by yanking them out of the narrative arc and leaving them to gasp and flop about on the shore. In their own element, each of these scenes builds on a picture of a Jesus who frighten faithful people.

Do not assume that Matthew was too stupid to recognize this. Do not assume that his portrait of Jesus is an accident. Matthew is carefully painting a picture of Jesus who reacts rigidly when he encounters anything he could call a lukewarm response. Honor the text by noticing this.

Inter-Text: The World We Think We Live In

Survivors of the slaughter in Rwanda sometimes frighten people who encounter them later. They look like extremists, they call for revenge, they are glad that their behavior and attitude frighten outsiders. "Can't we all just get along?" ask the outsiders, to cold glares.

Survivors of the slaughter in Rwanda often frighten other survivors, not because they are extremists or because they dream of revenge, but because they no longer care that revenge will create the next round of reprisals, and slaughter will follow slaughter and lead to answering slaughter, an endless cycle.

Listen to these urgent reflections out of Rwanda's neighbor Burundi:

> The lesson of history for Burundi today is this: you must take on the responsibility of long-term reconciliation or face a future of recurrent bloodbaths.[88]

These reflections come from 1974. This prayer in the aftermath of a prior slaughter went unanswered; the call to responsibility was ineffective. That is why survivors often frighten survivors.

Matthew's story was written in the aftermath of the crushing of the First Jewish Revolt against Rome. Families had been slashed apart. Tens of thousands had been killed, perhaps hundreds of thousands. The generation that first heard Matthew's story in this form would find the story of Jesus' childhood as a refugee to echo their own childhood. When Jesus sneers at the lapdogs of Empire, most audiences would join in the sneering, at least at first. When Jesus looks like an extremist, many in the audience would have understood. When Jesus called for rigidity and revenge, many would have nodded their heads, and would have looked around the room to make sure that everyone else nodded, too.

Matthew's storyteller takes time to throw red meat to those segments of the audience. Perhaps he is seeking to rally the faithful for the next fight against the enemies of the dominion of God. Perhaps he is up to something else. Read the end of Matthew's story and my discussion of Matthew's narrative arc before you decide what he is up to.

It is okay to be a little frightened by the look on Jesus' face in some of these scenes. I think Matthew intended that.

Provoking the Story

When you play this scene, weave the words of the survivors of the genocide in Rwanda into Matthew's text. Include both the words of those who demand revenge and those who fear the endless cycle of reprisals that might come. Let your audience wonder what the survivors would say to Jesus in the scene.

Proper 10 (15)
Matthew 13:1–9, 18–23

(see translation, p. 333)

Ritual Text: The Life of the Worshiping Community

There are two kinds of ritual here. There is the ritual of work, the ritual appropriate to the trade of planting seed. You know this is a ritual because of the triple repetition of the technical term for planting seed: sowing. The sower went out in order to sow, and in his sowing.... This is not some random person dropping seed in the direction of the ground (more or less) and hoping that gravity and good luck take care of the rest. This sower is sowing, which points to a practiced skill. The seed goes where it is supposed to go. No soil is left bare. No soil is overplanted. Even with such a sower, however, some of the seed lands by the road, or on stones, or on thorns. Not much landed there, I expect, but some did. This will have been part of an effort to waste no soil and waste little seed. Some seed is wasted, this will not have been a surprise to anyone. Some seed is wasted; but only a little. Find a National Geographic television special and watch the ritual of sowing. There is real skill to this trade.

The other ritual to watch is the ritual of teaching with story. Jesus is in a boat, and there is a crowd gathered to him. This "gathering" could imply many things. Some in the crowd will have been there because they knew what to expect, having heard Jesus many times before. Some might have been there because the crowd was so dense they couldn't get out of the area and found themselves trapped into listening to whoever this guy in the boat was.[89] There will have been people scattered all over any middle ground you can sketch between these two extremes.

But even if everyone in the large crowd was a devoted follower who knew what to expect and was eager to hear, still Jesus has to hold his audience. Any storyteller, and any teacher who is any good at all, has learned this basic truth: you have to hold your audience or the crowd will be much smaller at the end than it was at the beginning. Worse, the audience will be either drowsy or restless or both if the storyteller cannot hold her audience. Notice the vivid words, the simple beginning that is followed by elaboration, the way the little story rewards listeners who are following along and making guesses about how all this will turn out. What will happen when seed is sown on stones? Every sower in the audience knows, and stands waiting on top of the answer until Jesus gets there. This gives the audience a sense of power as they listen to the story. Note that Jesus gives the audience two chances to share this power in the case of the seed on the stones.

But the moment that catches my ritual eye most is the moment in the story when Jesus reports the harvest produced by the seed that falls on beautiful soil. Some seed produces a hundredfold. I imagine that the audience laughs at this point. Any farmer in the audience would have known that, if this seed is wheat, no wheat in the ancient world could produce a hundredfold. So, after the chuckle dies down, Jesus says: Well, then, how about sixtyfold? Another laugh. Sixty-fold is still too high. Again the chuckle dies down. Again Jesus takes another try, and this time names a yield that would (at least nearly) lie in the realm of possibility.

Jesus is playing with his audience. This is an old trick used both by teachers and by storytellers. When it works (which is most all of the time), the audience is hooked and pulled into the story. The storyteller gives a bit of herself away, specifically her stance as an unquestioned authority. In return, however, the storyteller gets an audience that plays along. This is a good thing to have when you are teaching out in the open with the noise and bustle of people going about their daily commerce. All of a sudden the audience keeps itself quiet and holds its attention on Jesus. Now all that remains is to figure out why he's telling stories about farming when he is sitting in a boat with a shore full of fishing folk in front of him.

Intra-Text: The World of Matthew's Story

Chapter 13 is a mass of parables. This is just the first of many. Because the storyteller has woven together a fabric of stories (some shared with other Gospels, some unique to Matthew's story), we have to read and play this story told by a storyteller inside a story told by Matthew's storyteller differently.[90] One chief theme of this mass of parables is the making of separations. Wheat is separated from weeds, rough fish are separated from good fish, and in the parable that begins it all, good soil is distinguished from other kinds of soil. Another chief theme of this mass of parables is growth.

Wheat and weeds grow together, mustard grows into a tree, leaven grows hidden in dough, and in the first parable in the string, seed grows as it is able when it hits the ground.

A third chief theme is perception of value. This is a theme that also operates in the sorting parables in this mass, so crops and fish are sorted according to their value. This is also a theme when treasure is found, or a pearl, and the finder reacts dramatically. The same thing happens in the first parable, that of the sower, but not so much in the parable itself as in the reason given for telling parables in the first place. "Why tell stories?" the disciples ask. Jesus responds by mapping the border between the disciples and "Them." The disciples know the mystery of the dominion of the heavens. The people who belong to Them do not. It has not been given to them. Since the mystery has not been given to Them, even what they have will be taken away. The disciples, on the other hand, may expect something different.

Inter-Text: The World We Think We Live In

This is a kind of application of a regularly observed pattern of life in society: the rich get richer and the poor get children, only this time the rich and powerful adherents of Empire are figured as the poor, and the disciples and other opponents of Empire are the ones who will be given more than they need. In Matthew's story, Jesus promises them that they will have too much. Isaiah is brought in to explain this strange state of affairs, with a decided twist. In Isaiah's day there was no "Us" that understood, and the "Them" that did not see or hear included the whole people of God. Before being given the charge to speak unsuccessfully to a people that cannot hear, Isaiah himself protests that he, like all of God's people, has "unclean lips." God sears his lips and sends him, but does not separate him from the chosen people. The disaster that will land on God's people will burn them as painfully as Isaiah was burned, and even more painfully, and the nation will see destruction everywhere. But in the midst of this destruction, God promises that even if all that is left is a stump, still out of the stump will grow new life. God's promises are firm, even in the face of deadly destruction.

Matthew has Jesus read Isaiah differently. Over against the Them that does not hear Jesus posits an Us: himself and the disciples. "Their eyes they shut," says Matthew's Jesus, "lest they should see, and hear, and understand and turn and be cured." He turns to the disciples. "Your eyes," he says, "Godlike in happiness: they see."

This distinction between Us and Them is an innovation. Isaiah remained linked to the people to whom he was sent. Matthew paints Jesus differently. The audience would have noticed.

Provoking the Story

Play the whole scene, including the verses in the middle that are omitted. Play the scene so that the audience sees and feels the divisions that are being made. These divisions could mean many things. Do not settle all those things this week, and don't exclude any possibilities. Customary readings expect that being separated out is exactly what a good Christian should hope for and expect. You don't have to protect this reading; it will take care of itself. You will, however, have to protect any reading that is disturbed by Jesus as he makes separations between Us and Them. Such readings are atypical and will not occur to most audiences unless they are given a good, clear look at the way Matthew's narrative arc sets up exactly that sort of discomfort. Practice finding ways to show the audience how disturbing Jesus' words would be to a community that was straining to hold itself together in the aftermath of the failed revolt against Rome. Such a community would have no great sympathy for those people who collaborated with Rome, but Matthew's Jesus is also taking shots at those members of the community who are not sure that Jesus offers the best and only way forward. Jesus is made into the criterion by which Us is separated from Them, and Matthew has Jesus tinker with Isaiah to get this result. Some members of Matthew's ancient audience, even those who were comfortable with using Jesus as the criterion of separation, might have been a little disturbed when Isaiah was getting rebuilt.

Show this discomfort to your audience and let them think about it.

Proper 11 (16)
Matthew 13:24–30, 36–43
(see translation, p. 337)

Ritual Text: The Life of the Worshiping Community

Since we are talking about the rituals and regular practices that make a trade into a trade (and not just a confused and hopeful sort of blundering about), it is worth nothing that this scene (like the previous one) will get a laugh out of people who know something about how grain grows. The grain is planted; the weeds are planted, too. The grain grows, and so do the weeds. Then the slaves make the ultimate town-kid suggestion: Maybe we should go out and pull the weeds now. This well-intentioned suggestion carefully forgets how grain is sown. It is broadcast, not planted in rows. If we were talking about soybeans, or corn, their suggestion might be worth considering. Farmers these days plant such crops in rows and (at least before the development of more specialized herbicides) would regularly remove weeds while the crop was still growing. When I was a kid, "bean walking" was a regular activity on farms around where I lived. The rows gave the "walkers" access to the whole field of beans and any volunteer corn that grew up from the last crop rotation was weeded out. If you tried something similar with broadcast grain the field would be a trampled mess by the end of the process, and the crop would be damaged, at least.

The problem is that you'd get the same result if you did what Jesus has the master of the house decide to do. In fact, the result might be worse. When the grain is growing, it can stand (a very little) trampling. When the grain is standing ready to harvest, drying heads balanced on fragile, dry stalks, any disturbing of the field will knock seeds out of the heads. They will fall to the ground where they will, by ritual custom, be left for any gleaners who can pick them out of the soil. Those that are not found will grow as volunteer plants that will have to be weeded out of the next crop planted in the field.

This is a strange little story. Maybe Jesus is a town kid who doesn't know that his story is odd. Or maybe not.

Intra-Text: The World of Matthew's Story

The first moment to notice in this story-within-a-story is the moment when the crop has begun to grow in the field. The soil has done what soil does: the seeds have germinated, taken root, and grown. And the wheat and the weeds stand side by side, growing vigorously.

In a world that does not use herbicide, this situation is normal and to be expected. Wheat grows. So do weeds. The situation is complicated, perhaps, by the specification that these weeds were not just "plants out of place," but were poisonous weeds. That makes the removal of the weeds a matter of more importance if the crop is to be used. But wheat and weeds, even poisonous ones, grow together in every field.

The slaves notice the weeds and ask a pointed question, a question that carries a back-of-the-hand rebuke to the landowner: if you sowed beautiful seed, how do you explain the weeds? There is not much available to the slaves in the way of back-talk, but they can ask questions like this one, questions that can be innocent if they need to be, but will furnish chuckles for slaves to share later when they laugh at the mishaps brought on by the one who imagines that he owns them.

From this moment of discovery and confrontation the parable grows. The master refuses to imagine that he could have sown adulterated seed, and asserts (without evidence beyond the existence of weeds) that an enemy has caused the problem. Of course, the parable has provided the audience with a glimpse of that enemy stealing into the field at night and sowing poisonous weeds, but the master has not seen this and the slaves have not seen this. For them, all they have is a master who can't imagine that he made a mistake when he inspected the seed before planting. "It was an enemy," he says. "That's the ticket."

The slaves give him a chance to give them a stupid order to match his unsupportable assertion: "So, do you want us to go out and gather the weeds?" Since it will be the slaves who do the work of farming, and not the master, I think it is wisest to assume that the slaves know that trampling the field full of grain in the head would be the wrong choice. That has never stopped bosses who were sure that they possessed the only intelligence in the room from ordering underlings to do stupid things. The conversation in the break room begins, "You won't believe what they had me do today." It goes on from there.

The master's answer bears some reflection. He does not give a stupid order. The fields will not be trampled today, in any case. But notice the order that he does give. When finally it is harvest time, the harvesters (slaves, again) will be ordered to gather the weeds first. As I noted in the previous section, if this means that the fragile field of ripe grain will be trampled, the result is just as bad. Grain doesn't stand too much trampling, especially when it stands ready to harvest. It is also possible, I suppose, that the master is giving a slightly different order. It is possible that he means to command the slaves working the harvest to cut the grain and then separate each handful into weeds and wheat, bundle each separately and proceed from there. This is an interesting possible reading. Perhaps the master feels the sting of the bowing sarcasm in the slaves' question about how the field got so messed up. If so, this is his response: "You can jab at me as much as you like, but I can make you stand in the hot sun and separate stalks of wheat from stalks of weeds, no matter how long it takes, and I can beat you if you drop too much wheat on the ground."

Such a reading delivers a rather different bite. The parable and its interpretation roll along, just as before, but the pull and push behind the scenes can be felt by everyone in the audience. The master has the power to assert that an enemy caused the problem discovered by his slaves. The master also has the power to make his slaves do anything he orders, whether it makes a great deal of sense or not.

And meanwhile, the wheat and the weeds are standing side by side, growing green in the field. Once again as so often happens in Matthew's story, Jesus looks at a mixed lot (this time wheat and weeds) and orders that a rigid separation be made. This time, as always in Matthew's story, those that are separated out are burned.

When the separation explicitly involves human beings, Jesus will add a specification that is nearly unique to Matthew's story. He will point out the wailing and gnashing of teeth that go with being sorted out. This time the audience has only weeds to look at, so they see them burned and are left to wonder about whether people would be burned, too, or only weeds.

Inter-Text: The World We Think We Live In

Interpreters have long noted the moral rigorism of Matthew's story. In Matthew's story, Jesus demands perfection modeled on God's perfection. Jesus advocates amputation before compromise of purity, even when it involves actual body parts. Some of this shows up in other Gospels as well, but in Matthew's story these elements crowd together in a dense throng that follows Jesus whenever he speaks, acts, or moves about. This pattern of making rigid separations in any audience that Jesus encounters brings the present scene into focus for interpreters. Where Jesus shows his audience a field of wheat and weeds mixed and mingled, interpreters see a community of faith with some weedy members mixed in. Interpreters typically pick this scene to buttress their argument that Matthew is advocating moderation in his audience because he has Jesus defer the separation for burning until the end of the age. There is moderation here, to be sure, at least if it is moderation to urge people to light the fire later rather than sooner. There is a sort of moderation here, but it is not very moderate. Until the angels finally arrive, however, the community is left to anticipate the final separation, left to make its own internal judgments about who is wheat and who is weed. The only thing that is forbidden is the actual lighting of the fire. The making of divisions continues apace.

Interpreters who take this line see the final scene in Matthew's story as throwing back an echo of the injunction to let weeds stand with wheat until the completion of the aeon. The mixed crowd on the mountain is left standing, though some doubted. On this reading, they will be gathered later, and burned. This is a possible reading of the scene. Possible, but not convincing to me. This reading misses the key difference between Matthew's final scene and this odd little parable in the middle of the story: in the middle of the story, the fire is actually lit, if only in the imagination of the audience. At the end, there is no such note. There is no fire, and no implication that one will be lit. For the first time in Matthew's story, Jesus meets a mixed crowd and does not make separations. Even when a division within the crowd is explicitly identified, he ignores it. He sends the whole mixed lot out to make disciples.

It is still possible that Matthew intends the audience to supply the fire all on their own, but the difference in the flavors of the scenes is too striking for me to buy that reading. Something has changed in the aftermath of the disaster of the crucifixion, which included Jesus' own collapse and disqualification as a perfect martyr. Something has changed, and Jesus behaves in a way that is quite new. Now there is gentleness that is not part of a rant. Now there is welcome that is not paired with rejection. Now there is a messiah who has been raised from the dead and promises to be with his mixed and imperfect community of disciples, even to the end of the age. Before you play the scene for this week, and before you decide how to read it, taste the difference between this week's scene and the scene at the end of Matthew's story. Bring everything you know about the making of religious divisions between Us and Them to your playing of this scene.

Provoking the Story

When groups of Us are separated from groups of Them, there is always a religious dimension to the separation. Sometimes the group of Them is clearly religiously different, and that makes the making of religious separation apparently easier. This easiness masks the real nature of religious separations between Us and Them. The real nature shows up when there is no religious distinction, no denominational fault-line that can serve as the dividing point between Us and Them. Then you encounter one of the most important facts about life in a community of faith, a fact that we forget to our peril.

When we divide Us from Them, God (by definition) is always on our side of the line. God is always one of Us.

That may seem obvious, but think about it. Many things that are obvious will reward a little slow thinking, a little pondering.

Even communities that affirm the radical otherness of God, that claim that God is above and beyond all human distinctions, even such communities assume that, if we must divide Us from Them, God is properly on our side of the dividing line. Carefully developed theologies, balanced and nuanced and properly in awe of the majesty of God, retire to the other room when Us/Them divisions are being made. Carefully developed and balanced theologies will return to the discussion after the dirty work is done, and then God will be figured as one who suffers with us the depredations visited upon Us by Them. Sometimes this theological line-drawing will even be stirring and inspiring. Sometimes it will even motivate people to listen to groups of Them as they do the same thing and develop their own theology of dispossession.

But always God is on our side, one of Us.

To hear what this sounds like, listen in again on the correspondence between Christians in Rwanda in the midst of the slaughter. Recall that these Christians were members of the same denomination. They were even all of them pastors. A group of pastors had written to their supervision pastor, expressing fear in the face of the growing violence. The answer came back, simple and direct and highly theological. "You must be eliminated. God no longer wants you."[91] They were Tutsis. Their supervising pastor was Hutu. To get a feeling for how this parable does its work, create for your audience (and for yourself) a group of people who will be the plants in the field. Some will be wheat; some will be weeds. Make the crowd of people/plants clearly distinguishable from each other, perhaps by using costume, or gender, or age, or something easily seen. Do not identify, however, which half is wheat and which half is weed. Simply make it clear that they are different and that half will be gathered and burned. Let your audience feel the force of this promised division. The bite will be stronger if you do not help the audience decide who is slated for destruction.

This parable does re-present a normal condition of life after all.

Proper 12 (17)
Matthew 13:31–33, 44–52
(see translation, p. 337)

Ritual Text: The Life of the Worshiping Community

Another parable from the complex of parables in chapter 13. Another reference to ritualized skilled practices: farming again, and (new to the complex) baking. Both of these skilled practices are wound in the rituals that govern such essential activities. The first might be a skilled practice done mostly by males. The second is very likely women's work.

There are surprises in these little stories, as you would expect, given the rituals that go with storytelling, but the surprises are surprisingly large.

First, the farming story. It seems so straightforward. Mustard is small when it is planted. Mustard is large when it grows. Matthew has Jesus exaggerate the growth (mustard does not become a tree, even a town kid would know this), so maybe this is the surprise that makes this a parable. When the parable is read this way, it is a story about the explosive growth potential of the dominion of the heavens (whatever exactly that might be). This is, judging from centuries of interpretation, a productive way to read this story. It might be a story about the way the Christian movement spread all over the Mediterranean basin. It might be a story about how Gentiles poured into the movement. It might be a more general story about how, with God, a little is never "too little."

As useful as all of this is, it misses the real surprise in this story. This is a story about a person sowing (there is that technical term for skilled planting again) mustard in his field. This is a story told by a Jewish storyteller to a Jewish audience who live in an area populated by Jews and Gentiles. In such places, it is both important and easy to tell the difference between the farms of the two different groups: they have different practices.

I used to live in rural Wisconsin. The area had been settled by Europeans from Norway and from Belgium, not usually in compact settlements, but farm by farm each group was sown around the county. Local people can tell which group the original settlers belonged to, just by looking at the farmsteads, even after all these years. Belgian farmers, when they could afford it, built houses out of a yellow brick very like the yellow brick they remembered from home. Norwegians did no such thing. White frame houses were the rule. Belgian farms were distinctive even when there was no yellow brick house. The houses were built very close to the road, sometimes with the barn on the other side of the road. Norwegians built their houses and barns farther back, up a little drive. Locals had conflicting explanations for why these practices had taken hold. The explanations do not matter. The predictive value of these observations was very, very high. The two groups farmed differently, and that is all there is to it.

The same is true for Jewish and Gentile farmers in the first century CE. Jews did not plant mustard in their fields, not in the first century of the Common Era, anyhow.[92] Mustard, as any farmer will tell you, is a wildly profligate plant. It spreads everywhere and grows wildly, so much so that it was a metaphor for lack of restraint. Jews used mustard in cooking in the first century, but they did not plant it in their fields. Living a Jewish life means living a life that witnesses to the stable and orderly love of God in all things. Planting a weed that was a symbol for wild disorder was judged to be an unnecessary compromise of the basic principles of a Jewish life.

This little story says one of two things: either Jesus is saying that the dominion of God is like a plant growing in a Gentile's field, or he is saying that the dominion of God is a sign and source of disorder and chaos that disrupts the community's ability to witness to God's love. Not much of a choice. Which ought we to choose?

The audience would have been given a clue in the telling of the next parable.

It is a story of women's work, the mysterious business of baking leavened bread. Leaven is not Red Star yeast, not a little packet of granulated powder. Leaven is a piece of bread that was placed in a warm, dark, moist place until it changed from bread into something that would cause bread to rise. Mold grew on it, and its power was a great mystery.[93] So far, so like the usual reading of the parable of the mustard, except for the part about being green and black. Perhaps the dominion of God is a mystery power that brings a gift to human community through the work of women.

But leaven is also the substance that is removed from a Jewish house when it is cleaned for Passover. Leaven is used as a metaphor by Paul and Jesus to refer to contaminating influences that ought to be avoided. And the rabbis used it as part of a customary cliché from the time: A little leaven leavens the whole lump. This cliché was the exact equivalent of the current cliché: One bad apple. . . . You know the rest.

The dominion of the heavens is like a weed that weakens your ability to witness to God's love. The dominion of the heavens is like a source of corruption. However you finally decide to read these little stories, pay attention to the provocation offered by the ritual meaning of mustard and leaven. Jesus tells very strange stories.

Intra-Text: The World of Matthew's Story

This selection of parables from Matthew 13 mixes parables of growing with parables of valuing. Mustard and leaven grow. Treasures, pearls, and good fish are valued. Both types of parables touch major themes in Matthew's story. What is intriguing is that these two complexes of parables, different as they are, still read each other in at least one interesting way.

When the net full of fish is hauled to shore, the rough fish are picked out and discarded. When mustard grows in a field, farmers (then and now) pick it out. When Passover time comes, Jewish families sort through all the food in the house and discard anything that has leaven in it. In the case of the fish, this is just standard practice: you don't keep what you can't sell. In the case of the mustard, this is also standard practice: unwanted mustard is a weed and it uses up moisture and nutrients that the intended crop will need if it is to grow successfully. In the case of the leaven at Passover time, this is an exercise in metaphoric cleansing and rededication. The house is cleaned and the family is purified so that they can share the celebration of God's promised deliverance from all oppression.

Why does Jesus compare the dominion of God to things that must be picked out and discarded before God's deliverance can be celebrated? Why make the dominion of God somehow parallel to the rotten fish? This oddity is hard to construe. In this scene Jesus picks two images to talk about God's rescuing presence in creation that are certain to offend his target audience. From the start of the story when he was associated with John the Purifier, Jesus has linked his project with that of carefully observant Jews. At key points he gives instructions for those who desire to be strict in their observance of Torah. And now he uses images that imply that the dominion of God defeats careful observance, maybe even makes it impossible to observe Passover and its celebration of deliverance. Why?

A few scenes ago Jesus ranted at towns who had heard him but had not responded enthusiastically enough. Perhaps their response was tempered by the images Jesus used there, as well. If observant Jews listen to Jesus and object, then this nest of parables gives us a clue as to why that might happen. Jesus doesn't sound like the savior of the world in this scene. He sounds like an immature disrupter. There is a difference.

Inter-Text: The World We Think We Live In

I had a friend in high school who went to Vietnam. Many of us had friends who went to Vietnam. My friend also came back from Vietnam, unlike some others I knew. He came back, but he did not quite come back. He came back from combat to the life that he had left and spent years looking for it. Whenever he found something that looked like the life that he had left, it was too quiet, too dull, empty of risk. "After you've been in combat," he said, "golf is a little dull."

He found the people around him a little dull, too, and a little too laid back. A little too fat, a little too comfortable. "Nobody lays their life on the line for anything here," he said one day.

I don't know where my friend is these days. I haven't seen him in years. The last I saw him he had joined a missionary group that was accepting volunteers to go to New Guinea. He hoped life would be harder and more dangerous there. Maybe it was. All I know is, when I see Jesus in this set of scenes, he looks a lot like my friend. Everyone he looks at looks too fat and happy; no one looks sufficiently committed to anything.

Remember that Jesus starts out in Matthew's story as a refugee from a combat zone that killed all of his contemporary cousins. Remember that he had run into violence and deep danger already at an age when most kids who live where I live haven't begun to cross the street by themselves. Take the Incarnation seriously. Expect that real life experience will have had a real life effect on Jesus and the way he carries himself in the world.

Imagine the eyes of someone who had seen such things. What would they look like? How would such a person enter a room? Where would he sit? How would such a person react to sudden sounds? Would he play golf?

Provoking the Story

Practice playing scenes without pulling punches. Do not always give the characters in the scene "Bible story voices"; do not always give villain voices to the people who question Jesus, and do not always give Jesus a well-modulated baritone voice, perfect for working on the radio. This scene is a good one to try this out. If you have a friend like mine who came back from Vietnam, but not quite all the way, give his voice to Jesus. Give Jesus also his eyes: eyes that shift sometimes and other times burn holes in the world. Give Jesus the little jump my friend had when a car backfired or someone touched him from behind.

Give your own worried voice to the people who ask Jesus tough questions.

Proper 13 (18)
Matthew 14:13–21

(see translation, p. 342)

Ritual Text: The Life of the Worshiping Community

What did the crowds hear? Matthew leaves the question open. Jesus heard that John had been murdered. He went out, away into the wilderness. Did the crowds hear that he had gone away, or did they hear that John had been killed? If so, their choice to follow Jesus into the wilderness is a powerful choice. Perhaps they are retreating. Perhaps they are mustering for battle. Perhaps they are simply following Jesus assuming that he knows what ought to be done next. Whatever the reason, they follow him into the wilderness. They flock to him, a large crowd, perhaps just as they flocked to John. Yet once more, Jewish faith drives people into the wilderness in the face of yet another threat to God's people and God's promises.

The wilderness is the place of ritual beginning for Jewish faith. Sarah and Abraham left the settled civilization of their families and wandered into the wilderness to look for the concrete reality of God's promise of descendants, land, and a blessing (both to them and through them). In the wilderness they encountered the threats that made their stories what they were. Some of the threats came from their childlessness, some of the threats came from the measures they took to overcome that childlessness, some of the threats came from the God who called them into the wilderness and then called Abraham to kill the son Sarah had born, the only son she bore, the son whom she loved, Isaac.

Isaac lived also in the wilderness, and favored his firstborn son, Esau (whom he did not try to kill). His second born, Jacob, was favored by his mother, Rebekah. Esau was well-suited for life in the wilderness, Jacob, not so well, but he learned to live there after he cheated Esau out of his birthright and fled from him into the wilderness where he wrestled with his father-in-law, his children, and an angel, who gave him a name and a limp, both of which he carried for life in the wilderness.

Jacob's children, the children of Israel (then and now),[94] were driven out of the land of promise into Egypt. After generations, they were led out of Egypt, out of one of the most advanced civilizations the world has ever seen, out of slavery, into the wilderness, led by Moses who had, himself, lived forty years in the wilderness after he had killed an Egyptian overseer. The people of Israel followed Moses into the wilderness, where they wrestled with the wilderness, with Moses, and with God through all their years of wandering. By the time they wandered out of the wilderness into the land of promise (either invading, or infiltrating, or both), they had been shaped by the time in the wilderness. The prophets of the eighth century BCE remembered this time of wilderness wandering as constitutive of Jewish faith, remembered the wilderness as the place where God shaped and trained, supported and gave life to the Jewish people. This understanding of the wilderness held the people together through the disasters of the eighth century (the destruction of the Northern Kingdom, Israel, in 722 BCE), the sixth century (the destruction of the Southern Kingdom, Judah, in 587 BCE), and all the centuries in which God's people have found themselves thrown into chaos.

And so Jesus — when he hears that Rome (through its stooge, Herod) has killed John, just as the previous Herod had killed all of Jesus' contemporary cousins at the beginning of Matthew's story — goes into the wilderness. Having been cast into chaos yet again, he goes where Jews go to wrestle with disasters, with angels, and with God and circumstances beyond their control. The faithful crowd follows him. When he looks up, and when they all look up, they see that there is a large crowd of faithful Jews, together again in the wilderness, ready for whatever wrestling is necessary.

Intra-Text: The World of Matthew's Story

When does Jesus go into the wilderness in Matthew's story? It is a good question to ask. Part of the answer is, "Not often." John is discovered in the wilderness and when he is imprisoned, Jesus reflects back on why people went into the wilderness to see him.

After Jesus went into the wilderness to be purified by John, he was driven by the breath of God into the wilderness alone. Now Jesus and the crowds hear that Herod has killed John, and Jesus and the crowds go into the wilderness. No matter whether they both go independently or whether the crowds simply follow Jesus, when this scene begins they find themselves in the wilderness together. Reading off the pattern that has been established in the story, we would do well to assume that this wilderness wandering will prepare Jesus and the crowds for something big that is just about to begin. That's what happened when Jesus and the crowds met John in the wilderness. Reading off the established pattern, we would do well to assume that Empire will not like what happens next. We shall see if this expectation is borne out. Perhaps it is. Perhaps not.

While we wait to see what happens next, note that this scene echoes another distinctive theme in Matthew's story: the theme of having too much. In the midst of the knot of parables in Matthew 13 Jesus promises that those who have will be given more, given too much even, so that they overflow. Those without (whatever exactly that means) will be robbed of what little they do have. Now again this excess is brought into the story, only this time it is food that is too much. The people were stuffed. There were twelve baskets left that no one could eat. And all of this excess happens in the wilderness where the disciples were concerned that there was not enough food.

Just for a moment, notice that the theme has been twisted. In Matthew 13 those with too much get more. In Matthew 15, those who have nothing get too much. This is a reversal, and worth paying attention to.

While we're in the neighborhood, there is another reversal to consider. Jesus has gone into the wilderness to meet John and goes there after he hears of John's death. He will go there yet one more time in Matthew's story and will encounter a crowd of four thousand people whom he will feed just as he feeds the five thousand in today's scene. Late in the story, however, he will counsel against going out into the wilderness to meet the messiah. Why the change? The

189

problem, of course, is easily solved: Jesus will be offstage by that time, and he is telling people not to go into the wilderness to meet a false messiah. Simple.

Nothing is ever quite that simple, however. The people who go on errands into the wilderness, both early in the story and late, go out to encounter God's intervention against Empire, or to recover from Empire's retaliation against God's people. Why should that stop? It is not simply that Jesus will be otherwise occupied at that later date and thus could not be expected to meet people in the wilderness. His prohibition cuts deeper than that. He himself has gone into the wilderness and has prepared for his contest with Empire. When he warns against future errands into the wilderness, he is engaged in the last days of his own contest. He is in Jerusalem, and Passover is at hand. If we read Jesus' words as part of the narrative arc of Matthew's story, he prohibits future wilderness wandering perhaps because he expects that his contest with Empire will make such future errands unnecessary. If that is his expectation, he will be disappointed.

Or, if we read his words as part of the history of Jewish attempts to overcome the crushing of the First Jewish Revolt against Rome, the bite is rather different. Then he is counseling against future retreats into the wilderness to repeat John's preparation for combat with Rome. The storyteller and the audience have both seen the results of such contests. Jesus, on this reading, advises his audience to give such adventures a miss.

Or finally, if we read his words, however, as part of the arc followed by the goat-like messiah of Matthew's story,[95] the bite becomes even more interesting. Now the reversal looks more like a hint of what will happen to Jesus after he discovers himself raised from the dead. Before his crucifixion, he feeds the people Passover at the site of Rome's contest with Jewish faithfulness and history. After his resurrection he sends a mixed lot of disciples out to purify and teach, thus making them into disciples. The time in the wilderness is finished. The resurrection has changed the terms of engagement. How odd.

Which of these options is the correct one?
Yes.

Inter-Text: The World We Think We Live In

This scene in the wilderness is not just a scene about hunger and nourishment. And it's not just a scene about providing food for the hungry. Every mouthful of this scene is rich with layers and layers of traditional flavors.

To begin with, it takes place in the wilderness. The word "wilderness" implies, in English, a certain wildness to the place, a certain untamed and untameable nature. The word in Greek (ερημος) is different: it implies devastation and depopulation. In a traditional Jewish text like Matthew's story, devastation and depopulation set off echoes that ring all the way back to the memory of the exiles in Babylon who remembered Jerusalem standing empty and desolate. In the Septuagint, the subtitle given to Lamentations locates it after the scattering of Israel and after the depopulation of Jerusalem. For Matthew's storyteller and Matthew's audience the memory of a battered and desolate Jerusalem would be more than a traditional observance. Matthew's story is told in the form we have it sometime soon after the crushing of the First Jewish Revolt against Rome in 70 CE. Vivid experience of disaster would be deepened by practiced memory of disaster and shaped by Passover celebrations that prepare to enter into the wilderness on the way to a return to the land of promise. When the crowds and Jesus meet in the ερημος, the desolate, depopulated place of mourning and preparation, they meet there with all of the Jewish members of Matthew's first audiences. The feeding that God provided in the post-Exodus ερημος likewise deepened and shaped the feeding that Jesus brought about for the crowds who met him. The food was sustenance, to be sure, but it was also a celebration of the memory of food on the way to the land of promise, food remembered (along with the memory of tears) in every Passover celebration, food that also gathered up the mourning and preparation that would have been proper to post-70 Jewish communities.

All this from a single Greek word.

There is perhaps even more sustenance to be had in the Hebrew word for wilderness. In Hebrew the word is *midbar*. To catch the bite of this word, you need to see how the word is composed. It has two parts: *mi-* ("away from") and *dabar* ("to speak a word"). The word implies a place away from words, a wordless wilderness as I sometimes translate it. This translation catches the silence of a stark place where people do not live, where plants and animals conserve moisture and move little in the daytime. But there is more to *midbar* than just silence. When God created the beautifully knit together cosmos in Genesis 1, God did the work of creating by speaking to the world not yet formed, speaking the way a mother speaks to her baby not yet born. When the world heard God's voice, it emerged out of chaos and rose up into order, beauty, and mutuality, each part supporting and being supported by every other part. Every part came out of the fertile soil and returned to it to nurture future life. All this because God spoke (*dabar*) to the creation.

In this scene, the crowds and Jesus are in the *midbar,* the place away from words, the place that has not yet heard and responded to God's call to order, beauty, and mutuality, the place that has not yet lifted itself up to nurture life. No wonder the people are hungry. Jesus' act of providing food in the *midbar* is a seed around which nurturance can crystallize even in the scarred aftermath of devastation and desolation, which are here figured as pre-creation states. There is more here than food, and more here than wilderness.

All this from a single word in Hebrew. This would not surprise the rabbis, who understand that God spoke to chaos in Hebrew and it responded gladly, as if to its mother's voice. A word can do a lot.

Provoking the Story

This scene draws its life from its roots, the old stories that reach deep into Jewish history and provide meanings for words like "wilderness" and for themes like "feeding in the desert." Play the scene with those old roots woven into the picture. Maybe you could weave in stories from the Exodus and the wilderness wandering so that your audience hears both the scene from Matthew and the memories that give it life.

Of course the roots of this story are not simply sunk in stories of miraculous Providence. "Wilderness" also would imply for Matthew's audience something about devastation and depopulation, and this is true at every level and in every century. Weave this also into your performance of the story. Show your audience the city of Jerusalem sitting lost and lonely in Lamentations. Show them Jerusalem devastated also by the Romans almost six hundred years later. You might also show your audience other times when human communities were devastated. Perhaps you could weave into the scene stories like those told of the Holocaust by Ida Fink, stories like the fictional "A Fine Spring Morning," which tells of the murder of a little child during a deportation to a camp, a murder the father was powerless to prevent. Perhaps you could sharpen the idea of wilderness by weaving in stories from the experience of the Lost Boys of Sudan who wandered for years trying to escape the devastation of a civil war that killed their parents and relatives.[96]

Weaving these stories into the telling of this scene will sharpen the audience's awareness of the bite that would have been felt by Matthew's first audiences. It will also honor the arc of Matthew's whole story, which begins with Matthew introducing a little refugee boy and naming him "God-With-Us" (Emmanuel).

Proper 14 (19)
Matthew 14:22–23
(see translation, p. 344)

Ritual Text: The Life of the Worshiping Community

Water is not only water, at least not when the storyteller is Jewish. Water is the necessity that humans must have for life, and we must drink it even though it can swallow us and all that we have built up, swallow it all in an instant. Water is the tense embodiment of the precarious balancing act that is life in God's creation. Water was

193

pushed up and back when God made a safe place for human life, according to Genesis 1, but water waits, just on the other side of the sky, waits to gush out and wash everything away. Water waits, in Jewish storytelling, to return God's creation to the formless void, the dangerous watery chaos, that existed before God began to create. When God looked out before beginning the work of bringing order out of chaos, God saw what humans see swirling around even the most stable of moments, the most joyous of times. God's promise never to destroy the entire creation by flooding it has not comforted those parts of it that get washed away in the storm surge.

Intra-Text: The World of Matthew's Story

The question is not whether Peter should have glanced at the whirlwind and become afraid. The question, I think, is whether he should have abandoned his place at the oars in order to attempt to do the impossible: walking on chaos and catastrophe without getting the least bit wet. This particular reading I owe to Steve Martens, a pastor of uncommon skill and insight, who is one of my teachers in a text study I lead. He noticed a parallel between this scene and the scene of testing at the beginning of Jesus' career. Both times a character who has been linked to the satan says to Jesus: if you are you, do something stupid. In the first scene, there are three stupid things Jesus could do: break his fast (and his teeth) on rocks, worship someone other than God, leap to his death. In this scene, Peter says something equivalent: If you are you, order me to do something stupid. And Jesus says: Okay, do something stupid. The question is: who fails in this scene of testing, Peter who sinks like his namesake (a rock), or Jesus who does not resist ordering Peter to do the impossible?

Inter-Text: The World We Think We Live In

This scene has always attracted speakers who wanted to motivate an audience to take risks. "You've got to step out of the boat," they say. "Miracles are waiting for you if you are willing to take the risk."[97]

This is not the worst thing one might do with this scene. Risk is indeed necessary, and willingness to try things that might be impossible (but also might not) is crucial to human progress. But to read this scene only this way is to misrepresent the disciples who remain in the boat. Most risk-taking interpretations sketch them as hanging on to their comfort and safety. That deliberately ignores the rowing they were doing and implies that in times of danger what we need are people who jump out of the boat and not people who do what seasoned veterans of difficult times have learned long ago. Grizzled vets know: in a storm, rowing is good, panic is bad. Risk-taking interpretations also fail to notice that Peter never attempts to walk on the water again. If the point of this story were to teach people to step out of the boat, the storyteller would have given us a look at another time when Peter does just exactly that, only this time he takes a longer walk before sinking. There is no such scene. Jesus and the disciples travel by boat later in the story, but nobody walks on the sea, or even tries to, ever again. Maybe they learned their lesson.

If you read risk-taking interpretations carefully, many of them are urging optimism. "If you expect to sink, you will sink," they say, implying the corollary, "If you sink, it's because you expected to sink." There is real mischief here. Stories of improbable success always charm us. Stories of risks that paid off always attract our attention, perhaps because we like to imagine that we, too, are just one risk away from fabulous wealth. Such stories are always told by people whose risk paid off. We do not hear, or want to hear, the stories of those people who also took risks, and sank to the bottom never to rise. And we do not want to imagine that those who took the risks and succeeded did so because they had ability and education and access to a moment in time that made their actions profitable. The story of Bill Gates, the college dropout who succeeded, ought not be read as an encouragement to cease being educated. Most people are not Bill Gates, and no amount of determined optimism will change that.

When this scene is read as a primer in optimism, real mischief erupts. I understand that Admiral James Stockdale was asked what he had learned during his time as a prisoner of war during the Vietnam war. He learned, he said, that optimists were the first to die. They died because they were sure that release would come soon, perhaps at Thanksgiving.

Or maybe Christmas. Or maybe Easter. Pretty soon it was Thanksgiving again, and pretty soon their ability to cope wore out. Optimistic expectation of success weakened them. It is worth asking whether Stockdale, Navy man that he was, would have climbed out of the boat with Peter.[98]

Provoking the Story

Water is not only water. Water is the chaos that kills people. And Jesus is walking on top of it. Consider this ritual picture carefully. If this scene is about Jesus' calm, Godlike control of chaos, then Jesus strolls through the storm without getting wet. His divine status makes him immune to the torture his disciples are suffering as they row for their lives in the boat. Chaos threatens to swamp them and Jesus is dry. He isn't even sweating. The theological implications of this way of playing this text are troublesome; the dramatic implications may be worse. A Jesus who can stroll on chaos without consequence can only condescend to the poor air-breathers who can drown.

This scene could be played another way. Perhaps Jesus does not hover untouched a millimeter above the surface of chaos. Perhaps "walking on the sea" means that Jesus walks on the water the way people walk on deep snow: sometimes on the surface crust, sometimes breaking through, sometimes floundering, stumbling as the almost-solid-enough snow gives way unevenly. This yields a very different picture. This Jesus gets wet, and works very hard indeed, as he struggles through the storm and the water, sometimes on the surface, sometimes wallowing almost to his waist, walking to help people who are also tortured by the waves. This way of playing the scene yields a very different picture, both theologically and dramatically.

But Jesus can still walk on the sea.

Proper 15 (20)
Matthew 15: (10–20), 21–28

(see translation, p. 347)

Ritual Text: The Life of the Worshiping Community

The woman is a Canaanite. That is most likely not what she would call herself. She might well have called herself a "Syro-Phoenician," as the storyteller in the Gospel of Mark does. She might have called herself a woman of Tyre, or a Sidonian. She might have called herself any number of things, but the odds are good that she did not call herself a Canaanite.

"Canaan" was the name of the land into which the wandering people of Israel went, led by Moses' successor, Joshua, after generations in the wilderness. Canaanites were the people who were dispossessed in that conquest. To name her as a "Canaanite" is to ritually erase centuries, even millennia of history, to erase her probable privilege as a person allied with Rome and before that with Antiochus IV and the Seleucids. To name her a "Canaanite" is to erase all of the complicated history of the Jewish people all the way back to the entry into the land, leaving only the painful memories that went with the return from Exile when the Jewish community emerged from the generations of captivity in Babylon to find people living on the land they had left behind. These people were charged with cultural accommodation, among other things. They were called "Canaanites," as well. Of course, to erase this complicated history is also to call it back to mind.

This woman, this mother, is a Canaanite. She is made to be an unacceptable hybrid; she is created as one of the people who were pushed off the land to make it the land of promise for the wanderers. This is odd. This naming reverses the power relationship, and with it, the ethical slope of this encounter. When the story is told this way, Jesus looks at a displaced person, displaced by the promise, and chooses to ignore her. When his disciples speak around her to ask Jesus to dispense with her, Jesus calls her a dog and disdains to

197

even address her in order to dismiss her. The rituals of cross-gender, cross-cultural, trans-millennial conversation in this scene are painful to behold. She has no voice, and represents no human presence, and Jesus and his disciples are doing a ritual dance that makes that crudely apparent.

Intra-Text: The World of Matthew's Story

Does Jesus listen to himself when he talks, or does he just talk? If what comes out of the mouth defiles a person, listen to what Jesus says to the woman in this scene. If duties to mother and father are the measure of a person's faithfulness to God, watch what Jesus does when he first meets the mother in this scene. He gets better later, that is true. But not until a Gentile mother schools him a little. Jesus should listen to himself more often.

This is an awkward thing for most Christians to say. Jesus floats through our stories and our sermons and comes to our Sunday Schools without a hair out of place. He is calm and in control of every situation. How else could he be, since he is identified as God in the flesh, and God is imagined as the "Unmoved Mover" who initiates all motion, but is never pushed into anything? This notion of God, which owes much more to Aristotle than it owes to biblical texts, is open to question. It has little to do with the passionate God we encounter in biblical stories, the God who decides, acts, listens, and has a change of mind every now and again. But if this unmoved God is the one that Jesus must embody, then he will surely need to be perfectly calm in the midst of every extremity. This notion of Jesus, however, seems never to fit with biblical texts. Surely there are moments that can be bashed into compliance with this notion of God, but they require significant bashing. More important, these images of Jesus are minority reports inside the Gospels. The Gospel stories show Jesus reacting and overreacting, planning and changing his mind. Customary interpretation, of course, masks this variability, this tendency toward change, but faithful readers of the Bible must notice (and make room for others to notice) the reality and importance of Jesus' variability.

I think faithful readers must go farther, however. I think faithful readers and performers of the Gospels must make room for the possibility that Mathew's storyteller paints a picture of a Jesus who learns things and changes for the better.

I have argued that Matthew's narrative arc draws Jesus through a transformation. At the beginning of the story he is a damaged character, wounded by Herod's slaughter of his extended family. In the middle he acts out the consequences of this damage, consequences that are customarily seen in survivors of such disasters. He is rigid; he is demanding; he is a perfectionist. At the end he is raised from the dead, and he is surprised. The surprise changes him. See the larger discussion of this surprise that is part of the exploration of the scene assigned for Easter Day, on page 129.

If this is the overall narrative sweep of the story, you should expect to see small instances of change and development in individual scenes in the story. The scene for today is one of those examples. In his words about what makes for cleanness and uncleanness, Jesus demonstrates remarkable openness, perhaps even risky openness. In his treatment of the mother who comes to him asking a favor, he acts out the nasty edge of exclusivism. Perhaps his actions are rooted in the memory of the support offered to Antiochus IV by people who lived around Tyre and Sidon. Perhaps he simply has never met a person from that region and assumes what people often assume about strangers. Perhaps he reacts as he does simply because she is a woman and he is not. Whatever the reason, the scene is painful at the beginning. The scene is perhaps less painful at the end. Jesus' actions, by the end, line up with his words in the previous scene. He seems to have learned a lesson, and this requires that he be a character who is able to change.

Stop and think what it means that Matthew is telling a story with a Jesus who can, and must, change if he is to accomplish his task along the narrative arc that Matthew sketches.

Inter-Text: The World We Think We Live In

Listen to these words from a man who changed his mind and his actions. If you've worked your way through this entire book, you'll remember the story from earlier on. The man is Dick Fiske, who was a survivor of the attack on Pearl Harbor. I met him at the Pearl Harbor memorial on Oahu. Until his death he spent most days at the Memorial telling his story of survival and reconciliation to visitors.

> "Some of those who bombed us are now my very close friends," said Fiske. "We are so close that we call each other family. Can you believe that?" he asked.
>
> Fiske talked about how it was back then and how it feels to live with the effects of war.
>
> "People don't seem to understand that we did what we were told to do, both of us [us and the Japanese]. I'm sorry for all the deaths I may have caused," Fiske explained tearfully.[99]

There are many things to hear in Richard Fiske's story. I wish I had met him earlier in my life or had talked longer with him. For now, notice the tears cried by this ex-Marine. Change that goes this deep often brings tears along with it.

Provoking the Story

Whatever you do, do not erase the face of the mother in this scene. She reacts to Jesus' words, and her reaction is an essential part of this scene. Too much biblical interpretation concerns itself with Jesus and Jesus only. His reactions are taken to be the central core of any biblical passage, and his actions are taken always to be salvific, his behavior exemplary. While there is surely value in this powerful, insistent focus on Jesus, such an approach does not take the Gospels seriously. These stories are scripture as a whole, not in atomized bits, and the mother in this scene is as much essential to scripture as is Jesus. If that were not the case, Matthew would have had Jesus float through and announce things. He would never have to meet anyone, and he would never, ever learn anything. Such an approach to these stories reveals a narrow and constrained view of scripture and its value. I would argue that the stories that come to us out of scripture are scriptural as stories. In their narrative entirety.

But that means that the woman's reactions are crucial to the scene. They are essential even if she scowls at Jesus. They are essential even if she does not shake his hand at the end of the scene. Her face is essential, especially if she looks the way so many women have had to look when they have been overlooked yet again. In this scene she is a mother seeking help for her daughter. She encounters roadblocks, to which she would react the way any mother would. Some of the roadblocks are thrown up by the disciples. Her face would track her reaction. The roadblocks that really matter are thrown up by Jesus himself, who ignores her at first and then insults her. Even if the painful history shared by Jews and Gentiles from around Tyre and Sidon, by Jews and Canaanites, is the background for the curt and dismissive remarks and insults, and even if the woman understands that painful history, still a mother will react as a mother will react. Honor the mother in this scene.

Proper 16 (21)
Matthew 16:13–20
(see translation, p. 353)

Ritual Text: The Life of the Worshiping Community

What are people saying that the son of Adam is? This is, in itself, a surprising question. He is who he is. Isn't he?

Neither the question nor the answer is simple. The area in which Jesus is active is small, but there is no evening news, no newspaper, no poster campaign. News travels by word of mouth. In such a media environment, people are who others say they are.

It is the set of answers that is the real surprise. The story assumes that everyone knows of John's imprisonment and seems to assume also that everyone knows of, and mourns, his murder by Herod. If people assume that Jesus is somehow John, they must have seen something stirring in John that would not be held even by death, the ultimate tool of imperial control. This is not a simple expectation of resuscitation, a naïve belief that death was a door that could swing both ways. To look at Jesus and see him as John is to see something moving in the world that is bigger than historical individuals. Empire has no ability to control what is happening.

The same perception lives within the other guesses that people have made: Jesus is Jeremiah or one of the prophets. The prophets spoke with breath that God breathed new into the world; they were animated by a new creative act that changed lives and perceptions throughout the Jewish people. The prophets in particular challenged God's people to open their eyes and see both the realities of the historical moment and the realities of their responsibility toward their neighbors.

It is striking, however, that Matthew carefully includes Jeremiah as the first prophet mentioned. Jeremiah warned of the coming destruction at the hands of the Babylonians in the sixth century BCE. Jeremiah lamented the destruction of Jerusalem. Jeremiah gave voice to the weeping of Rachel, wailing for her children who have been destroyed by centuries of conquerors, by empire after empire. All of these links are important, but because Matthew let Rachel mourn the story into motion after the slaughter of the children of Jesus' hometown, it seems most important to notice the linking of Jesus with Jeremiah and Rachel in mourning. Somehow in Jesus' sharp cries people heard not just a call to rigorous discipleship but (more importantly) the keening wail of a mourner.[100]

Peter hears something different. He has access to the same data. He is part of the same word-of-mouth world, and the same world of Jewish hope and demand. He looks at the link to the murdered John and the mourning prophet and sees in Jesus the action of God in the person of one anointed to be king. To be anointed as king in the midst of such a historical moment, with Rome controlling the land and the people, is to expect violent conflict. To speak of an anointed one in the context of a mention of Jeremiah is to link messiahship with mourning. This is a link distinctive in Matthew's story, a link made necessary by the way Matthew's story is slaughtered into motion. This link is especially poignant since Matthew's story is told (in the form we have it) sometime after the Temple has been destroyed and Jerusalem has been conquered yet again. A mourning messiah has definite responsibilities at such a moment.

Intra-Text: The World of Matthew's Story

What are people saying that the son of Adam is? The question bears asking again. It is worth wondering what the mother in last Sunday's scene would say, after all. In the end her daughter was healed and she got what she needed out of Jesus. But she had to break through his silence, overcome his rejection, and counteract his insult before that happened. Matthew's storyteller does not inform us of her reaction to Jesus or his healing after she finally gets him to respond helpfully, and this silence of the storyteller is worth remembering while we listen to the disciples and Peter as they respond to Jesus' question.

Now in the scene for this Sunday, Jesus elicits from Peter a recognition of Jesus as messiah. This recognition, he says, did not come from "flesh and blood," which surely refers to normal human powers of perception. But there is a note that must be heard here. "Flesh and blood" is a reference back to the creation story in Genesis 2, in which Mudguy was built as a fully articulated body that waited only for life to be breathed into it when God blew into its nose. The word for "body" in Hebrew is often translated into English as "flesh." And when the breath of God goes into the nose of Mudguy, it makes life, which resides in the blood. When Jesus says that "flesh and blood" cannot look at him and see anything that looks like a messiah, he is not just saying that human perception is inadequate to the task. He is saying that the gifts of perception given by God in creation are inadequate to the task. Something more is required, a revelation from his father in the heavens.

This is an interesting twist, given his interchange with the Pharisees and Sadducees at the beginning of the chapter. When they responded to Jesus' promising activity and asked for further clarification, Jesus called them names as if his identity should have been obvious to them and everyone else. When Peter responded to the same activity and saw what Jesus says God-given perception would not be able to see, Jesus commends him and builds his assembly on him. "Nobody with the eyes God gave him would be able to see what you just saw," Jesus says. Maybe that is why Jesus finishes this scene by scolding his disciples that they shouldn't tell anyone that he was the messiah. Maybe that's why the next scene in the story has Jesus talking about his crucifixion. Nobody would look at that death by torture and see God's deliverance of creation.

Inter-Text: The World We Think We Live In

In the scene that begins chapter 16 in Matthew's story, Pharisees and Sadducees band together to try Jesus. They ask for a sign out of heaven. Jesus responds harshly. "No sign will be given," he says, "except the sign of Jonah." Matthew's storyteller, doubling things up as he so often does, has led Jesus into this area before. In chapter 12 Jesus also speaks of the "sign of Jonah" and explicitly links Jonah's three days in the belly of the whale to Jesus' wait in the tomb for resurrection. This reads the sign of Jonah differently than does Luke's storyteller, who ties it to the response of the Ninevites to Jonah and sees that as pointing to the response of all of creation to Jesus. The storyteller gives no sign that we should read this second reference to Jonah differently, which will be important when we come to assess the importance of the way Matthew tells the story of the resurrection in his narrative arc.

Two things are more important at the moment. First, to imagine the Pharisees and the Sadducees collaborating on anything is an oddity that begs for interpretive attention. And second, to ask for a sign is not a bad thing.

Some time ago, there was a rash of burglaries at the college where I teach. Thieves from outside the college community were walking into campus buildings dressed as computer technicians and walking out with expensive hardware. We were all instructed to ask to see credentials whenever we encountered "computer technicians." It was a reasonable action to take; it was also effective. The thefts ceased. Some of the thieves were caught. When faithful Jews ask for a sign, they are just asking for Jesus' credentials. This is also a reasonable action to take. Matthew does not tell us that they are hostile, only that they ask for credentials. Their attention has been drawn to his teaching and healing, and they ask to see credentials that might validate their suspicions. Could this be the messiah? Jesus calls them representatives of a worthless generation. He figures them (offensively) as adulterous women, calling to mind both the judgment laid out by the prophet Hosea ("Israel is Not-My-People") and the offense of using a woman, a wife, as a metaphor.

These two oddities dance close together. If one reads with an eye on the propriety of asking for credentials, all of Israel (figured by linking two arguing segments) sees something in Jesus' activity that warrants further investigation. Jesus rebuffs them. If one reads this matter from the side of Jesus, who seems to assume that enough signs have been given already, then all Israel is united in refusing to see what is right in front of their face. Jesus brings down the memory of Hosea's condemnation on their heads. In either case, Jesus seals the matter by pointing to Jonah and to his own resurrection. If we read from Jesus' side, the scene sounds like a foreshadowing of a post-resurrection argument over the reality and meaning of the resurrection as proof of Jesus' identity. If we read from the side of those who ask, rightly, to see some ID, then there is an odd twist to this whole scene. Jesus is offering the resurrection itself as a sign, to be sure, but he is offering the particular telling of the resurrection to be heard from Matthew's storyteller, and in that telling, Jesus is changed by the resurrection. In particular, after the resurrection Jesus does not rebuff people who see signs and doubt them. Instead, he sends doubters and worshipers alike out to do the work of the dominion of God. Perhaps the "sign of Jonah" is more complex than it originally appeared. Perhaps it points both to Jesus' resurrection and to the change that is seen in Jesus. Jonah, after all, also changes, and not all that willingly. First, he changes when he consents to go and preach in Nineveh. Later he sits grumbling because the unworthy Ninevites had repented and now would not receive the punishment they deserved. Perhaps this points ahead to the transformation that awaits Jesus when he finds himself raised from the tomb.

Provoking the Story

Play this scene together with the scene at the beginning of chapter 16. When you portray the Pharisees and Sadducees, however, do not play them as villains from Central Casting. Do not play them as rigid rejecters of Jesus. Play them as honest people who look at Jesus with the eyes that God gave them and ask to see something more. Play Peter as the attentive younger brother who watches closely when the older siblings (Pharisees and Sadducees) get into trouble, and then carefully steers around the trouble when Jesus asks the disciples to identify him.

Proper 17 (22)
Matthew 16:21–28

(see translation, p. 354)

Ritual Text: The Life of the Worshiping Community

This scene is typically read as pushing up the continental divide between a nationalistic understanding of the work of a messiah and the work of a messiah as "reinterpreted" by Jesus. Nationalistic messiahs, we are told, conquer earthly powers and establish justice in human affairs. This, we are told in customary readings, is a limited, human view of things, and is rejected by Jesus. A proper messiah, we are told, does his work in the spiritual realm. This, we are told, is what it means to see things from God's point of view. If you ask whether this doesn't put God on the side of quietism in the face of injustice, whether this doesn't, in fact, guarantee the survival of the powers that are founded on injustice, making God an ally of the broken status quo, then typical readers roll their theological eyes at you and link you with Peter, the satan. All this because you thought that God intended to have a real effect on the creation, an effect other than extending the life of injustice. How odd.

What is even more odd is the recognition that Jesus' words, if you read them as they are written, and then play them as they are most naturally played, sound like they contemplate worldly violent clash with established powers. Peter's words, as they are most naturally played, sound like balanced counsel against picking fights that you cannot win.

Albert Schweitzer heard something like this in these words. He saw Jesus' entrance into Jerusalem as a desperate attempt to force God's apocalyptic hand, to turn the wheel of history by challenging Rome face to face. On the cross, Jesus and his project are crushed, rolled over by the reality of Roman power.

What is at stake here is the sense of how you stage the drama of messiahship. Does messiah simply and easily overturn the power of Empire? Or does messiah charge at the windmill in a quixotic quest for immortality? Or does messiah prepare a people to resist and finally rise against oppressive powers? There are many more options, but of these three, the first seems not to have happened in any case. Peter's words fit best with the third option since they seem to counsel not wasting the energy of messianic hope on a fool's errand. That leaves Jesus tilting at windmills and demanding that his followers similarly kill their own lives. The word does not imply losing one's life; the Greek is clear enough: followers are to actively kill their lives.[101]

These are very different ways of staging the drama of the messiah. Since the first option seems to be unavailable, the choice (for now) is between the last two. The option chosen by Jesus is heroic but desperate. Our traditional stories are full of such desperate heroism. "Once more into the breach, dear friends, once more, or fill the wall up with our English dead." So said Shakespeare's Henry V at the battle of Harfleur, and the English won the day. Desperate heroism is marvelous, when it succeeds. We would tell the story differently if the result were simply the filling of the wall with English dead. Not all desperation is heroic. Some is foolish. Some is wasteful. And some is simply wrong. If we are to read this scene as authorizing all desperation as messianic (and thus licit and even desirable), there will be consequences that we ought to consider ahead of time.

When Peter's counsel is read against Schweitzer's background, Peter emerges as less desperate, more patient, and more willing to trust God to make of this ragtag movement a messianic overturning of injustice. "May God be merciful to you," he says. "This must not be." Read this way, Peter is saying: "This is not the way to play out the drama of messiahship." This is not the way to turn the world right-side-up. This is not the way to honor the hopes that have kept Jews alive through the most desperate of times. Do not squander the hopes of generations on a suicide mission that has no hope of succeeding.

You can always decide later whether Jesus' project succeeded. Christians have invested two millennia of theological time and energy in demonstrating that Jesus succeeded perfectly well, thanks. But do not dismiss Peter's sober counsel too easily. He is neither a coward nor a short-sighted nationalist. If anything, he is the opposite. He is aware of the responsibility that goes with using the title "messiah." He knows that the "hopes and fears of all the years" do indeed rest on such a title, and that one ought to pick up such a title in a way that respects those who have staked their lives on the hopes that attach to the title. Peter, soberly, looks for a different way to play out the drama, if the drama must indeed be played.

Notice that Maurice Blanchot, in his century, also recognized the responsibilities that go with messiahship. A messiah must always be coming, but must never arrive, notes Blanchot.[102] That way the hopes are preserved and the imagination of the people is fired to reach for justice and balance in God's creation. That way the people are trained to resist powers too strong for them. I imagine that Peter would have read Blanchot's cautions and understood them well. I imagine that Peter had been required to take a step beyond waiting for the messiah who must always be coming, that he had been required to take the risk of welcoming a messiah who had arrived. In this scene Jesus announces that he intends to waste this risk, and that he expects all of his followers to do the same. "May God have mercy on you," says Peter. "This must not be."

Intra-Text: The World of Matthew's Story

In the scene for last Sunday, Jesus noted that no one who looked at him with the eyes that God gave to us would see him as the messiah. People were making remarkable guesses. John the Purifier, Elijah, Jeremiah: these are huge guesses as to Jesus' identity. Apparently people could use their God-given sense to look at Jesus and make such guesses. Perhaps Jesus continues the program of purification for resistance to Empire that had been begun by John. You can look at the story and see evidence that would support such a hypothesis. Perhaps Jesus represents the return of Elijah, that inconvenient prophet of God for whom a place is set at Passover Seder meals, just in case he should choose to attend and inaugurate the renewal of creation. If you could look at Jesus and see a demanding purifier very much like John, you could intensify things a little bit and link his activity with something fit for Elijah. And Jesus has been linked with Jeremiah (tacitly) since the beginning of the story. When Rachel shrieks for her children in century after century, it is Jeremiah's creative, mourning voice that invites her in. You apparently could look at Jesus and see him as Mourner-in-Chief in the mold of Jeremiah. Jesus apparently views such interpretations of his person and action as plausible. In any case he offers no rebuke and no special commendation. Peter sees Jesus as messiah, and Jesus says that God-given eyes could never see him in that role, so Peter's perception must depend on something beyond sight, a divinely sparked insight, perhaps.

On the face of things, you can see why Matthew's storyteller puts down these words for the character Jesus to speak. Prophets stir things up, or, as Jacquelyn Grant puts it, they "perturbate the system." But prophets live and die, and leave room for yet another much needed "perturbation" at some point in the future. As different as John, Elijah, and Jeremiah are (and they are quite decidedly different), they resemble each other strongly in this regard: they disturbed the world and changed it, and yet they left it needing future disturbance and change.

A messiah offers something different. A messiah does not merely stir things up; a messiah turns them right-side-up. This notion, surely, is shot through with conclusions clarified by centuries of Christian study, conclusions clarified (but differently) by separate Jewish exploration of the same matter. But in all of the possible permutations, messiahs turn things right-side-up, beginning with the relation of domination and subordination enforced by the Roman Empire. The way the world boiled around Simeon ben Kosiba (hailed as Bar Kokhba, the son of the star, the messiah) in the Second Jewish Revolt against Rome offers contemporary witness to this understanding. The work of James C. Scott shines a light on how subjugated peoples resist domination in any century, and the light picks up features in ancient Jewish hope and practice that are recognizable. Subjugated people wait and sing and pray and work for the world to be turned right-side-up. In ancient Jewish faith these resistant activities are gathered under the name of messiah.[103]

Jesus heals. And he teaches. And he purifies. And he stirs things up. But at the end of his activity, the world is still upside-down. On the face of things, you can see why ordinary, God-given human sense would not call Jesus messiah.

Inter-Text: The World We Think We Live In

This becomes even more true when you know how Matthew's story ends. Not only does Jesus not overturn Roman domination; he is tortured to death in a display of imperial invincibility. Rome used crucifixion to make it clear to anyone who had missed the point that opposition to Empire was useless. If the cash value of the term "messiah" is that the holder of this title turns the world right-side-up, then crucifixion is a bitter crushing of this expectation. A person who will be crucified is led through a whole series of assaults that serve to demonstrate that he has no supporters and can have none. Rome can crucify whomever it chooses to crucify. And family or supporters of the crucified are forced to stand helpless and watch as Rome acts out its absolute domination for all to see. This is another brutal demonstration of the unassailable fact of imperial dominance. During the years of race-based slavery in the United States, one of the tools used to enforce the dominance of the masters was the whipping of a child in the presence of the community of slaves, including most particularly the child's parents. The assault on the child is brutal, but the assault on the parents carries its own cruelty. They are taught impotence when the slaveholders demonstrate to all and sundry that no one has the power to defend the child.[104] Crucifixion acted out the same lesson in impotence. The victim was paraded through the streets to the place of crucifixion. The cross was placed where the community must walk past it. The obscenity of the torture was conducted in full public view. And all the time no one could act to protect the victim without being added to the list of candidates for crucifixion. The practice taught impotence. It also inculcated rage, but that rage had to wait, and wait, and wait for a moment when it could be released.

None of this belongs among the accomplishments of a messiah. Pilate knew that, and placed a placard above Jesus as he hung dying. The placard taunted him and all Jews by identifying Jesus as the king of the Jews.

Provoking the Story

At our distance of two millennia, crucifixion has become a safe and sanitized metaphor. No one is crucified any more. When terrorists wish to intimidate opponents and inflame public rage (which, when it leads to official retaliation, results in more offenses that they can claim to avenge), they behead their victim. Just to gauge the distance we have come since the first century of the Common Era, you might notice that beheading was the mode of execution reserved for Roman citizens who had committed a capital offense. It was understood as a form of execution preferable to the obscenity of crucifixion. If any group were to attempt to practice crucifixion, it would be taken as evidence of extreme barbarism and would be used to justify any form of retaliation against the offending group, any form at all. In the first century of the Common Era, crucifixion was practiced by the most civilized nation on the face of the earth. The word "civilized" even comes to us from Latin. The next time someone tells you how much worse the world is becoming, remember this.

Spend some time reflecting on what crucifixion actually was, what it sounded like, what it smelled like, what it did to human communities, both those that suffered it and those that inflicted it. You might read the article in the *Journal of the American Medical Association* that examines the physical realities of crucifixion from the point of view of a physician.[105] You might read James C. Scott's analyses of the technologies of domination in *Domination and the Arts of Resistance.* You might read Philip Gourevitch's descriptions of the bodies left behind after the slaughter in Rwanda in *We Wish to Inform You That Tomorrow We Will Be Killed with Our Families: Stories From Rwanda.* Whatever you read, read it slowly and imagine the sounds and smells, the taste of impotence left in your mouth.

After giving sufficient time to what will have been a painful exercise, go to Matthew's story and read Jesus' words to his disciples (verses 24–25, especially). For Matthew's first audience, these were not words about metaphorical crucifixion. They did not function as encouragement to practice self-denial. Find an actor to work with and look for all the ways these words can be said. Remember, they must taste bitter to be real and honest, and the smell in the room must be acrid. Go over and over this exercise before you tell this story.

Proper 18 (23)
Matthew 18:15–20
(see translation, p. 362)

Ritual Text: The Life of the Worshiping Community

The ritual in this scene is a boundary ritual. The scene starts as a consideration of the matter of forgiveness, which sounds so standard, so much an ordinary part of the life of a community of faith. The scene ends with the injunction to treat a sister or brother as a Gentile, as a tax traitor who collaborates with Empire against her own people. This ending is important. The question is: How did we get from the conventional beginning to this odd ending?

The next thing to notice about the ritual in this scene is that the ritual pattern of action that is commanded is both demanding and traditional. If a sister or brother should sin against you, and they surely will, given the realities of human life together, Jesus in this scene calls you to act with sober integrity. The most natural reaction is to line up allies first, to gossip and punish the wrong-doer indirectly. Such actions are to be avoided. "Go to your sister," says Jesus, "go to your brother, just the two of you, and reveal to her the cause of your dissatisfaction." It is so much more satisfying to skip this step and gather allies. No provision is made for the step we enjoy most. "Go to your sister," says Jesus, "and reveal to her." If this is sufficient to balance things, that's the end of it.

If the first step was not sufficient, take two or three witnesses with you. This step is founded upon the expectation that your sister might not have reason to believe you if you speak alone. This expectation is sober and wise. This requires the plaintiff to recognize the complexity of the situation. It is not simply that you have a complaint. The relationship is at stake. Your sister may have cause for complaint also against you. You are obliged to find witnesses, which implies that if there are no witnesses who will accompany you, the matter is at an end. If no witnesses see things the way you do, you will have learned something about your complaint. This bit of sober advice is buttressed by a citation of a principle that rings through Jewish writing from the bible to the Talmud to the rabbis today: "on the mouth of two witnesses, or three, shall stand every word."

If you find witnesses, and if your sister does not listen, still there is another step. You are directed to the whole gathered community, and you are directed there with a reminder that the next step involves severing your relationship with your sister or brother. Do not take this last step if you are unwilling to cut your ties should this fail. This is sobering advice. This is not simply a way to get people to listen to your complaint. There are plenty of ways to do that. Every community of which I have been a part has had festering sores that were the result of offenses that were never resolved. The plaintiff complains abundantly, but never as part of a ritual of reconciliation. The offender is kept around, not out of some desire to bring about reconciliation, but so as to be a permanent lightning rod for every wrong, every offense. As long as the community had an all-purpose offender who could be blamed for anything and everything, everyone else could escape blame and avoid the difficult work of reconciliation. And the sores festered continually.

Intra-Text: The World of Matthew's Story

This scene sets out a ritual of reconciliation that is quite marvelous in its sober earnestness. By itself, this scene offers to communities in conflict (finally all communities are in conflict) a way to nurture a life together even when the community suffers pain and offense. The final step of the ritual of reconciliation is drastic, but seems to float there in the distance to bring sobriety to the earlier steps of the ritual.

All of this sweetness and light persists until you play this scene in the midst of Matthew's story at this point. When you play this scene as it flows out of the scene that begins chapter 18, everything changes. Suddenly the final step, the step in which you cut off contact with your sister or brother, starts to sound like an echo of the command to cut off your hand when it offends you. First one hand and then another. First one foot and then another. First one sister and then another. One wonders what one is to do when one runs out of appendages. Perhaps one is to cut off the stump a little bit higher up the arm, though this does not solve the problem of how one is to hold the axe. One wonders what one is to do when one runs out of sisters.

Matthew's story is an odd mix of gentle, wise advice and seething anger. Even in the quietest scene you can hear the sound of axes being sharpened, axes of moral rigorism and revenge. If you determine (naïvely) to simply take the story as it comes, it will stir up forces that you had not anticipated. In any community of faith there are some members who know of another offense that deserves, on a biblical basis, the death penalty. In any religious communities there are a few people willing to carry out that penalty themselves. A naïve playing of this scene will energize those dangerous few who are entirely ready to begin cutting off the parts of the community that offend them (and, by extension, God, since anything that offends them must also offend God).

This is a good point to go back and reread my exploration of Matthew's narrative arc (in chapter 2). There is a transformation that is accomplished in the performing of this story. Jesus is changed, and it is the experience of death and resurrection that does it. But it is not only Jesus who is changed. The audience is also changed.

Imagine the process with me. When the story is begun, the rigorists in the crowd are given plenty to cheer for. Jesus sounds like their boy, and he throws them plenty of red meat. When he demands perfection, they attempt perfection. When he sends the imperfect to hell, the perfectionists volunteer to help the imperfect pack for the journey. When he calls for amputations, however, things change. The rigorists might well be willing to cut off sisters and brothers. This is a regular feature of fanatical religious groups. But far fewer will be willing to cut off hands and feet. Some will grow disenchanted with the whole perfection business just at that point. Others, however, will turn the force of the command to amputate into a weapon to be used against the members of the community who are less perfect than they are. Rigorists can always find someone less perfect than they are; in fact, they have to find such people in order to keep from cutting off their own hands and feet.

This uncomfortable process continues until Jesus reveals his own imperfection on the cross. This leaves the remaining rigorists (the craziest of the crazy) in an awkward position. They have no choice but to cut Jesus off, but as soon as they do, God raises him from the dead and he welcomes a mixed and imperfect crowd. What is a rigorist to do?

Matthew's story is a sucker punch that catches religious perfectionists where they have no defenses at all. At the end of the story they have to choose to be Christian without a messiah, or they have to scrap the whole perfection thing and accept forgiveness along with all the rest of us. They are left no other choices.

The scene for this Sunday is part of this sucker punch.

Inter-Text: The World We Think We Live In

This scene is read as a source of good advice and a model for good practice in a community of faith. Every congregation of which I have been a part has internal tensions that are related to hurts and offenses. In any community, people hurt each other, sometimes just because of the heat produced by friction. When people live and work close to one another, they rub up against each other and sometimes they rub each other raw, without malice or forethought. Other times the hurts are the result of simple nastiness. Human beings have a great potential for altruism. We also have a ready reserve of selfishness, and in a community that means that we sometimes hurt each other on purpose.

As useful as these readings might be, they forget the central dynamic in Matthew's story and in Matthew's audience. Matthew tells his story amid the rubble of the failed First Jewish Revolt against Rome. More to the point, Matthew tells his story in the midst of a Jewish community (part Christian, mostly not) on which the weight of Roman wrath had landed. Rome destroyed the Temple, expelled Jews from Jerusalem, killed perhaps a million people (this is a huge number out of any community, but proportionately very high for the relatively small Jewish community), thousands of them by crucifixion. During the siege of Jerusalem, Rome dug a trench around the city to trap any who would attempt to escape from the doomed city. Any Jews who were caught trying to escape, even if they presented themselves as desiring to cease hostilities, were nailed to crosses placed around the perimeter of the city, close enough to the walls so that their death could be heard inside the city, close enough so that everyone inside was made to feel their own inability to help a fellow Jew in desperate need. These victims were not simply nailed to crosses in orthodox Sunday School fashion. Perhaps the first ones were, but later victims were arranged in artful postures. The torturers were bored with customary crucifixion. They posed their victims to deepen the ridicule, to make it clear that Rome could do whatever it chose to do and would not stop with simple barbaric brutality. At the end, in the worst of the siege, Jews inside the walls killed each other. This also is a regular feature of siege warfare.

The effect on the community was predictable. When Rome landed its weight on the Jewish community, all the seams popped. Communities under such abominable pressure rupture at every possible weak point. Every disagreement becomes a flashpoint. Every difference of opinion or background becomes an occasion for conflict. Every disagreement and difference became the focus of the community's piercing gaze as it struggled to assess the reasons for the disaster. Communities under such unrelenting pressure try to assign blame and the buzzards circle, alert for anything that might be carrion.

It is in this setting that Matthew's storyteller performs this scene about offense and reconciliation, offense and amputation.

Listen to an assessment of the problems to be solved in the aftermath of yet another scene of slaughter, this time in Burundi, Rwanda's neighbor:

There was so much suffering and so many people killed in Burundi that all of us must ask the question, Who, if anyone, was to blame? What were the causes? Perhaps somehow we can find a way to prevent a recurrence of such a tragedy in Burundi and in other countries. In various reports one is able to identify some men who obviously played a role in ordering executions and/or eliminating people for reasons of personal vengeance. But the real villain was not any specific man or group of men but rather the type of alienation existing in the Burundi nation. This alienation — caused primarily by the two evils of

217

hate and fear — has time and again triggered massive violence of neighbor against neighbor in both Rwanda and Burundi. It is a kind of disease like malaria: as long as it remains in the body, there is a danger of it breaking out. Until the disease is eradicated, or at least brought under control, there is danger of other bloodbaths in Burundi.[106]

There was no intra-Jewish genocide in the aftermath of the crushing of the Revolt. But notice that the question is the same: Who is to blame? This natural and crucial question, asked in the presence of the hate and fear left behind after any such incident of barbarism, feeds the disease that will break out inside the body of the community in the future. Jews asked the question about blame for the disaster, and pointed at each other. This is understandable. And dangerous. Years later the rabbis settled the matter admirably: the cause of the disaster was sectarianism, which blames not people or groups of people but rather the very activity of dividing into groups. The disaster was caused, the rabbis concluded, not by this group or that group, but by the community's willingness to place the blame on this group or that group.

Matthew's storyteller would seem to agree. In this sucker punch of a Gospel, he baits the rigorist partisans relentlessly. At every occasion he draws them out, gets them to cheer as the story is performed, encourages more and more extreme reactions against the targets that seem to have been selected by the Christian partisans (particularly the scribes and the Pharisees, it would seem). Woes are pronounced, and condemnation is thrown out liberally. Amputations are encouraged.

At the end of the story, Jesus is raised to life apart from these partisans. He no longer breathes fire. He no longer condemns the imperfect. He no longer supports the program of revenge, which is the disease lurking in the body of the community of faith after the crushing of the Revolt.

He surprises everybody, perhaps even himself.

Resurrection is like that.

Provoking the Story

Before you play this scene, explore the dynamics of communities under pressure. You might look at movies, even lousy ones, that include scenes inside prison camps, for instance. You might read stories told by Sister Helen Prejean (the author of *Dead Man Walking*) about life inside penitentiaries, and about the way the justifiable need for revenge affects human beings and human communities. If you have ever had to spend much time in the family waiting room at the intensive care unit at a hospital, remember what the people there looked like and sounded like. Catch the physical shape of the interactions of people under pressure, the ways they hold themselves together by holding themselves apart from everyone around them. If you have had to spend much time in such places, you may well have learned that the pressure pops seams. When the patient is a child and the child dies, the mother and father of the child face a sustained period of pressure that leads to a high rate of divorce. Explore all these dynamics before attempting to play this scene about human life and human offense.

Proper 19 (24)
Matthew 18:21–35
(see translation, p. 362)

Ritual Text: The Life of the Worshiping Community

How did a slave ever run up that sort of a debt? It is a real question. If a talent is worth fifteen years of a laborer's wage, then this slave has amassed a debt worth 150,000 years of a laborer's wage. It has only been 2,000 years since this story was told. We have only another 148,000 years to go before we have run as long as a laborer would have to work to pay off that debt, which is disconcerting when you consider that Homo Sapiens Sapiens has only been around as a species for 195,000 years. For the slave to pay off the debt, the labor would have had to have started with the emergence of our particular species of hominid. How would a slave ever amass such a debt?

If we were to imagine that the laborer in question would earn, in contemporary terms, perhaps $20,000 per year, then this debt would add up to something like $200 million. In days of multi-billion dollar national deficits, a mere $200 million seems almost manageable. But the question remains: how would a *slave* ever have a chance to run up such a debt? Someone loaned him the money. Someone should have known better. Someone like the slaveholder in the parable. And now the slaveholder plans to sell the slave, his wife, and his children. "Because he can" is the answer to both questions that beg to be asked: why did the master let the slave go so far into debt? and, Why does the slaveholder decide also to sell the children and the wife of the slave in the story? Because he can.

The slave is released from the debt. The proposed sale of human beings would not have begun to touch the debt in any case. The slaveholder might just as well release him.

It is at this point that we get a glimpse of the slave's ability as a money manager. If we are to imagine that he is attempting to collect a debt of his own as part of an effort to raise the funds necessary to pay off his master, he looks hopelessly math-challenged. The fellow slave owes him roughly one-third of a year's wages. At this rate, he will only need to shake down 450,000 other slaves who also owe him money before he can pay back the debt from which he has been released.

This is an odd story. Do not solve the problem of the parable by leaping immediately into the vastness of the debt of human sin. We will get there in any case. But don't go there until you have reflected on the financial particulars of this case. There is a regular ritual to financial matters, a ritual governed by regulations and a shared sense of fair play. How did the slave ever amass such a debt? Who allowed this to happen? Who encouraged it to happen?

Intra-Text: The World of Matthew's Story

This story flows directly out of last Sunday's scene. The storyteller has set up a flow that swirls between the rocks of reconciliation and amputation. The stream is moving fast. Peter paddles into an eddy and asks how many times he ought to forgive this brother. His question has a bite to it. The way he asks it explicitly recognizes the importance of the familial relationship (whether biological or fictive) and the pain caused by offense within that relationship. His question places him in the camp of those who pull back from amputation, whether for a limb or a sibling, but shows that he feels the inadequacy of sentimental notions that forgiveness makes everything right and easy.

Jesus' answer is not easy to read. On the one hand, he lands solidly on the side of forgiveness and does not feed the anger of the fed-up rigorists who simply can't stand any more sloppiness. On the other hand, however, his demand for eternal forgiveness sets up the possibility for a new kind of religious athleticism to break out. Now people in the community have an opportunity to compete for the title of Forgiver of the Year. (Maybe it even comes with a Special Parking Place?) Ordinary people might be capable of forgiving even seven times, but someone who really has the gift of forgiving leaps beyond that without a thought. And a real forgiveness athlete aims for 10 x 7 x 7, or totality x completion x completion. That's a lot. Ordinary mortals would never be able to reach such heights, but spiritual athletes are not ordinary mortals.

So is Jesus' answer a gentle and wise counsel concerning the necessity of forgiveness, or is it yet another call to the Olympics of spiritual perfection? Unfortunately, the answer is "Yes."

Inter-Text: The World We Think We Live In

This scene makes no sense unless you recognize the role played by the slave-holding master in the parable. He is not just a person; he is a master. He has the power to own other human beings. He has the power to create a situation in which a person (the slave) who does not even (technically) own himself can run up a debt so great that the entire history of humankind would not be long enough to work it off as a laborer. The slave-holding master also has the power to sell the people he owns, not because the proceeds from the sale will cover the debt, but because he has the power to inflict the pain of permanent separation on the slave who owes so much money (because the master had the power to allow him to owe so much money).

The scene makes no sense until you pay attention to the dance of domination.

Something deep in our democratic bones objects to the power structure of this scene. Something deep in the history of the American republic refuses the notion that a human being can own other human beings, or even worse, that a human being can sell other human beings. But at the same time, we have grown accustomed to the excuses offered on behalf of corporate executives who plunder pension accounts "for the good of the company and the workers" and then complain, when they are caught, that they have been ruined financially since they are left with only three houses, vacation property in the south of France, a private jet and a golden parachute to use when they jump out of it. We are not surprised when those who object to such abuses of pensioners are accused of engaging in "class warfare."

The scene makes no sense until we realize that we, perhaps, are not so democratic as we imagine, that perhaps our republican virtues are not so deeply held after all. Perhaps, at the heart of things, we just wish we were the slaveholder in the story, the master who cannot be held accountable for anything by anyone.

This is a parable told to an audience that loves power, and loves to pretend that it does not. Matthew's story is told to an audience that hates Rome, and wishes it had the power to do to Rome what Rome did to them. Since that will never happen (that sort of messiah seems never to come), they have settled for abusing what power they have over their sisters and brothers in the community of faith. The point of the parable is made at the end: if this is how you wish to structure the world, you should expect God to fit right in. If the only question that really matters is who dominates whom, then, Jesus says, "Thus my father, my heavenly father, will do to you all."

Sucker punch.

Provoking the Story

In my first book, *Provoking the Gospel: Methods to Embody Biblical Storytelling through Drama*, I described a game my actors taught me. The game is called "Columbian Hypnosis." I do not know why it is called that.

In this game, players are placed in pairs: one person is the leader, the other the follower. The leader holds a hand before the follower's eyes and moves it up and down, around and around. The follower has a single purpose: to maintain a constant relationship to the leader's hand. If the leader moves quickly across the room, the follower follows the hand. If the leader moves the hand up and down while crossing the room, the follower undulates while following, maintaining an even distance between face and hand at all times.

After a suitable length of time, the roles are reversed. Leader becomes follower, and follower becomes leader.

Play this game with a group of people, and then explore the results. Sometimes when I have played the game with groups there are leaders who force followers to twist and contort themselves in all sorts of uncomfortable ways. This behavior does not persist. As soon as the roles are reversed, lessons are learned and the next role reversal brings either further retaliation (followed generally by a refusal to continue playing) or a recognition of the responsibilities that go with leading.

After playing Columbian Hypnosis several times and exploring the experience with your actors, play it again while reading the scene for this Sunday. Read the parable slowly. The master and slave are playing Columbian Hypnosis, only neither party quite gets it. First the master leads the slave into massive, irredeemable debt; then he leads him into the realization of what it means to be a slave: he will be sold, along with his wife and children, simply because that's what you can do with a slave if you are a master. Then the master simply drops the slave and forgives him the debt, again because he can. The slave has learned well the lesson of domination, of doing what you can simply because you can, and goes out and abuses his power over a co-slave who must be subordinate because he owes him money. The master then condemns the slave to prison, demonstrating that only he has the final power to dominate those under him.

It is a fascinating game, power.

Proper 20 (25)
Matthew 20:1–16

(see translation, p. 370)

Ritual Text: The Life of the Worshiping Community

There is an old joke from the former Soviet Union. As the nation slid toward collapse, nothing worked right: government was up for grabs, business and industry were in free-fall, money became nearly worthless. In the midst of the chaos, a government-paid worker was asked how he managed to keep going with everything falling down around him. He said, "It's just like always: we pretend to work and they pretend to pay us."

This is a joke because it recognizes that the ritual of work and remuneration is so basic that people can be supposed to dance their parts in the ritual even when there is no work and no actual remuneration. The ritual dance is powerful, basic to human life together.

This old joke and the much older ritual behind it provide the twist that makes this story a parable. In the story, everybody works (at least a little) and everybody gets paid. Customary interpretation sees in the master's action an enactment of grace because he graciously gives to each worker a full day's wage. But the master chooses to ignore the reality of the work done by the laborers who put in a full day's work. This choice twists the ritual, warps the dance that human communities do together to maintain balance and productivity. What isn't addressed in the story is what this twisting of the dance does to future work in the vineyard. Now that the master has twisted the dance, one might well assume that laborers will be unwilling to bear "the burden of the day and the heat." If the ritual has been bent so that work and remuneration no longer correspond to each other, only a chump will work through the heat of the day. Now that's what I call grace. Or maybe not.

Intra-Text: The World of Matthew's Story

There are many stories about powerful masters, or kings, or landowners in Matthew's story. All of them do exactly what they choose to do. All of them exercise their power without regard for what anyone else would think about it. In this scene, we encounter one more of these autocrats. At the end of the story he asks, "Isn't it appropriate for me to do what I want in my business?" The audience can tell that he assumes that the correct answer to his insolent question is "Yes, O most beneficent master, you can indeed do whatever you want to do with your power and we poor mortals are powerless to question you." The groveling goes on from there. And it has to go on, because the laborers will want to be hired again the next day, and the next, and the next. Of course the master may indeed have trouble hiring workers who will actually work in the future, but one may suppose that he will solve this problem when it arises, and that he will solve it through the use of the power that allows him to do what he wants in his business.

Matthew has given us other views of what masters and kings do when their will is frustrated. Judah wants to be done with Tamar, so he ignores her claim to clan support and sends her back to her father's house. David wants Bathsheba, so he takes her and kills her husband. Herod cannot control succession to the throne of the king of the Jews, so he kills all the toddlers in and around Bethlehem. A king invites guests to a wedding feast (Matthew 22:1–14, the scene for two Sundays from now) and when they do not come, he burns their city and does it before the wedding feast.

Look even at Jesus' own family: Joseph wants to maintain his reputation for strict observance so he decides to abandon Mary to her fate at the hands of a patriarchal clan and wash his hands of the whole business, at least until an angel gets his attention rather forcefully. Even Jesus, when he encounters a fig tree without fruit, blasts the tree for eternity (Matthew 21:19ff.). If he has the power to blast the tree for eternity, and even use this miracle as a sign of what can be accomplished by faithful people, couldn't he just as well perform a productive miracle and make the tree suddenly fruitful?

In Matthew's story, when people with power are frustrated, you should duck. This apparently even applies when it is Jesus who has the power. One might do well to reread the testing scene in the beginning of Matthew's story. Back then, Jesus resisted using power "just because he could." Now perhaps things are different?

So perhaps we are to draw the conclusion that the master, when next he needs to hire workers for his vineyard and encounters people who are unwilling to bear the burden of the whole day and the heat, will burn their house down. And after he does that, perhaps the master will again ask, "Isn't it appropriate for me to do what I want?"

Matthew's story seems to beg for someone, anyone, just once to respond, "No, perhaps it is not appropriate." Until someone finally responds appropriately, the abuses of power will just pile up and pile up.

Of course, the biggest abuser of power is still waiting in the wings for his big entrance. Pilate, the highest ranking Roman we will encounter in Matthew's story, stands behind all abuses of power in this narrative world. He will get his time onstage in a few chapters. He will demonstrate what abuse of power looks like when it is done by a professional. "This is what a Jewish king looks like," he will proclaim at the crucifixion. "This is what Jewish hope looks like." And then Jesus will die, having failed at delivering the revenge that messianic religion so often longs for. (This is, I think, an enduring characteristic of messianic religion, this longing for revenge, but this longing is done secretly, to prevent messianists from foaming at the mouth in public.)

At that point, Pilate could say, "You see, it doesn't matter whether what I do is 'appropriate' or not, does it? The point is that I can do it and you cannot stop me." Before you decide that the resurrection is God's answer to Pilate, remember that Matthew's audience will have heard Rome say the same thing as they crushed the First Jewish Revolt. Rome will have been right both times. What does that mean about the narrative contribution made by the raising of Jesus from the dead?

Inter-Text: The World We Think We Live In

Behind this odd little parable lies a world of power and economics too often ignored by interpreters. Jonathan Reed has given us a glimpse of this world by analyzing archaeological data available from ancient Galilee.[107] Sepphoris and Tiberius grew rapidly under Herodian sponsorship during the first century of the Common Era. Ancient cities, Reed argues, were consumer cities: they deformed existing subsistence economies and drove peasant landholders into debt and forced them to sell their land because they were ill-equipped to compete with the intruding elites who managed the money economy. The result was that powerful masters emerged and the former landholders became tenant farmers or day-laborers. The masters could indeed do whatever they wanted with their business, and the people who had lived on the land for centuries could do nothing about it. The dance of labor and life had already been twisted before this parable begins. The master continues the twisting, perhaps to the breaking point.

Just in passing, notice the roles played by debtors, day-laborers, and debt slaves in scenes in the Gospels.

Provoking the Story

Above all, play this scene so that the audience entertains the possibility that the parable is supposed to be offensive. If you play it so that the only authorized point of the story is: "God is good just like the owner of the vineyard, so shut up," everyone who owns a business, and everyone who works for a living, will file the interpretation under "Once Again, the Church Doesn't Get It." This is not the file you want biblical interpretation to land in consistently. If you are working with actors, you have an advantage. Their bodies, and especially their faces, are visible to the audience. Their reactions to the words and events become powerful and important. Be sure that you do not simply let them look greedy. Root their reaction in good business sense. If the landowner sets up an economy that does not reward hard work, he will get what he pays for. Work carefully as you explore the ways the landowner could say the line about "doing what he wants." Standard interpretation gives him a warm, baritone voice, easy to love. Give him Donald Trump's voice, or Leona Helmsley's. If you are not familiar with these characters from the American business stage, look them up online (Wikipedia has useful entries for each, for instance). Remember as you explore the scene that the actors playing the workers will be the audience's window into the meaning of the scene. Matthew's first audiences would more likely have included day-laborers than Roman landowners who had displaced Jewish subsistence farmers.

Proper 21 (26)
Matthew 21:23–32
(see translation, p. 378)

Ritual Text: The Life of the Worshiping Community

The ritual of granting and accepting authority is one that we choose to misunderstand whenever we can get away with it. Perhaps it is our vague commitment to democratic leveling of society; perhaps it is simply naïveté. We like to imagine that we believe that every person is equal to (and interchangeable with) every other person. "He puts his pants on the same way you do," we say, "one leg at a time." We say this to comfort ourselves when we face an imposing challenger, never noticing that we do not also say it when we encounter someone weaker, less imposing, less desirable. Our use of our own clichés demonstrates that we don't believe them.

It's probably good that we don't believe at least some of our rhetoric. There is a difference between someone who sacrifices his body for a football team and someone who loses a limb in combat. It does matter whether the surgeon is board certified or just well-intentioned. Some people should be leaders and some should be followers. And sometimes all bets are off. Sometimes our rituals force us to grant authority to people who ought not have it.

It is the ritual of authority that interests me the most. Authority is a dance that takes up space. Someone stands up; someone sits down. Someone bows; someone deigns to notice. Everyone learns that certain gestures have an effect even at a distance. A wave of a hand can send people scurrying. A finger pointed at a map can destroy homes and families. Because we know the ritual power of authority, we interrogate every claim carefully. And we punish pretensions to authority severely. You cannot impersonate a police officer, a physician, or an attorney and not expect to have the full weight of civil authority land squarely on your back. This, also, is part of the ritual.

Jesus and, before him, John have waved their hands, raised their voices, set the world swirling. Someone has to ask about their credentials. Not to ask would be irresponsible.

This, however, makes Jesus' answer troublesome. It is no proper answer. It appears to link Jesus' authority with that of John, and to make of them a team to be accepted or rejected. But it is just as possible to read Jesus' words about John as a dodge. John is safely dead, and the authorities no longer have to deal with him and his disruptions. But John, like anyone killed in the line of duty, has become unassailably authoritative in death. It seems likely enough that President John F. Kennedy would have tangled the nation in the Vietnam war just as deeply as did his successor, Lyndon Johnson. But President Kennedy was assassinated, not hounded from office. Dead people do not make any new mistakes, so they benefit from a reputation that polishes itself through time. There may have been many good reasons to question John, or his aims, or his tactics, or his wisdom, or his authority. But now that he was dead, it was safe enough to appreciate blandly "what he stood for." Listen to old segregationists blandly praise Martin Luther King Jr. in similar terms. Jesus' "answer" is aggressive, not responsive. There is a difference.

Intra-Text: The World of Matthew's Story

This follows immediately after the cursing of the fig tree. That means that the question about authority is not, as the pericope could lead you to believe, about the authority of Jesus' teaching and the refusal of Jewish authorities to accept that teaching. That may be a part of their concern, but the story as it is told sets up their question as a reaction to Jesus' unreasonable blasting of the fig tree, and of the Temple. The question is now much larger than is usually assumed.

Start simply. The fig tree stands there beside the road. It has leaves, but no fruit. In Mark's story, the storyteller makes it clear that it was not the season for figs, and interpreters have pointed out that the presence of leaves is the sign for this. Matthew's storyteller does not point out that this is not fig season, but may (or may not) rely on his audience to know that on their own. If it is not the season for figs, Jesus' act is irresponsible and disturbing, just the sort of thing that would lead anyone to ask to see some ID.

But even if Matthew diverges from Mark at this point, even if figs were in season, still the act is disturbing. Why are there no figs? Perhaps the tree had a bad year and bore little fruit. I lived for six years in Door County, Wisconsin, a marvelous place where tart cherries grow abundantly. A good friend of mine was an orchardman. He told me that the factors that make for a good crop of cherries come together about once in every seven years. The other six years, the harvests are smaller. Some years all the factors conspire against the tree, and the harvest is very small indeed. I imagine that the same thing could be true for fig trees. Why is Jesus blasting a fig tree because it was a bad year?

Or there could be no figs because the fruit has already been harvested. If this fig tree is part of someone's farm, it is questionable whether Jesus should have been looking to pick from it in any case. Again, my friend the orchardman tells stories of tourists who imagine that the cherry and apple trees alongside the road were planted just to enhance their fantasy vacation. Such tourists think nothing of pulling off the road and picking fruit for free. Such tourists are sometimes cranky when the orchard has already been harvested. It adds an odd spin to this scene if Jesus blasts the tree because he got there after the harvest had already been brought in.

Or maybe the tree isn't part of someone's farm. Maybe it is simply a random tree that stands alongside the road. In that case, the fruit was understood in ancient Jewish culture to be provided by God for transients and homeless people, for people who needed to glean in order to live. Jesus, perhaps, could be fit into that category, though it might be a bit of a stretch. But then it might be the case that there is no fruit on the tree because homeless people (God's intended recipients of the fruit of the tree) had picked the fruit and thanked God for the goodness of creation. Now the blasting of the tree looks even more problematical. He is resenting people who have no other source of food. That is crude, at least.

And in any case, at the end of the scene the tree will never bear fruit again. This will be a problem if someone owns the tree. It will be a bigger problem if the tree is a random tree that feeds gleaners, because such trees in any culture always dwindle in number. Listen to the arguments about public access to lakes and beaches to hear why it is hard to maintain random trees that feed the homeless.

After such a performance, someone ought to ask for credentials. What gives anyone the authority to blast a tree just because it has no fruit? And if a person has the power (and authority) to perform such a miracle, wouldn't it be a better use of that power (and authority) to bless the tree and make it marvelously fruitful? If I were at the door checking IDs, I would want to ask questions about the limits to imagination that lead to power being used only for destruction.

When the scene for this Sunday opens, Jesus is in the Temple and he is teaching. The chief priests and elders of the people ask for credentials. They could be asking for nothing more than a teaching certificate, but the audience has just seen the incident with the fig tree, so their question carries a greater impact. Jesus expands the scene even further when he stretches the frame of reference all the way back to John. This sets the scene into a rhythmic pattern seen throughout Matthew's story. Complexes of scenes in which Jesus teaches and heals are typically introduced by a scene that brings John back onto the stage (for instance, see Matthew 3, 11, and 14; note also that Matthew 16, 17, and 20 do the same thing, but substitute a Passion prediction for the reference to John). Now in this scene, Jesus is teaching, as he will be in the next chapter, and the next, and the next, and the next. Each time the swirl of teaching scenes finishes by taking a swing at authorities who do not simply accept what Jesus says. When this swirling pattern has run its course, the Passion narrative begins and Jesus is killed.

Inter-Text: The World We Think We Live In

When Jesus stretches the frame to include John, he does it, says the storyteller, because it will trip up his questioners. Customary interpretation picks up the potential humor in the behind-the-scenes dithering of the priests and elders. "On the one hand . . . ," the elders say, "but on the other hand. . . . " Back and forth they go, oscillating between being non-observant and being fearful. Finally they say, "We don't know." Quite an answer.

The comedy is worth playing and exploring. And it might be that Matthew means in particular to parody the political instinct that always checks the results of polls and focus groups before answering any question. This instinct deserves parody.

But remember as you explore this scene that the priests and elders are caught in the tightest of colonial nets. Rome was a skillful colonizer. The key to controlling a colony was (and is) to establish an organ of liaison between the colonizers and the colonized. This organ of liaison must be some group of people to whom the people at large will listen, so that when the colonizer wishes to give orders to the colonized the orders will be heard. Chief priests and elders fit this bill perfectly, and Rome had chosen them to be the organ of liaison to suit its own purposes.

But the choice of the organ of liaison is more complicated than has appeared. The colonizer is not simply concerned with the flow of information. In the end, the goal that matters most is the creation of submission among the dominated people. Nothing else matters next to this. If submission can be created by skillful manipulation of the organ of liaison, Roman swords can stay clean(er). But domination will be had, regardless. The fact that the priests were tied to the Temple thus made them the most practical choice. Because the Temple was the center of the Jewish world and of Jewish identity, it would also be the natural center for Jewish resistance to Roman domination. Colonizers thus select potential centers of resistance to be organs of liaison because this undercuts any resistance that might attempt to organize itself. If the people become accustomed to hearing Roman orders from the priests, they will learn not to trust them, and will not trust the priests if they attempt to organize resistance.

The matter goes even further. Colonizers reward the people who function as the organ of liaison, reward them handsomely. This guarantees that Rome will get a hearing from the group they intend to suborn. It also guarantees that the chosen group will fall out of favor with the people at large because they have been enriched by the colonizer. At the same time, colonizers know that this unaccustomed wealth will be addictive, and that this will further serve to guarantee that Rome will always have a mouthpiece and that popular resentment of the (newly) wealthy priests will be supported by real evidence.

When Jesus tells the story of the two sons against this colonial background, everything gets complicated. You can see why customary interpretation is glad to retreat to a world in which Roman domination vanishes from the screen. It is easier to talk about this as a story related to religious duties, easier when interpreters assume themselves to be part of the ideal audience, the audience that gets Jesus' point and takes it the right way.

But against the background of colonial domination and submission it is not so easy to be sure what one's religious duties might be. If the father is the embodiment of God in the story Jesus tells, and the sons are those who have duties to carry out, duties commanded by God, then what are those duties in a time of Roman domination? Ought observant Jews do their best to stay off the Roman radar screens? Or, since this complex of teaching is kicked off when Jesus introduces John the Purifier to the discussion, ought observant Jews be rabble-rousers like John?

The image used in the little story calls explicitly for the audience to consider this as a story about Torah observance, since the issue at hand is the sons' willingness to follow through on responsibilities they took on when commanded by the father. The rabbis tell stories in which God offers Torah to nation after nation, but gets a response only when God addresses the Jews. Torah is a gift, to be sure, but it is a gift that makes a people answerable for the way they live with the gift they have been given. In Jesus' story, the sons hear the father and respond. One accepts the burden; the other rejects it.

Perhaps this figures the reactions of the nations of the earth to the chance to take on the responsibility of Torah. This possibility would turn the story into a spur used to urge Jews to observe Torah more assiduously than is done by Gentiles who observe it by accident. Jewish faith, seen both in the rabbis and in the letters of Paul, expects that Gentiles will indeed observe Torah, if only by accident, and that this observance is pleasing to God. When the son who initially rejected his father's command finally fulfills it, the father is pleased.

Perhaps this little story figures the varying performance of different Jews to the responsibilities of Torah observance. Now the story still spurs greater observance, but the spur is applied by the observance of Jews who had been lax until John stirred them to live a Jewish life.

Both of these possibilities yield a coherent reading, but neither settles the thorniest problem: What does Torah observance demand when it comes face to face with the Roman demand for submission? Ought the rabble to be roused or quieted? Jesus, at least at this point in Matthew's story, clearly prefers the option that John chose. Rouse the rabble; pay back Empire for the slaughter of the innocent toddlers at the beginning of the story. This fits with the tone he takes when he announces that he brings a sword and division to the people. This is the tone of a perfectionist who expects Torah observance to include cutting off any part of a person or of the people that does not perfectly perform. This does not fit, however, with the tone taken by Jesus after he is raised from the dead. After the disaster of his death, he has apparently seen enough of swords. After his collapse on the cross, he seems not so interested in perfection. After God raised him, inexplicably, from death, he wraps his arms around the whole mixed community of disciples, both worshipers and doubters, and sends them all out to baptize and teach. He makes no more divisions.

Be sure to listen to all of these options in the context of Jewish faith that has seen the First Jewish Revolt fail.

Provoking the Story

If you are working with actors in your exploration of this scene (and I would strongly suggest that you do, especially for complicated scenes like this one), make sure that they understand the web that holds the priests as organ of liaison, make sure they feel the complications.

A twentieth-century point of contact might help. Consider the role played by the Judenrat, the Jewish council set up by the Nazis to manage the people who had been forced into the Nazi-created ghettoes. These people functioned as the organ of liaison for the Nazi conquerors. They managed day-to-day operations, and they were rewarded (with relative safety if nothing else). Sometimes day-to-day operations involved organizing operations to feed and house people in the ghetto. Sometimes they involved delivering people for transport to death camps. The role that was forced on the members of the Judenrat made them the focus of endless disputes. Were they Jews who were caught in a web, or were they partly willing collaborators with the Nazis? Unhelpfully, the answer is, Yes, they were both.

Play this scene so that the actors portraying the priests and elders embody the "caught-ness" of the members of the Judenrat. They must deliver peace and quiet. Their lives are forfeit if they do not. They must deliver Roman orders, even when those orders burn in their mouths. And if the people do not obey the orders delivered by the priests, Rome will kill the people as the priests watch. Now the dithering looks different. Now the audience will see the Roman sword that hangs over everyone in the scene. If the priests say that John, executed as a disturber of Empire, came from God, Rome will hear it. If the priests say that John was just one more religious crank, the people will raise an uproar, and Rome will hear this, too.

Which option would you choose?

Proper 22 (27)
Matthew 21:33–46
(see translation, p. 381)

Ritual Text: The Life of the Worshiping Community

Week after week we hear scenes about agricultural production, usually involving vineyards. If the lectionary had included all of Matthew's story, we would have had yet another vineyard scene. Now this week again we have a vineyard.

Week after week we have also heard scenes that dance with the ritual of labor. We have watched slaves laboring. We have listened as a landowner reminds day laborers that he can do anything he wants with his land and the rootless workers who depend on him. In this scene, the laborers are tenant farmers.

We misunderstand Matthew's story if we forget that the rituals of labor are different from any we customarily meet. If we imagine that the landowner in these scenes is the brother of the tenants, we miss the point. If we imagine that the landowner is the neighbor of the tenants, we ignore the reality of the story. If we forget how tenant farming came about in the ancient world, we miss the bite of the whole scene. Tenant farming arose when the economy changed and outsiders pushed hereditary landholders off the land their families had farmed since long ago. Sometimes these outsiders were "local outsiders" who saw which way the wind was blowing and threw their lot in with the colonial authorities who were building cities and collecting taxes and imposing their structures on the region. More often the outsiders were the colonizers themselves, and the tenants were the people who had formerly owned the land they now farmed for a foreigner. Imagine a French farmer who found herself obliged to send tribute to new Nazi overlords. Imagine a member of the Anishinabe nation losing the right to live on their hereditary homeland because they had not paid taxes to a conquering nation.[108]

The recognition of the ritual of domination and dispossession changes the sound of this scene. When the landowner builds his structures and leaves, Jewish audiences will hear an echo that goes back to Roman practice. When the tenants resist the landowner and kill the slaves sent to collect tribute, Jewish audiences will hear justifiable resistance to foreign domination.

Intra-Text: The World of Matthew's Story

In the previous scene, Jesus took the side of rabble-rousers who drew the wrath of Rome. In particular, he held up John the Purifier as the picture of Jewish faithfulness and made a person's response to John to be the criterion by which proper faithfulness was to be measured. His point appears to be: "Roman standards do not matter; God's do."

Now in the scene for this Sunday, he tells a story that flows in a different direction, at least once you recognize Rome behind the mask of the absentee landowner. It works, of course, to read the absentee landowner as God. This has worked for customary interpretation for centuries. On this reading, God comes to the vineyard, is rejected, and Jerusalem is destroyed in consequence. Jews are driven out and others are let in. In the most overeager versions of customary interpretation, this driving out extends beyond the expulsion of Jews from Jerusalem following the crushing of the Revolt and includes driving them out of the favor of God forever. Cardinal Michael von Faulhaber, the archbishop of Munich, drew Nazi wrath for arguing that Jews could properly be referred to as the "people of God," at least in a historical sense. But even this alleged friendly interpreter draws the line at the moment of Israel's "visitation." Then, says Faulhaber, the Jews were given a "bill of divorcement" and dismissed forever from divine favor.[109]

The customary interpretation delivers a potentially coherent reading, and this should give us pause. If the Nazis read Matthew correctly, perhaps it is time for the rest of us to read Matthew differently. But the images used in the parable are more complicated than that. If they call to mind the practices of God, they also (and equally) call to mind the practices of Empire. That would make this parable a sort of double parable and would force it to flow in two opposing directions simultaneously.

That is a real complication.

If Jesus sides with a rabble-rouser who was executed by Empire in the previous scene, this time he sides with Empire and (which is worse) brings God with him. If the penalty described at the end of the parable refers to the destruction of Jerusalem in 70 CE (and how could any Jewish audience *not* have heard it this way after the Revolt was crushed?), then God and the Romans are working the same side of the street. Jesus would not be the first prophet to point to a pagan enemy and see the judgment of God, but this parable would go further than that. The ancient prophets pointed to pagan conquerors as tools in the hand of a God who brought judgment to the chosen people. As painful as that reading of historical circumstances would be, it is nothing next to the alliance Jesus arranges in his little parable. The pagan enemy is not just a tool in God's hand; the pagan enemy is the owner of the vineyard, and the owner of the vineyard is God. Do the math. When you remove the shared middle term, God is identified with Rome, and the interests and actions of each are identical. This is a view, of course, that would have sat well with Rome, and with the enforcers of any absolutist or fascist regime. This was decidedly not the view taken by the Jewish community that suffered defeat at the hands of the Babylonians in 587 BCE. Read Psalm 137 to see how Babylon, God's tool of judgment, was viewed: "O Babylon, you devastator, happy shall they be who take your little ones and dash them against a stone."

So, which way is Matthew working this? Again, the answer is, "Yes."

Inter-Text: The World We Think We Live In

When the Hutus came for the Tutsis in Rwanda, there were Christians on both sides. By noticing this I do not mean to imply that Christian deaths are more important than other deaths. Rather, I mean to point out that the line between murderer and victim even cut through relationships that functioned like religious kinship. When the murderers belong to a foreign faith tradition and the victims belong to our faith tradition, we think that we understand the problem: the problem is Them. The problem is that They want to kill Us. And, gentle souls and good that we are, we cannot figure out why. Why do They hate Us so? Woe is Us.

But when the Hutus came for the Tutsis and killed them, there were Christians on both sides of the line, even members of the same Christian denomination. There were pastors of the same Christian denomination, pastors who knew each other well, on both sides of the line, and there were families and husbands and wives, and still the murderers did their work.

What is worse is that the murderers did their work and announced to their victims that God ordained the killing. "You must be eliminated. God no longer wants you."[110] So said one pastor in response to a plea for help.

When Matthew's story was first told in the form we have it, it was being told inside the Jewish community, because to be a Christian was to be a kind of Jew. To meet for worship and study was to meet with the Jewish community. That means that when lines are drawn between Us and Them in Matthew's story, both Us and Them are likely to be in the room when the lines are being drawn. At the least, everybody in the room knows relatives who are part of Us and relatives who are part of Them. When the line between Us and Them is marked off, the audience could hear the shiver of the sword being dragged across the stone floor.

Provoking the Story

Explore this scene by imagining that the voice telling the story of the vineyard is a Hutu voice. Imagine first how this voice sounds to Tutsis who hear this as a justification of the slaughter of eight hundred thousand Tutsis.

Next imagine how this voice sounds to Hutus who agree with its conclusions.

Now go take a shower.

Proper 23 (28)
Matthew 22:1–14
(see translation, p. 383)

Ritual Text: The Life of the Worshiping Community

The most difficult thing about playing this scene is the effort required to make sure that you are playing this scene from Matthew and not covertly playing the similar scene from Luke. In each case, there is a feast prepared. In each case, the invited guests decline to attend. In each case, the feast is filled with others who had not been invited. While this is an impressive list of similarities, the sharp differences are what matter in this scene.

In Matthew's story, this is a story about a wedding feast. In any century, and in any culture that I know anything about, this is an occasion to collect and connect community and family. In Matthew's story, the guests are summoned, notified that the preparations stand ready. But in Matthew's story when the guests decline to attend they do not have established, defensible reasons for their absence (as they do in Luke), and in Matthew's story the guests do not merely decline (as they do in Luke). In Matthew's story the first invited guests refuse to be diverted from the ordinary course of their affairs. If that is the characteristic that the decliners share, then this king has invited a strange group to the feast. If the characteristic they all share is a refusal to break with usual practice, then the behavior of the last invited guests is terrifying. They do not simply decline to attend: they rape the slaves; they murder them. If this is their customary practice from which they do not choose to deviate, then this is a strange world, with customs that are strange indeed.

Their behavior is so outrageous that the story Jesus is telling is interrupted, the slaughtered animals left hanging, while the king mounts a military campaign to destroy the guests and their city. Only after the conclusion of the campaign does the wedding resume. One might ask after the effect of the intervening slaughter on the joy of the festivities. Now the hall is full of guests, and the guests are explicitly described as being both worthless and worthy.

Intra-Text: The World of Matthew's Story

This parable opens an odd narrative world for the audience. If you stand far enough away, it is a simple little story about guests who decline an invitation to a wedding feast. Come closer, and both the guests and the host engage in ferocious acts of violence. One of the problems you will have to solve in interpreting and playing this scene is the problem created by injecting such violence into a story about a wedding and the feast attached to it. Weddings are occasions for delight. Feasts are foretastes of the culmination of all things. And Matthew cannot tell of either weddings or feasts without injecting beatings, rape, slaughter, and destruction. It makes me wonder what the food tasted like for the inhabitants of the parabolic narrative world, since in their world the feast could not proceed until a city had been razed and people slaughtered. That's got to put a strange flavor in the soup.

It makes me wonder about the son's memory of the wedding, and that of the daughter-in-law, since they will have gone through the day with the noise of the military adventure going on in the background. Probably not the happiest day of their lives, unless they are very odd people indeed.

Parables are often populated by odd people who live in odd worlds. This one is no exception. Notice, though, that this first oddity fits smoothly into one of the deepest oddities of Matthew's whole story. In the parable as in the Gospel as a whole, the narrative world is shot through with surprising violence. Some of the violence is crudely physical. Some is rhetorical. But whether toddlers are being killed, or people are being thrown into the outer darkness, always the audience is reminded that Jesus, in Matthew's story, brings a sword with him when he comes. And he uses it.

This parable fits into Matthew's larger story in another way, as well. Throughout the story, Jesus meets mixed crowds. There are faithful people in the narrative world, and there are unfaithful. There are those who strive to be perfect as God is perfect, and there are those who would never consider chopping off their hands if their hand offended them. There are sheep and there are goats, wheat and weeds, good fish and bad. In this scene, the banquet hall is filled with people, some of whom are worthy, some are not. This is not surprising since the slaves were sent out to invite any and all that they could find. Throughout Matthew's story Jesus meets mixed crowds, and when he does he points out, again and again, the fork in the road that is the main geographic feature of Matthew's narrative world. Those that are sorted onto the right fork find themselves gathered into the dominion of God. Those that are sorted onto the left fork are thrown into the outer darkness where people wail and gnash their teeth. This destination is distinctive to Matthew's story. The phrase occurs only once in all the other Gospels put together, but it occurs and recurs commonly in Matthew, some six times altogether. This scene is one of them.

So this scene fits perfectly with Matthew's narrative arc. Yes, and no. It fits with the arc at every point in the story except the most important point. It fits with everything except the end of the story, the moment that seals the story for the audience, the moment that nails the landing on the narrative arc. In his very last scene in Matthew's story, Jesus again encounters a mixed crowd. This one more mixed than others, because the storyteller explicitly tells us that some of those gathered on the mountain doubted. For the first time (and in his last scene) Jesus does not send anyone off to the outer darkness. This change alters the way we have to view the working of Matthew's narrative arc, including how this parable fits into the whole story.

Inter-Text: The World We Think We Live In

There is a man invited in off the street and he lacked a wedding garment.

Why is the man who was invited off the street and lacked a wedding garment bound hand and foot? I could convince myself that you could make a case for removing him from the hall, even for his own good, since his polyester doubleknit slacks and Hush Puppy shoes are causing giggles among the group wearing their dinner jackets. I could imagine that you could make such a case. But then escort him from the hall. Movies are filled with such moments. Julia Roberts can't quite navigate in polite society in the movie *Pretty Woman*. The audience feels bad for her. Dustin Hoffman can navigate only on his own utterly atypical terms no matter where he is in *Rain Man*. The audience roots for him as his brother learns to love him. I could make sense of escorting the guy without a wedding garment from the hall. But why bind him hand and foot? And beyond that, when he is thrown out the door, why does he land in the outer darkness? Why does the story suddenly warp from the banquet hall above the Elks Lodge to an apocalyptic location in another dimension? How are the slaves to find their way to the "outer darkness" while toting this poor schlump who doesn't own a tuxedo? If they were to stop to ask directions to the "outer darkness," which gas station is likely to be at all helpful to them? This is taking on all the features of science fiction, or perhaps the *Twilight Zone*. I'm waiting for Jesus to morph into Rod Serling and finish the episode for us. Maybe that's what he is doing at the end of the parable.

Provoking the Story

You might play the scene as a *Twilight Zone* episode. In any case, you will need to invent a way to play the scene that makes room for all of the insistent oddities, all the twists and surprises. It might be interesting to make Jesus into Rod Serling as he tells the story.

Proper 24 (29)
Matthew 22:15–22

(see translation, p. 384)

Ritual Text: The Life of the Worshiping Community

The boundary between Us and Them is carefully defended. In order to be safe, it is crucial that everyone be able to tell who is one of Us, and who is one of Them. There is a basic divide between Us and Them in Matthew's story, and it shows up in this scene: anyone to whom we must pay tribute is one of Them. Caesar is the chief representative of Them in this scene, and the issue of paying tribute was a painful reminder that being Jewish in the Roman Empire meant that you belonged to a conquered people.

The Pharisees in this scene are testing Jesus to see whether he knows how to keep to his people's side of the Us/Them boundary with Rome. This is an important test, one that you see often among communities that have been conquered. The particular test is complicated. If Jesus says that Jews ought not pay tribute, most people would agree with his ideals, but not with his sense of what is practical. Rome was not amused by refusals, especially when colonial submission was involved. But, on the other hand, if Jesus gives a practical answer, if Jesus submits to Roman tribute, it will cost him politically.

This is an old political ritual. American politicians regularly ask their opponents impossible questions in front of crowds in order to embarrass them. "If someone assaulted your daughter," they ask, "would you believe in the death penalty then?" "If you are so supportive of the military," they ask, "why did you take advantage of your father's influence to get a cushy state-side posting?" It is a game, a ritual. It is a trap, hidden in the bushes along the boundary between Us and Them.

Intra-Text: The World of Matthew's Story

There is a surprise in this scene, however, an Us/Them surprise. The Pharisees are seeking to trap Jesus. That is perhaps no longer a surprise. They have concluded that Jesus is dangerous trouble. The Pharisees are observant, resistant Jews. They live to maintain Jewish integrity even under Roman domination. Such a tenuous situation, however, requires being careful to pick only those fights you really want. Jesus is drawing unwelcome attention, and they give him a chance to fail publicly, a chance even to draw the fire of Rome. So far, no surprise.

The surprise comes when the Pharisees send their students to Jesus with a group of Herodians. The Pharisees would have had little use for the Herodians. The Pharisees resisted Empire; the Herodians benefited from it. The Pharisees argued, in Jesus' century and later, that Herod wasn't even properly Jewish, so how could he be king of the Jews? The Herodians asked calmly which side of this dispute had wealth and access to military power. Henry Kissinger famously said that power was the ultimate aphrodisiac. The Herodians, in their own way, said the same thing. Power provided the only evidence of religious observance that mattered.

And now the Pharisees send their students to Jesus in the company of Herodians. Why? It is possible that we are looking at hypocritical Pharisees who are not so observant and resistant as they might first appear. This, of course, would fit into the customary playing of this scene. The customary playing is too easy.

What if the Pharisees are, in fact, sending their students in disguise? What if the crowd of Herodians is the set-up? Now the test is doubled and tripled. The make-believe Herodians approach Jesus. They begin by buttering him up: "Teacher, we know that you are honest. . . . " One of the most important moments in anyone's life comes right after you have been complimented by someone with power. Integrity melts at such moments, and long-suppressed dreams suddenly awake. "Teacher," say the Pharisees disguised as possessors of power, "we know you are honest." And then they wait to see just how honest Jesus actually is. Will this be enough to get him salivating? If so, they will have learned everything they needed to know about him, and the crowds will have learned it, too. This is the first test.

There is another test going on at the same time. "You do not glance into people's faces," say the Pharisees in disguise. This creates an interesting moment. Say this line to someone, just as it is written. In my experience, people look down, look anywhere but back in your face. It is an interesting phenomenon. If Jesus does what most people do, if he looks down or away, he will not see through the disguise. And if he cannot see through the disguise, he will prove, in front of the crowds no less, that he is unable to tell the difference between Pharisees and Herodians. Such tests are common with outsiders who are pretending to know things that they obviously do not know. Town kids are sent out to milk the Herefords. And when they can't tell the difference, everyone laughs. This is also the way con men set up their patsies. Set up the situation so that ordinary people surrender their ordinary judgment lest they be thought unsophisticated. Can Jesus tell a Hereford from a Holstein? This is the second test.

And the third test is the most obvious one of all. "Herodians" ask Jesus whether they can be observant Jews while paying tribute. Any answer he gives will box him in. Any answer he refuses to give will set him up to be called a waffler.

Inter-Text: The World We Think We Live In

Jesus' eyes are better than they thought. He sees the pretenders and calls them actors, role players. He asks them for a coin. Commentators have noted helpfully that his question will scare hypocrisy out into the open. If they have a coin in their pocket, a coin with a graven image on it, they are revealed as non-observant despite all their protestations. This is helpful. It is worth noting, however, that it is not clear that the Pharisees have the coin in their own pockets at this point. The scene is even more delicious if they do not. Jesus makes a simple request: Give me a coin. That implies that he does not carry such blasphemous coinage in his own pockets. What if the Pharisees also do not have a coin, but have to ask the Herodians for help. Suddenly the difference between Herodian and "Herodian" comes clear. "Role players!" Jesus says. "You didn't even get the costuming right. A Herodian carries blasphemous coins. You should know that."

Now the observance of the ritual border between Us and Them gets sticky. Jesus divides between Caesar and God, and, I imagine, the crowd parts like the Red Sea, Herodians to this side, and "Herodians" to that. The whole point of the Pharisees' test is demonstrated. The line between Us and Them does indeed matter. The issue is not settled by inflexible ideals, neither is it dismissed by calling on cynical practicality. Real human beings are really caught in the political tangles of real life, but not so caught that they cannot distinguish between God and Caesar. The Pharisees and Jesus both know this. Jesus demonstrates that they largely agree. This was the real test. The Pharisees abandon him. Like him or not, agree with him or not, he will not be caught in colonial traps. His mama didn't raise no fool.

Provoking the Story

Human beings love to believe that there are two sides to everything. On the one hand, this is good because it saves us from imagining (all the time) that our opinion is the only possible one. It also allows us to think about catastrophic situations in which it is crucial that we decide which side we are on.

But our love of bipolar oppositions is also a great weakness of ours. There are not two sides to every question; there are fives sides for simple things and thirteen (at least) for complex things. The scene at hand has (at least) three sides. Jesus does get a side to himself, if only because the people he encounters are all trying to test him. But the people administering the test represent at least two more sides: the Pharisees and the Herodians. Jesus has scrapped with the Pharisees, but the scraps are the sort one has with people who are worth a good argument. The Herodians, on the other hand, are new to the narrative. But they bear the name of Herod. They are associated with the political descendents of the king who slaughtered all of Jesus' contemporary cousins.

There are also probably a few other groups that would show up if you looked closely at the crowd in this scene. There will be the Herodians and the play-acting Pharisees who are trying to look like Herodians. There will be the Herodians who are fooled by the Pharisees and those who are not. There will be Pharisees who are in on the joke, and there will be some who are not, and these two groups will watch the play-acting with different sorts of interest.

When you explore this scene, try to find and embody as many different sides as you can. When you finally play the scene, you may very well want to simplify things back down to three sides, but you need to know which three sides will matter most.

Proper 25 (30)
Matthew 22:34–46
(see translation, p. 387)

Ritual Text: The Life of the Worshiping Community

Customary interpretation plays this scene as the final battle in the war against Jesus. The Pharisees take their best shot and it misfires. Jesus fires back, and no one bothers to reload. It can work that way. But this reading ignores the ritual of argument that is going on here. The Pharisees are trying Jesus; they are testing him. Why? According to Matthew's storyteller, it was because they heard that he had poked a hole in the basic Sadducean argument about life, death, and resurrection. Jesus cites a passage from Jewish scripture that can be read to imply that somehow Abraham, Isaac, and Jacob stand simultaneously before God, which would be impossible if there were no resurrection and death were a dead end. It does not matter whether readers in our century are impressed with the cogency of his argument. The Pharisees are presented as being impressed. So they ask him a basic question, one that anybody with any Jewish education at all should be able to answer. Jesus apparently has a Jewish education. He can answer.

The question is too easy, as can be seen from the completeness of Jesus' answer. It is a good answer, but the first question in a rattling good argument ought to start a longer flurry of back-and-forth questions, probing for the contradictions to be had in too-easy questions. The question is too easy, and the Torah expert is left with no way to follow up on Jesus' response. In the awkward silence that followed this too-easy question, Jesus asks one of his own, one that is not at all easy. It is a question that might have been predicted, though, if you pay attention to the premise of the argument he used against the Sadducees. His argument with the Sadducees presupposes that in death, all bets are off. Basic relationships, even so basic as marriage, are altered in the presence of God (that's the point of his remark about being "like angels"; see Matthew 22:30). All generations are alike in being alive to God. Fathers and sons stand before God in the same generation and on the same footing. So what is to be made of David and his son who will bring all things to completion? All bets are off. Is the promise of God in the past or in the future? Yes. Is David the model for, or just one subject of, the ruler that will restore all things? Yes. All bets are off, and too-easy answers go the way of too-easy questions.

Nobody dares to ask him questions after that. No kidding.

Intra-Text: The World of Matthew's Story

This is the last time anyone asks questions of Jesus. Part of the tragedy of the story is carried in that short sentence. Interpreters sometimes imagine, along with adolescents worldwide, that everything would be better if They (whoever They might be) would just stop questioning everything I do. Adolescents imagine this because so much of what they do is questionable. Interpreters are led to this imagining by a theology that places God beyond question, and sometimes places Jesus beyond God. Leaders of organizations, whether companies or countries, who create a community that never questions their authority are headed for a fall. I have a colleague at Augustana College who came to teaching out of a distinguished career in banking. He says that one of the first lessons of leadership is this: If you and I agree on everything, one of us is unnecessary. Questioning is how disagreements become positive and productive, and a wise leader cultivates colleagues who will ask hard questions.

And now Jesus will no longer be questioned.

This is part of Matthew's tragedy because questions are a sign of respectful engagement, especially in a Jewish narrative world. This is crucial to understanding the story even though the Pharisees are figured in Matthew's story as listening to Jesus' answers and disliking them. This is crucial because they are figured in Matthew's story as asking worthy questions, questions that any leader would want someone to ask. "Should your teacher be eating with traitors who collaborate with Rome?" ask the Pharisees (Matthew 9:11). "Is it wise to trust an exorcist who eats with collaborators?" they ask. "Might he not just be in league with both Rome and the demons?" (Matthew 9:34). "Shabbat gives us a glimpse of a world turned right-side-up," they say. "Should you be teaching your disciples to disregard it?" (Matthew 12:2). "Show us your credentials," they demand (Matthew 12:38, 16:1). "Why are you not teaching your disciples to live like Jews?" (Matthew 15:2). "Aren't there some grounds that would justify divorce?" (Matthew 19:2). The questions swirl around the central issues of what it means to live an observant life under Roman domination. The disciples of John the Purifier are figured as asking similar questions (Matthew 9:14). Questioning each other is a gift that good colleagues give gladly, and in the scene assigned for this Sunday that questioning ends. This is part of the tragedy.

Another part of the tragedy can be seen in the next chapter of Matthew's story. Jesus turns to talk about the now silent Pharisees. It turns out that he has not valued their questions. He calls them pretenders and pronounces woes on them. The evidence he cites is important. When he begins, he points out the dodge that is necessary for showy strictness. Perfectionism only works if the perfectionist can, by sleight of hand, keep the audience's attention on the imperfection of others. At the outset, Jesus points to all the little dodges that allow perfectionists to bind heavy burdens and place them on other people's shoulders. "Don't seek honor," he urges, "but humility." So far, so good. He goes on to point out the compromises that perfectionists must make: an oath is to be avoided, and so an oath consists in using this set of words but not that set of words. "An oath is not an oath unless you say x, y, or z," he says. It is easy (and probably important) to make fun of such tap dancing. But then he goes on to draw the conclusion that this outward gleam of perfection must conceal bones and corpses and desperate impurity. This conclusion is telling. Only a perfectionist could make this leap. The woes that Jesus pronounces are predicated on the assumption of inner filth. Matthew has opened a curtain here, and the view is disturbing. And now the questioning ends.

Inter-Text: The World We Think We Live In

This scene is set up by a question asked of Jesus by the Sadducees in an earlier scene, a question that pokes at the logical, ethical, and social complications that would be created if the dead were to be raised. Notice two things. First, though the questioner pushes the matter to the extreme (a common feature in such questions in any century), the question is a good one. Images of the culmination of all things (both popular and biblical) include scenes of gathering and feasting, which are commonly taken to imply that we will join with those people with whom we have gathered and feasted throughout the only life we have known up to this point. If a child asks whether she will recognize her parents in heaven, the parents that I know have always said "Yes." And for good cause.

Second, notice that, though the Sadducees question is logical enough, Jesus simply rejects it out of hand. "You don't know the scriptures and you don't know the power of God," he says. "Learn

something about those basic matters and maybe I'll talk to you."
His answer at this point reveals the same structure of thought detected by Jacob Jervell in the book of Acts: without belief in the resurrection of the dead there is no authentic Jewish faith.[111]

The scene at hand begins with the Pharisees also noticing this. They see that Jesus has muzzled the Sadducees, and they are pleased. Though Matthew often places the Pharisees together as opponents of Jesus, the historical situation was more complicated than that, and this scene opens a window on that complication. The Pharisees hear that Jesus has stuck it to the Sadducees, and a Torah expert asks Jesus a basic Do-You-Have-A-Clue-About-Being-Jewish? question. The question is indeed too easy, but it is a respectful question. Jesus clearly has a clue about being a Jew.

This interchange puts Jesus on the Pharisees' side of several important debates within Jewish life. He affirms the resurrection of the dead, he expects moral seriousness, and he rejects Roman domination. So did the Pharisees. The Sadducees read Torah strictly and saw resurrection as a later cultural contamination. They are likely to have been as morally serious as anybody else,[112] but they had been chosen as the organ of liaison by Rome and rewarded for their efforts. Such people will always be suspected of all sorts of moral turpitude. It is a consequence of having been put in between the colonizers and the colonized. Because they came to represent the voice of Roman domination, they could not be figured as rejecting Rome. Because they could not be figured as rejecting Rome, they will not be presented as morally serious. And so a fault line in Jewish life ran between the Pharisees and the Sadducees.

And Jesus is recognized in this scene as landing on the Pharisees' side of this divide.

Provoking the Story

Find a different reason, a new reason, why people did not dare ask Jesus questions after this scene. Customary interpretation all the way back to the ancient world has supposed that they were silenced because they had been "totally confounded in their conversations" because they were plotters, not honest questioners.[113] Matthew's story will support such a reading, but as is often the case in Matthew, it will support other, quite different, readings as well. Find a new reason. Begin by noticing that the question asked by a Torah expert is not a trick question. If earlier questioning was designed to trap Jesus, this question reads more like a basic school question, an invitation to dance and think together.

If you begin there, why do people stop questioning Jesus when this scene is completed?

All Saints' Day
Matthew 5:1–12
(see translation, p. 291)

Ritual Text: The Life of the Worshiping Community

See the discussion for the Fourth Sunday after Epiphany. This text resurfaces for this day because All Saints is a day to remember the gifts given by all sorts of saints, some meek, some peacemakers, some anything but. All Saints is also a day to remember those for whom we are mourning, those who have died since last we celebrated All Saints' Day. American culture is so rigidly informal that we work mightily to lose anything that might be a helpful ritual, especially around heavily ritualized transformations like mourning. This makes All Saints' Day even more important than it has been in the history of the ritual life of the community of faith. This scene is tight with complications and contradictions. The mourners in your community will be listening to hear whether you recognize the complications or not. If you appear to imagine that it is natural and normal that mourners be called "Godlike in happiness" because they will be comforted (the traditional translation and reading), the mourners are likely to conclude that you are too inexperienced to be worth much, and they will nod and smile at you and wait for you to grow up.

If the mourners hear that you understand the tight tension that goes with pronouncing blessing on those who have lost the world they had always lived in, at least until death destroyed it, they may well conclude that you know a thing or two about the reality of loss, and about the odd things that happen to texts about resurrection when you have lost someone you needed.

Intra-Text: The World of Matthew's Story

See the discussion for the Fourth Sunday after Epiphany above on page 93.

If the mourners in your community hear you promise that they will be "called as witnesses" (the experimental translation that I am working with for παρακληθησονται), some of them in particular will have things that call for testimony in whatever court will hear the case. Remember that Jesus in Matthew's story also has things that should be heard in court, but it will have to be a court that can pronounce judgment on Empire, particularly in the person of Herod, who killed all Jesus' contemporary cousins. Remember, Jesus is a mourner in this Gospel, which might be why some people have linked him with Jeremiah.

Inter-Text: The World We Think We Live In

See the discussion for the Fourth Sunday after Epiphany.

Remember that Matthew's first audience would also have plenty to mourn about. They lived in the aftermath of the crushing of the Jewish Revolt against Rome. Even if the audience did not lose family members in the disaster, they lost the Temple and Jerusalem, and they lost the sense that resistance to Rome would turn out well for people who were faithful. That is a lot to lose.

Provoking the Story

See the discussion for the Fourth Sunday after Epiphany.

This might be the time to gather a team of players to work with you, even if all you do together is read the scene for the congregation. Select old people, people with depth and experience, people who know and show a thing or two about peacemaking and mourning, people who have learned (even painfully) the dangers that go with meekness. Practice reading and working together so that you find a way to show these hard-won discoveries to the audience.

Proper 26 (31)
Matthew 23:1–12
(see translation, p. 388)

Ritual Text: The Life of the Worshiping Community

If you want to know what a person believes, watch his feet, not his mouth. This basic criterion I was handed as a gift by Murray Haar, a friend and colleague, a teacher of mine. It is a good principle. Jesus hands his audience the same principle, only he intensifies it. The Pharisees are correct, he says. Listen to them, take them seriously. Do what they instruct you to do. But then actually do it. This is often taken to imply that the Pharisees were all talk and no action, or, as Molly Ivins says when she describes people who want to be Texans but aren't, all hat and no cattle. If you read it this way, this scene opens the door to rather customary scraps with Pharisees and, by implication and sermonic application, with religious leaders of every time and every place. And this scene flows directly into the next scene (omitted from the Revised Common Lectionary), which is both customary and disturbing at the same time: Woe to you, scribes and Pharisees, hypocrites.

Do not leap into the customary; you will arrive there soon enough in any case. Wait here a moment and notice that Jesus has just told his listeners that the Pharisees are correct. Let me repeat that: the Pharisees are correct. When the Pharisees say that Jews are always in the Temple, and should act accordingly, they are right. When the Pharisees judge that gifts of joyfulness should be given to God, not just out of wages, but also out of mint and dill and cumin, follow their advice. When the Pharisees look at Jesus and demand something substantial in return for the title *mishiakh,* trust their instincts. We will get to more customary urgings (customary at least for Christians) shortly. Linger here with this surprise.

Intra-Text: The World of Matthew's Story

The scene for this Sunday is cut off just at the end of the practical advice, which is to say it is cut just before the beginning of the woes. The beginning of this chapter of Matthew's story is remarkable because, as we have seen, Jesus acknowledges that the Pharisees are right. Throughout the story, they have asked questions. Throughout the story, they have shown concern for proper observance of Torah. In their last encounter with Jesus, the Pharisees (in the person of a Torah expert) ask Jesus to focus all of Torah observance in one commandment. The answer Jesus gives is the answer that is given also by rabbis through the centuries. Jesus' answer shows that he has a Jewish education, which matters if you are Jewish, and he is. Now Jesus grants the rightness of the teaching of the Pharisees. He approves of their teaching, but he does not approve of their practice.

In the part of the scene excluded from the assigned pericope, Jesus accuses the Pharisees of play-acting. This charge rings back to the time some Pharisees disguised themselves as "Herodians" and tried to trip Jesus up. Jesus caught them and seems to have taken this posing as a revelation of their true character. To be sure, the experience of watching Pharisees pretend to be collaborators with the Herodians (and with Rome) will have been one to remember, particularly for a person who barely escaped from their attack as a little kid, a person who will have grown up noticing again and again the holes in his family caused by Herod and his allies and masters. It will have cut him to see observant and resistant Jews pretending to have sold out. Imagine hearing your rabbi say, "Heil Hitler." Jesus calls the Pharisees role players, and blasts them for what he sees as shallow observance. On the one hand, everyone needs a good stirring now and again. On the other hand, Jesus stirs them and shakes them, and then goes on to attribute the worst motives possible to everything they do. He calls them whitewashed tombs. This attack merits attention. He is using good appearance itself as if it were evidence of nefarious motives. This is a regular characteristic of the boundary between Us and Them. When one of Them looks good, it is, by definition, evidence that she is shallow, or conniving, or manipulative. As I write this, George W. Bush is the president of the United States. Supporters talk about how he always has a happy smile on his face. Opponents are struck by his smirk. The previous president, Bill Clinton, was admired by his supporters for his ability to outmaneuver political opponents who tried to take cheap shots at him. His opponents called him "Slick Willie." The line between Us and Them is always drawn like this. To make real-world sense of this scene you have to notice that Jesus is doing exactly this. This matters because interpretation with integrity takes the reality of the real world very seriously.

Inter-Text: The World We Think We Live In

In Albert Camus' *The Plague*, a city is locked in the grip of the plague for endless months. The storyteller opens the gates of the city to us, his audience, and gives us glimpses of life in a time of plague. More than that, he gives us close views of people who live and find their way in a time of plague. We see a criminal who begins by attempting suicide. When the attempt is thwarted, he commits himself to serving the cause of life by fighting the plague, free from the law until the gates are again opened to the police and his past. We meet a man who saw his father argue in court for the execution of a criminal and was disgusted by the experience. In his flight from his father, he even became a revolutionary and found himself ordering and participating in executions of his own. Out of this experience, he came to call himself a "plague-bearer." He had come to realize, he said, that we all carry the plague and so we must all fight the plague, though "plague" has come to mean something much larger than anything that can be seen in a hospital or under a microscope. "All I maintain is that on this earth there are pestilences and there are victims, and it's up to us, so far as possible, not to join forces with the pestilences," he says.[114]

And there is a priest who begins his time in the locked city by announcing a rather customary message of judgment on the city, judgment from God. He says,

> "If today the plague is in your midst, that is because the hour has struck for taking thought. The just man need have no fear, but the evildoer has good cause to tremble. For plague is the flail of God and the world His threshing-floor, and implacably He will thresh out His harvest until the wheat is separated from the chaff. There will be more chaff than wheat, few chosen of the many called."[115]

The sermon goes on from there. It may sound a bit like things one hears in parts of Matthew, perhaps because it *is* a bit like things one hears in parts of Matthew.

Later in the story he preaches another sermon, this time to a much emptier church. The plague has increased people's desire for superstitious religious practices and decreased their willingness to sit still and wait for tradition (and traditional practices) to deliver what they promise. That is regrettable, because the second sermon is wiser than the first. For one thing, the long shared confinement in the city has broken down the priest's Olympian perch. He no longer addresses the people from a distance, from above, as "you." In his second sermon, he speaks, Camus notes, not of "you" but of "we."[116] This time he confronts the brutal durability of the plague. "Religion in a time of plague," he says, "could not be the religion of every day."[117] I wish at this point that the priest would listen to the character who has discovered that we are all plague-bearers, which makes the distinction between everyday life and the time of plague less easy to make, but still this new sermon is better than the old one. The priest talks about what it means to witness the senseless death of a child, to witness the death and be unable to do anything to help, to witness the death and recognize that perhaps all that medical intervention has given to the child is a longer time to suffer on the way to a senseless death.

Such a death, the priest argues, does not teach us resignation, nor does it inculcate that complicated virtue, humility. Such a death, says the priest, hands to us something far more difficult: it hands us humiliation.

This is what is in my ears when I hear Jesus speak of humbling and exalting in the scene for this Sunday. Matthew's story is being told (for its first audience, anyway) in a time and place where people were forced to confront the reality of the destruction that followed the First Jewish Revolt. This surely would have been true for Jews who lived near to the action, in the occupied land of promise. But it will also have been true for Jews who lived nowhere near the scenes of destruction because one of the casualties in that disaster was the notion that God should, would, and could intervene to turn the world right-side-up. That is the promise-value of the name "messiah." That is the spur that drove people out into the wilderness to hear John. That is the deep hope that had funded Jewish resistance to Antiochus IV and to oppressors before and after him.

Matthew's audience had watched that hope die in the eyes of a child they could not protect. They knew the humiliation that the priest knows.

Provoking the Story

Understand carefully the shot that Jesus takes at the Pharisees in this scene. Remember that he tells his followers to do what the Pharisees tell them to do, and remember that this includes tithing on the tiniest matters and carrying the heavy burdens that go with religious observance.

As you explore what it means to remember this injunction, play the scene at least two ways. Play it with a Jesus who becomes a stricter taskmaster than the Pharisees could ever be, because he not only binds heavy burdens on the people, but demands that they do them. But play it also from another angle. In the aftermath of any disaster, one thing that allows people to go on living until they can return to life is the performance of the ordinary little things that life is made of, the little rituals that may not mean much, perhaps, but provide a way to continue living. The details of Torah observance will have provided such little rituals for Jews trying to go on living after the disaster. You might play both Jesus and the Pharisees as people who were trying to get their feet back on the ground so that they could go on living. "Do what the Pharisees say," says Jesus. "It will help you figure out which way is up."

Proper 27 (32)
Matthew 25:1–13
(see translation, p. 401)

Ritual Text: The Life of the Worshiping Community

Before you play this parable, back off from it to a distance of at least twenty paces. Look this thing over carefully before you approach it. It is a story about people waiting for the bridegroom to arrive for a wedding feast, and as such, it may be a story about a common clan-and-community celebration. Whether the middle-of-the-night arrival would have been customary or not, interpreters disagree.

This is a story about the ritual involved when young, unmarried women attend a wedding. If this is a multi-clan gathering, then it is not just the celebration of the making of one marriage alliance between clans, but it is also the occasion for young, unmarried men to encounter young, unmarried women who belong to a clan with which their families might agree to have them begin marriage negotiations.

If this is a story about a meeting between clans who have a future interest in intermarriage, then this is a scene in which the young women have a huge interest in being noticed favorably. Folktales about such meetings are filled with competition between women placed in such situations. This competition may help explain the odd actions of the young women. Some had extra oil, some had none. The arrival was delayed. No one thought to extinguish all the lamps but one, and thus preserve the shared store of oil. When the bridegroom and his company arrived (along with the young, eligible men), the women who had oil refused to share with those who had none. This, by the way, violates the instructions that Jesus gives elsewhere for how participants in the dominion of God should treat each other: if anyone begs from you, give.

It may be worth noting that all of the company in this scene nodded off while they waited. When they awoke, some had oil, and some had none. But note that Jesus does not conclude this parable about competition for marriage partners by advising people not to be morons but to bring extra oil. Instead, he advises people not to fall asleep in the first place. How would this ritual change if no one had fallen asleep?

Intra-Text: The World of Matthew's Story

Half of the virgins were prudent. Half were morons. This transla-tion may have surprised you. Usually the first group is translated as "wise," and this works well enough, though "wisdom" usually extends to matters more complex than having enough oil on hand. What "wise" gives you, though, is an easy contrasting translation. If five are wise, the others (easily enough) must be foolish. "Foolish" is a gentle enough word, a silly word that touches everything from a demonstrated lack of ability to an implied dizziness that lends easy comedy to the scene, at least until the "foolish" virgins are locked out because they are not recognized. How were the others recog-nized? Perhaps it was simply because they were mixed in with the whole waiting crowd, in which case one of the secondary points of this parable is that you ought always to make arrangements to stay in the middle of the crowd.

Customary translations soften the impact of the words in the Greek. The virgins were not "wise" (σοφος), a word that would imply intellectual rigor, piercing insight, and a certain philosophi-cal distance from everyday distractions. The parable does not deny any of this to the virgins with enough oil, it simply attributes to them something else. These virgins, says the parable, are φρονιμος. This word implies a well-honed ability to navigate in the real world, making the best of the quick decisions that end up guiding a surprisingly large chunk of a person's life. They were, as I translate it, "prudent." There is a certain wisdom to prudence, but it is a useful and practical wisdom. This is why they had thought about the possibility that the bridegroom might be delayed and what that would mean, given the average rate of oil consumption in the type of lamp they were planning to bring. As a result of this hard and practical calculating, they brought enough oil.

The other virgins, the parable tells us, were morons. This word, μοραι, could well be translated as "foolish" if it were not the root of the English word "moron." The word carries, in Greek and in English, a sharp bite that "foolish" doesn't touch. It does not imply a happy little silliness that comes along with "foolish" in English. It is a harsher word, both in sound and in meaning. I take it as a first rule of translation that one ought always catch harshness when it is in the original. There is too much "making nice" in the practice of translating religious texts.

But what will we do with Matthew's Jesus calling some of these virgins morons? It is a good question, not one to be solved by finding a softer, kinder synonym that we can substitute. In Matthew's story, Jesus is often gentle and wonderfully kind. And he also can be remarkably harsh. He looks at the lilies of the field and sees God providing beauty for free. And he urges his followers to pluck out their eye if it should scandalize them. He calls all the weary and overloaded people in the world to come to him because his yoke is serviceable and his burden light. And then he tells his followers that they must be perfect as God is perfect. No matter how many times Jesus comforts or heals or welcomes in Matthew's story, still it is in Matthew that he casts people into the outer darkness, and he does so repeatedly.[118] The usual interpretive tendency, and not just in sermons, is to select the gentle kindness and claim it as the leading motif in the story, and then to translate and interpret the harsh moments out of existence. Such an approach disrespects the story that Matthew is telling. Worse, such an approach distrusts the story that Matthew is telling, and distrusts it so deeply that it presumes to rewrite his story into a form that is judged to be more palatable to our audiences. In the process, we make ourselves unable to read, play, and hear the story that Matthew is actually telling. And we pick up this inability to read, play, or hear the story because we want to be unable to read the story as Matthew tells it.

"The Jesus I know would never say such a thing!" So said a young woman in a course I was teaching when she encountered Jesus' dying words in Matthew's story. I hear the same assertion rather frequently when ideologues (on the left or on the right) encounter a word of Jesus that they think might give aid and comfort to their treasonous opponents. Ann Coulter, that highly paid purveyor of ugly attacks, has even labeled those people of faith who espouse liberal views "godless." Presumably she would include Jesus in this scurrilous attack, at least if he were found to have urged giving freely to the poor or to have said that riches make it difficult to enter the dominion of God. (Oh, wait, he did say such things. Oops.)

Matthew paints a harsh Jesus, a Jesus who emerges from his childhood damaged by Herod's attack. Matthew paints a Jesus who is an absolutist, a Jesus who sends his opponents to the outer darkness. More important, Matthew paints a Jesus who changes, but this change makes no sense unless interpreters and translators respect and preserve the biting harshness.

Of course, if it is important to preserve this harshness, then audience members ought to be rewarded for wondering why none of the virgins, prudent or moronic, thought to solve their shared problem by leaving only one lamp lit and sharing the available stock of oil. Audience members are to be encouraged to notice that perhaps no one would have had a problem at all if the bridegroom had not been late. When he subsequently high-handedly refuses to admit them to the feast, he is punishing them for his late arrival.

Even if I am wrong about the bite of Matthew's whole story (this is always possible), we will not discover a better reading by ignoring those parts of the story that give us hives.

Inter-Text: The World We Think We Live In

> We have been taught that Rabbi Menahem son of Rabbi Yose
> expounded the verse "The commandment is a lamp and the
> Torah is light" (Proverbs 6:23) as follows: scripture associates
> a commandment with a lamp and the Torah with light. A com-
> mandment is compared to a lamp in order to tell you that as
> a lamp gives light for a short time, so the performance of a
> commandment gives protection only for a short time. But the
> Torah is compared to light itself, in order to tell you that as
> light always illumines the world, so the study of Torah always
> brings enlightenment to the world (*B. Sotah* 21a).[119]

On this (albeit later) model, all the virgins have the commandments, but only the prudent virgins engage in study of Torah. The
morons, perhaps because they believe that they will always have time
to run quick and begin to study Torah, are caught short. Because
this interpretation springs directly from a straightforward reading
of Proverbs 6:23, it is more than possible that the first audience,
and Jesus himself, would have heard a story about studying Torah
and how it makes one ready to celebrate the wedding feast when it
is time.

The surprise in the scene, then, would be that women are expected
to study Torah.

Provoking the Story

Where did the moronic virgins get oil in the middle of the night?
There would be no shops open. Perhaps they had some at home
that they could retrieve, but their whole families would likely be at
the wedding feast, so who would accompany them home and let
them in?

And while you are at it, why did the bridegroom refuse them
entry?

Proper 28 (33)
Matthew 25:14–30

(see translation, p. 402)

Ritual Text: The Life of the Worshiping Community

We meet here a master. We meet here some slaves. Whatever else this scene is, it is a dance between master and slave. Such dances have several essential characteristics, the most important of which is the absolute power differential between master and slave. This is not a dance between employer and employee. Though some conditions of employment may approach slavery, there remains a difference. Employees can leave and not be subject to community-sanctioned hunting. Employees own something. However little and poorly made it might be, still they own it and it is theirs and the community will support them in defending it. Slaves cannot leave without permission and they cannot own anything. They are themselves property.

Some years ago, Robert William Fogel and Stanley L. Engerman caused an earthquake with their study of the material conditions of race-based slavery in the American South. The book, *Time on the Cross: The Economics of American Negro Slavery,* noted that careful study of historical records indicated that slaves on plantations where records were diligently kept ate about as well, and were clothed about as well, as low-wage workers in factories in New England. The earthquake was enormous,[120] and understandable. Readers heard in the book a defense of race-based slavery, heard echoes of the vile justification of slavery offered by "good massas" all over the South: I take better care of my slaves than they could take of themselves; if I were not so magnanimous, they would be living like animals in Africa. Such obscenely racist statements must always make Americans nervous: they come out of our history and we are only a century and a half from the days when the institution of slavery still existed. Missing, perhaps, in the earthquake of reaction, however, was a recognition that slavery was not wrong because human beings were economically deprived. Slavery *is* wrong

265

because human beings are properly free, and any social system that denies this freedom is an offense against creation and creation's God.

This is a scene about a master who has full freedom of movement and vast wealth. His leftover possessions, so trifling that he entrusts them to slaves, amount to 144 years of a laborer's wages, more than a common family would earn in seven generations. My own family records extend barely that far into the past, but I have no real understanding of what life was like for anyone more than four generations back even in my own family. The total expenditure of seven generations of working people is for me impossible to imagine. And this is just his leftover wealth. And he gives this leftover wealth, impossible to imagine in its excess, to people who do not, and cannot, own anything.

At this point, resist any sermonic/theological judgment about the absolute fealty humans owe to God ("the earth is the Lord's, and the fullness thereof," etc.). Resist the temptation to make of slavery a metaphor. Notice the offense. "You were faithful in your tending of a trifling little bit of money," says the master when discussing 144 years of a worker's wage. This master makes Donald Trump look like Mr. Rogers.

Intra-Text: The World of Matthew's Story

Jesus concludes this scene by throwing the "useless slave" into the darkness where there is wailing and gnashing of teeth. This is the last time anyone is thrown into darkness until Jesus is thrown there at the crucifixion. As the door is opened to throw the "useless slave" out, the wailing and gnashing of teeth that the audience hears is the last until Jesus screams on the cross and accuses God of abandoning him. In Matthew's story, Jesus recognizes abandonment when he experiences it because he has pronounced it so many times on those who did not measure up.

This scene in the middle of Matthew 25 is part of a swirl of scenes that sweeps Jesus out to Bethany and then back into Jerusalem and then into Pilate's presence and then onto the cross. Three chapters ago, Jesus was engaged in arguments with people who listened to him. The arguments were sometimes respectful, sometimes not. Sometimes the arguments mostly involved tripping and shoving. But he was still arguing, and arguing about the heart of Torah and human responsibility. These are activities that bind him to the whole of continuing Jewish history. But in Matthew 23, everything changed. Jesus began a pointed critique of the scribes and the Pharisees. He did not criticize them for being too strict and inflexible, but for being strict and inflexible only in their words. They make strong demands when it comes to Torah observance. In that regard, Jesus commends them and tells his audience to listen to them and to do what they are told. But they do not do what they teach others to do, says Jesus, and for this the scribes and the Pharisees are condemned. The tempo and volume of his attack increase until in the end he sounds very like John sounded in the wilderness at the beginning of the story. "Snakes," he calls them, "snakes and people fathered by poisonous snakes." This is vintage John. There is not a lot of gentleness to be had. Morons, he calls them, moronic and blind, and then he blames them and all Jerusalem for the deaths of prophets.

Matthew 24 continues the swirl to the end of the story. As the chapter begins, Jesus and his disciples go out from the Temple and the disciples are pointing out the buildings, the improvements. Jesus still dripping with sweat from his rant inside the Temple responds by promising the destruction of the Temple and the disordering of human life. Again he promises sharp and severe divisions. Some will be spared, some will be taken, perhaps by the invading Roman army that comes to destroy the city. All should flee before the siege starts and traps them in the city. He tells a story that ends with wailing and gnashing of teeth; he tells another that pushes out young women who went too late to buy oil for their lamps (calling them morons in the process). After the scene for this Sunday there is only one more scene before Jesus is pulled out into the river and swept off to Pilate and death.

All of this swirling activity spins the scene for this Sunday. The darkness at the end echoes the darkness seen repeatedly in Matthew's story when those who do not measure up are cast out. The harsh judgment on the slave who preserved his master's property against his return foreshadows the obscenity of the crucifixion. Both are possible because the master in each case can do whatever he wants, whenever he wants. Both punishments function as object lessons about the abuse of power. "Take from him the talent," Jesus says. "Those who have will have too much, and those who do not have will have everything stripped from them." The slave is thrown into darkness where people despair. The slave is probably lucky. Had he appeared in the next scene he would have been thrown into the eternal fire. Be thankful for small favors.

It is possible that this parable would sound different if it were found at a different point in Matthew's story. It is possible that you could read it as an exhortation to make the most of your talents before you lose them if you found the parable somewhere else in the story.

But the story shows up in this scene, as a part of this larger swirl to death, and that changes everything. Jesus blasts the Temple, built and improved by Herod, the slaughterer of all his cousins. And Jesus is being swept toward Pilate and a Roman execution, one of thousands of executions by crucifixion in the experience of Matthew's audience. Being swept up in that swirl forces a focus on the master and his wealth and his abuse of power. What master has that kind of wealth and power? Rome and only Rome. The added note about the indefinite absence of the master brings to mind Rome's military absence after the opening outbreak of the First Jewish Revolt against Rome. Rome found itself drawn away by military exigencies and left the rebels in a position to solidify their advantages and, according to some students of the period, secure the success of the Revolt. They did not make good use of the time and Rome returned and crushed them.

Inter-Text: The World We Think We Live In

Any attempt to play this scene will encounter lots of company. This scene has been played and interpreted, interpreted and applied, applied and spread throughout Western culture. How deep does this little parable go into our culture? The word for the unit of money given to each slave is ταλαντον. This word comes straight into English as "talent," which is a simple transliteration of the Greek word. The English word "talent," which refers to abilities or knacks or gifts (musically talented and musically gifted can mean the same thing), comes directly from this parable.[121] So says no less an authority than the *Oxford English Dictionary.* In English, at any rate, we cannot talk about abilities without being drawn into the playing, interpreting, and applying of this little parable. You will encounter lots of company.

Most of the company will be repeating interpretations that are what you already expect: This is a story about developing your talents, sometimes called "God-given" talents. This line of interpretation has been widely and wonderfully successful and useful. The story helps us see (using the eyes provided by the narrative) that it takes risk and investment to develop talent. Nothing grows if it is buried in the ground. Well, seeds grow if they are buried, but that is a different parable, a different interpretive paradigm. If you hide your talent away, you will never have more than potential, and (as the saying goes) when people say that you have potential, it only means that you haven't done a blasted thing yet.

I would like to introduce you to another interpretation of the terms of this parable. It is not only Jesus and the entire English-speaking world that talks about what you should do with talents given to you by a master. The Talmud also talks about what subordinates should do if a master entrusts them with significant cash. "Take no risks," says the Talmud. "Bury it in the ground." Why? Because the power differential makes it unsafe and unwise to do anything else. The master owns slaves. The slaves do the work; the master collects the gain. When the master turns over such a large amount of money to people who do not even own themselves, the slaves are under no obligation to put their lives and families and futures at risk. That is, perhaps, how the slave ran up such an impossibly large debt in the parable in Matthew 18:23–35. A slave does not have access to such a fantastic amount of money unless a master has put him in charge of it. The slave in Matthew 18 is scheduled to be sold, along with his wife and children, perhaps because when he invested the money handed to him the markets went sour. The Talmud recognizes such situations, and recognizes the abuse of power present in them, and advises that a person put in such danger would do well to bury the money to keep it safe.

This is not bad advice. The English-speaking world knows what you should do with the talents you have been given. The Talmud knows what you should do when a master, who puts you and your family in unnecessary danger. When you play this scene, spend some time getting to know this new companion in interpretation.

Provoking the Story

Consider this possibility.

Perhaps the slave who buried the money is the only slave who thought that the master was going to return. In the story the master goes away without saying for how long or under what circumstances. The parable has him return "after much time." The implication is that the absence was extensive. What if the first two invested the money because they thought that the money was theirs? Imagine the scene. Suddenly one day the master returns. This is a rather nasty surprise. The first two slaves had grown accustomed to wealth and realized that they had misunderstood things rather badly. The third slave had always expected such a day, and probably even remembered where he had buried the money (at least after a little nervous head-scratching). The first two gather together everything they can find and deliver it to the master who is presented in the story as harsh and inclined to profit at others' expense. Imagine their relief when the master is pleased. The third servant delivers his cache to the master, glad that he, at least, had prepared for exactly this day. Imagine his reaction.

Now consider something else. After the initial phase (quite successful) of the First Jewish Revolt against Rome, Rome went away. Its legions and attention were needed elsewhere in the Empire. Historians argue that had the rebels managed to consolidate their gains during the Roman absence they might have been able to achieve at least a provisional kind of independence. That is not what happened. The various rebel groups, perhaps assuming that the Roman threat was past and gone, began to scramble for control. Defenses were not improved, armies were not strengthened, but if Rome is never coming back then who needs armies? The rebels proceeded as if the city of Jerusalem were theirs to do with what they pleased. Then Rome returned and called them to account. The end result was the destruction of Jerusalem and the Temple, and the loss of many, many Jewish lives.

For Matthew's first audience, any story about an absent master who returns will have reminded them of Rome's return to destroy Jerusalem. Rome was indeed a hard master, harvesting what it did not plant and gathering the spoils of war to itself. The Arch of Titus in Rome shows a large menorah being carried into Rome. The menorah was plundered from Jerusalem when the Temple was destroyed in 70 CE. Can you play this scene so that the master is Rome?

Christ the King — Proper 29 (34)
Matthew 25:31–46
(see translation, p. 405)

Ritual Text: The Life of the Worshiping Community

Rituals of separation must be understood carefully. The end result of this ritual is clear enough: punishing for some and eternal life for others. The clear result at the end can lead one to expect that the

271

principle of separation is also similarly clear. This is a good place to pause and consider the scene.

What is the actual difference between the two groups? Of course, one group fed the son of adam when he was hungry, clothed him when he was naked, looked in on him when he was weak or in prison, and the other did not. This is simple enough, simple enough that sermonic interpretation proceeds to enjoin listeners to look for the face of Jesus in the hungry, naked, and imprisoned. At that point, sentimental sociology enters, and well-meaning Christians discover, often to their embarrassing surprise, their shared humanity, shared with the hungry, naked, and incarcerated. This shared humanity is taken, sermonically, to be the face of Jesus that we are commanded to see everywhere. This is not bad. One could do much worse. But before leaping to this interpretive conclusion, notice that these two groups who are separated from each other in this ritual share a single common trait: neither sees the face of Jesus anywhere. And, on the fair chance that the "son of adam" does not refer to Jesus, neither group sees the face of the "son of adam" anywhere, either. Their behavior is different, but their perceptions are the same. If the point of the scene is to command Christians to hunt everywhere for the face of Jesus, listeners have no model in the story for how to do this. If anything, they have a model for how not to do it.

This last notion will require a little exploration, but the exploration may reveal an essential difference between these separated groups. Both groups say, "When did we see you . . . ?" The words of the last group, however, play best if they imagine ahead of time that they ought to be looking for the face of Jesus and are surprised that they could have missed it. They seem to think that their flaw lay in faulty perception. The words of the first group, however, play differently. They seem surprised that they were supposed to be looking for the "son of adam" anywhere. The scene plays best if the first group thinks, initially, that they have failed the test because they were supposed to see the face of Jesus everywhere, and they missed it every time. The scene plays best if, after this initial surprise, the first group reacts by writing off the whole test as irrelevant.

What if this is the real difference between the two groups? On this model, the second group looked everywhere for the face of Jesus and saw him a lot, and discovered shared humanity in the deserving poor, discovered it repeatedly. The first group never looked for anything of the sort; in fact, they find the whole suggestion that they should have spent their lives looking for the face of Jesus to be a waste of time. They fed people because they were hungry, not because they were deserving. They clothed people because they were naked, not because they were unjustly deprived of their dignity. They visited people because they were sick, and they called on people because they were in prison, knowing that most of those in prison earned their way in and needed to be confined for the safety of those outside the walls.

The difference between the sheep and the goats in this story is not a matter of seeing the face of Jesus, but of visiting people and taking care of them.

Intra-Text: The World of Matthew's Story

There is a translational decision to be made in this scene. The "son of adam" is clear enough, as is the "throne of glory." What is not so clear is who exactly is gathered in front of his throne. The Greek says that it was παντα το εθνη. This phrase is usually translated as "all the nations," which makes this a scene of universal judgment at the culmination of all things. Such scenes are commonly part of Christian imagining of what the "end of the world" entails, and as such they set before all humanity a standard of performance that is expected to be met.

But the phrase could also be translated as I have translated it: "all the Gentiles." The word εθνη translates the Hebrew word *goyim*, and even that word could refer either to every nation that is not Israel, or every nation including Israel.

So which is it to be?

To my eye, either translation fits into Matthew's narrative arc. If the judgment is directed at every nation, all humanity, then Jesus is continuing his practice of making either/or distinctions. Either you are a sheep or you are a goat; either you inherit the dominion of God or you go into the eternal fire. Jesus has made such rigorous divisions from the beginning of the story, and here as before the criterion is based on behavior.

If, on the other hand, the judgment is only for the Gentiles, still Jesus is winnowing the chaff from the wheat, separating the worthy from the worthless, and still the criterion is based on behavior.

What is noteworthy is that the criterion is not "belief in Jesus," whatever that might exactly mean. The criterion is not membership in the Christian community, however that might have been accomplished. The criterion is not stated in any of the terms applied to discipleship either inside Matthew's story or outside. The criterion is simply the treatment one accords to other human beings.

I translate it as "all the Gentiles" because that provides an echo back to the Slaughter of the Innocents, the attack by the forces of the Empire on Bethlehem in an attempt to kill the king of the Jews, no more than a toddler at the time. Yes, the attack was carried out on the orders of Herod, the king of the Jews, and yes, Herod considered himself (with some three generations of established right) to be Jewish, but Herod held his post and acted out his role at the pleasure of the Roman overlords. And Herod's claim to be Jewish was rejected by ancient rabbis, partly because of the tangled background of his family's conversion, and partly because he was Herod, the violent king who ruled much as any pagan ruler under Roman domination, killing his own children and offending Jewish sensibility repeatedly. Even his building and elaborating on the Temple in Jerusalem was a source of controversy. The Temple was beautiful, but it could be viewed as a monument to Herod's Hellenistic rule even by those who loved it as the Temple of God placed at the center of the world. Jesus shows evidence in Matthew's story that he shares the view of later rabbis. When his disciples comment on the numerous improvements that have been made to the Temple, Jesus promised demolition for all of it. It is customary (and surely correct, at least in part) to read this promise as a prophecy *post eventu* (a promise of events the storyteller has already seen happen), but the identification of the improvements as the focus of attention makes it necessary to consider whether Jesus in Matthew's story might not have had cause to disapprove of the improvements made to the Temple by the man who killed all Jesus' cousins.

There are lots of "ifs" hanging around this scene, but a few things hold no matter how the phrase is translated. Jesus continues to divide his audience into the worthy and the worthless. The division, now as always, is sharp and absolute and permanent. This time it includes fire, but this is not new or unusual in Matthew's story. And the operating criterion is behavior. One could read this as an example of what Jesus (and the rabbis) say constitutes Torah observance: Love your neighbor as yourself, though the omission of the first half of that summary (love the Lord your God) would surprise both Jesus and the rabbis. One could also read it as a kind of summary of what is required of Gentiles (who do not have the Lord as their God). Though the instances cited do not deal with most of what is specified in the (later) Noachide laws[122] (for instance, there is no mention of idolatry or blasphemy), still the examples could be taken to embody the spirit of those laws. In either reading, the omissions are striking: there is no mention of loving God, and there is no mention of following Jesus.

Inter-Text: The World We Think We Live In

In this scene, sheep are divided from goats. Matthew's story has so many stories of dividing that one becomes accustomed to reading them. This is just one more. The pastoral imagery makes it seem calm and quiet. One of the goats lets out a bleat and the sheep jostle against each other. You can hear the little lambs baa-ing.

Remember that at the end of this scene the goats are not simply taken to a different pasture. At the end of this scene, the goats are burned in an eternal fire.

But the criterion for separation is sound and wise and functions to encourage responding directly to human need with no thought beyond the fact that a human needs your response. There is no sectarian special pleading, no arcane requirements of any sort, just the expectation that moments of random encounter with people in need are moments illuminated by eternity. But at the end of the scene the light from eternity is provided by the burning goats, and the goats are people.

After Auschwitz, the notion of burning people is not a metaphor. It was not a metaphor before Auschwitz, either, truth be told.

Remember the offense of this scene before you play it, before you interpret it, before you read it. Get as clear as you can what the exact offense is. Someone will ask whether it isn't God's perfect right, and even responsibility, to make judgments, especially on a criterion such as is used here. Someone will ask whether it isn't part of proper theology to leave such judgments to God. Someone will ask whether it isn't part of a proper fear of God to recognize that God is free to save and even to damn as God chooses, particularly when God works with such an obviously good and just criterion as response to human need.

But someone ought also to ask what it does to a human being to tell the story of this saving and damning. This applies to anyone who will tell the story of this scene today. There are only human mouths available to do that telling, and someone ought to ask about the human cost of taking this saving and damning into an actual human mouth. To play this scene you will need to put a human being in the midst of a crowd of people (whether the crowd is on the stage or only in the language, the effect is the same) and hand that person the task of dividing the crowd into those that will be burned and those that will not be burned. If we are to imagine that this scene aims to narrate something like universal final judgment (whether for Gentiles or for all humanity), the crowd of people to be divided will include people of all sorts who have had a whole life to establish a tendency to respond or not respond, to support each other or not to. But the crowd will also include old grandmothers holding the hands of little children who are hoping to go to the park. And the human being with the task of making deadly divisions will have to separate some children from some grandmothers to do the job that has been assigned. At such moments we typically spin up a quick theology that either grinds all humanity down into a loathsome slurry of desperate evil deserving nothing but death,[123] or exhausts itself in imagining that the glories of heaven will make the pain of separation between child and grandmother recede into the eternal distance.

And someone ought to ask what it would take for a human being to be able to walk calmly through the crowd of people and make simple decisions, simple as sheep from goats, about who burns and who does not. Do you know anyone who would be glad to make such decisions? Do you trust them? Would you trust them with your children?

I am not arguing that God ought not to recognize evildoers, or that we ought to pretend that doing evil does not matter. Far from it. I am only saying that to play this scene you have to imagine what it would take for a person to send people to be burned, and what it would do to any human being to imagine a moment in which she might have to make such a decision. Burning people is not a metaphor. When you stir such an image into a human imagination, it leaves marks.

Provoking the Story

And before you play this scene, or interpret it or read it, someone ought to notice that the person making the divisions in the scene is not God, it is the "son of adam." The phrase "son of adam" is, by ancient Aramaic convention, a way of referring to oneself obliquely. Sometimes it is a way of referring to all human beings abstractly. In the scene at hand, the speaker is Jesus, so if he is referring to himself he is (by continuing custom of Trinitarian theology) referring to God. Perhaps this means that all our worrying over the effect and meaning of these lines in a human mouth was for nothing. Perhaps Jesus is so thoroughly God in this little scene that he doesn't share human limitations.

But such a dodging solution forgets that ancient Christians rejected any theology that separated or diminished the human reality of Jesus. And Jesus himself rejects the dodge when he identifies the divider in the story as the "son of adam," a member of humanity, a human, one person. So the question has to be asked, not only about the person telling the story but also about Jesus himself: What does it do to a person to say these words, and what do you have to do to someone to make these words come out of her mouth?

Matthew provides a backstory for Jesus that forces these words out of his mouth. If he is judging the Gentiles, he is judging the people who killed all his cousins and drove him and his family out of their ancestral home. Play this scene interwoven with snippets from the Slaughter of the Innocents from the beginning of Matthew's story. If Jesus is judging all humanity, play this scene and interweave snippets from refugee stories of all kinds and centuries.

But make sure that you see what it costs a human being to say these words. Make sure you see what marks they leave.

You might also play this scene, at least in workshop, using an exercise that I suggested earlier. Since the scene involves sheep and goats, work with actors who can clearly be divided into two groups, distinguished perhaps by costume, age, or gender. But do not identify which of the groups is the sheep or which is the goats. Leave that matter up in the air.

THE GOSPEL OF MATTHEW TRANSLATED

Chapter One

¹Book of the birthing of Jesus Messiah
   son of David
     son of Abraham.
²Abraham fathered Isaac
Isaac fathered Jacob
Jacob fathered Judah
   And his brothers
³Judah fathered Perez and Zerah
   out of Tamar
Perez fathered Hezron
Hezron fathered Aram
⁴Aram fathered Aminadab
Aminadab fathered Nashon
Nashon fathered Salmon
⁵Salmon fathered Boaz
   out of Rahab
Boaz fathered Obed
   out of Ruth
Obed fathered Jesse
⁶Jesse fathered David
   the king.

David fathered Solomon
  out of the wife of Uriah
[7]Solomon fathered Rehoboam
Rehoboam fathered Abijah
Abijah fathered Asaph
[8]Asaph fathered Jehoshaphat
Jehoshaphat fathered Joram
Joram fathered Uzziah
[9]Uzziah fathered Jotham
Jotham fathered Ahaz
Ahaz fathered Hezekiah
[10]Hezekiah fathered Manasseh
Manasseh fathered Amos
Amos fathered Josiah
[11]Josiah fathered Jechoniah
  and his brothers
  at the time of the Babylonian deportation.

[12]After the Babylonian deportation,
Jechoniah fathered Salathiel
Salathiel fathered Zerubbabel
[13]Zerubbabel fathered Abiud
Abiud fathered Eliakim
Eliakim fathered Azor
[14]Azor fathered Zadok
Zadok fathered Achim
Achim fathered Eliud
[15]Eliud fathered Eleazar
Eleazar fathered Matthan
Matthan fathered Jacob
[16]Jacob fathered Joseph
  the man of Maria
  out of whom was fathered
    Jesus
    the one spoken of as Messiah.

17Therefore all the generations from Abraham up to David:
  fourteen generations.
And from David up to the Babylonian deportation:
  fourteen generations.
And from the Babylonian deportation up to the Messiah:
  fourteen generations.

18The birthing of Jesus the Messiah was this way:
  After his mother was promised in marriage to Joseph,
    before they came together
      she was found having a baby in her belly
        out of a holy breath.
19Joseph,
  her man,
  being strict and not wanting to expose her publicly,
chose secretly to divorce her.
20After he had planned this,
  look
    a messenger of haShem[124]
      in a dream
      appeared to him,
  he said:
    Joseph,
      Son of David,
    do not be afraid to take Mary, your wife:
      The thing fathered in her
        out of a breath
      is from the holy one.
      21She will give birth to a son
      and you will call his name Jesus,
        for he will rescue his people from their sins.
      22This whole thing has happened
      in order that it might be fulfilled,
        the word spoken by haShem,
          through the prophet

who said:

²³Look the virgin will have a baby in her belly
and she will give birth to a son
and they will call his name
Emmanuel
which is, translated, God is with us.

²⁴When Joseph got up from sleep
he did as it was ordered him
by the messenger of haShem.
He took his wife.
²⁵He did not know her
up until she gave birth to a son.
He called his name Jesus.

Chapter Two

¹When Jesus was born
in Bethlehem of Judea
in the days of Herod
the King,
look
Magi from the East arrived in Jerusalem;
²they said:
Where is the one who was born King of the Judeans?
For we saw his star in the East
And we came to worship him.

³After the King, Herod, heard this
he was shaken
and all Jerusalem with him.
⁴After he gathered all the high priests
and scribes of the people
he inquired from them
where the Messiah is born.
⁵They said to him:
In Bethlehem of the Judeans
For thus it stands written through the prophet:

⁶You, Bethlehem, land of Judea

you are not least among the leaders of Judea,

for out of you will come one who leads,

one who will shepherd my people, Israel.

⁷Then Herod,

after secretly calling the Magi,

learned exactly from them the time when the star appeared.

⁸After he sent them into Bethlehem

he said:

After you go, inquire exactly about the child.

As soon as you find him,

report to me,

so that even I might go and worship him.

⁹After they heard the king they traveled.

Look:

the star,

the one they saw in the East,

it led before them

up until,

as they came,

it stationed itself over where the child was.

¹⁰After they saw the star,

they rejoiced a joy exceedingly great.

¹¹After they came into the house,

they saw the child

with Mary his mother

and

falling

they worshiped him.

After they opened their treasuries they brought to him gifts:

gold and frankincense and myrrh.

¹²Because they were warned in a dream not to return to Herod,

by another road they departed into their own region.

¹³After they departed,

look

a messenger of haShem appeared
>> in a dream
to Joseph.
He said:
>> Get up,
>> take the child,
>>> and his mother,
>> and flee into Egypt
>> and be there until I should speak to you.
>>> For Herod is about to seek the child
>>> in order to kill him.

14He got up;
took the child and his mother during the night
and departed into Egypt,
15and he was there until the end of Herod,
>> in order that the word might be fulfilled,
>> the word from haShem,
>> the word through the prophet,
>> which says:
>>> Out of Egypt I called my son.

16Then Herod saw that he was ridiculed by the Magi.
He was furious.
He sent;
he killed all the children in Bethlehem
>> and in all her region,
all the children from two years old and down,
>> according to the time which he had discovered from the Magi.

17Then was fulfilled the word through Jeremiah the prophet
>>>> which says:
>> **18**A voice in Ramah is heard,
>>> wailing and great mourning,
>> Rachel shrieking for her children,
>>> and she will not be comforted:
>> they are not.

19After the end of Herod,

look,
    a messenger of haShem appears in a dream to Joseph in Egypt,
    he says:
        ²⁰Get up,
        take the child and his mother
        and go into the land,
          Israel:
        They are dead,
          those who were seeking the life of the child.
    ²¹He got up
    and took the child and his mother
    and went into the land, Israel.
    ²²But after he heard that Archelaus was ruling over Judea
        instead of his father Herod,
    he was afraid to go there.
    After he was informed in a dream,
    he departed into the area of Galilee,
    ²³he came
    he made his home in a city called Nazareth.
        Thus was fulfilled the word through the prophets:
          He will be called Nazarene.

Chapter Three

¹In those days
    there arrives
        John the Purifier.
        He arrives preaching in the wilderness of Judea;
        he arrives saying:
          ²Change
          for the dominion of God is so near.
    ³For this is the one spoken
        through Isaiah the prophet who said:
          A voice bellows in the wilderness:
            Prepare the road of haShem;
            Make straight his paths.

⁴This same John customarily had his garment from camel hair
  and a leather belt around his hips;
his food was grasshoppers
  and honey from the field.
⁵Then there came out to him
  Jerusalem
  and all Judea
  and all the region surrounding the Jordan
⁶and they were purified
  in the Jordan river
    by him
      while they confessed their sins.
⁷When he saw many of the Pharisees and Sadducees
  coming to be purified
he said to them:
  People fathered by poisonous snakes:
  who warned you to flee from the erupting wrath?
    ⁸Make fruit therefore worthy of change.
  ⁹And don't presume to say to yourselves:
    A Father we have:
      Abraham.
  I say to you:
      God is able from these rocks
      to raise children to Abraham.
        ¹⁰Already the axe to the roots of the trees is laid.
          Every tree not bearing fruit
            good fruit
          is cut down
          and into the fire it is thrown.
        ¹¹I purify you in water
          to change you.
        The one coming after me is stronger than I;
          of him I am not worthy to carry his sandals.
        He himself will purify you
          in holy breath and in fire.

¹²His winnowing shovel is in his hand.

He will purify his threshing floor.

He will gather his grain into the bin.

The chaff he will incinerate in unquenchable fire.

¹³Then arrives Jesus

from Galilee

to the Jordan

to John

in order to be purified by him.

¹⁴John was trying to prevent him;

he said:

I have need by you to be purified

and you are coming to me?

¹⁵Jesus answered;

he said to him:

Let it happen now.

For thus it is proper

for us to fill up all strictness.

Then he let it happen.

¹⁶After Jesus was purified,

BANG

he came up out of the water

Look:

The heavens were opened;

he saw a breath of God

coming down like a pigeon,

coming upon him.

¹⁷Look:

A voice out of the heavens

She¹²⁵ said:

This is my son

the beloved

in whom I am well-pleased.

Chapter Four

¹Then Jesus was driven up into the wilderness
  by the breath
to be tested
  by the prosecutor.
²After he fasted forty days and forty nights
  he was hungry.
³The tester came;
  he said to him:
    since a son you are,
      a son of God,
    speak in order that these stones
      become loaves of bread.
⁴Jesus answered;
  he said:
    It stands written:
      Not on bread only lives a human being
      But on all words coming out
      through the mouth of God.
⁵Then he takes him,
  the prosecutor does,
into the holy city;
  he stood him on the highest place at the Temple.
⁶He says to him:
  Since a son you are,
    a son of God,
  throw yourself down;
    for it stands written:
      "To his messengers he commands
        concerning you,"
    And
      "On their hands they will lift you
      that you never strike your foot against a stone."
⁷Jesus kept saying to him:

Again it stands written:
    "Do not try haShem
      your God."
8Again he takes him,
    the prosecutor does,
into a very high mountain.
He shows him
    all the dominions of the beautiful world
      and all the glory of them.
9He said to him:
    These to you,
    these all I will give,
      if after you fall you worship me.
10Then he says to him,
Jesus does:
    Take it to court,[126] haSatan,
      For it stands written:
        "haShem your God will you worship
        and him only you will serve."
11Then he released him,
    the prosecutor did.
    Look:
      messengers coming to him,
      messengers deaconing to him.
12After he heard
    that John was handed over,
he departed into Galilee.
13After abandoning Nazareth,
he came and lived in Capernaum by the sea
    in the region of Zebulun and Naphtali,
      14in order that it should be fulfilled,
    the word spoken
      through Isaiah the prophet
        saying:

¹⁵"Land of Zebulun and Naphtali,
Road of the sea,
Area of Jordan,
Galilee of the Gentiles
¹⁶the people that sits in darkness
light it sees, great light.
And to those sitting in a region
and shadow of death,
light dawns on them.

¹⁷From then Jesus began to proclaim and to say:
Change,
for the dominion of the heavens is so close.
¹⁸As he walked along beside the sea of Galilee
he saw two brothers:
Simon,
the one called Peter,
and Andrew
his brother.
They were throwing their casting net into the sea
(They fished for a living.)
¹⁹He says to them:
Come after me
and I will make you fish for people
²⁰Right away
they abandoned their nets;
they followed him.
²¹After they went forward from there
he saw two other brothers
James,
the son of Zebedee,
and John
his brother.
They were in the boat
with Zebedee
their father.

They were mending their nets.
He called them;
    22right away
  they abandoned the boat
    and their father.
  They followed him.
23He went around in the whole of Galilee
  teaching in their synagogues,
    proclaiming the good news of the dominion,
  healing every illness
    and every softness in the people.
24His fame went out
  into the whole of Syria.
They brought to him all those in a bad way
  oppressed with various illnesses
    and torments
    demonized
    moonstruck lunatics
    paralytics.
He healed them.
25They followed him,
  crowds,
  great crowds,
      from Galilee
      and the Decapolis
      and Jerusalem
      and Judea
      and the region of the Jordan.

Chapter Five

1Because he saw the crowds,
  he went up into the mountain.
After he sat down,
  his disciples came to him.
2He opened his mouth;

he taught them;
he says:
　　³Godlike in their happiness,
　　　　the poor in breath:
　　　　　　theirs is the dominion of the heavens.
　　⁴Godlike in their happiness,
　　　　the mourners:
　　　　　　they will be called as witnesses.
　　⁵Godlike in happiness,
　　　　the gentle ones:
　　　　　　they will inherit the earth.
　　⁶Godlike in happiness,
　　　　the hungry ones,
　　　　the thirsty ones,
　　　　　　hungry and thirsty for strictness:
　　　　　　　　they will be sated.
　　⁷Godlike in happiness,
　　　　the merciful ones:
　　　　　　they will receive mercy.
　　⁸Godlike in happiness,
　　　　the purified in mind:[127]
　　　　　　they will see God.
　　⁹Godlike in happiness,
　　　　those making peace:
　　　　　　sons[128] of God they will be called.
　　¹⁰Godlike in happiness
　　　those who have been hunted
　　　on account of strictness:
　　　　　theirs is the dominion of the heavens.
　　¹¹Godlike in happiness
　　　you are
　　　　whenever they reproach you
　　　　and hunt
　　　　and speak all evil against you
　　　　　lying on account of me.

¹²Rejoice and rejoice exceedingly:
  your reward is great in the heavens
    for thus they hunted the prophets before you.
¹³You are the salt of the earth;
  if ever the salt were made tasteless
  by what means would it be salted?
    It is capable of serving no purpose still
      except to be thrown out and trampled by people.
¹⁴You are the light of the beautiful world.
  It is not possible to hide a city sitting on a mountain.
    ¹⁵They don't light a lamp
    and place it under a bucket,
  but on a lampstand
    and it lights all those in the house.
    ¹⁶Thus let your light shine before people
  so that they should see your beautiful works
    and glorify your father in the heavens.
¹⁷Do not suppose that I came to tear down the Torah
  or the prophets.
I did not come to tear down,
  but to observe it fully,
¹⁸for Amen I am saying to you:
  up until the heaven should come to an end
    and the earth,
  not one iota or one horn of the Torah
  will ever come to an end
    up until all these things happen.
    ¹⁹Whoever loosens one of these commandments,
      even one of the smallest ones,
        and teaches thus to people,
  smallest will be called
    in the dominion of the heavens.
  Whoever observes and teaches
    this one will be called great
      in the dominion of the heavens,

²⁰for I am saying to you:

    unless your strict observance

    exceeds beyond that of the scribes

       and the Pharisees,

    never will you enter the dominion of the heavens.

²¹You heard that it was said to the old ones:

    "Do not murder;

    whoever murders will be caught in judgment."

²²I say to you:

    everyone who is furious with his sister or brother

    will be caught in judgment;

    whoever should say to his sister or brother:

       Idiot!

    will be caught in the Sanhedrin;

    whoever should say:

       Moron!

    will be caught into Gehenna of fire.

²³Therefore if ever you are bringing your gift on the altar

    and there you remember that

       your sister or brother has something against you,

²⁴abandon there your gift

    before the altar;

go first,

    be reconciled with your sister or brother,

then come,

then offer your gift.

²⁵Be kind to your opponent in court;

    do it quickly

    when you are with him in the road,

so that he won't hand you over to the judge,

    and the judge to the helper,

and you be thrown into prison.

²⁶Amen I am saying to you:

    You will not get out of there

       up until you hand over your last penny.

²⁷You heard that it was said:
"Do not commit adultery."
²⁸I am saying to you:
Everyone who glances at a woman
to lust for her
already has committed adultery in his plans.
²⁹If your right eye scandalizes you,
tear it out and throw it from you,
for it is profitable to you
that one of your members be destroyed
and your whole body not be thrown into Gehenna.
³⁰If your right hand scandalizes you,
cut it off and throw it from you,
for it is profitable to you
that one of your members be destroyed
and your whole body not go away into Gehenna.
³¹It was said:
"Whoever releases his wife
give her a written notice of divorce."
³²I, however, say to you all:
Everyone who releases his wife
(except because of a report of fornication)
makes her commit adultery.
And whoever marries a released woman
commits adultery.
³³Again you heard that it was said to the old ones:
"Do not swear falsely;
you will give to haShem your oaths."
³⁴I, however, say to you all:
Do not swear at all,
neither by heaven,
because the throne it is the throne of God;
³⁵neither by the earth,
because the footstool it is,
the footstool of his feet;

neither by Jerusalem,
>because the city it is the city of the great king;

36neither by your head shall you swear,
>because you are not able
>to make one hair white or black.

37Let your word be yes
>if you mean yes

no
>if you mean no;

that which goes beyond this is from the worthless one.

38You heard that it was said:
>"An eye for an eye
>and a tooth for a tooth."

39I, however, say to you:
>Do not stand against the worthless one
>But who slaps you on your right cheek
>>turn to him also the other.

40To the one who wants
>to be brought to trial with you
>>to take your undershirt
>>>let go to him also your outer clothing.

41Whoever presses you into service one mile,
>lead on with him two.

42To the one who asks you, give.

The one who wants to be lent money from you,
>do not turn him away.

43You heard that it was said:
>"Love your neighbor;

Hate your enemy."

44I, however, say to you all:
>Love your enemies.

Pray for those that hurt you.
>>**45**Thus you will become children of your father,
>>>your father in the heavens,
>>because his sun he rises

on the worthless
and the worthy.
It rains on the strictly observant
and on the unjust.
46If ever you love the ones that love you,
what reward do you have?
Don't even tax collecting traitors[129] do that?
47If ever you greet your sisters or brothers only,
what extra are you doing?
Don't even Gentiles do that?
48You all be perfect,
as your father
your heavenly father
is perfect.

Chapter Six

1Devote yourself
that your strict observance
you not do in front of people
in order to be seen by them.
If they see you
you will not have a reward
with your father,
your father in the heavens.
2Whenever you do acts of mercy,
don't trumpet before yourself
as the role players do
in the synagogues
and in the alleys
so that they might be honored by people.
Amen I say to you:
They have their full reward.
3When you do acts of mercy,
don't let your left hand know
what your right hand is doing

⁴so that your act of mercy will be in secret.
  Your father
    the one who sees in secret,
    he will pay you back.
⁵Whenever you pray,
  don't be like the role players,
    because they love
        in synagogues
        and on the corners of wide streets
    to stand and pray
        so that they will be seen by people.
  Amen I say to you all:
    They have their full reward.
⁶You, however, whenever you pray,
  go into your storehouse;
  lock the door.
  Pray to your father,
    your father who is in secret.
      Your father,
        your father who sees in secret,
      he will pay you back.
⁷When you all pray,
  do not babble
    the way Gentiles do.
      They imagine that
      by their talking a lot
      they will be heard.
⁸Do not be like them.
  He knows,
    God does,
    God your father knows
  what all you need
    before you ask him.
⁹So pray like this:

Father
    Our father
    Our father in the heavens
Be consecrated!
    your name.
10Come!
    your dominion.
Happen!
    your will:
        as in heaven,
        also on earth.
11Our bread for tomorrow,
    give to us today.
12Let go for us our obligations
    as we let go those obliged to us.
13Do not carry us into testing.
Rescue us from the worthless one.
14If ever you let go for those people their failures,
    he will let them go also for you,
        your father,
            your heavenly father will.
15If ever you all do not let go for people,
    neither will your father let go your failures.
16Whenever you fast,
do not become like the role players:
    gloomy.
    They make their faces invisible
    so that they may be seen by people
        as they are fasting.
    Amen I say to you all:
    they have their full reward.
17You, however, when you fast,
    anoint your head;
    wash your face;

18so that you may not be seen
  by people
as you are fasting;
  but by your father,
    your father in secret.
Your father
  your father who sees in secret
he will pay you back.
19Do not treasure for yourselves
treasures on the earth,
  where moth and rust make things disappear,
  where thieves dig through and steal.
20Treasure for yourselves
treasures in heaven,
  where neither moth nor rust makes things disappear,
  where thieves neither dig through
    nor steal.
21Where your treasure is,
  there will be your mind.
22The light of the body is the eye.
If ever your eye should be healthy,
  the whole body will be shining brightly.
23If ever your eye should be worthless,
  the whole body will be blind.
    If therefore the light,
      the light in you.
    is dark,
      how dark is that?
24No one is able to slave for two masters,
for either he will hate the one
  and love the other,
or stick tight to one
  and despise the other.
    You are not able to slave for God
    and for the god of riches.

²⁵Because of this I say to you all:
  do not worry for your life:
    What will you eat?
  or:
    What will you drink?
  Neither for your body:
    What will you wear?
  Is not your life more than food,
    and your body more than clothes?
²⁶Take a look at the birds of heaven:
  they neither plant
      nor harvest
      nor gather into storehouses.
  Your father,
    your heavenly father,
  feeds them.
    Aren't you superior to them?
²⁷Which one of you all is able,
  by worrying,
to add to your height,
  say, eighteen inches?
²⁸Why do you worry about clothing?
  Consider carefully the wild lilies,
    how they grow:
        not laboring [like men]¹³⁰
        not spinning [like women].
    ²⁹I say to you all:
      not Solomon in all his glory
      had a robe thrown around him equal to one of these.
      If wild grass
        (today alive,
        tomorrow thrown into the oven),
        ³⁰if God thus clothes wild grass
          will God not much more clothe you,
            Little Faithfulness?

³¹So do not worry.

Do not say:

What will we eat?

What will we drink?

What will we throw around us?

³²All these things Gentiles seek.

He knows,

your father,

your heavenly father knows

that you need of all of this.

³³Seek first the dominion

and the strict observance

of your father

and all these things will be added to you.

³⁴So do not worry about tomorrow.

Tomorrow will worry about itself.

Enough for the day is the day's disgrace.

Chapter Seven

¹Do not make divisions,

so that you will not be divided.

²By the criterion with which you make division

you will be divided.

By the measure you mete out

it will be meted out to you all.

³Why do you see the piece of chaff

in your sister or brother's eye,

the log in your eye

you don't notice?

⁴Or how will you say to your sister or brother:

Allow it that I throw out the bit of chaff

from your eye?

Look:

there's a log in your eye.

⁵Role Player!

Throw out first
   out of your eye
the log.
   Then you will see clearly to throw out
   the bit of chaff
   from the eye of your sister or brother.
⁶Do not give the holy to dogs.
Do not throw your pearls in front of pigs[131]
   lest they trample them with their feet
   and turn and tear you to pieces.
⁷Ask:
   it will be given to you.
Seek:
   you will find.
Knock:
   it will be opened to you.
   ⁸Every one who asks, receives.
   The seeker finds.
   To the knocker it will be opened.
⁹Or who is among you a person
   whom your son asks for bread:
     you wouldn't give him a stone, would you?
   ¹⁰or he asks for a fish:
     you wouldn't give him a snake, would you?
¹¹Since you
   who are worthless
know to give worthy gifts to your children,
   how much more will your father,
     your father in the heavens,
   give worthy things to those who ask him?
¹²So all this:
   Whatever you want people should do for you,
     thus also you do for them.
     This is the Torah and the prophets.

¹³Go in through the narrow gate

because wide the gate

and broad the road

the road leading to destruction;

many are the ones who go in through it.

¹⁴But narrow the gate

narrow the road

the road leading into life;

few are those who find it.

¹⁵Hold yourselves away from the false prophets:

They come to you all

in clothing of sheep;

inside they are seizing wolves.

¹⁶From their fruit you will know them:

neither do they gather

from thorn bushes

grapes,

or from thistles

figs.

¹⁷Thus every worthy tree makes beautiful fruit;

the rotten tree makes worthless fruit.

¹⁸A worthy tree is not able to carry worthless fruit;

neither is a rotten tree able to carry beautiful fruit.

¹⁹Every tree that doesn't make beautiful fruit

is cut down and thrown into the fire.

²⁰Then from their fruit you will know them.

²¹Not everyone who says to me:

haShem, haShem

will go into the dominion of the heavens,

but the one who does the will

of my father

my father in the heavens.

²²Many will say to me in that day:

haShem, haShem

was it not in your name we prophesied?

In fact, in your name we cast out demons;
in your name we did many deeds of power.
²³Then I will agree with them:
I never knew you.
Depart from me,
Underminers of Torah.¹³²
²⁴So everyone who listens to these words of mine
and does them,
he will be compared to a practical man
who built his house on a rock.
²⁵The rain came down;
came the rivers;
blew the whirlwinds;
and they attacked that house.
It did not fall:
it stands founded on the rock.
²⁶Everyone who hears these words of mine
and does not do them
will be compared to a moronic man
who built his house on the sand.
²⁷The rain came down;
came the rivers;
blew the whirlwinds;
they struck that house.
It fell;
its fall was great.
²⁸It happened when Jesus completed these words
the crowds were driven out of their minds
by his teaching,
²⁹for he was teaching them as one who had authority,
not as their scribes.

Chapter Eight

¹When he went down from the mountain
many crowds were following him.

²Look:
   a man with leprosy
      coming to him.
   He worshiped him;
   he said:
      haShem
         if you want to
         you are able to cleanse me.
   ³He extended his hand;
   he touched him;
   he said:
      I want to.
      Be cleansed.
         Right away
   his leprosy was cleansed.
⁴He says to him, Jesus does:
   See here:
      speak to no one,
      but go:
         show yourself to the priest;
         offer the gift Moses commanded
            to be a witness to them.
⁵When he went into Capernaum,
   he came to him
      a centurion.
   He asked him;
   ⁶he said:
      haShem,
         my boy
         has been thrown in the house
         paralyzed
         terribly tortured.
⁷He says to him:
   I will come.
   I will heal him.

8He answered;
the centurion said:
  haShem,
    I am not worthy
    that you enter under my roof,
    but only speak with a word:
    my boy will be cured.
  9For I
    myself
am a person in a chain of command.
    I have under me
      Soldiers.
    I say to this one:
      Go,
        he goes;
    to another:
      Come,
        he comes;
    to my slave:
      Do this,
        he does it.
10After Jesus heard he was astonished;
  he said to those following:
    Amen I say to you all:
      with no one did I find
      this sort of faith
      in Israel.
    11I say to you all:
      many from the East
      and the West
      will come and recline at table
        with Abraham
        and Isaac
        and Jacob
      in the dominion of the heavens,

¹²but the sons of the dominion
    will be thrown out
    into the outer darkness.
      There will be wailing
      and the gnashing of teeth.
¹³Jesus said to the centurion:
    Go.
    As you have been faithful,
      It happened to you.
      The boy was cured in that hour.
¹⁴After Jesus came into Peter's house,
    he saw his mother-in-law
    thrown and fevered.
¹⁵He touched her hand;
    the fever abandoned her;
      she rose;
      she deaconed to him.
¹⁶When evening came;
    they brought to him
    many demonized.
He cast out the breaths with a word.
    All those in a bad way he healed.
¹⁷Thus it was fulfilled
    that which was said by Isaiah the prophet,
      who said:
        "He himself took our weaknesses
        Our illnesses he took away."
¹⁸After Jesus saw a crowd around him
he ordered to go away to the other side.
    ¹⁹There came to him
      one scribe
    he said to him:
    Teacher
      I will follow you wherever you go.

²⁰He says to him
 Jesus does:
  Foxes have dens
   and birds of heaven, nests.
  The son of adam does not have anywhere
  to lay his head.
²¹Another of the disciples said to him:
 haShem
  Permit me first to go away
  and bury my father.
²²Jesus says to him:
 Follow me
  Let the corpses bury their own corpses.
²³As he got into the boat
 his disciples followed him.
  ²⁴Look:
   a great earthquake happened in the sea
    so that the boat was covered by the waves.
   He was asleep.
²⁵When they came to him,
 they raised him.
 They said:
  haShem
   save;¹³³
   we are being destroyed.
²⁶He says to them:
 Why are you cowardly,
  Little Faiths?
 Then after getting up
 he ordered the whirlwind and the sea:
  there was a dead calm.
²⁷The people were astonished,
 they said:
  What kind of person is this?
   The whirlwind and the sea obey him.

309

²⁸After he came into shore
  into the area of the Gadarenes.
There met him two demonized people;
  out of the tombs they came
    exceedingly dangerous
    so that no one was strong enough
    to pass by through that road.
²⁹Look:
  they screamed;
  they said:
    What to us and to you
      Son of God?
    You came thus
      before time
    to torture us?
³⁰There was a long way from them
  a herd of many pigs grazing.
³¹The demons asked him;
  they said:
    Since you are casting us out,
    send us into the herd of pigs.
    ³²He said to them:
    Go.
The ones who came out
went away into the pigs.
  Look:
    the whole herd rushed
      down the steep bank
    into the sea.
    They died in the water.
³³Those who were grazing the pigs fled.
They went away into the city.
They reported all
  even the things about the demonized people.
    ³⁴Look:

all the city came out
    in order to meet Jesus.
After they saw him,
    they asked that he go away from their region.

Chapter Nine

[1]After getting into the boat,
  he crossed over;
  he came into his own city.
    [2]Look:
      they were carrying to him
      a paralyzed man,
        thrown on a bed.
After Jesus saw their faithfulness
he said to the paralyzed man:
  Be confident, child,
    your sins are let go.
[3]Look:
  some of the scribes said among themselves:
    this guy blasphemes.
[4]Because Jesus knew their reflections,
  he said:
    to what end are you reflecting on worthless things
      in your minds?
    [5]What is easier:
      to say:
        Your sins are let go;
      or to say:
        Get up and walk?
    [6]So that you might know
    that the son of adam has authority on earth to let sins go . . .
Then he says to the paralyzed man:
  Get up;
  pick up your bed;
  go to your house.

311

⁷After he got up,
  he went off to his house.
⁸When the crowds saw
they were afraid
  and they glorified God,
    God who gave such authority to people.
⁹When Jesus was passing by there
he saw a person sitting in a tax collecting traitor's booth,
  Matthew he was called.
He says to him:
  Follow me.
    He rose and followed him
¹⁰It happened when he was reclining at table in the house.
  Look:
    many tax collecting traitors
      and sinful men
    coming and reclining at table
      with Jesus
        and his disciples.
¹¹When the Pharisees saw,
they were saying to his disciples:
  On account of what
    with tax collecting traitors
    and sinful men
  does he eat,
    this teacher of yours?
¹²After he heard,
he said:
  No need they have,
    the strong ones,
      no need of a doctor,
    but the ones who are in a bad way.
¹³Go,
  learn what this is:

"Mercy I want,
    not sacrifice."
   I did not come to call the strict,
    but sinners.
14Then they came to him,
  the disciples of John.
They said:
  On account of what
    Do we and the Pharisees fast,
  But your disciples do not fast?
15He said to them,
Jesus did:
They're not able
  the sons of the wedding chamber
  to mourn
    so long as the bridegroom is with them.
  The days will come
    when seized from them will be the bridegroom.
  Then they will fast.
16No one throws a patch of unshrunk cloth
  on an old garment:
    the patch tears away from the garment;
    a worse tear happens.
17Neither do they throw new wine
  into old wineskins.
    If they did:
    the skins burst;
    the wine is poured out;
    the skins are destroyed.
But they throw new wine into new wineskins;
  both are kept safe.
18As he was saying these things to them,
  Look:
    a leader
      one who came to him

worshiped him.
He said:
    My daughter just died,
    but if you come
      and place your hand on her
    she will live.
[19]After he got up,
Jesus followed him.
    His disciples followed, too.
    [20]Look:
    A woman,
      hemorrhaging twelve years,
    woman who came to him.
      From behind she touched the tassel of his garment.
      [21]She was saying in herself:
        If only I touch his garment
        I will be rescued.
[22]Jesus,
    turning and seeing her,
said:
    Be confident, daughter,
      your faithfulness has rescued you.
      The woman was rescued from that hour.
[23]After Jesus came into the house
and saw the flute players and the crowd thrown into disorder
he was saying:
    [24]Go away.
    The little girl is not dead but asleep.
They laughed at him bitterly.
[25]When the crowd was thrown out,
    he went in;
    he grasped her hand;
      the little girl was raised.
[26]Her fame went out the whole of that land.
[27]When Jesus was passing by there,

they followed him:

two blind men

screaming,

saying:

Have mercy on us

son of David.

28When he came into the house,

the blind men came to him.

He says to them

Jesus does:

You are faithful[134] because I am able to do this?

They say to him:

Of course, haShem.

29Then he touched their eyes.

He said:

According to your faithfulness,

let it happen to you.

30Their eyes were opened.

Jesus snorted at them indignantly;

he said:

See here:

let no one know.

31Those who went out famed him about

in the whole of that land.

32After they came out,

look:

they brought to him

a man unable to speak

because of a demon.

33After the demon was cast out,

the mute man spoke.

The crowds were astonished;

they said:

Never has it appeared thus in Israel.

³⁴The Pharisees were saying:
  By the leader of the demons he casts out demons.
³⁵Jesus was passing by all the cities and villages.
He was teaching in their synagogues
  proclaiming the good news of the dominion
  healing all illness and all softness.
³⁶After he saw the crowds
  he felt it in his gut for them
    because they were skinned alive
      and throw down,
      like sheep without a shepherd.
³⁷Then he says to his disciples:
  The harvest is large,
    the workers few.
    ³⁸So ask the lord of the harvest
  so that he cast out workers
    into his harvest.

Chapter Ten

¹After he called to him his twelve disciples
he gave them authority of unclean breaths
  so as to cast them out
  and to heal all illness
  and all softness.
²Of the twelve sent out
  the names are these:
    first, Simon
      (the one called Peter),
    and Andrew
      (his brother),
    and James
      (son of Zebedee),
    and John
      (his brother),
    ³Philip and Bartholomew,

Thomas and Matthew
   (the tax collecting traitor),
James
   (son of Alphaeus)
and Thaddeas,
⁴Simon
   (the Canaanite),
and Judas
   (the Iscariot)
     (the one who handed him over).
⁵These twelve Jesus sent out.
After ordering them,
he said:
   Do not travel on a Gentile road.
   Into a Samaritan city do not go.
    ⁶Go more to the sheep,
     the lost sheep,
    of the house, Israel.
  ⁷As you go,
  proclaim;
    say:
     The dominion of the heavens is so close.
    ⁸Weak ones,
     heal them.
    Dead ones,
     raise.
    Lepers,
     Cleanse.
    Demons,
     cast out.
  As a gift you received;
   as a gift, give.
  ⁹Do not acquire gold
   or silver
   or copper

into your belt;
   [10]no knapsack for the road,
   no two undershirts,
   no shoes,
   no walking stick.
Worthy is the worker,
   worthy of his food.
[11]Into whatever city or village you go,
inquire who in it is worthy,
   and there remain up until you leave.
[12]When you come into the house greet it:
   [13]if the house be worthy,
     let your peace come upon it;
   if the house be not worthy,
     let your peace to you return.
[14]Whoever does not receive you,
   and will not hear your words,
     as you are going out of the house
       or that city,
     shake off the dust of your feet.
[15]Amen I say to you all:
more bearable it will be
   for Sodom and Gomorrah
     in the day of separating
       than for that city.
[16]Look:
I am sending you all out
   as sheep in the midst of wolves
So be sensible,
   like snakes.
Be guileless,
   like pigeons.
[17]Beware of people:
   they will hand you over into sanhedrins
   and in their synagogues they will flog you.

¹⁸Before leaders and kings you will be driven
> because of me
>> for a witness to them
>> and to the Gentiles.

¹⁹Whenever they hand you over,
> do not worry how or what to say.
>> It will be given to you all
>> in that hour what to say.

²⁰It is not you who speaks
> but the breath of your father
>> the breath speaking in you.

²¹Brother will hand brother over to death,
> and father, his child.
> Children will rise up on their parents
>> and they will kill them.

²²You will be hated by all
> because of my name.
The one who endures to the completion,
> that one will be rescued.

²³Whenever they hunt you all
> in that city
>> flee into the other one.
Amen I say to you all:
> No way will you complete the cities of Israel
>> up until the son of adam comes.

²⁴A disciple is not over the teacher
> Nor is the slave over his master.

²⁵It is enough for the disciple
> that he become like his teacher,
> and the slave like his master.
If they called the master of the house
> Beelzebul
how much more the members of the household?

²⁶So do not fear them:

nothing is hidden
    that will not be revealed;
nothing secret
    that will not be known.
27What I say to you all
    in the dark,
you will say in the light.
What you hear into the ear,
    proclaim on the house.
28Stop being afraid
    because of those who kill the body,
        the life they are not able to kill.
Continue to fear more the one who is able
    both life and body to destroy in Gehenna.
29Aren't two sparrows offered for sale at one-half penny?
    One of them does not fall on the earth
        without your father.
30Of you even the hairs of your head
    all are counted.
31Stop being afraid.
You are worth more than many sparrows.
32Anyone who agrees with me
    before people
I also will agree with him
    before my father
    my father in the heavens.
33Whoever denies me before people,
    I also will deny him before my father
        my father in the heavens.
34Do not suppose
    that I came to throw peace on the earth.
    I did not come to throw peace,
        but rather a sword.
35I came to divide
    a person against his father

a daughter against her mother
a bride against her in-laws.
³⁶A person's enemies?:
 the members of his household.
³⁷The one who loves father
 or mother
  over me
 is not worthy of me.
The one who loves son
 or daughter
  over me
 is not worthy of me.
³⁸Who does not receive his cross
 and follow after me
 is not worthy of me.
³⁹The one who found his life
 will destroy it;
the one who destroyed his life
 because of me
  will find it.
⁴⁰The one who welcomes you
 welcomes me.
 The one who welcomes me
  welcomes the one who sent me.
⁴¹The one who welcomes a prophet
 honoring the name of a prophet
  the reward of a prophet will receive.
The one who welcomes a strict one
 honoring the name of strictness
  the reward of strictness will receive.
⁴²Whoever waters one of these little ones
 with a cup of cold water
  honoring the name of a disciple.
Amen I say to you all:
 he will not lose his reward.

Chapter Eleven

¹And it happened when Jesus completed commanding his
     twelve disciples,
he departed from there
 in order to teach and proclaim
  in their cities.
²After John heard
 in prison
the works of Jesus,
 he sent through his disciples;
 ³he said:
  You are the coming one,
   or ought we to expect a different one?
 ⁴Jesus answered;
 he said to them:
  Go report to John what you hear and see:
   ⁵the blind see again,
   the lame walk,
   the lepers are cleansed,
   the deaf hear,
   the dead are raised,
   the poor get good news.
  ⁶Godlike in happiness
   is anyone who is not
    scandalized by me.
⁷As these disciples were going,
Jesus began to say to the crowds about John:
 What did you go out
  into the wilderness
 to see?
  A reed shaken by a whirlwind?
 ⁸But what did you all come out to see?
  A person dressed in softie's[135] clothing?
  Look:

322

the people wearing softie's clothes
   are in the house of kings.
9But why did you come out?
  To see a prophet?
  Yes, I say to you all:
   and more than a prophet.
   10This one is the one about whom it stands written:
   Look:
      "I am sending my messenger before your face
       who will prepare your road in front of you."
  11Amen I say to you:
  There has not arisen
   among the birthings of women
greater than John the Purifier.
   The smallest in the dominion of the heavens
    is larger than he.
  12From the days of John the Purifier
   up until now,
the dominion of the heavens suffers violence.
   People who use violence seize it.
  13All the prophets and the Torah
   up until John
they all prophesied.
  14Since you want to welcome the idea,
   he is Elijah who is about to come.
    15The one who has ears should hear.
16To what shall I compare this birthing?
  It is like children sitting in the market
  who call out to others.
  They say:
    17We played the flute;
     you did not dance.
  We mourned;
   you did not beat your breast.

¹⁸John came:
>not eating
>not drinking;
they are saying:
>He has a demon.
¹⁹The son of adam came:
>eating
>and drinking;
they are saying:
>Look:
>>a person,
>>>a glutton,
>>>a drunk,
>>>a friend of tax collecting traitors,
>>>and sinful men.
>Wisdom is declared strict
>>from her works.
²⁰Then he began to revile
the cities in which his very many deeds of power happened
>because they did not change:
>²¹Woe to you,
>>Chorazin.
>Woe to you,
>>Bethsaida.
>>Because if in Tyre and Sidon
>>>had happened the deeds of power
>>>that happened in you,
>>long ago in sackcloth and ashes
>>they would have changed.
>²²Only I say to you all:
>>for Tyre and Sidon it will be more bearable
>>>in the day of division
>>than for you all.
>²³And you, Capernaum:
>>are you not exalted up to heaven?

   Down to Hades you will go.
   Because if in Sodom had happened
   the deeds of power that happened in you,
    it would remain until today.
  ²⁴Only I say to you all:
   for the land of Sodom
    it will be more bearable
     in the day of division
    than for you.
²⁵In that time Jesus answered;
he said:
 I agree with you
  father
  haShem of heaven
   and the earth,
 because you hid these things
  from the wise ones
  and those with understanding
 and you revealed them to babies.
²⁶Yes,
  father:
thus it happens to be pleasing
 before you.
²⁷All those things
 to me
have been handed over
 by my father,
and no one knows the son
 (except the father)
and neither does anyone know the father
 (except the son)
  and whoever the son wills to make revelation to.
²⁸Come to me
 all those who are exhausted [by work]
 and loaded heavy.

I,
 even I,
I will rest you.
²⁹Pick up my yoke on you;
learn from me:
 I am gentle
  and lowly in mind;
 you will find rest for your life.
³⁰My yoke is serviceable;
 my lead is light.

Chapter Twelve

¹In that time Jesus went
 every Shabbat
through planted fields.
 His disciples were hungry:
 they began to pluck heads
  and eat.
²The Pharisees,
 when they saw,
said to him:
 Look:
  your disciples are doing
  what is not appropriate to do on a Shabbat.
³He said to them:
 You haven't read what David did
  when he was hungry
   and those with him?
⁴How he went into the house of God
  and the breads of presentation
   they ate,
    which was not appropriate for him to eat,
    neither was it for those with him,
     but only for the priests.
⁵Or you haven't read in the Torah:

Every Shabbat the priests
   in the Temple
profane the Shabbat
   and are guiltless?
[6]I say to you:
   greater than the Temple is here.
[7]If you had read,
   What is:
     "Mercy I want
       not sacrifice,"
you would not condemn the innocent.
   [8]Master,[136]
     indeed during Shabbat,
   is the son of adam.
[9]After he moved from there he came into their synagogue.
   [10]Look:
   a person who had a withered hand.
They asked him;
they said:
  If it is appropriate
    every Shabbat
  to heal?
It was in order to charge him.
[11]He said to them:
  Who will be the person among you
  who will have one sheep
  and if ever it falls,
    this one sheep,
    every Shabbat
  into a ditch,
  will not grasp it and lift?
   [12]To what degree does a person differ from a sheep?
Thus it is appropriate
    every Shabbat
to act beautifully.

13Then he says to the person:

    Extend your hand.

He extended,

it was restored,

    healthy as the other.

14Pharisees came out;

they took a plan against him,

    how they might destroy him.

15Because Jesus knew,

    he departed from there.

They followed him,

    many did;

he healed them all.

16He ordered them that they not make him visible

17in order that it might be fulfilled,

    the thing said through Isaiah the prophet,

    he said:

        18Look:

            my boy

                whom I choose;

            my beloved

                by whom my life is pleased.

        I will place my breath on him.

            He will announce separation to the Gentiles.

        19He will not quarrel;

            he will not scream;

                no one will hear his voice in the wide streets.

        20A crushed reed he will not break;

            a smoking wick he will not extinguish,

                up until he casts out division into victory.

        21In his name Gentiles will hope.

22Then there was brought to him a demonized person:

blind,

mute.[137]

He healed him,
   so that the mute person spoke and saw.
²³All the crowds were beside themselves;
they were saying:
   Is not this the son of David?
²⁴When the Pharisees heard they said:
   This guy does not cast out demons
      except by Beelzebul, leader of demons.
²⁵Because he knows their reflections
he said to them:
   Every dominion
      divided against itself
   is made into a wilderness.
   Every city or house
      divided against itself
   will not stand.
²⁶If haSatan casts out haSatan,
   he is divided on himself:
   how will his dominion be able to stand?
²⁷If I
   by Beelzebul
cast out demons,
your sons,
   by whom do they cast out?
   Through this they will be your judges.
²⁸If by the breath of God
I cast out demons,
   then it came first upon you all,
      the dominion of God did.
²⁹Or how is anyone able to go into the house of the strong one
   and seize his property,
if he does not first tie up the strong man?
   Then he will plunder his house.
³⁰Anyone who does not gather with me
   scatters.

³¹Because of this I say to you all:
   every sin
   every blasphemy
     will be let go for people.
   The blaspheming of the breath
     will not be let go.
³²Whoever speaks a word
     against the son of adam,
   it will be let go for him.
   Whoever speaks against the breath
     the holy breath
   it will not be let go for him,
     not in this aeon,
     not in the coming aeon.
³³Either you make the tree beautiful
     and its fruit beautiful,
or you make the tree rotten
     and its fruit rotten.
     Out of the fruit
       the tree is known.
³⁴People fathered by snakes,
     how are you able
     to speak worthy things
       while you are worthless?
     Out of the overflow of your minds
     your mouth speaks.
³⁵The worthy person
     out of a worthy treasury
casts out worthy things.
The worthless person
     out of a worthless treasury
casts out worthless things.
³⁶I say to you all:
     every ineffective word
     that people speak,

they will give account of it
    in the day of separation,
37for out of your words
    you will be made strictly observant,
    out of your words you will be condemned.
38Then they answered to him,
some of the scribes and Pharisees;
they said:
    Teacher,
      We want
        from you
      to see a sign.
39He answered;
he said to them:
    Worthless birthing.
    Adulteress.
    It seeks a sign.
    It will not be given a sign,
      except the sign of Jonah the prophet;
    40for just as Jonah
      was in the belly of the sea monster
        three days
        and three nights,
      thus the son of adam will be
in the heart of the earth
        three days
        and three nights.
    41Men,
      Ninevites!
will rise up in the separation
    with this birthing.
      And condemn it,
      because they changed
      in honor of the proclamation of Jonah.

Look:

more than Jonah is here.

[42]A queen of the South

will be raised in the separation

with this generation

and will condemn it,

because she came

out of the end of the earth

to hear the wisdom of Solomon.

Look:

more than Solomon is here.

[43]Whenever the unclean breath goes out from a person

it goes through waterless places,

seeking rest,

not finding it.

[44]Then it says:

Into my house I will return,

from where I came out.

After it goes,

it finds it at leisure,

swept clean,

having been put in beautiful order.

[45]Then it goes and takes with it

seven different breaths

more worthless than itself.

After going in

it settles there.

It happens:

The last things

for that person

are worse than the first.

Thus it will be for this birthing

this worthless birthing.

[46]While he was still speaking,

look:

his mother
>and his brothers
stationed themselves outside;
they sought to speak with him.
⁴⁷Someone said to him:
>Look:
>>your mother
>>>and your brothers
>>are stationed outside
>>seeking to speak with you.
⁴⁸He answered;
he said to the one talking to him:
>Who is my mother?
>Who are my brothers?
⁴⁹Extending his hand on his disciples
>he said:
>>Look
>>>my mother
>and my brothers.
>>⁵⁰For whoever does the will of my father,
>>>my father in the heavens,
>>he is my brother,
>>and sister,
>>and mother.

Chapter Thirteen

¹In that day when Jesus came out of his house
he sat by the sea.
²There were gathered to him many crowds
>so that he
>>after getting into a boat
>sat.
All the crowd was standing on the shore.
³He spoke to them many things in parables;
he said:

Look:
    The sower went out in order to sow.
    [4]In his sowing,
        some fell by the road:
            the birds came
                they ate them.
      [5]Others fell on the stones where it did not have much earth:
        right away
        it sprang up,
            because it did not have deep earth.
      [6]When the sun rose it was scorched;
            because of not having roots
            it was dried out.
      [7]Others fell on the thorns:
            the thorns went up;
            they choked them.
      [8]Others fell on beautiful earth:
            it gave fruit,
                some one hundred,
                some sixty,
                some thirty.
  [9]The one who has ears should hear.
[10]His disciples came;
they said to him:
    On account of what
      in parables
  are you speaking to them?
[11]He answered;
he said:
    To you has been given to know the mystery
      of the dominion of the heavens;
  to them it has not been given.
  [12]Anyone who has
    it will be given to him,
    it will be too much.

Anyone who does not have
   even what he has will be seized from him.
¹³On account of this
   in parables
I speak to them:
   when they see,
     they do not see;
   when they hear,
     they do not hear;
       they do not understand.
¹⁴It is being fulfilled in them,
   the prophecy of Isaiah,
that says:
   "In hearing
   you hear,
     but do not understand;
   when you look
   you look,
     but do not see.
¹⁵The mind of this people is made fat
   with ears they heard heavily;
   Their eyes they shut,
     lest they should see with eyes
     and with ears should hear
     and with mind understand
       and turn and be cured."
¹⁶Your eyes,
   Godlike in happiness:
     they see.
Your ears:
     they hear.
¹⁷Amen I say to you all:
   many prophets
   and strictly observant

desired to see what you see;
   they did not see;
and to hear what you hear;
   they did not hear.
¹⁸So you:
hear the parable of the sower:
   ¹⁹while all were hearing the word of the dominion
     and not understanding
  the worthless one comes and seizes what was sown in his mind.
    ²⁰This is what was sown along the road.
  That which was sown on the rocks:
    this is the one who hears the word
      BANG
    with joy receives it;
      ²¹he does not have roots in himself,
     but is transitory.
    When affliction comes,
    or harassing,
      because of the word,
    BANG
    he is scandalized.
²²That which was sown into the thorns:
    this is the one who hears the word
      and the worries of the aeon
      and the trickery of wealth
      choke the word
      it becomes fruitless.
²³That which was sown on beautiful earth:
    this is the one who hears the word
    and understands
    who bears fruit
    and makes
      some one hundred,
      some sixty,
      some thirty.

²⁴Another parable he put before them;
he said:
> The dominion of the heavens was compared to a person
> who sows beautiful seeds in his field.
²⁵While the people were sleeping,
> this enemy came
> he sowed poisonous weeds in the midst of the grain and
>> went away.
²⁶When the grass sprouted
and made fruit,
> then appeared also the poisonous weeds.
²⁷When the slaves of the master of the house came
they said to him:
> haShem,
>> didn't you sow beautiful seed in your field?
>>> Where did it get poisonous weeds from?
²⁸He said to them:
> An enemy,
> a person did this.
The slaves are saying to him:
> So, do you want us to go out and gather them?
²⁹He said:
> No
>> lest in gathering the poisonous weeds you should uproot
>>> with them
>> the grain.
³⁰Let both grow together
>> up until the harvest:
> in the time of the harvest
> I will say to the harvesters:
>> Gather first the poisonous weeds;
>> bind them into bundles
>>> to burn them up.
> The grain gather into my barn.
³¹Another parable he placed before them;

he said:

   The dominion of the heavens is like a grain of mustard

     which,

         when a person takes it

         and sows it in his field

        32is smaller than all seeds;

    whenever it grows

       is larger than garden herbs

       and becomes a tree,

          so that birds of heaven come

         and nest in its branches.

33Another parable he spoke to them:

   The dominion of the heavens is like leaven

     which a woman takes,

     she hides it

        in three sacks of wheat flour

          up until when the whole is leavened.

34All these things Jesus spoke in parables to the crowds;

apart from parables he spoke nothing to them,

    35so that it might be fulfilled

   the thing said through the prophet;

   he said:

     "I will open in parables my mouth;

     I will belch hidden things from parables."

36Then leaving the crowds,

he came into his house.

They came to him,

   the disciples did,

they said:

   Make quite clear to us the parable of the poisonous weeds

             of the field.

37He answered;

he said:

   The one who sowed the beautiful seed

     is the son of adam.

³⁸The field is the beautiful world.
The beautiful seed,
   these are the sons of the dominion.
The poisonous weeds are the sons of the worthless one.
³⁹The enemy,
   the enemy who sowed them is the prosecutor.
The harvest is the completion of the aeon.
The harvesters are messengers.
   ⁴⁰So just as the poisonous weeds are gathered
     and in fire burnt up,
  thus it will be in the completion of the aeon:
     ⁴¹the son of adam will send out his messengers;
     they will gather out of his dominion all scandals
       and those undermining Torah;
     ⁴²they will throw them into the fiery furnace.
     There
       there will be wailing and the gnashing of teeth.
     ⁴³Then the strictly observant will shine
       like the sun
     in the dominion of their father.
The one who has ears should hear.
⁴⁴The dominion of the heavens is like
  a treasure hidden in the field,
    which when a person finds it,
    he hides it.
      From his joy he goes
      he sells as much as he has
      he buys that field.
⁴⁵Again the dominion of the heavens is like
  a merchant who seeks beautiful pearls.
    ⁴⁶When he found one very valuable pearl,
      he had gone away
      he had sold all
        as much as he had
      and he bought it.

⁴⁷Again like is the dominion of the heavens to
  a dragnet thrown into the sea
    and out of all kinds it gathers,
  ⁴⁸which, when it was filled
    they pulled it up on the shore.
    They sat;
    they gathered the beautiful into containers,
    the rotten they threw out.
  ⁴⁹Thus it will be in the completion of the aeon:
    the messengers will come
    and separate the worthless ones
      out of the midst of the strictly observant.
    ⁵⁰They will throw them into the fiery furnace.
      There
      there will be wailing
      and the gnashing of teeth.
  ⁵¹Did you understand all these things?
    They say to him:
    Yes.
  ⁵²He said to them:
    Because of this every scribe
      who is a scholar in the dominion of the heavens
    is like a person,
      a master of a house,
    who casts out
      out of his treasury
    new and old things.
⁵³It happened when Jesus completed these parables
 he went away from there.
⁵⁴After he came into his native place,
he taught them in their synagogues
  so that they were driven out of their minds
  and said:
    Whence to this one this wisdom
      and these acts of power?

⁵⁵Isn't this one the son of the builder?
Isn't his mother called Mariam?
   and his brother James and Joseph and Simon and Judas?
   ⁵⁶and his sisters
      aren't they all with us?
⁵⁷They were scandalized by him.
Jesus said to them:
   A prophet is not unhonored
      except in his native place
      and in his house.
⁵⁸He did not do there many acts of power
   because of their unfaithfulness.

Chapter Fourteen

¹In that time Herod heard,
   Herod the tetrarch,
heard the report of Jesus.
²He said to his boys:
   This one is John the Purifier;
he was raised from the corpses.
      On account of this
      the acts of power are worked in him.
³For Herod,
   after seizing John,
bound him
and placed him in prison
   because of Herodias
      the wife of Philip,
         his brother,
   ⁴for John was saying to him:
      It is not appropriate for you to have her.
⁵While he wanted to kill him,
   he was afraid of the crowd,
      because as a prophet they held him.

6When the birthdays of Herod happened
the daughter of Herodias danced
 in the middle.
  She was pleasing to Herod.
7Because of this, with an oath
 he agreed with her
 to give whatever she might ask.
8She had been instructed
 by her mother:
  Give to me,
 she said,
  here
   on a board
  the head of John the Purifier.
9The king, sorrowful,
 because of his oath
 (and because of those reclining at table)
 ordered it be given.
10After sending,
 he beheaded John in prison.
  11His head was brought
   on a board
  and given to the little girl
   and she carried it to her mother.
12After his disciples came to lift up
the fallen corpse
 and bury him,
after they came,
 they reported to Jesus.
13When Jesus heard,
he left there in a boat
 into a wilderness place
  all alone.
When the crowds heard

they followed him
  by land from the cities.
14When he came out
he saw a large crowd.
   He was moved in his gut by them;
  he healed the sickly among them.
15When it was evening
his disciples came to him;
they said:
   A wilderness
     this place is.
   The hour is already passed by,
  so release the crowds
     so that they can go away into the villages
    and buy food for themselves.
16Jesus said to them:
   They have no need to go away.
   Give to them
     yourselves
  something to eat.
17They say to him:
   We do not have here,
     except five loaves
    and two fish.
18He said:
   Bring them to me here.
19After ordering the crowds to recline at table
  on the grass,
after taking the five loaves and two fish,
after looking up into heaven,
  he blessed.
After breaking,
  he gave to the disciples
    the loaves,
  and the disciples to the crowds.

²⁰All ate and were stuffed.
They lifted up the excess of broken pieces:
  twelve baskets full.
²¹Those who ate were
  men
    about five thousand
  (not to mention women and children).
²²Right away
  he forced the disciples
  to get into the boat
  to go ahead of him
    to the other side
      up until he should let the crowds go.
²³After he released the crowds,
  he went up into the mountain
    all alone
  to pray.
When evening came,
he was there alone.
  ²⁴The boat
    was already many stadia
    distant from land,
      tortured by the waves,
     for it was against them,
        the wind was.
  ²⁵In the fourth watch of the night
  he came toward them
  walking on the sea.
²⁶When the disciples saw him on the sea walking,
they were terrified
  they said:
    It is a phantom.
  They screamed from fear.
²⁷BANG
Jesus spoke to them;

he said:
    Be confident;
    it is I am;
    stop being afraid.
28He answered to him,
    Peter did,
he said:
    haShem
      if you are you,
        order me to come toward you
          on the water.
29He said:
    Come.
He got down from the boat.
Peter walked on the water
    and came toward Jesus.
30When he glanced at the whirlwind,
    he became afraid;
when he began to drown,
    he screamed,
    he said:
      haShem
        rescue me.
31Right away
Jesus
    after extending his hand
took hold of him;
he says to him:
    Little Faith,
    to what end did you doubt?
32When they got into the boat,
    the whirlwind stopped.
33Those in the boat worshiped him;
they said:
    Truly God's son you are.

³⁴When they had crossed over
they came on the land
into Gennesaret.
³⁵When they recognized him,
the men of that place
sent into the whole of that surrounding region.
They brought to him
   all those who had it bad.
³⁶They kept asking him
that only they touch the tassel of his garment.
   As many as touched it were thoroughly rescued.

Chapter Fifteen

¹Then they came to Jesus
   from Jerusalem
Pharisees and scribes.
They said:
   ²On account of what
   do your disciples transgress
   the traditions of the elders?
   They are not washing their hands
   whenever they eat bread.
³He answered;
he said to them:
   On account of what
   do you transgress the commandment of God
     through your traditions?
   ⁴For God said:
   Honor your father
     and your mother;
  and:
   The one who insults father
     or mother
   let him be put to death.

⁵But you say:

    whoever says to his father

      or mother:

    what is owed from me

    is a gift.

    He does not honor his father

      or his mother.

⁶You cancel the word of God through your tradition.

⁷Role Players.

Well did Isaiah prophesy concerning you

when he said:

    ⁸This people with their lips honors me;

      their heart is far, far distant from me.

    ⁹In vain they worship me.

      When they teach as teachings human commandments.

¹⁰After he called the crowd,

he said to them:

    Hear and understand:

      ¹¹It is not the thing that goes into the mouth

        that defiles a person,

      rather it is the thing that comes out of the mouth.

      This defiles a person.

¹²Then when the disciples come to him,

they say to him:

    Do you know that

    the Pharisees

      when they heard the word

    were scandalized?

¹³He answered;

he said:

    Every plant that does not grow,

my father,

    my heavenly father,

    tears out by the roots.

¹⁴Leave them:
   they are blind guides:
      whenever they lead
      both fall into the ditch.
¹⁵Peter answered;
he said to him:
   Explain to us the parable.
¹⁶He said:
   Still
   you
      (even you!)
   are without understanding!
¹⁷Don't you know that
   everything that goes into the mouth
      goes out into the belly
      and into the latrine is cast out?
¹⁸The things that come out of the mouth
   come out of the mind
      those things defile a person.
¹⁹Out of the mind come:
   adultery
   worthlessness
   thievery
   lying
   blasphemy.
²⁰These things are the defilers of a person.
   Handwashing for eating
      does not defile a person.
²¹After he went out from there,
Jesus moved into the region of Tyre and Sidon.
   ²²Look:
   a woman
   a Canaanite
      from the mountains.
   She came out;

she screamed;
she said:
    Have mercy on me
      haShem
      son of David,
    my daughter is badly demonized.
[23]He did not answer her a word.
After his disciples came to him,
they asked him;
they said:
    Release her,
      because she is screaming after us.
[24]He answered;
he said:
    I was not sent out
      except to the lost sheep
      of the house of Israel.
[25]The woman who came out
worshiped him
she said:
    haShem
      Help me.
[26]He answered;
he said:
    It is not right to take
    the children's bread
    and throw it to the dogs.
[27]She said:
    Yes,
      haShem,
    even the dogs are eating
    the crumbs that fall
      from the table
        of their masters.[138]

²⁸Then Jesus answered;
he said to her:
> O woman
> great is your faithfulness.
> Let it happen for you as you want.

Her daughter was cured from that hour.
²⁹After moving from there,
Jesus came by the Sea of Galilee.
After going up into the mountain,
he sat there.
³⁰Many crowds came to him
who had with them
> lame people
> crippled people
> blind people
> deaf mute people
> > and many others.

They flung them at his feet.
He healed them,
> **³¹**so that the crowd was amazed
> when they saw
> > deaf mutes speaking
> > cripples cured
> > lame walking
> > blind seeing.

> They glorified the God of Israel.

³²After Jesus called his disciples to him,
he said:
> I am moved in my gut by the crowd
> because already three days they are with me
> and they have nothing to eat.
> I do not want to release them hungry,
> > lest they be weary in the road.

³³The disciples say to him:

How will we have
   in the wilderness
this many loaves
   so that such a crowd will be stuffed?
34He says to them,
Jesus does:
   How many loaves have you?
They said:
   seven and a few fish.
35After instructing the crowd to sit down on the earth,
36he took the seven loaves and the fish
and after giving thanks,
broke them and gave them
to the disciples,
   and the disciples to the crowds.
37All ate and were stuffed.
The excess of fragments they lifted up:
   seven baskets full.
38Those who ate were four thousand men
   (not to mention the women and children).
39After releasing the crowds
he went up into the boat
he came into the region of Magadan.

Chapter Sixteen

1They came,
the Pharisees and Sadducees,
   testing him.
They asked him a sign out of heaven[139]
to show to them.
2He answered;
he said to them:
   When it is evening you say:
      Fair weather,
      because the heaven is fiery red;

³and in early morning:

   A sign of stormy weather,

   the heaven is fiery red and gloomy.

The face of the heaven you know to discern,

   the signs of the times you are not able.

⁴Worthless birthing.

Adulteress seeks a sign!

   A sign will not be given to her

      except the sign of Jonah.

He left them;

he went away.

⁵After the disciples came into the shore

   they forgot to take bread.

⁶Jesus said to them:

   See here:

   Hold yourselves away from

   the leaven of the Pharisees

      and Sadducees.

⁷They were arguing among themselves

   because they did not take bread.

⁸When Jesus knew,

he said:

   Why are you arguing among yourselves,

      Little Faiths,

   because you have no loaves?

⁹You don't understand yet?

Neither do you remember

   the five loaves of the five thousand,

      and how many bushels you took?

   ¹⁰Neither the seven loaves of the four thousand,

      and how many baskets you took?

¹¹How do you not understand

   that it wasn't about loaves that I spoke to you?

Beware of the leaven of the Pharisees and Sadducees.

¹²Then they understood
that he did not say beware of the leaven of bread
  but of the teaching of the Pharisees and Sadducees.
¹³After Jesus came into the area of Caesarea Philippi
he asked his disciples;
he said:
  What are people saying that the son of adam is?
¹⁴They said:
  Some say:
    John the Purifier;
  others:
    Elijah;
  and then others:
    Jeremiah or one of the prophets.
¹⁵He says to them:
  But you, what things are you saying that I am?
¹⁶Simon Peter answered;
he said:
  You,
    you are the Messiah,
      the son of God,
      the living God.
¹⁷Jesus answered;
he said to him:
  Godlike in happiness are you,
    Simon Barjona:
      flesh and blood
      did not reveal to you,
        but my father
          my father in the heavens.
¹⁸Indeed to you I say:
  You, you are Peter
  and on this rock I will build my assembly.
  The gates of Hades
  will not overpower it.

¹⁹I will give to you
  the keys of the dominion of the heavens.
  Whatever you bind on the earth
    will have been bound in the heavens.
  Whatever you loose on the earth
    will have been loosed in the heavens.
²⁰Then he scolded the disciples
that to no one should they say
that he is the Messiah.
²¹From then he began,
  Jesus Messiah did,
to show to his disciples that it is necessary
  that he go into Jerusalem
  and suffer many things
    from the elders
    and chief priests
    and scribes
  and be killed
  and
    in the third day
  be raised.
²²When Peter took him to himself,
he began to scold him;
he said:
  May God be merciful to you,
    haShem:
      this must not be to you.
²³After he turned,
he said to Peter:
  Take it to court;¹⁴⁰
  behind me,
    haSatan:
      you do not intend
        the things of God
        but the things of people.

²⁴Then Jesus said to his disciples:
    If anyone wants to come after me,
        Deny yourself.
        Lift up your cross.
        Follow me.
    ²⁵For whoever wants to rescue his life
        will destroy it.
    Whoever destroys his life
        on account of me
    will find it.
    ²⁶For what good will it do a person
    if the whole beautiful world he gains,
        but his life is confiscated?
    Or what will a person give
        in exchange for his life?
    ²⁷The son of adam is about to come
        in the glory of his father
            with his messengers.
    Then he will give to each
        according to his business.
    ²⁸Amen I say to you all:
        There are some of those here standing
        who will not taste of death
            up until they see that the son of adam
            came in his dominion.

Chapter Seventeen

¹After six days Jesus takes with him
    Peter
    James
    John
        his brother;
he brings them up
    into a high mountain
        all alone.

²He was changed in form in front of them.

His face shone like the sun.

His clothes became white as light.

³Look:

There appeared to them

Moses and Elijah

who were talking with him.

⁴Peter answered;

he said to Jesus:

haShem,

it is beautiful that we are here.

If you want

I will make three tents

for you

one

for Moses

one

for Elijah

one.

⁵While he was still speaking,

look:

a shining cloud overshadowed them.

Look:

a voice out of a cloud;

she said:

This is my son

the beloved

in whom I am well pleased.

Hear him.

⁶After the disciples heard,

they fell on their faces.

They were terribly afraid.

⁷Jesus came to them;

after he touched them,

he said:

Get up.

Stop being afraid.

8When they looked intently,141

they saw no one,

   except Jesus only.

9As they were going down out of the mountain,

Jesus commanded them;

  he said:

    To no one

    tell what you saw

    up until the son of adam

    out of the corpses is raised.

10They asked him,

  the disciples did,

they said:

  So why are the scribes saying

    that Elijah necessarily comes first?

11He answered;

he said:

  Elijah comes and restores all things.

  12I say to you:

    Elijah already came.

    They did not know him,

      but they did in him

        what they wanted.

  Thus also the son of adam

    is about to suffer by them.

13Then the disciples understood that about John the Purifier he

          spoke to them.

14After they came to the crowd

there asked him,

  a person did,

  a person who fell to his knees

  15a person who said:

    haShem

have mercy on my son:
    he is a lunatic
    and in bad shape.
For many times he falls into the fire,
many times into the water.
    16I brought him to your disciples
        they were not powerful to heal him.
17Jesus answered;
he said:
    O birthing,
        unfaithful,
        distorted,
            up to when will I be with you?
            Up to when will I endure you?
    Bring to me him here.
18Jesus rebuked him;
there came out from him
    the demon.
The boy was healed from that hour.
19Then after the disciples came to Jesus,
    all alone,
20they said:
    On account of what were we
        (We!)
    not powerful to cast it out?
He says to them:
    On account of your little faith.
        Amen I say to you all:
            If you were to have faithfulness
            as a mustard seed,
            you would say to this mountain:
                Move from there,
            and it would move.
        Nothing would be impossible for you.
22When they came together in Galilee,

he said to them,
Jesus did:
　The son of adam is about to be handed over
　into people's hands.
　23They will kill him;
　　in the third day he will be raised.
They became distressed exceedingly.
24After they came into Capernaum
they came,
　the ones bringing the two drachma coin,
to Peter.
They said:
　Your teacher is not paying two drachmas tribute?
25He says:
　Yes.
When he came into the house
Jesus spoke first,
he said:
　What does it seem to you, Simon?
　　The kings of the earth
　　from whom do they take tribute and tax:
　　　from their sons
　　　or from the sons of someone else?
26He said:
　from the sons of someone else.
Jesus kept saying to him:
　Then the sons are free.
　27So that we not scandalize them,
　　go into the sea,
　　throw a fish hook.
　　　After the first fish comes up,
　　　　lift it.
　　　After you open its mouth
　　　　you will find a stateira.

> After taking it,
>> give to them
>>> for me and you.

Chapter Eighteen

¹In that hour
the disciples came to Jesus;
they said:
   So who is greatest in the dominion of the heavens?
²After he called a child
he stood it in the midst of them;
³he said:
   Amen I say to you all:
      if you do not turn
         and become like children
      you will by no means enter
      into the dominion of the heavens.
   ⁴So anyone who humbles himself as this child
   this one is greatest in the dominion of the heavens.
   ⁵Whoever receives one child of this sort
      upon my name
   receives me;
   ⁶whoever scandalizes one of these little ones,
      these little ones who are faithful into me,
   it would be profitable to him
   that he hang a donkey millstone around his neck
      and plunge into the open water of the sea.
   ⁷Woe to the beautiful world
      from scandals
         for it is necessary that scandals come.
   Still woe to the person
      through whom the scandal comes.
   ⁸When your hand or your foot scandalizes you
      cut it off
         throw it from you.

It is beautiful for you
    to go into life
      as a cripple
      or lame;
  or is it beautiful,
      having two hands
      or two feet,
  to be thrown into the eternal fire?
[9]When your eye scandalizes you
  take it out;
  throw it from you.
    It is beautiful for you
      one-eyed
    into life to go
    or is it beautiful,
      having two eyes,
  to be thrown into fiery Gehenna?
[10]See here:
  do not despise one of these little ones.
For I say to you all:
  their messengers in the heavens
  continually look at the face of my father
    my father in the heavens.
[12]How does it seem to you?
  If there happened to belong to some person
    one hundred sheep
      and one of them is led astray,
  won't he abandon the ninety-nine on the mountain
  and go
    seek the strayed one?
[13]If ever he should happen to find it,
  Amen I say to you all:
    he rejoices on it
      more than on the ninety-nine
      those who did not stray.

¹⁴Thus it is not desired
    in front of your father
        your father in the heavens
that one of these little ones be destroyed.
¹⁵If ever your sister or brother should sin,
    go expose him
        between you and him only.
    If ever she or he hears you,
        gain your sister or brother.
¹⁶If ever she or he does not hear,
    take with you still one or two
        that on the mouth of two witnesses
            or three
        should stand every word.
¹⁷If ever she or he should ignore them,
    speak to the assembly.
If ever she or he should ignore also the assembly,
    let him be to you as the Gentile
    or the tax collecting traitor.
¹⁸Amen I say to you all:
    As many things as ever you bind on the earth
        will be bound in heaven.
    As many things as ever you release on the earth
        will be released in heaven.
¹⁹Again Amen I say to you all:
    If ever two speak together out of you all
        on the earth
        about any matter which you ask,
            it will happen to you
                from my father
                    my father in heavens.
²⁰Where there are two or three gathered
    into my name
there I am in the midst of them.
²¹Then Peter came;

he said to him:

    haShem

        how many times well he sin against me,

           this brother of mine,

        and I will release for him?

          Up to seven times?

[22]He says to him;

Jesus does:

    I do not say to you seven times.

    Rather, up to seventy times seven.

[23]Because of this

    the dominion of the heavens may be compared to a person

                 who rules,

      who wanted to cast up accounts with his slaves.

      [24]When he began to cast up,

        there came to him

           one

           one debtor

             of ten thousand talents.

      [25]Because he did not have anything to pay with,

        the master[142] ordered him to be sold

          also his wife

          and children

          and all as much as he has

        and to be given back what was due.

      [26]So after he fell,

        the slave worshiped him;

        he said:

          Be bighearted on me.

            And I will repay all to you.

      [27]After he felt it in his gut,

        the master of that slave

          released him

and the loan he let go for him.

28After he went out,

that slave found one of his co-slaves,

   one who owed him one hundred denarii.

He grabbed him;

he choked him;

he said:

   Pay back if you owe anything.

29So after falling

this co-slave asked him;

he said:

   Be bighearted on me

      and I will repay you.

30He did not want to.

Rather,

   After going out

he threw him into prison

   up until he should repay the debt.

31When his co-slaves saw what happened,

   they were exceedingly pained.

After they came

they explained to their master all that had happened.

32Then he called him,

   his master did,

he says to him:

   Worthless slave.

   All that debt I let go for you,

      when you asked me.

   33It wasn't necessary also for you

   to have mercy on your co-slave,

      as I had mercy on you?

34His master became angry

he handed him over to the torturer

   up until he should repay

   all the debt to him.

³⁵Thus my father
 my heavenly father
will do to you all,
 if ever you do not let go
  each to his brother
from your minds.¹⁴³

Chapter Nineteen

¹It happened when Jesus completed these words
he picked up and went from Galilee
and came into the region of Judea
territory of the Jordan.
²There followed him many crowds.
He healed them there.
 ³There came to him
Pharisees
 testing him.
They said:
 Is it appropriate to release his wife
  for any cause?
⁴He answered;
he said:
 You never read:
  The creator
   from the beginning
  "male and female he made them"?
⁵And he said:
 On account of this:
  "a person abandons
   father and mother
  and will be welded to his wife."
 They will become
  the two of them
 a single body.

⁶So that no longer are they two
  but one body.
So that which God yoked together
  let not a person separate.
⁷They say to him:
  So why did Moses command
  to give a book of departure
  and to release?
⁸He says to them:
  Moses
    with regard to your hardheartedness
  permitted you to release your wives.
    From the beginning it has not happened thus.
⁹I say to you all:
  whoever releases his wife
    except because of fornication
  and marries another
  commits adultery.
¹⁰They say to him;
the disciples do:
  Since it is thus,
    the case of a person with the woman,
  it is not profitable to marry.
¹¹He said to them:
  Not everyone has room for this word,
    but it has been given to whom it has been given.
    ¹²They are eunuchs,
      those who are eunuchs out of their mother's belly
      they were born thus.
  And they are eunuchs,
    those who were castrated by people.
  And they are eunuchs,
    those who castrate themselves
      because of the dominion of the heavens.

  The one able to have room
   should make room.
13Then there were brought to him
 children
  in order that he lay his hands on them
  and pray.
The disciples scolded them.
14Jesus said:
 Let the children go;
  do not prevent them coming to me.
   Of such is the dominion of the heavens.
15After placing his hands on them,
he went from there.
 16Look:
 one came to him
 he said:
  Teacher,
   What worthy thing should I do
    in order that I should have life eternal?
17He said to him:
 Why are you asking me about a worthy thing?
  One is the worthy one.
 Since you want
  to go into life
   Guard the commandments.
18He says to him:
 Which ones?
Jesus was saying:
 Do not murder.
 Do not commit adultery.
 Do not steal.
 Do not lie.
 19Honor father and mother.
 Love your neighbor as yourself.

²⁰He says to him,

the young man does:

  These all I guard.

    What still do I lack?

²¹Jesus said to him:

  Since you want to be complete,

    Go;

    sell your possessions;

    give to the poor.

      You will have treasure in the heavens.

    Come;

    follow me.

²²After hearing this word,

The young man went away pained:

  he had much real estate.

²³Jesus said to his disciples:

  Amen I say to you all:

    Wealthy?

    With difficulty

      he goes into the dominion of the heavens.

    ²⁴Again I say to you all:

    Is it easier:

      a camel through eye of a needle

        to go in

    or:

      a rich person

        into the dominion of God?

²⁵After hearing,

the disciples were driven out of their minds

exceedingly;

they said:

  Then who is able to be rescued?

²⁶After looking around

Jesus said to them:

With humans this is impossible;
   with God all things are possible.
²⁷Then Peter asked;
he said to him:
   Look:
     we,
      we abandoned all things.
      We followed you.
   Then what will be to us?
²⁸Jesus said to them:
Amen I say to you all:
   You
     you who followed me,
   in the resurrection
     whenever the son of adam
       sits on a throne of his glory,
    you will sit
     yourselves
   on twelve thrones
   dividing the twelve tribes of Israel.
²⁹Everyone who abandons
   home
    or brothers
    or sisters
    or father
    or mother
    or children
    or fields
      on account of my name,
many times over they will receive
   and life eternal they will inherit.
³⁰Many will be first
   who are last,
and last who are first.

Chapter Twenty

¹Similar is the dominion of the heavens
to a person,
   a house despot,
who comes out
   just at dawn
to hire workers into his vineyard.
²Negotiating together with the workers
   a wage of a denarius for the day,
      he sent them into this vineyard.
³He came out around the third hour;
he saw others standing
   in the marketplace
   idle.
⁴To these he said:
   Go,
      you too
   into the vineyard
      and whatever is strictly right
         I will give you.
They went away.
⁵Again he came
around the sixth
and the ninth hour;
   he did the same thing.
⁶Around the eleventh
he came out
he found others standing;
he says to them:
   Why thus have you stood
   the whole day
   idle?
⁷They say to him:
   Because no one hired us.

He says to them:
  Go
    also you
  into the vineyard.
8When it was evening
he says,
  the master of the vineyard does,
to his overseer:
  Call the workers.
  Repay the payment.
  Begin from the last ones
  up to the first ones.
9After those around the eleventh hour came,
  they received a denarius apiece.
10After those first came,
  they supposed that they will receive more.
They received a denarius apiece,
  them too.
11After they received
  they grumbled against the house despot.
12They said:
  Those last ones did one hour.
  You did the same to us
    us:
      we bore the burden of the day
      and the heat.
13He answered to one of them,
he said:
  Buddy,
  I did not hurt you.
  Didn't you negotiate together with me for a denarius?
  14Take yours and go.
  I want
    to this last one
  to give as I gave to you.

15Isn't it appropriate for me
to do what I want in my business?
   Or is your eye worthless
   because I am worthy?
      16Thus the last ones will be first
      and the first ones last.
17When Jesus was about to go up into Jerusalem
he took the twelve aside
  all alone.
In the road he said to them:
  18Look:
    we are going up into Jerusalem.
    The son of adam will be handed over
      to the chief priests
      and scribes.
    They will condemn him into death.
    19They will hand him over to the Gentiles
      into mocking
      and into flogging
      and into crucifying.
        In the third day he will be raised.
20Then she came to him,
  the mother of the sons of Zebedee,
    with her sons,
she worshiped;
she asked something of him.
21He said to her:
  what do you want?
She says to him:
  Speak
    so that they might sit,
      these two sons of mine,
    one at your right
    one at your left
      in your dominion.

²²Jesus answered;
he said:
    You do not know what you are asking.
      Are you able to drink the cup
      that I am about to drink?
They say to him:
    We are able.
²³He says to them:
    My cup you will drink.
      Sitting at my right
      and at my left,
        it is not mine to give this thing,
        but to those for whom it was prepared
        by my father.
²⁴After the ten heard
they were moved with indignation
    about the brothers.
²⁵Jesus called them;
he said:
    You know that the rulers of the Gentiles
    exercise mastery over them,
    the great ones exercise authority over them.
      ²⁶Not thus is it among you all.
    Rather,
      whoever wants
        among you,
      to become great
        will be your deacon.
      ²⁷Whoever wants
        among you
      to be first,
        will be your slave.
²⁸So that the son of adam did not come to be deaconed to
    but to deacon
      and to give his life as a ransom instead of many.

²⁹As they were going out from Jericho
there followed him a large crowd.
>³⁰Look:
>>two blind men
>>>sitting by the road.
>After they heard that Jesus is passing by,
>they screamed;
>they said:
>>haShem
>>>have mercy on us
>>>>Son of David.

³¹The crowd scolded them
>so that they would be silent.
They screamed even more;
they said:
>haShem
>>have mercy on us
>>>son of David.

³²Jesus stood;
he called to them;
he said:
>What do you want
>that I should do for you all?

³³They say to him:
>haShem
>>that our eyes be opened.

³⁴Jesus was moved in his gut;
he touched their eyes;
right away
>they saw;
>they followed him.

Chapter Twenty-One

¹When they were so close
  into Jerusalem,
they came into Bethphage
  into the olive mountain.
Then Jesus sent two disciples;
²he said to them:
  Go into the village opposite you
  BANG
  you will find a donkey that has been tied
    and a colt with her.
  After loosing
  bring them to me.
  ³If ever anyone should say to you all:
    Why?
  Say:
    haShem has need of them.
      BANG
    he will send them.
⁴This happened in order that what was said be fulfilled,
  what was said through the prophet,
    who said:
    ⁵Speak to the daughter of Zion
      Look:
        Your king is coming to you
        gentle
        and mounted on a donkey
          and on a colt
          a son of one under a burden.
⁶The disciples went
they did exactly as Jesus instructed them
⁷They led the donkey and the colt
they laid on them their clothing.
He sat on them.

⁸The largest crowd spread out their own clothing
in the road.
Others cut branches from the trees
and spread them out in the road.
⁹The crowds,
   those crowds that went before him,
   those crowds that followed,
screamed;
they said:
   Hosanna to the son of David.
   Blessed the one coming in the name of haShem.
   Hosanna in the highest.
¹⁰After he went into Jerusalem
it was shaken
   all the city.
They said:
   Who is this?
¹¹The crowds were saying:
   This is the prophet
     Jesus;
       he from Nazareth of Galilee.
¹²Jesus went into the Temple.
He cast out all those selling
   and buying
   in the Temple.
The tables of the moneychangers he overturned,
also the chairs
   of those selling pigeons.
¹³He says to them:
   It stands written:
     "My house
     a house of prayer let it be called."
   You
   you are making it a bandit cave.

14They came to him
   the blind
   the lame
     in the Temple
he healed them.
15When they saw,
   chief priests and scribes,
the marvels that he did:
   the children screaming in the Temple
   saying:
     Hosanna to the son of David;
they were irritated;
16they said to him:
   Do you hear
     what those people are saying?
Jesus says to them:
   Yes.
   You never read:
     Out of the mouths of babies
     even nursing infants
     I will furnish praise.
17After abandoning them,
he went out,
   out of the city,
into Bethany.
   He was lodged there.
18Early in the morning
   when they returned into the city,
he was hungry.
19After he saw one fig tree
   on the road
he came upon it.
He found nothing in it
   except leaves only.

He says to it:
    No longer from you
    let fruit be born,
    not into eternity.
It was dried up at once,
    the fig tree was.
20When the disciples saw,
they were astounded;
they said:
    How
      at once
    was the fig tree dried up?
21Jesus answered,
he said to them:
    Amen I say to you all:
    If you were to have faithfulness
      and not be scattered,
    not only the thing with the fig tree will you do,
      but even if
        to this mountain
      you were to say:
        Be lifted up;
        Be thrown into the sea;
      it will happen.
22All things,
    whatever you should ask,
      in your prayer
      as you are faithful
    you will receive.
23When he came into the Temple
there came to him
    while he was teaching
the chief priests
and the elders of the people;
they said:

On what authority are you doing this?
Who gave you this authority?
²⁴Jesus answered,
he said to them:
  I will ask you all
    yes, me too,
  one word,
    which if you should speak to me
    I also
      to you all
    I will say
    on what authority
    I am doing these things.
²⁵The purification,
  John's purification,
    where was it from?
      Out of heaven
      or out of people?
They discussed among themselves,
they said:
  If we should say:
    out of heaven,
    he will say to us,
      so why were you not faithful to him?
²⁶If we should say:
  out of people,
  we are afraid of the crowd
    for everyone
    as a prophet
    holds John.
²⁷When they answered to Jesus,
they said:
  We don't know.
He said to them,
he in his turn:

Neither do I say to you all
on what authority
I am doing these things.
    28What does it seem to you all?
      A person used to have two children.
        After he came to the first
        he said:
          Child,
          go
            today
          work in the vineyard.
        29He answered;
        he said:
          I do not want to.
        Later
          because he was sorry
        he went.
        30He came to the other.
        He said likewise.
        He answered:
          I
            HaShem;
        and he did not go.
    31Which of the two
    did the will of the father?
They say:
    The first one.
  He says to them,
  Jesus does:
  Amen I say to you all:
    The tax collecting traitors
      and prostitutes
    are going before you all
      into the dominion of God.

³²For John came to you all
   in a strictly observant road.
You were not faithful to him.
   The tax collecting traitors
     and prostitutes
   were faithful to him.
You
   though you saw
you were not sorry later
   in order to be faithful to him.
³³Hear another parable:
A person there was
a house despot
who planted a vineyard:
   a fence for it he placed around it;
   he dug in it a winepress;
   he built a tower.
   He gave it out to tenant farmers.
   He went on a journey.
³⁴When the right time
was close for fruit,
   he sent his slaves to the tenant farmers
   to receive his fruit.
³⁵When the tenant farmers received the slaves,
   one they flayed
   one they killed
   one they stoned to death.
³⁶Again he sent other slaves,
   more than the first ones;
they did to them the same.
³⁷Later he sent to them his son;
he said:
   They will pay deference to my son.
³⁸When the tenant farmers saw the son
they said among themselves:

This is the inheritor;
come
let us kill him
and let us have his inheritance.
³⁹After they received him
they cast him out
out of the vineyard.
They killed him.
⁴⁰So, whenever the master of the vineyard should come,
what will he do to those tenant farmers?
⁴¹They say to him:
Those evil ones,
evil doing calls for evil destruction for them.
The vineyard he will give out
to other tenant farmers
who will give over to him
the fruits in their time.
⁴²He says to them,
Jesus does:
You never read in the scriptures:
A stone
that the builders tried and rejected,
this one
became the head of the corner.
From haShem this happened.
It is astounding in our eyes.
⁴³On account of this I say to you all:
It will be lifted from you,
the dominion of God will be.
It will be given to a Gentile nation
that is doing the fruits of it.
⁴⁴The one falling on the stone will be crushed.
Upon whomever it should fall
it will scatter him like chaff.

⁴⁵When the chief priests and the Pharisees heard his parable,
they knew that he is speaking about them.
 ⁴⁶Though they were seeking him to seize him
 they feared the crowds,
  since honored as a prophet they used to hold him.

Chapter Twenty-Two

¹Jesus answered,
again he said
 in parables
to them,
he said:
 ²The dominion of the heavens may be compared
to a person who rules
 who made a marriage feast for his son.
 ³He sent his slaves to call
 those who had been called
  into the wedding feast.
   They did not want to come.
 ⁴Again he sent other slaves,
he said:
 Say to those who have been called:
 Look:
  my morning meal has been prepared.
  My bulls
   and the grain-fed ones
  have been slaughtered.
 All things are prepared.
 Come into the wedding feast.
 ⁵The clueless ones went away,
 one into his own field,
 one on his business,
 ⁶the rest seized his slaves:
 they raped them,
 they killed them.

⁷The king was furious;
he sent his army;
he destroyed those murderers,
and their city he burned.
⁸Then he says to his slaves:
   The wedding is prepared.
     Those who have been called were not worthy.
    ⁹So go on the outlets of the roads:
     whomever you find,
      call into the marriage feast.
¹⁰The slaves went out into the roads;
they gathered all whom they found,
   both worthless and worthy.
The bride chamber was filled with people reclining to eat.
¹¹When the king went in to see the people reclining to eat
he saw there a person not dressed in a wedding garment
¹²He says to him:
   Buddy,
    how did you come in here
     not having a wedding garment?
The person was muzzled.
¹³Then the king said to his deacons:
   Bind him feet and hands.
   Cast him out
    into the outer darkness.
    There
     there will be wailing
     and gnashing of teeth.
    ¹⁴For many are called;
few are chosen.
¹⁵Then after the Pharisees came;
they took counsel
  how they might trap him in a word.
¹⁶They send to him their disciples,
  with the Herodians.

They said:
  Teacher,
    we know that you are honest
    the road of God in frankness you teach.
  It is not a matter of concern for you
    with reference to anyone,
      for you do not glance into people's faces.
  ¹⁷So tell us
    what does it seem to you?
      Is it appropriate to give tribute to Caesar
      or not?
¹⁸Jesus knew their worthlessness,
he said:
  why are you testing me,
    Role Players?
  ¹⁹Show me the coin of the tribute.
They brought to him a denarius.
²⁰He says to them:
  Of whom is this image
    and this inscription?
²¹They say:
  Of Caesar.
Then he says to them:
  So repay the things of Caesar
    to Caesar,
  and the things of God
    to God.
²²When they heard
they were astonished.
When they abandoned him
they went away.
²³In that day they came to him,
  Sadducees did,
    (they say there is no resurrection).
They asked him;

they said:
  ²⁴Teacher,
    Moses said:
      If ever anyone die
        (not having children)
      his brother will marry his wife;
        he will raise seed to his brother.
  ²⁵There were with us seven brothers.
    The first after marrying died.
      Because he did not have seed,
        he released his wife to his brother.
      ²⁶Likewise the second
    and the third,
    up to the seventh.
  ²⁷Later
    than all of them
died
    the wife.
  ²⁸So, in the resurrection
    of whom among the seven
    will she be wife?
      They all used to have her.
²⁹Jesus answered,
he said to them:
  You are led astray because you know
    neither the scriptures
    nor the power of God.
  ³⁰For in the resurrection
    neither do they marry
    nor are they given in marriage.
  Rather they are like messengers in the heavens.
    ³¹About the resurrection of the corpses
      you do not read the thing said to you
        by God
        who said:

³²"I am

    the God of Abraham;

    the God of Isaac;

    the God of Jacob."

God is not God of corpses but of the living.

³³When the crowds heard

they were driven out of their minds by his teaching.

³⁴When the Pharisees heard that he muzzled the Sadducees,

They were gathered in the same place.

³⁵One of them

    a Torah expert

asked,

testing him:

    ³⁶Teacher,

        which commandment is great in the Torah?

³⁷He said to him:

    You will love haShem

        your God

    in the whole of your mind

    in the whole of your life

    in the whole of your thought.

       ³⁸This is the great

          and first

       commandment.

    ³⁹The second is like to it:

       You will love your neighbor as yourself.

    ⁴⁰In these

       the two commandments

    the whole Torah is hanging.

    The prophets, too.

⁴¹When the Pharisees gathered

he asked them,

    Jesus did,

he said:

⁴²What does it seem to you concerning the Messiah?
　Of whom is he the son?
They say to him:
　Of David.
⁴³He says to them:
　So how does David
　　in breath
　call him haShem
he says:
　　⁴⁴he said
　　　haShem,
　　to my haShem
　　　sit at my right
　　　up until I should place
　　　your enemies
　　　under your feet.
　⁴⁵So since David calls him haShem,
　　How is he his son?
⁴⁶No one was able to answer him a word,
Neither did anyone dare
　from that day
to ask him any more questions.

Chapter Twenty-Three

¹Then Jesus spoke with the crowds
　and his disciples
he said:
　²On the seat of Moses
　sit the scribes and the Pharisees:
　　³so, everything
　　　whatever they should say to you all,
　　do it and guard it.
　　But according to their works do not do.
　　　For they say
　　　　and they do not do.

388

⁴They bind heavy burdens
they place them on the shoulders of people.
They
   however,
with their finger,
   they do not want to move them.
⁵All their works they do
   in order to be seen by people.
     They make broad their phylacteries;
     they enlarge their tassels;
     ⁶they love the places of honor,
       when reclining at banquets,
     and the seats of honor
       in the synagogue,
     ⁷and the greetings
       in the marketplace,
     and to be called
       by people:
        Rabbi.
⁸But as for you
do not be called Rabbi;
   one is your teacher;
all of you are brothers and sisters.
   ⁹Father
     do not call
       yours
       on earth.
One is of you
   the father:
     the heavenly father.
¹⁰Neither call
   teachers,
because your teacher
   is one:
     the Messiah.

¹¹The greater of you will be your deacon.
¹²Anyone who exalts himself
  will be humbled.
Anyone who humbles himself
  will be exalted.
¹³Woe to you all,
  Scribes and Pharisees,
    Role Players:
      you lock the dominion of the heavens
      in the face of people;
        for you do not go in,
        neither do you allow
        those who are going
        to go in.
¹⁵Woe to you all,
  Scribes and Pharisees,
    Role Players:
      you go around the sea
      and the dry land
      to make one single convert.
      Whenever it happens
        you make him a son of Gehenna
          twice what you are.
¹⁶Woe to you all,
  guides who are blind,
  who say:
    Whoever should swear by the sanctuary,
      it is nothing.
    Whoever should swear by the gold of the sanctuary,
      it is owed.
¹⁷Morons!
Blind!
  What is greater?
    The gold of the sanctuary,
    or the sanctuary that makes the gold holy?

¹⁸And:
  Whoever should swear by the altar,
    it is nothing.
  Whoever should swear by the gifts on it,
    it is owed.
¹⁹Blind!
  What is greater?
    The gift,
    or the altar that makes the gift holy?
    ²⁰So the one who swears by the altar
    swears by it
and by all that is on it.
    ²¹And the one who swears by the sanctuary
      swears by it
      and by that which occupies it.
    ²²And the one who swears by the heaven
      swears by the throne of God
      and by the one who sits on it.
  ²³Woe to you all,
    Scribes and Pharisees,
    Role Players:
      you give a tenth
        of mint
        and dill
        and cumin
      and you let go the heavier matters of the Torah:
        the divisions,
        the mercy,
        the faithfulness.
      These things it was necessary to do
        not letting go the others.
  ²⁴Guides who are blind!
    Who filter out a gnat,
    the camel you swallow.

²⁵Woe to you all,
  Scribes and Pharisees,
    Role Players:
      you purify the outside of the cup
      and the dish,
        inside they are full of rape
        and incontinence.
²⁶Blind Pharisee:
  purify first
  the inside of the cup
    in order that also its outside be purified.
²⁷Woe to you all,
  Scribes and Pharisees,
    Role Players:
      you resemble plastered tombs:
        outside they appear in youthful bloom;
        inside they are full of bones of corpses
        and all impurity.
²⁸Thus also you:
  Outside you appear to people
  to be strictly observant.
  Inside you are full of role playing
  and refusal of Torah.
²⁹Woe to you all,
  Scribes and Pharisees,
    Role players:
      you construct the tombs of the prophets
      and decorate the memorials of the observant,
³⁰You say:
  If we,
    we,
      in the days of our fathers,
  we,
  we would not have shared with them
    in the blood of the prophets.

³¹So that you testify to yourselves
   that you are sons
      of those who murdered the prophets.
³²You,
you fill up
   the measure of your fathers.
³³Snakes
   fathered by poisonous snakes,
   how might you flee from the separation of Gehenna?
³⁴On account of this,
   look:
      I send to you
         prophets
         and wise people
         and scribes.
            Some of them
               you kill
               and crucify
            some of them
               you flog in your synagogues,
               you hunt from city to city.
³⁵How might it come on you
   all observant blood shed on earth,
      from the blood of Abel
         (who was strictly observant)
      up to the blood of Zachariah
         son of Barachiah
            whom you murdered
            between the sanctuary and the altar.
³⁶Amen I say to you all:
   All these things will come upon this birthing.
      ³⁷Jerusalem,
      Jerusalem:
         the killer of the prophets,
         the stoner of those sent to her.

How many times I wanted
to gather your children
under my wings.
    You did not want.
[38]Look:
    it is let go to you,
      your house.
[39]I say to you all:
    You will not see me
    from now on
      up until you should say:
        Praised is the one coming
        in the name of haShem.

Chapter Twenty-Four

[1]Jesus went out from the Temple;
he was going
  and his disciples came to him
    to point out to him the improvements of the Temple.
[2]He answered;
he said to them:
  Don't look at all these things
  Amen I say to you all:
    There will not be left here
      stone on stone
        that is not demolished.
[3]When he was sitting on the olive mountain,
they came to him, his disciples did,
    all alone.
They said:
  Tell us:
    when will these things be?
    what is the sign
      of their arrival
      and of the completion of the aeon (eternity)?

⁴Jesus answered;
he said to them:
    Look out lest you be led astray.
        ⁵For many will come
           upon my name,
        they will say:
           I am the Messiah.
        They will lead many astray.
    ⁶You are about to hear wars
        and reports of wars.
See here:
    do not cry out.
        For it is necessary that this happen
        But not yet is the completion.
        ⁷There will be raised Gentile against Gentile,
           dominion against dominion.
           There will be famines
               and earthquakes,
                  place by place.
    ⁸All these things are the onset of labor.
    ⁹Then they will hand you all over
        into oppression
        and they will kill you.
    You will be hated by all the Gentiles
        because of my name.
    ¹⁰Then they will be scandalized,
    many will,
        each other they will hand over.
        They will hate each other.
    ¹¹Many pseudo-prophets will be raised;
    they will lead many astray.
        ¹²Because of the increase of Torah rejection
           it will breathe faintly,
               the love of many.

¹³The one who endures into the completion,
   that one will be rescued.
¹⁴It will be proclaimed,
  this good news of the dominion,
in the whole of the civilized world,
  into a witness
  to all of the Gentiles.
Then will have come the completion.
   ¹⁵Whenever you should see the disgusting thing of desolation
   the thing spoken through Daniel the prophet
  standing in the holy place
        (Storyteller, understand),
   ¹⁶then those in Judea:
    flee into the mountains;
  ¹⁷the one on the roof:
   do not come down to pick up the things out of the house;
  ¹⁸the one in the field:
   do not turn behind you to pick up a coat.
  ¹⁹Woe to those who have in belly
 and to those nursing
  in those days.
²⁰Pray
  in order that it may not happen,
   your flight,
  during the winter
   or on Shabbat.
     ²¹For there will be then great oppression
    such as has not happened
     from the beginning of the beautiful world
     up until now.
      It has never happened, period.
²²If those days were not shortened
all flesh would not be rescued.
  Because of the chosen ones
  those days were shortened.

²³Then if anyone should say to you all:
Look:
    here is the Messiah,
        or here;
do not be faithful.
    ²⁴They will be raised up,
        pseudo-Messiahs,
        pseudo-prophets;
    they will give great signs
        and monsters
            so as to lead astray
                if possible
            the chosen ones.
²⁵Look:
    it stands spoken beforehand
    to you all.
²⁶If they should say to you:
    Look:
        in the wilderness he is;
            do not go out.
    Look:
        in the storeroom,
            do not be faithful.
²⁷For as the lightning comes out
    from the East and appears
        up to the West,
thus it will be,
    the arrival of the son of adam.
        ²⁸Wherever should be the corpse,
        there will be gathered the eagles.
²⁹Right away
after the oppression of those days
    the sun will be made dark,
    the moon will not give its splendor,

the stars will fall from the heaven,
    the powers of the heavens will be made to totter.
³⁰Then it will appear,
    the sign of the son of adam in heaven;
then they will be cut off,
    all the tribes of the earth;
and they will see the son of adam
    as he comes on the clouds of heaven
        with power
        and much glory.
³¹He will send his messengers
    with a great trumpet.
They will gather
    his chosen ones
        out of the four winds,
        from the ends of the heavens,
        up to their ends.
³²From the fig tree
learn the parable:
    whenever already her branches
    become tender
        and the leaves grow out,
    you know that summer is near.
³³Thus also you,
    whenever you see all these things,
you know that near it is,
    upon the door.
³⁴Amen I say to you all:
    By no means will it pass by,
        this birthing
    up until all these things happen.
        ³⁵The heaven and the earth will pass by.
        My words
            let them not pass by.

³⁶Concerning those days and hours
no one knows,
   neither the messengers of the heavens,
neither the son,
except the father only.
³⁷For as the days of Noah
thus it will be,
   the arrival of the son of adam.
³⁸For they were in those days,
   those days before the flood,
     they were gnawing,
      and drinking;
     they were marrying,
      and causing to marry,
       until the day when Noah went into the ark.
³⁹They did not know
   up until the flood came
    and lifted everything.
Thus it will be,
   also,
   the arrival of the son of adam.
    ⁴⁰Then there will be two in the field:
     one is seized,
     one is left.
    ⁴¹Two women are grinding in the mill:
     one is seized,
     one is left.
⁴²So stay awake.
  You do not know
  in what day
  haShem,
   your haShem,
  comes.
⁴³That thing you know:

if the house despot knew
  in what guard
    the thief comes,
  he would have stayed awake;
    he would have allowed his house to be dug through.
⁴⁴Because of this
  you also,
  you be prepared,
    because you do not presume to know in what hour
    the son of adam comes.
⁴⁵Who then is the faithful slave
and prudent,
  whom haShem will set down
  on his household slaves
    to give to them nourishment at the right time?
⁴⁶Godlike in happiness
  is that slave
  whom
    when he comes
  haShem
    his haShem
  will find thus doing.
⁴⁷Amen I say to you all:
  on all his possessions he will set him down.
⁴⁸If ever he should say,
  that evil slave,
in his mind:
  he is delayed,
    my haShem,
  ⁴⁹he will begin to beat his co-slaves;
  he would eat
  and drink with drunks.
⁵⁰He will have come,
  haShem of that servant,

in the day when he is not waiting,
  in an hour when he does not know.
[51]He will cut him in two,
his slave will be set with the role players.
  There will be wailing and gnashing of teeth.

Chapter Twenty-Five

[1]Then it will be compared,
the dominion of the heavens will be,
  to ten virgins:
    Each takes her lamp,
    she goes out
      into the meeting of the bridegroom.
  [2]Five of them were morons;
five were prudent.
    [3]The morons,
      though they took their lamps,
    did not bring with them oil.
    [4]The prudent,
    they brought oil in the flasks,
      each with her lamp.
  [5]When the bridegroom is delayed,
    they all nodded off;
      they slept.
  [6]During the middle of the night
a cry has happened:
    Look:
      the bridegroom.
      Come into the meeting!
  [7]Then they were raised,
    all those virgins,
and they will beautify their lamps.
    [8]The morons
      to the prudent
    said:

Give to us
 out of your oil
because our lamps are extinguished.
9They answered,
 the prudent did;
they said:
 Lest there surely not be enough for us and you,
 go
  rather
 to the sellers,
 buy for yourselves.
10When they went off to buy
the bridegroom came.
Those who were prepared
went in
 with him
  into the marriage feast.
The door was locked.
11Later they came also,
 the leftover virgins;
they said:
 haShem
 haShem
  open to us.
12He answered;
he said:
 Amen I say to you all:
 I do not know you.
13So keep awake:
 You do not know the day
 or the hour.
14As a person who goes on a journey
 called his own slaves
 he handed over to them his possessions
  15to whom he gave five talents,

    two,
    and one,
      to each according to his own capabilities.
He went on a journey.
Right away
¹⁶after going
    the one who received five talents
    worked in them
      and gained five others.
¹⁷Likewise
    the one who received two
    gained two others.
¹⁸The one who received one went off;
    he dug in the earth;
    he hid the silver of his haShem.
¹⁹After much time,
    he comes,
      haShem of those slaves;
    he takes up accounts with them.
    ²⁰After coming to him
      the one who received five talents
      brought five other talents.
        He said:
          haShem,
            five talents you gave to me.
            See, another five talents I gained.
²¹He said to him,
his haShem:
    Good
    worthy slave
    faithful:
      on a few you were faithful;
      on many I set you down.
        Go into the joy of your haShem.
²²After coming to him

also the one who received two talents said:
  haShem

    two talents you gave to me.

    See, another two talents I gained.

²³He said to him,

his haShem:

  Good,

  worthy slave,

  faithful:

    on a few you were faithful;

    on many I set you down.

      Go into the joy of your haShem.

²⁴After coming to him,

also the one who had received one talent,

he said:

  haShem

    I knew you,

      that hard you are as a person:

        harvesting where you did not plant,

        gathering what you did not scatter.

    ²⁵Because I was afraid

      after going out

    I hid your talent in the ground.

      See, you have what is yours.

²⁶His haShem answered;

he said to him:

  Worthless slave;

  Lazy:

    you knew that I harvest where I did not plant,

    and gather what I did not scatter?

²⁷It was necessary that you throw my silver

to the money changers,

    so when I came

    I would recover what was mine

      with interest.

²⁸So lift from him the talent.
Give it to the one who has ten talents.
²⁹For to everyone who has,
  it will be given,
    it will be excessive.
  From the one who does not have
    even what he has will be lifted from him.
³⁰As for the useless slave,
  throw him into the outer darkness.
    There, there will be wailing
    and gnashing of teeth.
³¹Whenever he should come,
  the son of adam
    in his glory
      and all the messengers with him,
then he will sit on the throne of his glory.
³²They will be gathered before him,
  all the Gentiles.
He will divide them from each other,
  as the shepherd divides the sheep
    from the goats.
³³He will set the sheep at his right
the goats at his left.
³⁴Then he will say,
the king, to these at his right:
  Come, praised of my father,
  Inherit the dominion prepared for you
    from the founding of the beautiful world.
    ³⁵For I was hungry
      and you gave me to eat;
    I was thirsty
      and you watered me;
    a stranger I was,
      and you gathered me;

[36]naked,
   and you threw something around me;
weak,
   and you looked in on me;
in prison I was,
   and you came to me.
[37]Then they will answer him,
  the strictly observant;
they will say:
  haShem
    when did we see you hungry
     and we nourished?
    or thirsty
     and we watered?
   [38]When did we see you a stranger
    and we gathered?
    or naked
     and we threw something around you?
   [39]When did we see you weak
    or in prison
     and we came to you?
[40]The king will answer;
he will say to them:
  Amen I say to you all:
    So far as you did to one of these
    my sisters or brothers
     the littlest,
    to me you did it.
[41]Then he will say also to those at his left:
  Go from me you who have been cursed,
  Go into the eternal fire
    the fire prepared for the prosecutor
     and his messengers.
   [42]For I was hungry,
    and you did not give to me to eat;

I was thirsty,
  and you did not water me;
⁴³stranger I was,
  and you did not gather me;
naked
    and you did not throw anything around me;
weak
  and in prison,
    and you did not look in on me.
⁴⁴Then they will answer;
They will say:
  haShem,
    When did we see you hungry
    or thirsty
    or stranger
    or naked
    or weak
    or in prison
    and we did not deacon to you?
⁴⁵Then he will answer them;
he will say:
  Amen I say to you all:
    As far as you did not do
    to one of these
      the littlest,
    neither did you do it to me.
⁴⁶They will go away into eternal punishing,
the strictly observant into eternal life.

Chapter Twenty-Six

¹It happened when Jesus completed all these words,
he said to his disciples:
  ²You know
  that after two days the Passover happens.
  The son of adam is handed over into crucifixion.

³Then they gathered,
  the chief priests
  the elders of the people,
into the courtyard of the chief priest
  (who is called Caiaphas).
⁴They consulted together
in order that Jesus
  by cunning
might be seized and killed.
⁵They were saying:
  not in the festival
    in order that an uproar not happen in the people.
⁶When Jesus happened to be in Bethany
  in the house of Simon the leper,
⁷there came to him a woman
  a woman who had an alabaster of perfume,
    heavy with price.
She tried to pour it on his head
  as he was reclining to eat.
⁸After the disciples saw they were angry;
they said:
  To what end this waste?
  ⁹For it was possible to sell for much
    and to give to the poor.
¹⁰After Jesus knew,
he said to them:
  Why cause trouble to the woman?
    A beautiful work she did in my honor.
  ¹¹Always the poor you have with you.
    Me, not always you have.
  ¹²When she threw the perfume on my body,
    she acted in order to entomb me.
  ¹³Amen I say to you all:
    Wherever this good news is proclaimed
      in the whole beautiful world,

it will be spoken
>also
what she did
>as her memorial.

¹⁴Then he went,
>one of the twelve,
>the one called Judas Iscariot,
to the chief priests;
¹⁵he said:
>What do you want to give to me?
>>For my part,
>>>I will hand him over to you.
They placed to him thirty silver pieces.
¹⁶From then he tried to seek
a good time
>in order to hand him over.

¹⁷In the first day of the unleavends
they came to Jesus,
>the disciples did;
they said:
>Where do you want us to prepare for you
>to eat the Passover?
¹⁸He said:
>Go into the city
>>to the person we will not name.
>Say to him:
>>The teacher says:
>>>My right time is near,
>>>with you I make the Passover
>>>>with my disciples.
¹⁹They did,
>the disciples,
as Jesus ordered them.
They prepared the Passover.

²⁰When it was evening,
    he was reclining to eat
        with the twelve disciples.
²¹While they were eating
    he said:
        Amen I say to you all:
            One of you will hand me over.
²²They were exceedingly pained;
they began to say to him,
each one:
        You can't mean me,
            haShem?
²³He answered;
he said:
        The one who dipped with me
        the hand in the deep bowl:
            that one will hand me over.
        ²⁴The son of adam goes exactly as it stands written
                    concerning him,
        but woe to that person
        through whom the son of adam is handed over.
            Beautiful it would be for him
            if that person was never born.
²⁵Judas answered
    (Judas the one who hands him over);
he said:
    You can't mean me,
        rabbi?
    He says to him:
        You said it.
²⁶While they were eating,
after Jesus took bread,
after he blessed it,
    he broke it
after he gave to the disciples;

he said:
    Take it;
    eat it;
    this is my body.
27After taking a cup,
after giving thanks,
    he gave to them;
he said:
    Drink out of it,
      all,
    28for this is my blood
      of the covenant
      my blood for many poured out
        toward the releasing of sins.
    29I say to you all:
      I surely will not drink
        from now on
      out of this that grows of the vineyard,
        not up until that day
        whenever I drink it,
          with you all,
        new in the dominion of my father.
30After singing a hymn
they went out into the olive mountain.
31Then he says to them,
Jesus does:
    All you will be scandalized in me
      in this night.
    For it stands written:
      "I will strike the shepherd
      they will be scattered,
        the sheep of the shepherd."
    32After I am raised,
    I will go before you into Galilee.
33Peter answered;

he said to him:
   If they all are scandalized in you,
      I,
   I will never be scandalized.
34He said to him,
Jesus did:
   Amen I say to you:
     In this night
       before the rooster sounds
     three times you will deny me.
35He says to him,
Peter does:
   Even if it were necessary that I
     with you
  should die,
    I will not deny you.
      The same all the disciples said.
36Then he goes with them,
Jesus does,
  into the region called Gethsemane.
He says to the disciples:
sit here,
up until when
   after going away there
   I will pray.
37After taking Peter
and the two sons of Zebedee,
   he began to be pained
   and to be in great distress.
38Then he says to them:
   Surrounded by pain
   is my life
     up until death.
   Remain here.
   Keep awake with me.

³⁹After he went forward a little way
he fell on his face;
he prayed;
he said:
    My father
    if it is possible,
    pass by from me
      this cup.
    Still,
      not as I want,
    but as you want.
⁴⁰He comes to the disciples.
He finds them sleeping.
He says to Peter:
    Thus you are not strong
      one hour
    to stay awake with me?
    ⁴¹Stay awake.
    Pray,
      in order that you not go into trial.
        The breath is zealous;
      the body is weak.
⁴²Again a second time
after going away
he prayed;
he said:
    My father,
    since it is not possible
    that this pass by
    if ever I should not drink it,
    let it happen, your will.
⁴³After he came
    again
he found them sleeping
    for their eyes were heavy.

⁴⁴He abandoned them
 again
he went away
he prayed a third time
 the same thing he said
 again.
⁴⁵Then he comes to the disciples
he says to them:
 Sleep forever.
 Take your rest.
 Look:
  the hour is so close.
  The son of adam is handed over into the hands of sinners.
 ⁴⁶Get up.
Let's go.
 Look:
  the one who hands me over is so close.
⁴⁷While he was still speaking,
 Look:
  Judas
   (he one of the twelve)
  came,
   with him, a large crowd
   with swords and clubs
    from the chief priests
    and elders of the people.
 ⁴⁸The one who hands him over
 gave to them a sign;
 he said:
  Whomever I kiss,
   he is it.
    Grab him.
 ⁴⁹Right away
he came to Jesus;
he said:

Greetings
   Rabbi.
He kissed him.
50Jesus said to him:
   Buddy,
     why are you here?
Then they came to him;
they threw hands on Jesus;
they grabbed him.
51Look:
   One of those with Jesus
   extended his hand;
   he drew out his sword;
   he struck the slave of the chief priest;
   he took away his ear.
52Then he says to him,
Jesus does:
   Return your sword into its place,
   for all who take the sword
   by the sword are destroyed.
   53Or do you think that I am not able
     to ask my father
     and he would station by me
     from that moment
       more than twelve legions of messengers?
   54So how then would the writing be fulfilled
   that thus it is necessary to happen?
55In that hour he said,
Jesus did,
to the crowds:
   Am I a bandit
   that you came out with swords and clubs?
   Daily in the Temple
   I used to sit teaching
     and you did not seize me.

⁵⁶This whole thing has happened
   in order that they might be fulfilled,
     the writings of the prophets.
Then the disciples all abandoned him,
   they all fled.
⁵⁷The ones who seized Jesus led him away
to Caiaphas (the chief priest),
when the scribes and the elders were gathered.
⁵⁸Peter follows him from a distance
   up to the courtyard of the chief priest
     and,
       after going inside,
     he tried to sit with the servants to see the end.
⁵⁹The chief priests
   and the whole Sanhedrin
were examining false testimony against Jesus
   that sought to kill him,¹⁴⁴
     ⁶⁰They did not find anything reliable:
   it was false witness after false witness.
At last two witnesses came forward;
⁶¹they said:
   This one said:
     I am able to destroy the sanctuary of God
       and through three days to build it.
⁶²After he stood up,
'the chief priest said to him:
   Ought you not answer what these witness against you?
⁶³Jesus held silent.
The chief priest said to him:
   I am binding you by an oath according to God
     the living God
   that
     to us
   you should say if you are the Messiah,
     the son of God.

⁶⁴He says to him,
Jesus does:
> You said.
> Indeed I am saying to you all:
> > from now you will see the son of adam
> > seated at the right hand of power
> > > and coming on the clouds of heaven.

⁶⁵Then the chief priest ripped his garment;
he said:
> He blasphemed.
> Why still have we need of witnesses?
> > See now you all heard the blasphemy.

⁶⁶What to you does this seem?
Those who answered said:
> Guilty of death he is.

⁶⁷Then they spat into his face
and hit him with fists.
They hit him with clubs;
⁶⁸they said:
> Prophesy to us, Messiah,
> > who is the one who struck you?

⁶⁹Peter was sitting outside in the courtyard.
There came to him
> one woman
> > a little girl,
she said:
> > You also were with Jesus,
> > > the Galilean.

⁷⁰He denied before all,
he said:
> I do not know what you are saying.

⁷¹After he went out into the gateway
> there saw him another woman.
> She said to those there:

this one was with Jesus
    from Nazareth.
⁷²Again he denied with an oath:
    I do not know the person.
⁷³After a little while there came to him those who were standing,
they said to Peter:
    Truly also you are one of them:
        your dialect makes you stick out.
⁷⁴Then he began to curse and swear:
    I do not know the person.
        BANG
    the rooster sounded.
⁷⁵Peter remembered the word Jesus had spoken:
    Before the rooster sounds three times,
        you will deny me.
After he went out he wept bitterly.

Chapter Twenty-Seven

¹When it was early morning
a consultation they took,
    all the chief priests
    and the elders of the people,
a consultation against Jesus
so as to kill him.
²After they bound him
they led him
and handed him over to Pilate the ruler.
³Then he saw,
Judas did,
    Judas the one who handed him over,
that he was condemned.
He regretted;
    he returned the thirty silvers
        to the chief priests
        and elders,

⁴he said:

   I sinned by handing over harmless blood.

They said:

   What to us?

   You will see.

⁵After throwing the silvers into the sanctuary

   he went away.

   He went out.

   He hanged himself.

⁶The chief priests took the silvers.

They said:

   it is not appropriate to throw them into the treasury,

      since the worth of blood it is.

⁷A consultation they took,

they bought with them the field of the potter

   to be a grave for strangers.

      ⁸Therefore it was called,

         that field was,

      "field of blood"

         up to today.

⁹Then it was fulfilled,

   the word through Jeremiah the prophet,

who said:

   "They took the thirty silvers,

      the worth of the one that has been valued

         whom they valued from the sons of Israel.

      ¹⁰They gave them into the field of the potter,

         exactly as haShem set it in order for me."

¹¹Jesus was stood in front of the ruler.

He asked him,

the ruler did,

he said:

   You are the king of the Jews?

Jesus said:

   You say.

¹²While the chief priests and elders stated the charges against him,
he answered nothing.
¹³Then he says to him,
Pilate does:

> You don't hear what sort of things they're saying about you?

¹⁴He did not answer to him,

> not even one word,
>> so as to amaze the ruler exceedingly.

¹⁵Feast by feast
the ruler was accustomed to release one to the crowd,

> a prisoner whom they wanted.
>> ¹⁶They had then a remarkable prisoner
>>> who was called Barabbas.

¹⁷So when they were gathered together,
he said to them,
Pilate did:

> Which one do you want me to release to you:
>> Barabbas
>> or Jesus,
>>> the one called messiah?

¹⁸Pilate assumed that it was because of malice that they handed
him over.¹⁴⁵

¹⁹After he sat on the rostrum,
his wife sent to him,
she said:

> It is nothing to you and to that strictly observant man.
>> For many things have I suffered today
>>> dream by dream
>> because of him.

²⁰The chief priest
and the elders
persuaded the crowds that they choose Barabbas,

> Jesus they destroyed.

²¹The ruler answered,
he said to them:

Which of the two do you want from the two that I release
for you?
They said:
Barabbas.
²²He says to them,
Pilate does:
so what should I do to Jesus,
who is called messiah?
They say,
all of them:
Let him be crucified.¹⁴⁶
²³He said:
What bad thing did he do?
They kept screaming excessively;
they said:
Let him be crucified.
²⁴When Pilate saw that he was gaining nothing,
but rather a riot was happening,
he took water;
he washed his hands against the crowd;
he said:
I am innocent of this one's blood.
You will see.
²⁵The whole people answered;
they said:
His blood will be on us
and on our children.
²⁶Then he released to them Barabbas;
Jesus he flogged;
Jesus he handed over to be crucified.
²⁷Then the soldiers of the ruler took Jesus into the praetorium;
they gathered upon him the whole cohort.
²⁸After they stripped him,
a scarlet robe they put around him.

²⁹They wove a crown out of thorns;
   they placed it on his head,
      a reed in his right hand.
      Bowing in front of him they ridiculed him:
         Hail, king of the Jews.
   ³⁰After spitting on him
      they took the reed and struck him on his head.
   ³¹When they ridiculed him,
      they stripped from him the robe,
      put his own clothes on him,
         and drove him away to crucify.
³²As they were coming out they found a person,
   a Cyrenian
      (Simon by name),
this person they forced into service
   in order that he carry his cross.
³³After they came into a place called Golgotha
   (which is called Skull Place),
³⁴they gave to him to drink wine that had been mixed with gall.
He tasted it,
   he did not want to drink.
³⁵They crucified him,
   they divided his clothing
      by throwing lots.
³⁶They sat down,
   they watched him there.
³⁷They placed above his head the accusation that had been written
                  against him:
   This man is Jesus,
      the King of the Jews.
³⁸Then they crucified with him two bandits,
   one at his right
   and one at his left.
³⁹Those passing by blasphemed him
by shaking their heads

and by saying:
    ⁴⁰You are the one who destroys the sanctuary
      and in three days builds it.
        Rescue yourself,
          since son you are,
          son of God.
        Come down from the cross.
⁴¹Likewise the chief priests ridiculed,
with the scribes
and the elders,
they were saying:
    ⁴²Others he rescued,
      himself
      he is not able to rescue.
    King of Israel he is.
      Let him come down now from the cross
        and we will be faithful on his model.
    ⁴³He has trusted in God,
      let God shield him now
        if he wants him.
          For he said:
            of God I am son.
⁴⁴The same way even the bandits
    who were crucified with him
reproached him.
⁴⁵From the sixth hour darkness came upon all the earth up until the
               ninth hour.
⁴⁶About the ninth hour he bellowed,
Jesus did,
in a great voice,
he said:
    Eli Eli lema sabachthani?
    This is:
      My God, my God,
      to what end have you abandoned me?

⁴⁷Some of those standing there
after they heard were saying:
 Elijah! This one is calling Elijah!
⁴⁸Right away
there ran,
 one of them,
took a sponge,
filled it with vinegar
 and placed it around a reed.
  He gave it to him to drink.
⁴⁹The others were saying:
 Leave off.
  Let's see if Elijah comes to rescue him.
⁵⁰Jesus again screamed in a great voice.
He let go the breath.
 ⁵¹Look:
  the curtain of the sanctuary was ripped in two,
   from above to below.
  The earth was shaken.
  The rocks were ripped.
  ⁵²The tombs were opened,
  and many bodies of the holy ones who had slept were raised.
   ⁵³They came out of the tombs after their rising;
   they went into the holy city
    and were seen by many.
⁵⁴The centurion
and those with him watching Jesus
 when they saw the earthquake
 and the thing that happened
they were exceedingly afraid;
they said:
 Truly this one was son of God.
⁵⁵There were there women,
 many of them,
  keeping vigil from a distance.

These women had followed Jesus from Galilee
  to deacon to him.
    56Among these women was Mary Magdalene,
      also Mary the mother of James and Joseph
      and the mother of the sons of Zebedee.
57When it was evening there came a person, rich,
from Arimathea,
by the name of Joseph,
  who himself was a disciple to Jesus.
58This person came to Pilate;
he asked the body of Jesus.
  Then Pilate ordered it be given.
59After taking the body,
Joseph wrapped it up in a clean linen burial cloth.
60He placed it in his new tomb
  which was hewn in the rock.
After rolling a great stone in the door of the tomb
  he went away.
    61Mariam Magdalene was there
    and the other Mary.
    These women sat by the grave.
62In the next day,
  which is after the preparation,
they gathered,
  the chief priests,
  the Pharisees,
to Pilate.
63They said:
  Master,[147]
    we remember that that one,
      the liar,
    said
      while he was still living:
        After three days I will rise.

⁶⁴Order that the grave be secured up until the third day,
    lest his disciples after coming should steal him
    and should say to the people:
        He has been raised from the corpses;
    and the last lie will be greater than the first.
⁶⁵He said to them,
Pilate did:
    You have a sentinel.
    Go.
    Secure as you know how.
⁶⁶Those who went secured the grave by sealing the stone
                with the sentinel.

Chapter Twenty-Eight

¹Long after Shabbat,
    in the time of growing dawn,
        into the first of Shabbats,
there came Mariam Magdalene
    and the other Mary
to observe the grave.
²Look:
    an earthquake happened,
        a great one,
    for a messenger of haShem
        came down out of heaven.
    The messenger came forward.
    The messenger rolled away the stone
        and sat on it.
        ³His appearance was like lightning
           and his clothing white as snow.
⁴From fear of him the watchers were shaken
and they became like corpses.
    ⁵The messenger answered;
    he said to the women:

Stop being afraid;
for I know that you are seeking Jesus
   the crucified one.
⁶He is not here.
He has been raised,
   exactly as he said.
Come see the place where he was lying.
⁷Quickly when you women go,
say to his disciples:
   He has been raised from the corpses
And:
   Look:
      he is going ahead of you into Galilee.
         There you will see him.
  Look:
   I spoke to you.
⁸When the women went away quickly from the tomb
with fear and great joy they ran to report to his disciples.
  ⁹Look:
  Jesus met them.
  He said:
   Greetings.
  The women who came to him seized his feet.
  They worshiped him.
   ¹⁰Then he says to them,
  Jesus does:
   Stop being afraid.
   Go,
      report to my brothers and sisters
         in order that they go away into Galilee,
         and there they will see me.
¹¹While they were going
  Look:
   some of the sentinel went into the city;
   they reported to the chief priests everything that had happened.

¹²After gathering with the elders
   and taking a decision
   they gave much silver to the soldiers;
   ¹³they said:
      Say:
         His disciples came during the night.
         They stole him while we were sleeping.
      ¹⁴If ever this should be heard before the ruler,
      we ourselves will persuade
         and you we will make without care.
   ¹⁵They took the silver.
They did as they had been taught.
They famed this word about among the Jews to the present day.
¹⁶The eleven disciples went into Galilee,
   into the mountain where Jesus pointed out to them.
¹⁷When they saw him they worshiped,
   but some doubted.
¹⁸When he came to them,
Jesus talked with them.
He said:
   There has been given to me all authority in heaven and on earth.
   ¹⁹So go,
      instruct all the Gentiles
      by purifying them into the name of the father
         and of the son
         and of the holy breath,
      ²⁰and by teaching them to watch all whatever I ordered you.
Look.
   I myself with you
      I am
   during all the days
      up until the culmination of the aeon.

Appendix

LECTIONARY TEXTS IN STORY ORDER

Notes

Preface / Life Leaves Marks: Truth, Integrity, and Performance

1. See his article "Performance Criticism: An Emerging Methodology in Biblical Studies," at the website of the Society of Biblical Literature: *www.sbl-site.org/PDF/Rhoads_Performance.pdf.*

2. I owe the phrase "play them for true" to Kathy H. Culmer, a marvelously gifted storyteller and a colleague of mine in the Network of Biblical Storytellers Scholars Seminar. She says that to tell a story, you have to do two things: tell it true and tell it for true. I am still learning all that she means by that fascinating set of directives, but I know what it looks like and feels like from watching her perform. When she tells a story true, it trues up everything in the room, and when she tells a story for true, the audience can feel what the truth of the narrative world feels like, and what breezes must blow through such a world for this thing to be true. See her website at *www.kathyculmer.com.* Accessed August 24, 2006.

Chapter One / Authority and Revenge

3. Philip Gourevitch, *We Wish to Inform You That Tomorrow We Will Be Killed with Our Families: Stories from Rwanda* (New York: Picador, 1999), 15f.

4. Ibid., 237f.

5. Ibid., 34.

6. See *www.nps.gov/usar/survivors.html.* This website was accessed on February 27, 2006.

7. Gourevitch, *We Wish to Inform You,* Odette, 237.

8. The article is "Remembering Rachel's Children: An Urban Agenda for People Who Notice," found in *Word & World* 14, no. 4 (Fall 1994): 377–83. The article is available online at *www.luthersem.edu/word&world/Archives/14-4_City/14-4_Brueggemann.pdf.* Accessed August 28, 2006.

9. Online at *www.hnn.navy.mil/archives/010803/survivors_080301.htm*. Accessed September 27, 2005.

10. Online at *www.pearlharborchild.com/buy/phw_rfiske.asp*. Accessed September 27, 2005.

11. See online at *www.starbulletin.com/2004/04/05/news/story6.html*. Accessed September 27, 2005.

12. See Gourevitch's painful account, and pained reflection on this, in *We Wish to Inform You*, 17.

13. Ibid., 249.

14. Primo Levi, 1958, *Survival in Auschwitz: The Nazi Assault on Humanity* (New York: Simon & Schuster, 1996), cited on p. 275 of Gourevitch, *We Wish to Inform You*.

15. Primo Levi, *The Drowned and the Saved* (New York: Summit Books, 1988), cited on p. 275 of *We Wish to Inform You*.

Chapter Two / Matthew's Narrative Arc: From Rachel to Resurrection

16. For the oldest, and to my eye, still one of the best, exploration of how this works, read Aristotle's *Poetics*. For Aristotle the End, whether in narrative or in nature, determines everything.

17. This sketching of the arc of a television drama, by the way, is owed entirely to Aristotle's *Poetics,* as readers of Aristotle might already have noticed. It is a great testimony to the power of his writing that his analysis should so accurately trace the working of stories from ancient Greek tragedies to contemporary American television. Who knew Aristotle would be on TV?

18. I remember reading this somewhere in the rabbis. The rabbis asked why God rested on the Shabbat as part of creating the world. It should be impossible, after all, for the Holy One, the Almighty, to become tired enough to need to rest. Wouldn't it be blasphemy to suggest that God was exhausted and needed to sit down for a while? So why did God rest on Shabbat? "It's obvious," said the rabbis, "God rested on the seventh day because it was Shabbat. What else would you do on Shabbat?" The rhythm is so basic that even God follows it.

19. Here note Jack Kingsbury's assessment: "Matthew employs the genealogy to assert that God has guided the whole of Israel's history so that it might culminate in the birth of 'Jesus,' the protagonist of his story, who is 'Messiah,' 'Son of David,' and 'Son of Abraham.' " *Matthew as Story* (Philadelphia: Fortress, 1988), 48.

20. For example, see Martin Luther's understanding of this matter: "For God has always been accustomed to collect a Church for himself even from among the heathen. Thus Ruth was a Moabitess and Rahab was a Canaanite woman. They are numbered in the genealogy of Christ." *Luther's Works,* vol. 8: *Lectures on Genesis,* chaps. 45–50, ed. Jaroslav Pelikan (St. Louis: Concordia Publishing House, 1966), 135f.

21. For example, see the Cathedral Sermons of Severus, Homily 94. He refers to "fornication and adultery" and says, "By this means the genealogy revealed that it is our very sinful nature that Christ himself came to heal." Cited in *Ancient Christian Commentary on Scripture,* New Testament volume I-a, ed. Manlio Simonetti (Downers Grove, IL: InterVarsity Press, 2001), 6. For another reading of this matter, see Janice Capel Anderson, "Matthew: Gender and Reading" in *A Feminist Companion to Matthew* (Sheffield: Sheffield Academic Press, 2001), 25–51.

22. Even Warren Carter, who notes carefully the crimes of David (among others) in his treatment of the genealogy, still refers to Bathsheba as an "adulterer." *Matthew and the Margins: A Socio-Political and Religious Reading* (Sheffield: Sheffield Academic Press, 2000), 59. Apart from this, however, Carter's charting of the genealogy and its interpretation is extremely helpful.

23. In this I follow the translation of Everett Fox, which seems to me to catch the nature of the abuse committed in the scene. Fox, *The Five Books of Moses* (New York: Schocken, 1995), 182. The New Revised Standard Version also translates this way.

24. Remember that the point of the commandment about "honoring your father and your mother" has far more to do with the behavior of middle-aged children toward their elderly parents than with little children and theirs. "Your days will be long in the land" only if you have children who have learned from you how to care for their aging parents.

25. Gerhard von Rad, *Genesis* (Philadelphia: Westminster Press, 1972), 359.

26. Emmanuel Levinas, *Totality and Infinity* (Pittsburgh: Duquesne University Press, 1969), 199. Levinas rewards careful and slow reading. His work is difficult, but worth the effort.

27. Leon Kass, *The Beginning of Wisdom: Reading Genesis* (New York: Free Press, 2003), 534. The signet apparently was a seal used to sign clay documents.

28. Note, for instance, Warren Carter, *Matthew and the Margins,* who writes that "Joseph exemplifies the mercy required of Jesus' followers," 68. For an ancient voice, hear Chrysostom in his homily on the Gospel of Matthew: "Nevertheless Joseph was so free from the passion of jealousy as to be unwilling to cause distress to the Virgin, even in the slightest way." Cited in Simonetti, *Ancient Christian Commentary,* 14. See also Raymond Brown's careful discussion of this in *The Birth of the Messiah* (New York: Doubleday, 1977), 125–32.

29. It is clear that later legal codes provided for the execution of women in Mary's position. It is, of course, not clear that those later codes were in force during Mary's lifetime. It is also not clear that the practice during Mary's life was not harsher and more violent. The later codes could well have come

into force to restrain earlier practice. We do not know. Here see Tractate Kethuboth 44b–45a in the Talmud. *The Talmud: The Steinsaltz Edition*, ed. Rabbi Israel V. Berman, trans. Rabbi Israel V. Berman, vol. 10, part 4 (New York: Random House, 1994).

30. If you want some fascinating reading, do an Internet search on "God is a warrior" and "gender." Some of the hits are irrelevant, some are solid discussions of the serious topic of the metaphoric gender of God, and some sound like ravenous, drooling wolves eager to attack and devour their opponents. It is apparently risky to disagree with some people.

31. Here see especially the argument advanced by Emil Fackenheim in *The Jewish Bible after the Holocaust* (Bloomington: Indiana University Press, 1990). See also the delicate exploration of the figure of Rachel carried out by Walter Brueggemann in his "Remembering Rachel's Children: An Urban Agenda for People Who Notice" in *Word & World*, 14, no. 4 (Fall 1994): 377–83.

32. Note here the interpretation given to this scene by painters. The scenes show the slaughter of whole families. Those who must imagine the bodies involved have a harder time forgetting the "collateral damage." See the collection of images in Nigel Spivey's *Enduring Creation: Art, Pain, and Fortitude* (Berkeley: University of California Press, 2001), 136–53.

33. See Aristotle's *Poetics*.

34. For evidence (probably unintended) see the recent movie *The Gospel of John* (2003, directed by John Saville). Jesus, in that movie, smiles a lot and is warm, and when he speaks harsh lines the crowd concludes that he is crazy. Indeed.

35. For example, see Raymond Brown, *The Birth of the Messiah: A Commentary on the Infancy Narratives in Matthew and Luke* (New York: Doubleday, 1979), 49.

36. Commentators are fascinating on this point. Kingsbury says "At Golgotha and on the cross, Jesus does not permit concern for self to put him at odds with God's appointed plan that he relinquish his life" and hears his accusation that God has abandoned him as a cry of trust; *Matthew as Story*, 88–89. Carter hears it as "the anguished cry of the righteous sufferer who... feels abandoned by God. God seems unable and/or unwilling to deliver the sufferer (Ps 22:2) and does not reply to Jesus' cry" (*Margins* 534). Chrysostom wrote that "to his last breath he honors God as his Father and is no adversary of God... by all things Jesus shows how he is of one mind with the Father who had begotten him"; while Origen notes that "Certain people, in an outward display of piety for Jesus, because they are unable to explain how Christ could be forsaken by God, believe that this saying from the cross is true only as an expression of his humility"; cited in Simonetti, *Ancient Christian Commentary*, New Testament vol. Ib, 293–95. For a typically thorough

survey of the options, see Raymond Brown's *The Death of the Messiah* (New York: Doubleday, 1994), 2:1043–58.

37. Check, for instance, what George Steiner makes of the role of the divinity in the making of a narrative's sense of wholeness.

38. Here remember the observation from Judith Guest's novel: "So truth is in a certain feeling of permanence that presses around a moment." *Ordinary People* (New York: Ballantine Books, 1976), 87.

39. See Richard G. Bowman and Richard W. Swanson, "Samson and the Son of God, or Dead Heroes and Dead Goats: Ethical Readings of Narrative Violence in Judges and Matthew," in *Semeia 77: Bible and Ethics of Reading* (Atlanta: Scholars Press, 1997), 59–74.

Chapter Three / The Texts in Their Con-Texts

40. Which makes Jesus the first member of Medécins Sans Frontières (Doctors Without Borders).

41. Each of these texts comes to us from around the year 100 CE. What matters most is that each of these texts is composed after the Temple was destroyed in 70 CE. That lends to each of these texts the same powerful grieving for the stable center of the world that was destroyed by the Romans, and the same powerful demand for a divine response adequate to meet the real needs of God's people in the midst of chaos.

42. This essay is included in *Jesus the Christ,* ed. Donald H. Juel (Minneapolis: Fortress, 1991).

43. Andrea Halverson, a student of mine at Augustana College, explored contemporary honor killing in her senior honors thesis. As a part of her research, she gathered an impressive and disturbing bibliography, a portion of which I offer here to you to help you in your own research.

> Agence France Presse. "Honor Killings, Feuds Claim Nearly 1200 Lives in Turkey" (2006) Lexis Nexis (March 21, 2006).
>
> Amnesty International. "Turkey: Women Confronting Family Violence" (2004). Online at *www.web.amnesty.org/library/index/engeur440132004* (March 21, 2006).
>
> Anil, Ela, et al. "Turkish Penal and Civil Code Reforms from a Gender Perspective: The Success of Two Nationwide Campaigns." Women for Women's Human Rights (2005).
>
> An Na'im, Abdullahi Ahmed. "Toward a Cross-Cultural Approach to Defining International Standards of Human Rights." In *Human Rights in Cross-Cultural Perspectives,* ed. Abdullahi Ahmed An Na'im. Philadelphia: University of Pennsylvania Press, 1992.
>
> BBC Online. "Survey Shows over 35 Percent Back Honor Killings in Southeastern Turkey" (2005) Lexis Nexis (March 21, 2006).

Kardam, Filiz, et al. *The Dynamics of Honor Killings in Turkey*. Ankara: United Nations Development Program and United Nations Population Fund, 2005.

Moore, Molly. "In Turkey, Honor Killing Follows Families to Cities." Washington Post Foreign Service (2001) Lexis Nexis (March 21, 2006).

Nussbaum, Martha C. *Women and Human Development: The Capabilities Approach*. New York: Cambridge University Press, 2000.

U.S. State Department. "2004 Country Report on Human Rights Practices in Turkey." Lexis Nexis (March 21, 2006).

44. The violence of this giving of symbolic names is stunning, and sometimes ignored by interpreters. The names are treated as messages, and the children are forgotten. But the children had to endure a lifetime of hearing their names called out, a lifetime of knowing exactly what the names meant.

45. This story was reported on National Public Radio and may be heard at *www.npr.org/templates/story/story.php?storyId=5043032*. There have been several news stories in recent years about this practice, and a quick Google search will yield a frightening number of results. For instance, see *www.news .nationalgeographic.com/news/2002/02/0212_020212_honorkilling.html*, or *www.service.spiegel.de/cache/international/0,1518,344374,00.html*, or *www .amnestyusa.org/amnestynow/legalizedmurder.html* for similar stories from reliable sources. All sites accessed on March 30, 2006.

46. For detailed study of the role and nature of angels, consult Jarl Fossum, *Name of God and the Angel of the Lord: Samaritan and Jewish Concepts of Intermediation and the Origin of Gnosticism* (Tübingen: J. C. B. Mohr [Paul Siebeck], 1985).

47. European American culture often aims to calm and domesticate violent emotions, especially grief, which leaves us without an easy way to imagine the cries of Rachel or of the bereaved mothers of Bethlehem in this scene. The story about honor killing done by National Public Radio includes, near the end of the story, an audio clip from a morgue in Baghdad. In that clip a mother may be heard shrieking for her executed daughter. Do not listen to the clip unless you are willing for her wailing to change you forever. Incidentally, it will also change the way you are able to listen to this scene from Matthew's story. The clip may be found at NPR's website (*www.npr.org/ templates/story/story.php?storyId=5043032*). Accessed March 30, 2006.

48. Gourevitch, *We Wish to Inform You*, 17.

49. Ibid., 21f.

50. The class identification, of course, is an anachronism. The middle class will not arrive for centuries, but Pharisees seem to have come from the merchant class, from people with some little property, more often than they came from among the richest or poorest of the people.

51. Amos Oz, *How to Cure a Fanatic* (Princeton, NJ: Princeton University Press (January 16, 2006).

52. See on this Jonathan L. Reed, *Archaeology and the Galilean Jesus: A Re-Examination of the Evidence* (Harrisburg, PA: Trinity Press International, 2000).

53. We are told that Simon had a mother-in-law, so we assume that he had a wife, though we never meet her. If he had a wife, it is reasonable to assume that he also had children, given ancient realities involving what is now called "social security" and given general human averages.

54. Tim O'Brien's description of the chaos and of its multiple causes is terrifying. See *If I Die in a Combat Zone* (New York: Broadway Books, 1975).

55. Note Michael D. Jackson's analysis of the ways Hutus and Tutsis tell shared folktales in his *The Politics of Storytelling: Violence, Transgression, and Intersubjectivity* (Copenhagen: Museum Tusculanum, 2002).

56. Gourevitch, *We Wish to Inform You,* 249.

57. O'Brien, *If I Die in a Combat Zone,* 119.

58. Or 450, the text mentions both numbers.

59. The phrase "beautiful world" translates a single Greek word, κοσμος, which comes into English both in the cosmos and in cosmetology. My translation attempts to catch the insistence on the beauty of the universe that is carried in this single strong word.

60. Quoted in James C. Scott, *Domination and the Arts of Resistance: Hidden Transcripts* (New Haven and London: Yale University Press, 1990).

61. See ibid.

62. Well, okay, not really, but you get the point: once the poles of the plot are boiled down to "good guys" and "bad guys" the complications that structuralist analysis allowed us to see collapse into a simple bipolar opposition. Any culture raised on cowboy movies has been prepared to collapse everything into simple bipolar opposition.

63. The original quotation refers to divine grinding, but Empire will function as the only divinity that matters in practical terms. Though the notion of the divine right of kings is of later English origin, Empire always makes it clear enough that God and Empire agree on any matter touching the lives of their subjects.

64. You can find this story in many places. See, for instance, the version available at *www.ctssar.org/patriots/nathan_hale.htm* and note the unspoken parallels between the Provost-Major William Cunningham, who executed Hale, and Pontius Pilate, who executed Jesus. Both were later punished for their brutality. This only sharpens the contrast between Jesus' behavior and that of certified martyrs.

65. O'Brien, *If I Die in a Combat Zone,* 186.

66. Michael Barnett, *Eyewitness to a Genocide: The United Nations and Rwanda* (Ithaca: Cornell University Press, 2002), 1.

67. See Dave Grosman, *On Killing* (Boston: Little, Brown, and Company, 1996).

68. Peace, Dan Brown and all those excited by *The DaVinci Code*. For all the playful fun opened up by the book and its surrounding media event, Brown's notion that Jesus was promoted to godhood by the emperor Constantine some three hundred years after his death is just simply wrong.

69. See the exploration of the resurrection scene for Easter Sunday on page 129.

70. See, e.g., his interview in Der Spiegel Online, *www.service.spiegel.de/cache/international/0,1518,407315,00.html*. Accessed August 15, 2006.

71. See Jacob Neusner, *A Rabbi Talks with Jesus* (New York: Doubleday, 1993).

72. The Greek text says that they were eating in "the house." The house belongs to someone, and this way of referring to the house would normally indicate that the house belongs to Jesus.

73. Remember that the naming of Matthew as the author of this story is a matter of legend, not history or scripture. However tempting it might be to see in this scene a cameo appearance by the person who tells the story, such an emendation of the text is strictly conjectural. That doesn't mean you shouldn't experiment with this possibility that comes to us out of legend. Experiment with everything. Just remember that Matthew's story does not identify itself as "Matthew's Story," much less does it wave a flag and point to Matthew the tax traitor as Matthew the storyteller.

74. See my *Provoking the Gospel of Mark: A Storyteller's Commentary* (Cleveland: Pilgrim Press, 2005), especially the exploration of Mark's narrative arc.

75. See especially the studies of this scene gathered in Amy Jill Levine, *A Feminist Companion to Matthew* (Cleveland: Pilgrim Press, 2004).

76. See 1 Kings 22 and 2 Chronicles 18.

77. Gourevitch, *We Wish to Inform You*, 21f.

78. Ibid., 28.

79. From Michael Barnett's *Eyewitness to a Genocide: The United Nations and Rwanda* (Ithaca, NY: Cornell University Press, 2002), 2.

80. Gourevitch, *We Wish to Inform You*, 249.

81. Ibid., 250.

82. Neusner, *A Rabbi Talks with Jesus*.

83. For encouragement, you might want to check out the chapter called "How to Make Mistakes" in my how-to, why-to book, *Provoking the Gospel: Methods to Embody Biblical Storytelling through Drama* (Cleveland: Pilgrim Press, 2004).

84. For instance, see Larry Hurtado's reading of this matter in his *How on Earth Did Jesus Become a God? Historical Questions about Earliest Devotion to Jesus* (Grand Rapids, MI: W. B. Eerdmans, 2005).

85. Toni Morrison, *Sula* (New York: Vintage Books, 2002).

86. See the fuller exploration of the lives of these women on page 38.

87. For the background and detail of the following discussion of what "softie" means, see the discussion in Robert Brawley, ed., *Homosexuality and Biblical Ethics: Listening to Scripture* (Louisville: Westminster John Knox Press, 1996). This collection of essays is solid, varied, and probably the best collection I have seen.

88. Thomas Patrick Melady, *Burundi, the Tragic Years: An Eyewitness Account* (Maryknoll, NY: Orbis Books, 1994), 87f.

89. This is a good time to remember the importance of the doctrine of the Incarnation for Christians who will interpret Gospel texts. If Jesus is truly an ordinary human being, then people in the crowd must be expected to have reacted to him in all the ways they would react to any ordinary human being. My actors call this the SGNB principle (pronounced "sig-nib"). To be true to the implications of the Incarnation, Jesus must be played as if he were "Some Guy Named Bob" (SGNB). This is a good principle to remember.

90. This does indeed get complicated. To get a good glimpse of the complications, see Yvàn Almeida, *L'Opérativité sémantique des récits-paraboles: Sémiotique narrative et textuelle, herméneutique du discours religieux* (Louvain, Belgium: Editions Peeters, and Paris: Editions du Cerf, 1978). For another angle on the same problem, see Paul Ricoeur, "La Bible et l'imagination," *Revue d'Histoire et Philosophie Réligeuse* 62, no. 4 (October–December 1982), which is translated into English in *Figuring the Sacred: Religion, Narrative, and Imagination,* trans. David Pellauer (Minneapolis: Augsburg Fortress, 1995). You might also check my application and exploration of the work of Almeida and Ricoeur in my *Provoking the Gospel of Mark*. If you believe that stories have no particular importance and help merely to idle away useless hours, then parables inside a story pose no particular problem. People who are wasting time get to watch narrative characters waste narrative time. But if you understand, as I do, that storytelling has world-creating power (see my discussion of the authority of biblical story in *Provoking the Gospel of Mark, Provoking the Gospel of Luke,* and the present volume in the series: each contributes to a cumulative consideration of narrative authority), then a parable creates a world inside a world. All narrative worlds are in some measure disruptive, which is why I find it productive to provoke stories: when poked, they poke back. But that means that responsible playing of this scene will wonder about how the story pokes the narrated audience, and also how it pokes the audiences to Matthew's story, both ancient and contemporary.

91. Gourevitch, *We Wish to Inform You,* 28.

92. See Bernard Brandon Scott, *Hear Then the Parable: A Commentary on the Parables of Jesus* (Minneapolis: Fortress Press, 1990).

93. Ibid., 324.

94. Note that in the Seder meal, every family sharing the meal claims the "wandering Aramean" as father, not as distant fictive ancestor. And note that once this father is welcomed to the table, it is recounted that "we" went down to Egypt and were held in slavery.

95. See the discussion of the scene assigned for the Sunday of the Passion at the beginning of Holy Week, found on page 118.

96. You might consult the many websites devoted to these remarkable young people. For instance: see *www.lostboysofsudan.com/,* or *www.redcross .org/news/in/africa/0108lostboyspage.html.* Accessed August 15, 2006.

97. Note the interpretations of this passage offered on various websites. For instance "The decision to grow always offers us the choice between risk and comfort. Has God been asking you to do something? Have you been avoiding it because you are just too comfortable right now? Remember, you will never grow as long as you stay in the comfort zone. You will never grow unless you are willing to get out of the boat and onto the water" (*www.agapeindia.com/ miracle_01.htm*). "But God tells us again and again that we can do anything, with faith. We can see miracles, we can walk on water, if we put our trust, our faith, our hope, our very lives, in God's hands" (*www.bethquick.com/ sermon8-11-02.htm*). "This is a passage of promise: If you respond in faith to the call of God, you can walk on water. The lesson? If you want to walk on the water, you've got to get out of the boat" (*www.annerobertson.com/BSNT/ GetOutOfTheBoat.htm*). There are other readings of this scene, to be sure, but most of the readings available on the web as of today (June 29, 2006) treat this scene as a tool for motivational speakers.

98. The story is told many places, by many people. For one telling, see on-line *www.jogena.com/articles/articles0602/art0602s.htm.* Accessed August 15, 2006.

99. *www.hnn.navy.mil/archives/010803/survivors_080301.htm* Accessed September 27, 2005.

100. Though it appeared too late to be fully incorporated into the argument I am making at this point, consult the recent article, "Righteous Bloodshed, Matthew's Passion Narrative, and the Temple's Destruction: Lamentations as a Matthean Intertext," by David M. Moffitt in the *Journal of Biblical Literature* 125, no. 2 (2006): 299–320. Moffitt explores the link that Matthew (alone) makes to Jeremiah, and argues that this provides a connection to Lamentations, which functions as an interpretive template for Matthew's story.

101. No matter how many times this word is translated into submission as "set loose" or "lose," still απολλυμι will always mean "I destroy utterly," "I slay," "I demolish."

102. Blanchot says: "Jewish messianic thought (according to certain commentators), suggests the relation between the event and its nonoccurrence.... With the Messiah, who is there, the call must always resound: 'Come, Come.' His presence is no guarantee. Both future and past (it is said at least once that the Messiah has already come), his coming does not correspond to any presence at all." *The Writing of the Disaster,* trans. Ann Smock (Lincoln: University of Nebraska Press, 1995), 141–42.

103. See Scott's *Domination and the Arts of Resistance.*

104. See Scott's discussion of this technology of domination in ibid.

105. William D. Edwards, MD, Wesley J. Gabel, MDiv, and Floyd E. Hosmer, MS, "On the Physical Death of Jesus Christ, *Journal of the American Medical Association* 255, no. 11 (March 21, 1986).

106. Melady, *Burundi, The Tragic Years,* 71.

107. See Reed's *Archaeology and the Galilean Jesus.*

108. For a more recent example of this, see the Louise Erdrich's novel *Tracks: A Novel* (New York: Henry Holt, 1988).

109. *Nazi Culture: Intellectual, Cultural, and Social Life in the Third Reich,* ed. George L. Mosse (New York: Grosset & Dunlap, 1966).

110. Gourevitch, *We Wish to Inform You,* 28.

111. See Jacob Jervell, *Die Apostelsgeschichte* (Göttingen: Vandenhoeck & Ruprecht, 1998).

112. If the group that collected the Dead Sea Scrolls was a group of disaffected Sadducees (they call themselves "sons of Zadok," which is likely related to the term "Sadducee"), then Sadducees are clearly devoted to moral rigor.

113. This notion comes from Jerome, but Origen reads the same way. See *Ancient Christian Commentary on Scripture,* 162.

114. Albert Camus, *The Plague,* trans. Stuart Gilbert (New York: Random House, 1948), 229.

115. Ibid., 87.

116. Ibid., 200.

117. Ibid., 202.

118. This act of condemning and excluding occurs six times in Matthew. Outside of Matthew, it occurs only once in Luke, and nowhere else at all.

119. At *www.jtsa.edu/community/parashah/archives/5761/emor.shtml.* Accessed July 20, 2006.

120. Robert William Fogel and Stanley L. Engerman, *Time on the Cross: The Economics of American Negro Slavery* (Boston: Little, Brown, 1974). The earthquake, in fact, continues. You might check out the customer reviews of the book online, perhaps at *www.amazon.com.* The kinds of responses provoked by this book offer a disturbing diagnostic look at American understanding of this era in our history.

121. See the *Compact Oxford English Dictionary,* available online at *www.askoxford.com/concise_oed/talent?view=uk.* Accessed July 14, 2006.

122. These basic principles of behavior are traced back to the story of Noah. For one statement of the Noachide Laws, see *www.ahavat-israel.com/am/goyim.php* (accessed July 15, 2006). The laws include the following:

- *Avodah Zarah:* Prohibition on idolatry.

- *Birchat HaShem:* Prohibition on blasphemy and cursing the Name of G-d.

- *Shefichat Damim:* Prohibition on murder.

- *Gezel:* Prohibition on robbery and theft.

- *Gilui Arayot:* Prohibition on immorality and forbidden sexual relations.

- *Ever Min HaChay:* Prohibition on removing and eating a limb from a live animal.

- *Dinim:* Requirement to establish a justice system and courts of law to enforce the other six laws.

123. The classic American example of this is Jonathan Edwards's sermon, "Sinners in the Hands of an Angry God." This sermon must, however, be read carefully and in the context of the rest of Edwards's work. It does simply mean what it would appear to mean, or what it would mean in the mouth of a present-day religious ranter.

The Gospel of Matthew Translated

124. The word is Hebrew; it means "the Name" and is one of the ways observant Jews refer to God without emptying God's name of its transcendent meaning. The word is used wherever the biblical text has the consonants of the Divine Name, YHWH. These consonants appear without vowels so that no reader would accidentally misuse God's name. To further protect God's name, the practice developed of inserting the vowels of the word "adonai" (which means "lord" or "master") into the consonants of the Divine Name, and it was from this that the practice in English Bibles developed. Most English Bibles use the title "the LORD" when the original text has YHWH. In my translation of Matthew, I have used "haShem" wherever the text has κυριος, which is Greek for "lord" or "master." The term is often used to translate the Divine Name, so sometimes it will be clear enough that God is being referred to. Other times, however, the term must just mean "boss," and at those times my choice still to translate it as "haShem" will mostly be annoying. Feel very free to read each of these instances as "lord" or "master." Sometimes that will just work better.

125. Though I'd be glad to make an argument about the ways gendered language must be used to refer to the transcendence of God, in this case I am

doing something simpler. The word translated here is a participle, and it is feminine in gender because the word "voice," to which it refers, is feminine in gender. Because a Greek-speaking audience would have heard a feminine participle at this point, an English-speaking audience needs to have the same experience, just in case there is something going on in Matthew's story that might pop into view if I translate as I have.

126. This is a possible translation of the Greek word that appears at this point, and I have chosen it because of the courtroom metaphor being invoked by the role played by haSatan, the prosecutor.

127. The usual translation locates this purity in the heart, but English-speaking metaphorical anatomy is different from the metaphorical anatomy presupposed by this ancient Greek-speaking Jewish storyteller. For the story-teller, the heart is the organ of intellection and ethical decision making.

128. This idiom could be translated several ways, probably better than the translation I have chosen. It could be rendered as "children of God." It could be "daughters and sons of God." It could even be "Godlike, they will be called." I leave it to your choice.

129. To translate these people as just collecting taxes is to miss the point. Those who collected taxes did so for Rome, and benefited handsomely in the bargain. The translation I have chosen catches also the traitorous nature of the work they did.

130. The words in brackets in this and the next line are not in the Greek text, but they are implied in the words that are chosen.

131. The reference to dogs and pigs brings in a coded reference to Gentiles, who sometimes are called dogs, and who eat pigs. Before you get too irate with this form of address (if you are a Gentile), consider carefully how much you understand about Judaism. How well do you know the Zohar? Could you make your kitchen kosher? Do you know why the bread is covered at the beginning of the Shabbat meal? Do you know why sharing Shabbat meal calls for using the good china? There are pearls in Jewish life that Jesus would have known easily and dearly that most of his followers would mistake for small marbles or large tapioca.

132. This is a translation to savor. The usual reading takes the Greek as it finds it: "workers of lawlessness." This is a perfectly good translation, but it misses the Jewish meaning of "working lawlessness," which is the creating of chaos in the creation. For Gentiles to create chaos is no big surprise. For a Jew to create chaos is to undermine Torah, a serious matter indeed.

133. Just in passing, note that this Greek phrase translates the Aramaic phrase that will be sung as Jesus approaches Jerusalem: hosanna.

134. I have made it a regular practice for the last decade to translate the words πιστις and πιστευω so that the element of "faithfulness" stands out more than does the element of "faith." This is important because the texts

I work with are Jewish texts, and faithfulness is a key theme in all Jewish thought. "Faith" in Christian hands has come to mean a great many things, some of them stirring, some of them insipid, especially when the matter of "faith" is reduced to a matter of believing the right things against all evidence to the contrary. Most of the time, the translation works very well. In the case of this verse, however, it seems to work less well. Perhaps this is a time to shift back and translate it as "you believe that I am able to do this." Feel free.

135. The adjective μαλακος means "soft" or "weak" or "effeminate." The surface-level implication is that real people wear work clothes, while people Spiro Agnew once called an "effete corps of impudent snobs" (and "nattering nabobs of negativism," once he got rolling) wear soft clothes and are thus to be suspected of all sorts of things. Though I am reluctant to link Jesus too closely with a rightly disgraced former vice president, the reflex is the same in this scene. The reference is not merely to the softness of the clothes, but also to the supposed softness of the character that went with wearing anything other than work clothes.

136. The word here is κυριος, and perhaps ought (for consistency) to be translated as "haShem" as I have done everywhere else. It seemed right to make this exception.

137. Given the way the scene develops from this point, this is a good translation, but the word could just as easily mean "deaf." This is not too surprising, given the interconnection between hearing and speaking.

138. The word here is κυριος again. The oddity is that, in socio-economic or political terms, the woman was Jesus' master in her home region. Jews lived in this Gentile-dominated area at the sufferance of the dominant Gentile culture, and ate the crumbs from that table.

139. In an ambiguity not easily caught in English, the people testing Jesus ask for a sign from heaven (meaning from God) and Jesus gives them a sign in the sky. The word is the same.

140. This atypical translation picks up the courtroom theme that was developed in the scene of testing by haSatan in the wilderness. The word is the same as was used in that scene.

141. The text says that they lifted up their eyes, which could mean nothing more than that they had been looking down and now they changed the angle of their vision. But the phrase also reproduces a common Hebrew idiom for intensifying activity, and I have translated it thus here.

142. κυριος again.

143. Or: "With a will."

144. This translation pushes the edges of what can be borne, but it catches clearly and well the real situation faced by the Sanhedrin under Roman domination. That situation is so often lost or ignored, and it is time that Christian readers recognized it. Hence this way of reading the scene.

145. This translation, again, makes an argument about this scene, and pushes the text hard in one direction. Pilate is in charge in this scene; responsible historical analysis can read things no other way. Pilate, like all dominant colonial powers, understands and misunderstands everything thoroughly. In this scene, he makes assumptions that are simply wrong. The Jewish officials handed Jesus over because Pilate made it dangerous to do anything else.

146. Note that this statement is made in the passive voice, which recognizes the implacable force of the dominant colonial power, so dominant that it demands that its subordinates use an ersatz form of the "divine passive" when speaking about what Rome is going to do in any case.

147. Again, the word is κυριος. It is possible that Matthew intends to absolutely discredit the Jewish authorities by having them address the Roman ruler with the Divine Name, but it seems more likely that this is best played as a scene in which Rome demands such obeisance from its subjects.

PROVOKING THE GOSPEL series by Richard W. Swanson, *published by The Pilgrim Press*

The PROVOKING THE GOSPEL series spurs efforts to provoke pastoral leaders and religious educators with new and lively readings of the Gospels, and challenges them to experiment with interpretive tools such as embodied ensemble exploration. Each volume is composed of three chapters plus the author's provocative translation of that specific gospel. An appendix identifies the location of each text in the cycle established by the Revised Common Lectionary. Contains a companion DVD with illustrations of the process of script analysis and the performance that lies behind this way of storytelling.

Other titles in the PROVOKING THE GOSPEL series:

PROVOKING THE GOSPEL OF MARK
A Storyteller's Commentary, Year B

> In this study of Mark's story, the text is treated as the beginning point for contemporary oral performance, as sheet music that must be explored through performance to be truly comprehended.

ISBN 0-8298-1690-9
Paper over board — with DVD, 352 pages, $35

PROVOKING THE GOSPEL OF LUKE
A Storyteller's Commentary, Year C

> This exploration of the Gospel of Luke begins and ends with a repentance and rethinking rooted deep in the heart of Jewish faith, for the sake of Christians, Christianity, and the integrity and honesty before God and the world.

ISBN 0-8298-1689-5
Paper over board — with DVD, 368 pages, $35

Also by Richard W. Swanson:

PROVOKING THE GOSPEL
Methods to Embody Biblical Storytelling through Drama

> A "how-to" and "why-to" book about exploratory ensemble biblical storytelling that grew out of Swanson's six years of work in the PROVOKING THE GOSPEL PROJECT, a collaborative venture involving a multigenerational team of storytellers.

ISBN 0-8298-1573-2
Paper, 160 pages, $18

* * *

To order these or any other books from The Pilgrim Press, call or write to:

The Pilgrim Press
700 Prospect Avenue
Cleveland, OH 44115-1100

Phone orders: 800.537.3394 (M-F, 8:30am–4:30pm ET)
Fax orders: 216.736.2206

Please include shipping charges of $6.00 for the first book
and 75¢ for each additional book.

Or order from our web site at www.thepilgrimpress.com

Prices subject to change without notice.